Modern Radio Production

Modern Radio Production

Production, Programming, and Performance

NINTH EDITION

CARL HAUSMAN
Rowan University

FRITZ MESSERE
State University of New York–Oswego

PHILIP BENOIT
Millersville University-Pennsylvania

LEWIS O'DONNELL
Late, Professor Emeritus, State University of New York at Oswego

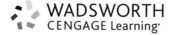

WADSWORTH
CENGAGE Learning·

Australia • Brazil • Japan • Korea • Mexico • Singapore • Spain • United Kingdom • United States

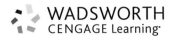
WADSWORTH
CENGAGE Learning·

Modern Radio Production: Production, Programming, and Performance, Ninth Edition
Carl Hausman, Fritz Messere, Philip Benoit, Lewis O'Donnell

Senior Publisher: Lyn Uhl

Assistant Editor: Erin Bosco

Editorial Assistant: Rebecca Donahue

Media Editor: Jessica Badiner

Marketing Program Manager: Gurpreet Saran

Design and Production Services: PreMediaGlobal

Manufacturing Planner: Doug Bertke

Rights Acquisition Specialist: Mandy Groszko

Cover Image: John Rensten/Getty Images

Compositor: PreMediaGlobal

For product information and technology assistance, contact us at
Cengage Learning Customer & Sales Support, 1-800-354-9706
For permission to use material from this text or product, submit all requests online at **www.cengage.com/permissions**. Further permissions questions can be emailed to **permissionrequest@cengage.com**.

Library of Congress Control Number: 2011941520

ISBN-13: 978-1-111-34439-9

ISBN-10: 1-111-34439-6

Wadsworth
20 Channel Center Street
Boston, MA 02210
USA

Cengage Learning is a leading provider of customized learning solutions with office locations around the globe, including Singapore, the United Kingdom, Australia, Mexico, Brazil, and Japan. Locate your local office at **international.cengage.com/region**.

Cengage Learning products are represented in Canada by Nelson Education, Ltd.

For your course and learning solutions, visit **www.cengage.com**.

Purchase any of our products at your local college store or at our preferred online store **www.cengagebrain.com**.

Instructors: Please visit **login.cengage.com** and log in to access instructor-specific resources.

Printed in the United States of America
1 2 3 4 5 6 7 15 14 13 12 11

About the Authors

Carl Hausman is Professor of Journalism at Rowan University in Glassboro, New Jersey. He holds a Ph.D. from the Union Graduate School and did his postdoctoral fellowship at New York University. He is the author of 20 books, including several texts on broadcasting and journalism. His works also include investigative and explanatory books, articles, and columns; he has appeared on a variety of talk shows, including *The O'Reilly Factor*, ABC's *World News Now with Anderson Cooper*, CBS Radio's *Capitol Voices*, and CNN's *Outlook*. A former talk show host and anchor, Hausman has also done voice-over work for a variety of corporate and institutional clients. His academic specialty is media ethics, and he has written two books on the subject and testified before Congress on ethics issues.

Frank (Fritz) Messere is founding dean of the School of Communication, Media and the Arts at the State University of New York at Oswego. A member of Oswego's communication studies faculty since 1977, Messere is a former coordinator of its broadcasting and mass communication program and two-time department chair. Messere received both his bachelor's and master's degrees from Oswego and did postgraduate work at Cornell University. He is the coauthor of five textbooks on electronic media and communication, including *Broadcasting, Cable, the Internet and Beyond*. He is a nationally recognized expert on broadcasting regulation and telecommunications. Messere has served as external assistant to FCC Commissioner Mimi Wayforth Dawson, as senior fellow of the Annenberg Washington Program in Communication Policy, and on the Rural Policy Research Institute's National Experts Panel on Telecommunications.

Philip Benoit (M.A., State University of New York, Oswego) is an adjunct professor of English at Pennsylvania's Millersville University. He was the director of public affairs at Middlebury College in Vermont, and associate vice-president for communications at Franklin & Marshall College in Lancaster, Pennsylvania. Benoit has a broad background in radio, television, and public relations, and he was the first director of the broadcasting academic program at SUNY Oswego. He was executive officer of the American Forces Network in Europe and American Advisor to the Vietnamese Armed Forces Radio Network.

Lewis O'Donnell The late Lewis B. O'Donnell, who was Professor Emeritus of Communication Studies at SUNY Oswego, was coauthor of most previous editions of this book. O'Donnell, a former president of a radio station ownership group, worked in a variety of management and performance positions in radio and television. He was awarded the Frank Stanton Fellowship by the International Radio and Television Society and he received the New York State Chancellor's Award for Excellence in Teaching.

Brief Contents

Contents

Preface

One of the authors of this book was recently talking to a pioneer broadcaster, now in his nineties, about the early days of broadcasting, and the author mentioned how exciting it must have been to be on the ground floor of the invention of a new medium—what exciting times those must have been.

The veteran's answer was a surprise: You *are* on the ground floor, he said. These are the days of the invention of a new medium, and the path it takes will be the path you blaze.

And that's true. While much of "traditional" radio remains the same exciting medium that has captivated audiences for decades, there is an entirely new angle to the business: Digital technology has lowered the barriers to entry into radio production and, to a certain extent, broadcasting.

Today, anyone who has access to a reasonably up-to-date computer and some moderately priced—or even free—software can produce radio. You can record your own music, edit the music, produce commercials, create podcasts, all on your computer, or even on your tablet device and in some cases on your smartphone.

Those are the new horizons open to today's radio producer.

At the same time, radio continues to be "the magic medium" that is the listener's lifestyle companion, the friendly voice, the music that captures our moods, and the voice of news that reaches us in the car or at home when the electricity's out.

This ninth edition of *Modern Radio Production* remains true to the theme we articulated when we wrote the first volume: We focus on technology but never lose track of the fact that radio production is about communication, not gadgets. Technology is great, but it's not an end in itself.

So while it is critical for anyone in the radio business to adapt to advancing technology, it is even more important to grasp the underlying factors of how to use the medium for communication. That way, the basic principles will last a lifetime, and you can stay current easily throughout your career.

FEATURES

This new edition has recurring boxed features throughout the text that are designed to highlight aspects of radio production and performance we consider essential for the modern radio communicator. Among them are the following:

- "Think About It": Ethics scenarios that look at situations important for communicators in the modern digital era, when quick decisions can have global reach
- "Tuning In To Technology": Boxes that highlight the very latest in technological developments, including—new to this edition—mobile applications and services that allow an individual to set up his or her own radio station on the Internet
- "You're On": Step-by-step guidance for on-air performance
- "Industry Update": Summaries of the newest trends in the radio business, both terrestrial and Internet
- "Radio Retro": Glances back into radio's heritage designed to show you how the past connects with the present and will connect with the future.

NEW TO THIS EDITION

Throughout the book, we make sure everything is up-to-date but do not limit our focus to technology. For example, quite a bit has been added relevant to the new economic models for radio and, for that matter, all media.

Here are some of the highlights of the new materials introduced at the suggestion of students and reviewers:

- Historical perspective on how technologies have changed radio in the past, and what that might mean for our future (Chapter 1).
- A more contemporary approach in which all inputs are examined in one chapter (Chapter 2), mirroring industry technological trends by adding such inputs as satellite and network programming and making the concepts more teachable.
- A similar approach in which outputs are examined in one chapter (Chapter 3).
- Detailed discussion of Web-based radio programming, discussed throughout the book.
- Comprehensive explanations of the new Web-based "long-tail" economy and the effect on radio economics. These references are woven throughout the book, with the most extensive treatment in Chapters 7 and 8.
- Flash memory and its uses in production, explained in Chapter 9.

- Many updates to the techniques discussed in Chapter 10, and updates of new practices.

- New sections exploring the HD ProTools system in Chapter 6.

- Special attention's to apps and plug-ins that allow the radio producer to perform extremely sophisticated operations on iPads, iPhones, and similar tablets and smartphones (mostly in Chapter 15).

- Discussion about mobile and cloud capabilities and flash memory; discussion about SonicFire Pro and Garageband for creating production beds; more discussion about interactive media and radio programming (iheartradio, aolradio, etc.) mostly in Chapter 9.

- The very latest on new technologies to enable voice tracking, including software that allows a remote announcer to talk over music intros and outros, dealt with primarily in Chapter 8.

- An updated discussion of satellite programming in Chapter 8.

- An editing software comparison chart in Chapter 6.

- Updates of all discussions of software throughout the book.

- The latest on interactive programming, such as techniques in which on-air play is keyed to Facebook "likes."

- New discussion of radio formats, mostly in Chapter 8.

- A complete explanation of the new digital infrastructure and how it affects radio in Chapter 17

- A discussion of text messaging as a radio tool in Chapter 18.

ACCOMPANYING RESOURCES

Resources for Students

Student Companion website. This free study tool includes chapter-specific assets such as glossaries, interactive flash cards, and links to relevant Web resources.

Resources for Instructors

Instructor Companion website. The password-protected instructor website includes electronic access to the Online Instructor's Manual, as well as a downloadable test bank.

Online Instructor's Manual. Modern Radio Production's electronic and down-loadable instructor's manual includes chapter summaries, teaching suggestions, sample syllabi, and test questions.

Please consult your local Cengage sales representative for more information. You may also contact the Cengage Learning Academic Resource Center at 800-423-0563, or visit us at http://www.cengagebrain.com.

ACKNOWLEDGMENTS

There are many people who helped us as we prepared this edition of *Modern Radio Production*. We're grateful to everyone who shared their knowledge and helped by answering questions about the current state of the industry. We want to thank Professor David Moody at SUNY Oswego, along with Fred Vigeant, Kate Percival, Jason Smith, and Matt Lavonier of the WRVO group of stations for their insights. Thanks also goes to Mark Williams at Avid Corporation, Jeff Laity at TEAC Corporation of America, Davida Rochman at Shure Inc., Brian Dickman at Smartsound.com, and Zac Wheatcroft at BIAS, Inc. They helped us with information about the current state of radio software and technology.

We also thank everyone at Cengage Learning for their support throughout the revision process, but we would be remiss in not thanking Erin Bosco for her tremendous help. This revision would not be possible without her guidance. Thanks also to Michael Rosenberg, Publisher; Rebecca Donahue, Editorial Assistant; Gurpreet Saran, Marketing Program Manager; and Sandeep Pannu, Project Manager with PreMediaGlobal.

We especially appreciate the feedback from reviewers of this new edition: Dave Lennie, Bradley University; Gina Sierzega, Muhlenberg College; and Sherry Williford, Stephen F. Austin State University.

Foreword

I got my start in radio, and learned so much about the magic medium from one of the coauthors of this fine tome, Dr. Lewis O'Donnell, when I was a broadcasting major at the State University of New York at Oswego. In fact, "Doc," as we called him, told me in my freshman year that "I had the perfect face for radio!" I actually consider that a compliment.

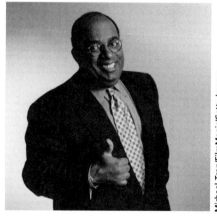

My colleagues at the time, Carl Hausman and Philip Benoit, shared, if not my facial deficiencies, then certainly my enthusiasm for radio—and I think the authors' view of radio shines through in this latest edition of their text.

This edition has been expanded to include more guidance about programming and on-air performance. Those are vital areas for anyone who wants to go into broadcasting, because in today's competitive marketplace, you need a complete arsenal of skills.

And of course *Modern Radio Production* still does what it did from the start: It provides a jargon-free, user-friendly introduction to the process of communicating with radio. While there's plenty of high-tech here, there's also a lot of down-to-earth information. I hope you enjoy this book. I know I have. And I'm not saying that just because Phil Benoit still has in his possession certain negatives from my college years that might prove embarrassing.

Al Roker
NBC's Today Show

Modern Radio Production

1

Production in Modern Radio

The phrase, "when one door closes, another opens" is an obvious cliche, but like many cliches it holds a grain of truth. Digital technology has turned virtually all entertainment and news industries on their heads. It will come as no news to you that changes in delivery systems have left executives in all media scrambling to find new revenue models. For many services and industries, the news is all grim.

But things look much better in radio, and the future—while no one can predict it with certainty—seems bright. Why? If you're entering radio today, new options are open to you, options unthinkable when the first version of this book was produced more than 20 years ago. For example, if you're involved in music you might get a job at a "traditional" radio station or record label, or you might start your own recording studio. A recording studio even 15 years ago involved staggering sums invested into mixing consoles, filters, and other paraphernalia to shape the audio signal. Today, even a modestly priced computer along with software that is often available for free can produce roughly the same product.

Are you fascinated by radio programming? You may elect to enter "traditional" radio and work your way up to program director. Conversely, you could also start your own radio station over the Internet. There are several modestly priced options that are within the range of almost anyone, financially and technically, who wants to start and maintain an Internet station.

The choices are yours, and you'll find all the options explained in detail throughout this book.

Chances are, you are indeed looking to enter the radio industry, and, as noted above, in the midst of media turmoil radio is one of the few media businesses to see an upturn. In 2010, radio revenue marked its first increase since 2000, posting, according to the trade group the Radio Advertising Bureau, a 6 percent increase over 2009.

"Spot" advertising, commercials placed by an advertiser at stations of the advertiser's choosing, was up 6 percent, and network radio was up 3 percent last year. Advertising on digital radio (i.e., websites), streaming audio over the Internet, and HD ("hybrid digital") were up 24 percent.

Listening patterns, though, are changing from previous years. Faced with a wide variety of choices, the average American has cut back on the number of hours he or she spends with radio from about 16 per week a decade ago to about 13 per week now. At the same time, there's been almost no decrease in the number of Americans age 12 and over who listen to radio. The figure currently stands at about 91 percent.

Traditional radio, which we often call "terrestrial" radio, is losing share to Internet, iPods, and other digital media, and shares of audience are dropping as traditional radio finds that it can offer two, three, or four channels with digital signals as well as virtually unlimited market segments on the Internet. Clearly, this is both a closing door and an opening one. Highly specific markets can often be exceptionally profitable. What such markets lack in numbers they make up for in appeal to advertisers who desire a focused demographic with predictable buying habits.

Speaking of reaching specific demographics, new developments in targeting radio listeners hold terrific promise for the future of radio—or whatever we choose to call radio in the digital future. We're talking about algorithm-based radio, a service that uses a sample of listener preferences to predict preference in music and, of course, purchases. Pandora, probably the most successful of algorithm-based radio, recently raised more than $100 million for an initial public offering (an initial public offering, or IPO, is a change in company financing in which stock is sold to the general public).

After a few tough years, Sirius, the satellite-relayed subscription service, in early 2011 had passed a whopping 20 million subscribers. Offering clear, high-quality audio mostly to listeners in cars, Sirius serves up an astounding array of channels, ranging from jazz and easy listening to sports and comedy.

Services that serve up on-demand music orders are beginning to take off as well. A service called Thumbplay, which offers what is essentially an all-you-can eat menu of music for $10 per month, was recently sold to radio giant Clear Channel Communications.

But we haven't yet touched on what promises to be the biggest game changer in the radio industry, an invention that brings the "radio" back to "radio." We're referring to the mobile market, the fertile ground for advertisers seeking to reach predominately young audiences. Some mobile smartphones ("phone" may in fact be becoming a quaint term) are now equipped with HD radio receivers, some with FM, and almost all are capable of receiving and playing back an audio signal of some sort. Mobile radio could be an advertiser's dream, because in addition to reaching people anywhere, a traditional strength of radio, all new smartphones are equipped with GPS location-sensing devices. While the privacy implications have to be sorted out, delivering ads based on the location of the listener has obvious profit potential.

Imagine: a portable device that reaches the listener with music suited to that person's preference and lifestyle. If that sounds familiar, note that a half-century ago, when radio was reeling under the crush of television, a new invention called the transistor allowed youthful listeners to take their music with them and immerse themselves in a lifestyle based on their music. The rest was history. And the rest of the story is the future.

Welcome to Radio 2.0.

THE DURABILITY OF RADIO

While this is clearly an unstable time for most media, radio has some unique strengths that bode well for the future. First, radio is still one of the few media that can be accessed reliably and safely in the car, where we spend an ever-increasing proportion of our time, and second, it is the constant companion of multitaskers. An ever-increasing share of radio time is devoted to using radio along with some other medium, particularly computer-based media.

Radio also retains a strong hold on what's called *business-to-business advertising* (B-to-B), essentially, one firm selling to other firms that use a particular product. Because radio reaches a high proportion of business owners and executives during drive time—the periods when people are traveling to and from work—it's a great medium for B-to-B.

So even though the media landscape is as shaky as it's ever been, remember that radio poses some unique advantages that bode well for its evolution. The fact that the Internet has spawned alternatives to so-called "terrestrial" radio is old news; but the *new* news is that the ability to offer a wider variety of radio choices on demand for the Internet portion of the radio offering—or an exclusive Internet channel— creates new opportunities in radio production, programming, and performance.

This chapter will put the ever-changing and ever-exciting world of radio in perspective, leading you through a bit of history and sketching the way radio came to do what it does so well today: target a specific audience that loves what a particular station has to offer.

Perhaps the most interesting facet of studying radio is seeing how it has adapted to technological change, sometimes evolving in ways no one expected and occasionally using threats from other media to its advantage. Throughout this book, we will be using a feature called Radio Retro to illustrate how the past has influenced the present in radio. This chapter's entry looks at radio's earliest origins.

Lessons from History as We Move into the Digital Future

There's something of a "sky is falling" atmosphere in what we might call the "traditional" or "legacy" media, including, of course, radio.

This is not to minimize the disruption that the digital age has imposed on radio, television, and newspapers, as well as on the traditional economic model that supported those media. Indeed, times are tough for many (though not all) media outlets, and predictions that things will get better are cold comfort to someone faced with paying the bills this week.

Having said that, it's important to remember that media rarely disappear. Usually, they come back in a stronger form, adapting themselves to new technologies, often altering their content in such a way as to make the new medium and the new message profitable.

Do the words in the preceding paragraph sound familiar? They echo a theory proposed by Marshall McLuhan, who coined the famous aphorism "the medium is the message."

Let's take a minute and walk through a century-and-a-half of media history to show what that means to media that not only are changing their physical method of delivery but their content as well. The point: This has all happened before, and while even the inventors of new media have never been very good at predicting the future, the future that evolved was generally a profitable one.

Here's an example of how medium became the message, dating back to the run-up to the American Civil War.

How the Technology Changed Content

The telegraph had made widespread delivery of news a reality, and a new organization, the Associated Press, leveraged this development to form a news "cooperative," in which newspapers pooled their news, being both providers and consumers.

But there was a problem: News before the telegraph was typically not in what would be characterized as an objective style; it was biased toward local views and often echoed a party line. Vestiges of this heritage remain in what remains of modern newspapers (two examples are *The Rochester Democrat and Chronicle* and *The Springfield Republican*).

Slanted news had an undeniable local appeal, but was not a marketable commodity among states sharply divided in political views not only pertaining to slavery but to tariffs, land-use policies in the expanding West,

and national banking. As a result, the AP instructed reporters to adopt a straightforward, "objective" approach to news so that the product could cross political lines.

There was a technological complication, too: Time on the telegraph was sharply limited because there weren't enough lines or operators, and service was often compromised by sabotage or censorship as the nation's conflicts evolved into a shooting war.

Wartime realities thus changed the structure of news again. The leisurely, rambling narrative common to pre-war coverage was replaced with a top-heavy "summary lead" that put the who, what, where, when, and why up front—in case the transmission was shortened or interrupted.

The inverted pyramid is still in common use today; the February 20, 2010 edition of the *New York Times* online had, in rough eyeball estimation, about a third of the news stories presented in the inverted pyramid format. A quick perusal of AP stories shows that most still utilize the format developed from about 1840 to 1865.

So what?

Let us answer with another story.

In late 2009, the Associated Press began reconfiguring how it writes leads and headlines. Irony and humor are discouraged. Repetition of key terms is encouraged. The reason: Search engines are not very good at detecting ironic meanings and generally lean toward ranking stories near the top if those stories contain relevant keywords.

Ecological and Technological Change and the Future of Radio

Technology and social structure have made an interesting loop in 150 years, and a study of the past, while certainly not providing a direct signpost for where media are or should be headed, does illuminate some twists the path may take in terms of technology, content, and economics.

The medium and message connection has become ecologically mixed in communication structures to the point where it is hard to discern without taking a deliberate step back. (*Note:* Here we use *ecological* in its literal meaning—an interdependent mixture of things that create a new, co-dependent entity. The word was rescued from its presumed synonymous relationship with the environment by media and communication scholar Neal Postman, who not only wrote about media ecology but evolved a respected academic department at New York University by that name. His contention was that media interacts ecologically with society by changing the system, not as an additive but as a mixture, in much the same way that eliminating a certain breed of fish affects more than just the fish; it may eliminate a food source for a certain species, which may then die off and give free rein to other creatures that were once its prey.

An ecological understanding of media really does provide an interesting insight into the factors that affected the development of communication technologies. Radio is a good example, and perhaps the perfect example.

As mentioned, "experts" in media have usually had a pretty poor track record of predicting where things are going—even with their own inventions and innovations. Thomas Edison thought his phonograph was a top-notch revolution in the business world—as a business dictation machine—and was dismissive of people who thought it would be fun (and profitable) to play music in the home.

David Sarnoff, perhaps radio's most influential pioneer, as a young man wrote a memo to his bosses saying radio—which was at the time viewed as a very profitable device for communication among ships—would someday be a "music box" where people could listen to their favorite songs. His idea was dismissed out of hand.

When it became apparent that people did enjoy listening to music via radio, early radio executives were unsure that the medium would ever be suitable for advertising. They didn't believe anyone would respond to a short commercial, and in any event thought that many products—such as toothpaste—were "too personal" to be advertised on such an intimate medium and would offend people.

The point: Expect the unexpected, and understand why we are so poor at anticipating the paths media will take.

Media May Eat, But They Rarely Kill

Media developments move in unexpected directions that frequently confound the "experts," and while the invention of new media is always expected to kill old media, that doesn't usually happen. Television almost killed radio for a while, but then radio adapted into a lifestyle medium and for a time became stronger than ever. Radio used to be a mass entertainment medium, broadcasting drama and variety nationwide. But when

it became apparent that television could do that task much better, radio evolved into a medium that targets specific listeners in a narrow range.

To demonstrate this effect in other media: Home video was once expected to kill movies. In fact, home video probably made the movie industry stronger by infusing production capital from up-front sales of home video rights.

Regulation Will Play a Role

The challenge for radio and all media in the coming years will be to evolve not only in directions the technology may take but in ways the government allows and sanctions, ways that will allow radio to have a competitive advantage. Again, the history of radio illustrates this concept clearly. Radio was initially developed as a method of ship-to-ship and ship-to-shore communication. Young Guglielmo Marconi and his backers made a fortune by taking out very restrictive licenses on his process and equipment. A ship could not just buy a radio; the shipping company had to buy a Marconi system and carry an operator in the employ of the Marconi Company—and all of this came at a premium price.

Some ships couldn't afford Marconi radio systems, and after a few of these ships sunk and their crews drowned because they couldn't send out an SOS or, if they could, they could not reach a Marconi-equipped rescue ship, the government stepped in and decreed that this new technology could not be cornered by one man or one company. Radio was then redeployed as a mass medium. When interference among radio stations endangered the future of the medium, the government stepped in with various pieces of legislation that governed the assignment of radio frequencies and dictated, to an extent, how stations should operate in a way that would assure mutual survival. Years later, when FM radio—a promising technological development that was going nowhere because not enough people owned FM receivers—the government mandated that auto manufacturers make car radios FM compatible. The rest, as they say, is history.

Radio and the Digital Future

As detailed elsewhere in this chapter, what we now call "terrestrial" radio is struggling to evolve. But as also detailed above, struggle and evolution are generally precursors to prosperity. As this chapter is being written in spring of 2011, radio is beginning to embrace new horizons. Satellite radio, for example, has already proved its viability. Internet radio, once a curiosity, has now become a mainstream venue for traditional radio enterprises as well as entrepreneurs. HD radio is off to a slow start (reminiscent of FM), but this evolving digital technology holds enormous potential in its ability to allow a broadcaster to produce several distinct channels in the spectrum space previously occupied by one.

The Real Lesson of History
The takeaway: Creativity—the ability to exploit the medium to communicate, entertain, and persuade—and

the acquired skill of developing a message that meets the needs and expectations of an audience is a skill that can be adapted to just about any technology. But the technology cannot be adapted to provide a producer with those skills. Throughout this book, as we have done for more than two decades, we will stress the message first, and then provide explicit guidance on how to adapt it to the medium.

Despite the galloping advance of digital technology, some things never change.

Portions of this section adapted from Carl Hausman's forthcoming book, The Future of News.

SOUND OF THE STATION

The station's sound is created by using various sources of sound to create a specific result—a targeted product that appeals to specific listeners. It's how these sources blend that makes one station different from the others that compete for a listener's attention.

The unique sound of a station emerges from a combination of the type of music programmed, the style and pace of vocal delivery used by the station's announcers, the techniques used in the production of commercials and public service announcements, the sound effects used in the presentation of newscasts, and other special recording techniques and sound production methods.

FORMATS

Commercial radio stations make their money by targeting audiences for advertisers who buy time on the stations' airwaves (there is, of course, much more on this in later chapters of this book). The audiences are "delivered" to the advertisers. They are measured by rating services, which use sampling techniques to provide a head count of the audience, including data on such characteristics as age, gender, and level of income.

A commercial radio station's programming goal is to put something on the air that will attract audiences, which then can be "sold" to advertisers.

If the programming doesn't achieve this goal, there will be few advertisers and, of course, little money coming into the station's coffers. Without money, the station cannot operate. So, the name of the game is to attract and hold an audience that will appeal to advertisers. This crucial aspect of radio programming—developing a format—is a highly specialized field of its own.

RADIO RETRO • RADIO CAPTURES LISTENERS—AND IMAGINATIONS

Radio's beginnings in the early part of the last century gave no hint of the role it would play in today's world. Early radio experimenters such as Guglielmo Marconi and Reginald Fessenden never envisioned an era when their electronic toy would become a means of providing entertainment and information to audiences in their cars, in their boats, and in their homes—much less to joggers in their stride.

Early radio programming started as a novel attempt to bring the cultural offerings of major cities into the living rooms of all America. Gradually, radio assumed its status as a personal companion. Early radio programming consisted of live symphony broadcasts, poetry readings, and live coverage of major news events, along with the same kinds of drama, situation comedy, and other programming that form so much of today's television schedules.

Some historians maintain that radio assumed its present form in 1935, when Martin Block first aired his *Make-Believe Ballroom* show on New York City's WNEW. The idea for the program came from a West Coast station. A planned remote broadcast of a band performance at a local ballroom was canceled. To fill the time, the enterprising broadcaster obtained some of the band's recordings and played them over the air. He identified the program as coming from a "make-believe" ballroom, and the time was filled. When Block brought the idea to New York, it was the birth of the **disc jockey (or DJ)** era in radio.

Radio production reached its zenith during the 1930s and 1940s, the so-called Golden Age of Radio. Radio programs of that era often originated in large studios, where production staff and performers created elaborate programs whose effectiveness depended on sophisticated production techniques. Dramas were broadcast live because audio tape recorders hadn't been invented yet. Music was provided by studio orchestras that performed live as the program aired.

Sound effects were imaginatively created by production staff who worked in the studio alongside the actors and musicians. Coconut shells, for example, were used to re-create the sound of horses' hoofbeats, and the crackling of cellophane near the microphone re-created the sound of fire. The arrangement and orchestration of various sound sources combined to create the desired effect in the minds of the listening audience. Budgets were elaborate, scores of people were involved, and scripts were often complex. Production is what made the Golden Age golden.

Today, the mainstay of radio is recorded music, interspersed with news, talk, and information—and, of course, commercial messages, which pay for the operation of commercial stations. When television took over the living rooms of American homes and supplied, in a far more explicit way, the drama, variety, and other traditional program fare that had marked radio in its heyday, the DJ format became dominant on radio. Music, news, and personality, in a careful blend known as a **format**, became the measure of radio's ability to attract listeners.

The development of **solid-state** technology, and later of **microchip** electronics, freed radio from bulky stationary hardware. At the beach, in the car, and on city streets, radio can be the constant companion of even the most active of listeners. Freedom from the long (half-hour and hour) programs that once characterized radio, and still typify television programming, means that information cycles quickly in radio. For example, when people want to find out about a breaking news event, they often turn first to the radio.

All this has great significance for anyone who wants to understand the techniques of radio production. **Production** in radio is the assembly of various sources of sound to achieve a purpose related to radio programming. You, as a producer in radio, are responsible for the "sound" of the station.

Just as commercial radio must attract and hold a specific audience to be successful in the marketplace, public radio stations must use the same fundamental techniques to design programming that will meet the needs of their audiences. Though public radio stations do not sell time to advertisers, they must successfully package their programming to obtain program underwriters and individual subscribers.

TUNING IN TO TECHNOLOGY • A TiVO™ FOR RADIO?

Could a Web-based TiVo for radio radically change listening habits?
Entrepreneur Michael Robertson recently launched a new service called DAR.fm, in which "DAR" stands for "digital audio recorder."

The site works by letting users record programs from several hundred radio stations that have online streams. Users can program the order in which they want the elements played back. Through a companion site, users can also store and stream their own content. Content plays back through apps for popular smartphones and some audio devices.

Not surprisingly, the launch of the site has raised eyebrows in the music industry, inviting possible legal action, reports the *San Francisco Chronicle*. While Robertson said he believes he is on solid legal ground because of court cases dealing with cable-TV digital recording services; in one such case, a court ruling said, in essence, that if the user hits the button it's not a copyright violation.[1]

---

1. http://www.sfgate.com/cgi-bin/article.cgi?f=/g/a/2011/02/23/ businessinsider-the-music-industry-isnt-going-to-be-pleased-about-darfm-2011-2.DTL Feb. 23

REACHING A SPECIFIC AUDIENCE

Unlike television, which tries to appeal to broader, more general segments of the public with its programs, radio has developed into a medium that focuses on smaller groups, the so-called *target audiences*. For example, a station may choose to program rock music to attract a young **demographic**. (Demographics are the statistical characteristics of human populations; the word is commonly used in the singular in the broadcasting industry to designate any given segment of the audience.) By appealing to one segment of the public (such as people of a certain age, gender, or income) that shares a preference for a certain type of music, a station can hope to attract advertisers wanting to sell products to people of that group.

HOW TARGET AUDIENCES AFFECT FORMAT

Much research and effort has gone into determining the types of programming that attract different types of audiences. The result of these efforts has been identification of formats that appeal to specific audiences.

A format is the arrangement of program elements, often musical recordings, into a sequence that will attract and hold the audience segment a station is seeking. For example, a format labeled "Top 40" or "CHR" (contemporary hit radio) is constructed around the most popular recordings currently being sold to an audience mostly in its teens and early twenties. By programming these recordings successfully, a station will attract a number of these listeners in these age groups. The more teenagers and young adults who listen to the station, the more the station can charge the advertisers who want to use radio to reach this valuable target audience.

There are a great many formats, including CHR (a newer and more inclusive version of the Top 40 format), adult contemporary (which reaches adults with modern music), urban, country, classic rock (now a fixture on FM), Christian, Latin, modern rock, dance, and classical. There are other specialized formats, too, such as urban contemporary, ethnic, smooth jazz, and news, which has developed several forms, including all-news, news-talk, and other hybrids.

While there are some very narrow formats, and the names used to describe them vary widely, at latest four formats—news-talk, adult contemporary, popular hits, and black-specific—accounted for more than half of all radio listening.

Format, remember, is more than music. The formula for constructing a format might be expressed as production, personality, and programming. How the production, personality, and programming are integrated into a format depends on a marketing decision by the station's management. This decision is usually based on a careful analysis of the competition in a given market and an ascertainment of which audience segments can realistically be expected to become listeners to a particular station. A format is then sought that will position the station to attract a large share of listeners in that market.

Stations switch formats frequently. Switching usually occurs because of a decision to go after a more profitable demographic segment; in other instances, the tastes of audiences may shift. Perhaps there is too much competition in a particular format, and a station elects to go after a segment of the audience for which there is less competition. Often, the switch comes about because station management believes the listenership is skewing too old.

Rightly or wrongly (and there is good evidence that it is wrong) the presumption is that older audiences are less likely to change buying habits than younger listeners and are tighter with their discretionary income.

HOW FORMATS ARE CONSTRUCTED

Stations assemble their formats in several different ways. Some simply obtain recordings and program them in some sort of sequence throughout the schedule. Other stations carry different formats for different parts of the day. A station that plays mostly music throughout the day may feature a talk show during the morning drive time.

The different times of the broadcast day are called **dayparts**. Research has shown that different populations or demographics listen to different dayparts. We tune into one station because we want to hear traffic reports in the morning, but we may prefer another station in the afternoon because of the music that particular station plays. We tune into a third station at night because it carries a sports broadcast we're interested in hearing.

A very big industry that has grown up in recent years provides stations with "ready-to-use" formats. Firms known as **syndicators** will, for a fee, provide satellite feeds, music tapes, or program features ready for broadcast. The music has been carefully planned and produced in a pattern designed to attract the maximum numbers of listeners in the desired audience segments. Some formats are delivered to stations via satellite. Some of these services have all the music and announcer segments included, with spaces for local commercials and newscasts. Others simply supply music on compact discs or through Internet audio files.

Computer automation in radio has made it possible to use programming from syndicators. This means only a minimum number of people are needed at the station level to get the program on the air. Many stations whose programming appears to involve many people performing various functions over the air are actually staffed by a sole operator, babysitting a computer that stores the station's music, voice tracks, commercials, and promotional announcements on a large hard drive.

Radio formats enjoy a particular advantage in the media world because they reliably reach an identifiable audience as well as reach a large share of the population. This is an attractive mixture for advertisers, who know that they can count on radio advertising hitting a sizable share of the population: According to the Radio Advertising Bureau, close to three-quarters of the population of Americans over the age of 12 listens to radio at some point during the day. The concept is known as *radio reach,* a concept discussed at some length in Chapter 16.

Moreover, the individual formats constructed for radio have a built-in appeal for certain audiences. News/talk/information, for example, currently garners the largest percentage (about 17 percent) of radio listeners and is a tried-and-true vehicle for reaching businesspeople. Adult contemporary, usually featuring softer versions of current music, reaches about 15 percent of radio listeners and is a staple of on-the-job listening—a perfect venue for, let's say, advertising for vacation destinations.

INDUSTRY UPDATE • COUNTRY RADIO AND THE NEW MEDIA

Bill Mayne, executive director of the Country Radio Broadcasters trade association, is bullish on the future of radio—country radio in particular—and the advances of new technologies.

Mayne told the *Nashville Tennessean* newspaper: "In the past, radio was confined to the geography of the power of [the] transmitter and the height of [the] tower—what's called the coverage area. The Internet provides a mega-transmitter and mega-tower that allows radio to serve the entire world."

That changes the industry's business model "tremendously," Mayne told the *Tennessean*. "It's now about going after nontraditional revenue. You can go to even small market stations, and they're making money from advertising on their streaming sites. We also need to understand how our listeners operate, especially with new media and social networking."

Despite technological advances, Mayne still sees a role for the human touch: "[A] music service like Pandora is just music, whereas a radio station provides a lot of entertainment and information and human contact. That's one of radio's great strengths."

Mayne tells the *Tennessean* that when recordable cassettes first appeared, there was widespread speculation that radio would be out of business. "But that's not the case, because people like that companionship factor. You may be able to order shoes online, but that doesn't mean you'll quit going to Off Broadway Shoes because you like to go down the aisle and reach in the bins and have that tactile experience. It comes down to who serves up the best program."[2]

_____

2. Nashville Tennessean, http://www.tennessean.com/article/20110227/BUSINESS06/102270353/Country-broadcasters-keep-touch Feb. 27, 2011

NETWORKS

In the 1930s and 1940s, radio networks were major sources of programming for affiliated radio stations around the country. They supplied news, comedy, variety, and dramatic shows, along with music programs of all types. At one point, local origination on many stations merely filled the hole in the network schedules. In fact, rules were developed by the Federal Communications Commission (FCC) to prevent the domination of radio station schedules by network programming.

Today's radio networks serve a function quite different from those of the earlier era. Stations depend on a wide array of networks as ancillary sources of programming and use them to supplement locally originated programming. Many stations take news from networks, and this allows them to provide a type of national and international news service that usually would not be available from a strictly local operation. In addition, radio networks often offer short feature programs to their affiliated stations; these programs may be carried directly from the network or used later.

Many radio networks have begun to offer blocks of radio programming to local stations. Networks, for example, offer stations programming blocks featuring political-entertainment formats like Rush Limbaugh. Increasingly, networks are also providing other forms of programming, such as music or holiday specials; this programming is used by affiliates to supplement their local schedules. In return, networks expect their affiliates to carry the networks' advertising. Such advertising is the networks' basic source of revenue.

Networks also take advantage of modern technology to offer programs to their affiliates via satellite (see Figure 1.1), which provides excellent-quality sound reproduction. And though radio networks are certainly less of a programming centerpiece than in pre-television days, growth in services is occurring rapidly. Many foresee the day when network services will not differ greatly from those of format syndicators.

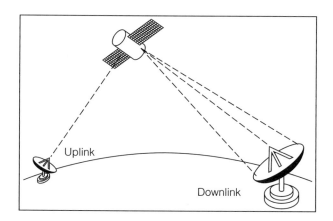

Uplink

Downlink

FIGURE 1.1

Signals from the earth are transmitted from a satellite 22,000 miles above the Earth. The signal is received on the satellite's transponder and retransmitted to a satellite dish on the Earth's surface.

Apps, or applications—or, to be precise, small programs that run on various devices, including mobile devices—are the emerging frontier of radio.

Some contend that apps for terrestrial are just a fad, reports Mike Stern of MediaLifeMagazine.com. Critics say that the real strength in apps is in personalized services such as Pandora, not in repackaging radio station content through streams.

App fans argue that apps reach the customer everywhere through mobile phones and are a powerful advertising vehicle because they can reach listeners on the move and closer to points of purchase. But Stern notes that apps will be more attractive if they offer a true two-way relationship with the station: "That may sound pie-in-the-sky, but in fact that sort of relationship is very much a part of radio's history, actually more so than with any other media.

"Besides being a reliable source for local information, radio was the original social medium, connecting listeners to stations and DJs with requests and dedications. Apps can fill that role by allowing them to shoot requests and comments to the station via the Internet," Stern writes.[3]

3. http://www.medialifemagazine.com/artman2/publish/Radio_46/Are-apps-the-great-hope-for-radio-.asp Feb. 15, 2011

OTHER PROGRAMMING DEVELOPMENTS IN RADIO

Format syndication, network programming, and locally produced elements form the bulk of programming sources in modern radio. Variations, such as syndicators who specialize in short health features, food shows, business reports, and so on, emerge almost daily. Nonmusical formats, such as all-news, sports, and all-talk, also thrive.

Radio production is a medium of great vitality, a medium that is still developing rapidly. It is exciting and full of career opportunities. Production—using sound elements to create an effect or deliver a message—has always been and will always be a key element in radio.

SATELLITE RADIO COMES OF AGE

Today, satellite radio, with myriad channels, is redefining radio by introducing new niche formats. Sirius and XM merged in late 2008, and the company provides continuous programming broadcast from geostationary satellites in space directly to your car or home receiver.[4]

The ability to drive long distances without changing the channel could change the way people listen to radio. For example, if your taste is strictly swing music, you could drive from Bridgeport, Connecticut, to Eugene, Oregon listening to the same channel.

4. Jon Fin, "Requiem for Old-Time Radio," *BusinessWeek*, March 10, 2008, 79.

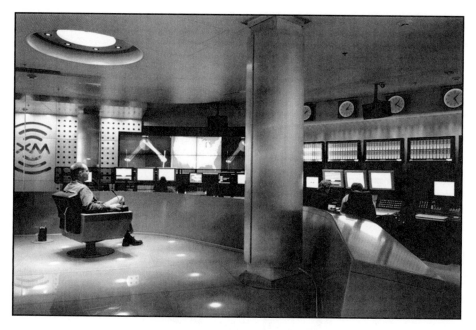

FIGURE 1.2

XM Radio's broadcast operations center controls two satellites and more than 170 digital channels of radio.

SOURCE: XM Radio

Because the satellite system offers more than one hundred channels of proprietary programming, listeners have quite a variety to choose from. Sirius–XM Radio has stations featuring programming from a range as wide as Sinatra, radio drama, heavy metal, hip-hop, Spanish-language, French-language, Howard Stern, comedy, and all-news. Sirius has moved into the business of covering special events, too. In May 2011, Sirius announced it was going to offer flag-to-flag coverage of the Indianapolis 500.[5]

Other innovations separate satellite radio from analog AM or FM. First, satellite radio sounds better than terrestrial radio because the signals are digital. Another difference is the production facilities. Satellite radio studios are among the most modern in the industry (see Figure 1.2). In addition to offering crystal-clear sound quality, satellite radio receivers are capable of displaying the title of the song and the name of the artist. You'll never have to wonder about the artist name or song title of that last selection.

But there are a couple of catches. You need a special receiver for satellite service, and currently available satellite receivers are only compatible with single

5. http://artsandentertainmentplayground.com/2011/05/26/sirius-xm-radio-to-offer-live-coverage-of-the-indianapolis-500/

TUNING IN TO TECHNOLOGY • WEB RADIO

The World Wide Web has turned the radio industry upside down, and while at first radio management often viewed the Web as a threat, many stations as well as chains such as Clear Channel Communications view the online world as an exciting new opportunity, providing listeners with additional features and listening options. (see Figure 1.3).

There are two main technological approaches to Web radio: streaming and podcasting. **Streaming** means putting out a digital signal in real time.

The quality is quite good and reaches into large buildings that often thwart a standard radio signal. This results in bigger midday audiences, as well as a chance to use the middle of the day to promote the drive times in the morning and afternoon, when people will be listening to the terrestrial signals in their cars.

Podcasting means distributing a program in MP3 or other formats. The term refers to Apple's iPod device, but you don't need an iPod to listen to podcast

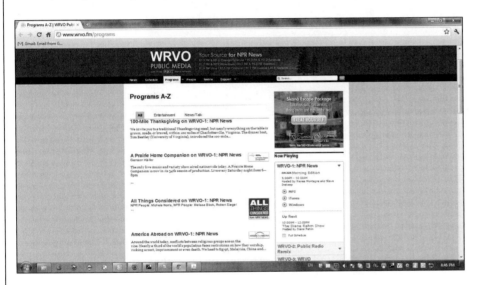

FIGURE 1.3

Podcasting has become a useful way for stations to reproduce programming.

SOURCE: WRVO-FM, Oswego, NY.

services. Radios made for XM Radio cannot tune into all of Sirius programming, and vice versa, although, as a result of the merger, the two companies have started to combine and share program resources. Also, satellite radio is not local, so if you need to listen for special weather or traffic information, you'll still need to tune into good old AM or FM radio.

Satellite radio has had an unusual history over the past couple of years. It has not lived up to its expected potential, although it certainly is a force to be reckoned with. As 2008 drew to a close, satellite radio had more than 18 million subscribers.

content. Any digital storage and playback device will do, and the term has caused some real consternation to manufacturers who are Apple's rivals and bristle at having to use the name.

Podcasting is very different from streaming in that the program is sent out as a *recording*. While that offers convenience for listeners, it plays havoc with music licensing. Currently, the major music licensing agencies won't allow music to be podcast because it amounts to distributing a recording, which can then be easily redistributed from one person to another. While streaming audio was once a problem for licensing agencies, standard agreements have been worked out that allow big-label music to be streamed from websites.

In a classic example of how technology and regulation shape programming, podcasting is developing into a first-rate news and information service. National Public Radio (NPR) offers many features on podcast, and major talk shows also distribute excerpts. Clear Channel distributes some original comedy via podcast, including a daily prank telephone call program that has received a total of about half a million downloads.

With about 20 percent of the population using digital recording devices and the number expected to go nowhere but up, the service we call podcasting may in fact be the future of radio.

Anyone beginning a career in radio should acquire skills in Web operations as soon as possible. Check out http://www.radio-locator.com and www.webcasting.com to get an overview of what's out there. Also, see what's happening at http://www.clearchannel.com and http://www.cbsradio.com. Both are good examples of the role of the World Wide Web in the commercial radio industry. And make a stop at http://www.apple.com/podcasting for a primer on podcasting.

About one in five radio listeners regularly tunes into podcasts, according to various surveys, and those involved in new media sometimes actually view podcasts as "old fashioned" in that they provide an essentially linear experience. In other words, it's a beginning-to-end program rather than something interactive.

Having said that, it's interesting to note that song "tagging" on live radio may soon effectively marry the linear podcast to the interactive radio scene. By digitally identifying a song for download, both parties in the radio listening transaction have something to gain.

But when you get right down to the base product—a song or series of songs stored digitally—the iPod and other MP3 players are a force to be reckoned with and certainly a threat to terrestrial and satellite radio. More cars are coming off the assembly line with jacks for MP3 players. In addition, cell phones can increasingly be used as MP3 players and plugged into those jacks. Cell phones are also becoming destinations for streaming music because of the availability of high-speed data networks.

One final note about podcasting: Some recent research shows that teenagers are particularly fond of MP3 and computer listening. Teenagers' use of the devices is increasing and at the same time their reliance on terrestrial radio is dropping.

Digital radio has performed below the expectations of many industry observers also, but the technology is still being developed and certain aspects are intriguing. For example, the latest technology on the horizon involves using a display screen for Internet or broadcast digital radio to "bookmark" radio content in order to return to it later, much the same way a TiVo marks content on video.

There are many advantages to a digital display screen that advertisers and producers can exploit, not the least of which are its capacities to display memorable images related to the product.

The ability of a digital engine to mix and match data about listeners' preferences is also in its infancy but promises to bring about sweeping changes in advertising for Internet radio. A good example of this is the service Pandora, which builds playlists based on previous listening habits. If you haven't tried it, it's uncanny: based on a few songs you select, the service will serve up more that are keyed to your tastes. Mated with other technologies, such services promise to open a new cash stream in the radio business.

Online listening is increasing yearly. The music and radio trade journal *Billboard* reports that in early summer of 2008, survey data showed that 46 percent of the general public listened to online radio, up from 28 percent in 2002. The major reason cited by those who tune to radio online is the ability to control the music being played (21 percent), with 17 percent saying they listened online to hear music not available elsewhere.[6]

HD radio is lagging behind industry expectations, but there are some bright spots on the horizon. First, the industry is lobbying for automakers to include the technology in more vehicles. A similar action was responsible for the growth of FM radio, which, believe it or not, almost died out before the widespread introduction of the devices into cars. Also, many programmers are experimenting with adding additional channels to their HD offerings. A typical HD channel can add two and sometimes three extra streams to the signal. Some of these extra channels appear to garner large and loyal audiences, though this cannot be assured.

THINK ABOUT IT • ETHICAL ISSUES IN MODERN RADIO

National Public Radio's firing of senior news analyst Juan Williams fueled a 2010 controversy over the ethics of his remarks as well as the moral justification for his dismissal.

Speaking to conservative firebrand Bill O'Reilly on his Fox show *The O'Reilly Factor*, Williams said that seeing people in full Muslim dress at airports made him "nervous" and "worried," according to the CBS report.

Williams was fired quickly by NPR, whose head, Vivian Schiller, said that NPR reporters and analysts should not be expressing their opinions in media appearances since it damages the public trust in their objectivity.

NPR's own coverage of the Williams firing noted that he also said during the O'Reilly program that Muslims should not be stereotyped as terrorists.

Williams, who quickly accepted a job offer from Fox News, said that other NPR commentators had made similar remarks that did not result in firings, reports the Canadian Press.

Williams contended that NPR commentator Nina Totenberg said 15 years ago that if there is "retributive justice," former North Carolina Senator Jessie Helms would get AIDS from a blood transfusion. An NPR spokesman told the Canadian Press that Totenberg repeatedly had apologized for the comment.

Conservatives immediately protested Williams's termination, and some in Congress called for an end to government funding for NPR, according to a report in *The Atlantic*.

Some defenders of NPR's action said that the network was well within its rights to determine what is acceptable behavior for its employees.

Schiller apologized on Monday for her handling of the incident, but not for the firing itself.

Question for discussion: Do you think it was fair for NPR to fire Williams?[7]

---

7. http://www.globalethics.org/newsline/2010/10/25/fox-npr-firing/

---

6. Antony Bruno, "Clear Channel, CBS Expand Online," *Billboard*, May 24, 2008, 26.

FOLLOW THE MONEY • TRENDS IN RADIO REVENUE

Revenue in 2010 disclosed some interesting trends, according to Radio Advertising Bureau data tabulated by *Radio World* magazine.

Total revenue for commercial U.S. radio added up to $17.3 billion. That's up 6 percent from 2009. The jump is welcome news because it comes after six years of decline or stagnation.

- Digital radio revenue was up 24 percent. However, digital revenues accounted for only $615 million of the $17.3 billion total. (*Digital* refers to Web radio, streaming media, and HD radio.)

- Local spot radio makes up the biggest chunk of revenue by far: $14.1 billion.

- The major component of local spot radio was auto advertising, contributing $1.8 billion.[8]

8. http://www.radioworld.com/article/114036 Feb. 18, 2011

NONCOMMERCIAL RADIO

Much of what we have said so far about the radio industry pertains to that segment of the industry geared toward making a profit for its owners. Noncommercial radio exists for other reasons.

Noncommercial radio includes a relatively small number of stations that gain their financial support strictly through the generosity of donors. Some of these outlets are affiliated with nonprofit organizations, such as religious organizations or community organizations. These radio stations receive most of their funds from their parent organizations or listeners, with occasional grants from foundations or businesses.

ECONOMICS OF RADIO

The majority of stations in the United States are licensed to broadcast commercially. They program a wide variety of entertainment and informational material. Commercial stations make money by selling advertising time within the programming to reach specific listening audiences. This has been the basic economic model for radio since 1927, and it is important to note that increased consolidation over the past 10 years has made the radio market more profit centered. Large corporations purchase radio stations to make money and to make it more efficiently: When a corporation owns many radio stations, it can achieve economies of scale by consolidating functions such as management, technology, and programming. Such consolidations have resulted in the loss of many jobs in the radio market. However, new economic trends mean that there is still a role for multitalented production staff members who are skilled at in-demand tasks, such as computer-assisted editing.

But there is another vibrant force in radio that is noncommercial. Public radio is the segment of the industry most people think of when they think of noncommercial radio. Public radio is characterized by its participation in a funding structure that includes two major sources of revenue: government funds and private funds. Government funds are distributed to public radio for use in station operations and programming costs. The formulas and procedures that govern how this funding is distributed are complex, and it serves no purpose to go into the details here. The other major source of funds for public radio is through solicitation of donations from listeners and other private sources.

Unlike commercial radio outlets, noncommercial radio stations are not tightly wedded to specific formats designed to increase listenership. Two types of noncommercial radio stations exist.

Public radio stations provide programming that is not generally available through commercial outlets. This philosophy is reflected in the broad scope of programming that is heard on NPR or Public Radio International (PRI). Extensive daily news programs like *All Things Considered*, live broadcasts of classical music or jazz, and coverage of such events as National Press Club luncheons are some examples of the kinds of programming that most commercial stations would shun, fearing lack of substantial audience interest.

The second type of noncommercial station is sponsored by nonprofit organizations such as colleges, churches, and local community groups. These stations present an eclectic assortment of programming that does not fit into specific format categories. These stations often serve as important training grounds for people interested in radio as a career. While both public and college radio stations rely on volunteers to help operate the stations, frequently content is provided by students in college stations. Another major programming difference between noncommercial stations and mainstream radio is the absence of commercials. At one time, it was a sacrosanct principle in public radio that promoting commercial products and services was inappropriate. In recent years, however, this prohibition has relaxed with the recognition that more underwriters could be persuaded to give more money for programming if they were allowed to use some of the time allocated for announcing their donations to get in a short pitch for their products and services.

The absence of commercials hasn't prevented some listeners from criticizing public radio stations for their on-air fund-raising efforts. At increasingly frequent intervals, it seems, most public radio stations take breaks from their scheduled programming to air lengthy appeals for donations from listeners. Some listeners say they would prefer product commercials to what they sometimes label as harangues that appeal to guilt and threats to drop programming unless listeners contribute.

Some stations have experimented with alternative methods of soliciting donations, such as promising to shorten or eliminate scheduled on-air fund-raising drives if they meet a certain donation level before the time drives are scheduled to begin. Efforts like these have had limited success in some areas, but the bottom line is that there will always have to be some way of appealing for funds if public broadcasting is to continue to survive.

Noncommercial broadcasting offers many opportunities for radio production people. Depending on whether you work at a small or large station or at the network level in public broadcasting, you are likely to find a wider variety of radio production taking place in noncommercial radio than in commercial radio.

TUNING IN TO TECHNOLOGY • ARE TEXT MESSAGES RADIO'S NEW CASH COW?

Writing in the radio trade journal *RadioInk.com*, marketer Bob Bentz notes that Americans are now sending more text messages per month than they use minutes per month on their cell phones. Nielsen research puts the average rate per user at 523 text messages per month.

With this in mind, Bentz reports, radio stations are turning to texting as a tool to reach their P-1 listeners—meaning members of the audience who listen to the station more than other stations. Text messaging is an ideal tool for collecting a database of those listeners. For one thing, it is an opt-in system, meaning that you are not spamming people of out the blue.

One common method to build the database is to hold a text-message-based sweepstakes. A text sweepstakes is less annoying than *phone based contests* to

listeners, because they don't have to spend a lot of time on hold or hearing a busy signal.

Now, writes Bentz, you can monetize that database. One way is to sell to a sponsor 40 of the 160 available characters in the texts you send out to your listener database. The sponsor's message appears for a certain amount of time—usually 15 days—in all messages sent out by the station.

The beauty of the system is that you can have the station's sales staff sell the messages or, if that fails, you can turn to your mobile service provider, who often is able to insert national spots to offset the costs of the text messaging sweepstakes.[9]

---

9. http://www.radioink.com/article.asp?id=2121537=spid=24698 (Accessed September 12, 2011)

Drama is still aired on public radio, for example, and many stations record musical performances on location. Such projects challenge radio producers in ways that commercial radio never will. Some noncommercial situations may also have more news production. And, of course, **airshifts** (discussed on page 21) require the ability to operate the equipment in an on-air studio.

Today many noncommercial stations and NPR itself, along with various nonprofit agencies, also maintain an Internet presence using many facets of technology, including podcasts and RSS (Really Simple Syndication) feeds. A prime example of a nonprofit exploiting radio technologies to their fullest is AARP, a huge association for older adults. AARP syndicates a radio program in many markets and maintains an enormous bank of downloadable programs. You can check out AARP's radio operation at http://radioprimetime.org/index.htm.

THE ROLE OF THE PRODUCER IN MODERN RADIO

With all the excitement over automated radio and prerecorded formats, it may appear that little remains to be done in radio production at the local level. In fact, the opposite is true.

Production skills form the basis of producing a station's sound. Without those skills, the unique sound can't be created. But skills alone won't suffice, and that's why we've begun this production book with a discussion of programming. Good production is an extension of the station's programming, and a **producer**—anyone who manipulates sound to create an effect or deliver a message—must tailor that production to reinforce the station's sound.

An increasingly important area of radio station operations is promotion. Today's climate of intense competition among all forms of media for audience attention means that stations must work harder than ever to make themselves stand out. Production plays a key role in this process. Audience promotion takes many forms—websites, on-air contests, bumper stickers, and other premiums bearing the station's identifying graphics; billboards; television advertising; and the like. But a key resource for audience building is the station's airtime. Production people can play a major role in helping a station promote itself by creating imaginative uses of sound to create a clear identity for the station in listeners' minds.

In this text, we explore the nuts and bolts of radio broadcasting. By learning the elements of radio production, you will be exploring the essence of radio programming. Production, from a mechanical standpoint, is a method of combining various sources of sound into a product that accomplishes something specific. Anyone in a radio station can perform this function. The sales manager who records and assembles a commercial is a producer, as is the person who constructs a newscast. The staff announcer who runs the console (known as a **combo** operation) is also a producer. In larger stations, the bulk of the production may be the responsibility of a production manager, who specializes in producing such items as commercials, public service announcements (PSAs), or talk shows. Some very large stations and networks have full-time producers who exclusively handle specialized programming, such as news, concerts and sporting events (see Figure 1.4).

The particular responsibilities of a producer depend on the station where he or she is employed. Radio stations vary in sophistication, from small, daytime-only stations with minimal and aging equipment to high-tech powerhouses in

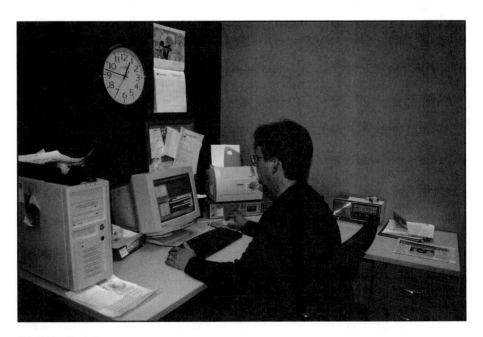

FIGURE 1.4

Modern newsrooms often are computer workstations. Here a reporter files a story on the central news computer. Next he will go into a production booth to voice an actuality.

SOURCE: Fritz Messere

major cities. But regardless of the size of the station, the role and importance of production and the producer is the same.

A producer may be called on to create and execute a commercial that sells a sponsor's product, to put together a newscast introduction that arrests the listener's attention, or to combine a number of previously recorded elements with live vocal delivery in a distinctive package known as an **airshift**. All these functions, and more, create the radio product in small, medium-sized, and large markets.

By becoming proficient at these tasks, you will be opening the door to a variety of opportunities in the radio field. And although our focus is radio broadcasting, the skills and knowledge in this text can be applied in various other professional situations. Studio recording; sound production for streaming and podcasting; multimedia presentations; audio for television; and specialized sound production for advertising agencies, production houses, and other commercial clients also require many of the skills covered in this text.

Overall, you will be exploring a field that requires a variety of skills, and you'll need to invest some time in learning them. But understanding the basics is just the beginning. Real proficiency in radio production requires professional commitment, experience, creativity, and a certain sense of adventure. A truly effective production bears the identifying mark of its producer. It is unique. The skills involved are tools. The way you use the tools makes the difference.

Even though some frustration may be involved in trying to come up with a production that sounds the way you've heard it in your mind, much satisfaction results when the magic happens and you can hear the finished result of your efforts and say, "Yes! That's it!" Many radio veterans feel that production is one of the most satisfying parts of their jobs. It's a chance to be, at once, an artist, a technician, and a performer. Production is one of the key jobs in any radio station. The people who do production well are those who form the foundation of radio broadcasting.

In addition, audio production opens up career opportunities in areas other than radio broadcasting. Film and television also require competent audio producers, and business and industry require the services of skilled in-house producers.

So enjoy yourself while you learn how to produce the magic. You'll work hard, but the rewards will be long lasting. You will acquire skills that will last a lifetime. You may also develop an enduring passion for this exciting and rewarding activity and for a profession that is a vital part of our world today.

SUMMARY

Radio has moved from a mass-audience medium to a more specific medium; that is, it reaches a specific target audience that is more narrowly defined than is the audience targeted by the modern mass medium of television.

Formats during the Golden Age featured imaginative and often lush production effects, including full symphony orchestras. The Golden Age was also the heyday of the "theater of the mind"—when radio dramas transported listeners through imaginative storytelling and live sound effects. Producers came to appreciate the full value of the medium's impact.

YOU'RE ON! • TECHNIQUES FOR EFFECTIVE ON-AIR PERFORMANCE: THE ROLE OF THE ANNOUNCER IN MODERN RADIO

The "You're On!" features in this edition of *Modern Radio Production* will help you understand the workings of on-air communication as they apply to the content of specific chapters. Though not every radio producer will go on-air, many will. For example, even if you don't run a live airshift, you may find yourself recording commercials, promotions, or other announcements. Perhaps you might do an occasional newscast. And if you do not go on-mic yourself, as a producer you will certainly be working with on-air talent and will need to understand these techniques, skills, and requirements.

To begin this exploration of the role of the announcer in modern radio, we need to travel briefly to the past.

Early Announcers

The first announcers on radio were part salespeople, part masters of ceremonies (MCs), and part sophisticated guides to the world's events. Announcers would perform varied duties, such as acting as MC of a variety program, announcing the cast of a drama, or serving as the introducer of a play (see Figure 1.5). The announcer was seen as performing, rather than talking, when on the air. This perception resulted in the development of a stylized form of speech that was emphatic and dramatic. Announcers used a distinctive style that was heard nowhere else but in radio.

The Modern Medium

When television arrived in the 1950s, radio found it could no longer fulfill the mission of being the medium of choice for everyone. Gone were the days of grand

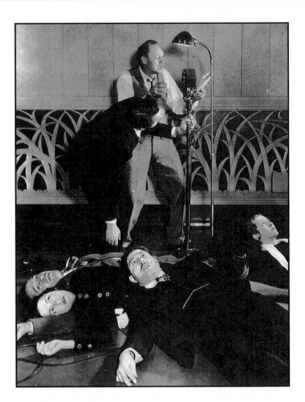

FIGURE 1.5

Radio drama enacted in NBC radio studio with the aid of a sound effects man and groaning victims (on floor) on Lights Out.
SOURCE: Bettmann/CORBIS

The sound of a radio station is the overall blending of music, vocal delivery, timing, pacing, and other production elements that combine to create a cohesive, identifiable signature. Today's commercial radio station carefully develops and fine-tunes its format to reach a quantifiable target audience—an audience that is, in turn, "sold" to buyers of radio-station advertising time. Noncommercial radio provides programming choices that are alternatives to these specific formats.

radio variety programs or weekly comedies. Almost by accident, radio began serving as a lifestyle companion for people who enjoyed a certain type of music. Up until the 1950s, the idea of playing recorded music on radio did not occur to many industry executives, but the desperation wrought by the arrival of television— media's 800-pound gorilla—impelled them to try.

And radio for the individual turned out to be a smashing success. The medium, now portable because of the introduction of the transistor radio, surrounded the listener with non stop music that reinforced a particular lifestyle. Today, we see an increasing specialization of radio and formats that are tailored toward highly specific audiences.

What This Means to the Announcer

For the on-air performer, the evolution of radio has several very clear implications:

1. Reaching the individual is the key. One-to-one contact is the name of the game in radio. Two people—the announcer and the listener—are sharing music and a lifestyle. As a result, the announcer's style must be intimate, communicative, and personal. There is very little room in radio today for the old-style, affected, booming "announcer voice."
2. Understanding the material is critical. The old-style announcer had to be glib and facile in handling an incredibly wide variety of tasks, from introducing classical music and announcing polka selections to moderating a local quiz program. Today, an announcer will be handling only one style of music, and further, usually only a specific niche within that style. (For example, "hot" rock-style country occupies a different niche than generic country music.) It is difficult or impossible to fake knowledge of music for such a concentrated audience, and audiences will not tolerate announcers who don't know the material.
3. Technical competence is important. At one time, announcers would simply read copy. They did not touch equipment, and, in fact, were often prohibited from doing so by union rules. There was sometimes good reason for this—early radio equipment was complex, jury-rigged, and often dangerous if mishandled. Later on, as equipment became simplified and standardized, it became part of the announcer's duty to run his or her own "board," or console. Today, you'll need to know your way around a computer because it is likely that you'll be executing some commands via computer-run editing programs or even having the computer "fire" your next music cut.

In summary, the days of the booming, golden-throated announcer are gone, and it is important that you avoid sounding like the stereotypical "hello-out-there-in-radio-land" announcer. That style is extinct and exists only at camp when someone is making fun of it.

The impact of networks declined considerably after the Golden Age, but satellite transmission capabilities, streaming, podcasting, and other technical advances have given new life to the network concept. Many stations now integrate network programming in a blend that complements their formats, allowing stations to localize the network feed.

2

The Console

Probably nothing in radio production is more intimidating than one's first exposure to the **console**—a complex network of switches, knobs, and meters—or sometimes, a dauntingly complex computer screen. However, operating the console, or **board**, soon becomes second nature. In fact, most radio professionals will tell you something like, "When I first started in radio, all I thought about was running the board and what would happen when I changed jobs and had to learn a new board. But after a few months, I found out that running the board was really one of the simplest aspects of the job. And when I changed stations, I picked up the new board in an afternoon."

We think it's important to emphasize that one does acquire familiarity with the console because many newcomers to radio production become discouraged with their first few experiences at the controls and never gain the confidence they need to experiment, to use the board as a versatile tool, and to "play" it like a musical instrument.

Remember, anyone can learn to run a console. You don't have to be an engineer or a technician; all you need is an understanding of what the console does and some practice in the necessary mechanical operating skills.

FUNCTION OF THE CONSOLE

Whether digital or analog, the audio console is simply a device for amplifying, routing, and mixing audio signals. It's important to keep the distinction between *audio* and *sound* firmly in mind. **Audio** is the term used to refer to the electrical signals that are involved in the reproduction or transmission of sound. **Sound** is a vibration through air or another medium.

Amplification

Amplification is the boosting of a signal to a usable level. The tiny voltage produced by a computer workstation, a CD player, a microphone, or some other audio input is not strong enough to send to a loudspeaker or over the air. This is precisely why your MP3 player needs to be connected to an amplifier and speakers to play without headphones. But unlike an MP3 player, the console gives the operator convenient control over the **volume** of various signal sources such as microphones, computers, CD players, digital cart machines, and other playback units. The operator can control one source in relationship to all the others.

Routing

The console allows the producer to determine the path of the signal or, in other words, to **route** it. As you will see, the console can send a signal over the air, to a computer for recording, or into a cue channel, which lets the operator preview an audio source without having the signal go over the air. In addition to routing signals through the console, the operator can turn signals on and off.

Mixing

The console can put two signals out at once—the announcer's voice and music, for example. The console also allows the volume of both to be controlled separately, or **mixed**, so that the music doesn't drown out the announcer.

Through amplification, routing, and mixing, the console operator can produce a final product that will be sent out over the air (as in the case of a radio announcer doing an airshift) or routed to a computer or some other recording device (as someone would do when producing a commercial to be played back over the air later).

UNDERSTANDING CONSOLE FUNCTION: SOME HYPOTHETICAL EXAMPLES

The preceding discussion of amplification, routing, and mixing is fine as a theoretical explanation of how a console works, but how do they function in practice?

To explain, let's take an approach that is a bit unusual: We will present a series of hypothetical consoles used at equally hypothetical radio stations. We'll briefly touch on the use of CD players, microphones, and playback units, but detailed instruction about these devices comes in later chapters. So don't worry about anything except understanding what the console does and why it does it. The purpose of these examples is to demonstrate how a console carries out certain operations.

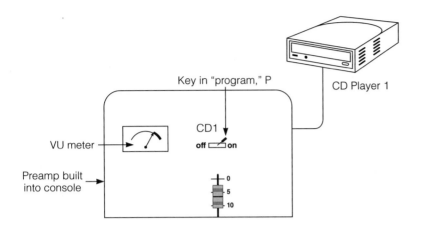

Key in "program," P

CD1

off on

VU meter

Preamp built into console

0
5
10

FIGURE 2.1

Console *A* at a station that uses only one CD player (CD1).

We will show standard "physical" consoles that resemble what are commonly used in most stations today. We should note here that digital consoles can convert analog audio into data or use data straight from a digital input source, such as a computer or digital audio cart; however, for the purposes of our discussion, we'll assume that analog and digital consoles function the same way. Later in the chapter we'll discuss digital consoles in more detail.

We'll make one more distinction here. Broadcast consoles and audio mixing consoles essentially do the same thing, but audio consoles for broadcasting usually look very different than audio consoles designed for mixing music. Right now we're going to focus on broadcast consoles.

Hypothetical Console *A*

At our first hypothetical radio station, hypothetical console *A* plays only one sound, the same disc, over and over. The only equipment owned by this station consists of a **CD player** and console *A* (see Figure 2.1). The following are the features on console *A*.

Preamplifier   The signal from some input devices is very weak, so a device called a **preamplifier** (usually shortened to *preamp)* boosts it to a more usable level. Here console *A* has a CD player connected to it. It could just as easily be a computer or an iPod™.

Potentiometer   In engineering terms, a **potentiometer** is a variable resistor; in lay terms, it's nothing more than a volume control. The potentiometer is almost always referred to as the **fader**. You might hear some radio professionals refer to it as a "pot." That's because older consoles had rotating potentiometers (like volume controls) instead of faders. Usually, a slide fader adjusts volume, just as a rheostat dimmer adjusts the level of lights in a dining room. The fader raises the volume of the console's output; it is therefore an adjustment for the VU meter (discussed shortly) and not a control for the monitor.

On Button or Routing Switch   The on button is essentially a switch that puts the signal out over the air when it is pushed. Some audio consoles identify it as a "program" button instead. Other consoles have an on button right below the slide fader and a program select switch at the top of the fader. We'll discuss other functions of the routing switch in later examples.

Volume-Unit Meter   You know that the fader allows adjustment of the level of volume, but how do you know what level is correct? Volume is a pretty subjective judgment.

The **volume-unit meter** (usually called a **VU meter**) gives an objective visual representation of loudness. It's a very important component of the console, and the ability to read it properly is critical to every phase of radio production. VU meters may be analog or digital (like the one pictured in Figure 2.2), with an illuminated bar graph.

Essentially, the most important aspect of reading a VU meter is to know that zero on the top scale is the reference for proper volume. A close-up of the meter

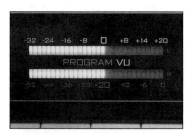

a. Proper-level reading.

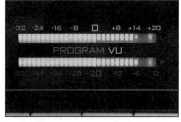

b. Reading "in the red".

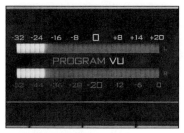

c. Reading "in the mud."

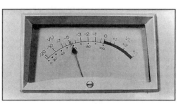

d. This VU meter displays percent of modulation on the bottom scale.

FIGURE 2.2

VU meter readings.

SOURCE: Philip Benoit

on console *A* (see Figure 2.2a) shows that the CD is playing at proper volume or level of sound.

The meter in Figure 2.2a displays numbers from −32 to +20 with 0 zero approximately in the middle. A reading of +14 on the top scale means that the signal is playing too loudly; if it goes much higher, the signal could sound distorted. (A volume unit is a relative measurement of audio loudness and is similar to a decibel, a measurement we discuss in Chapter 5.) A reading above zero is known as being "in the red" because the part of the scale above 0 is often colored red or the light-emitting diodes (LEDs) shine red. A reading of +4 or 5 indicates that matters are worse, and +14 (see Figure 2.2b) will put the meter all the way to the right, known as "pinning the meter," and could cause severe distortion.

On the other hand, too low a reading (down at −32 or −24) will result in too low a music level and too much noise. Noise is always present in electrical components. Even digital components have some noise. When there's not enough signal volume, the noise becomes much more apparent; this is known as an unacceptable signal-to-noise ratio. This is the ratio of the amount of signal in a channel compared to noise in a channel. A greater signal-to-noise ratio is better. A reading consistently lower than −20 or so (see Figure 2.2c) is known as running "in the mud." The operator of console *A* is responsible for keeping the peaks as close to zero as possible. This isn't particularly difficult because the VU meter is built to respond to averages. The color bars (or needle) tend to float around, seeking an average volume level.

The operator should not crank up the pot each time the level drops below zero or crank the pot down each time the needle goes into the red. Riding the pot too closely will result in an elimination of loud and soft passages in music, especially classical music.

LED meters react more quickly to overall levels than do the mechanical VU meters, and the scales may be showing both the peak volume level or the average loudness. In Figure 2.2b the rightmost LED bar is showing the peak volume level and the continuous bars are showing the average volume level. Usually LED VU meters will display green when the signal is within the acceptable range and orange or red when it is over 0 on the scale. Always check with the station engineer to determine the appropriate level for your console.

By the way, some VU meters indicate the percentage of modulation (Figure 2.2d). **Modulation** can be thought of as the imprint of sound on a radio signal, and 100 percent is the ideal. Modulation as measured by our VU meter is a percentage measure of voltage passing through the console to a transmitter or to a recording device. One hundred percent represents the maximum voltage permissible; the fluctuating VU meter can compare the sound imprint of our source to that of the maximum desired level.

Note that 100 percent corresponds to 0 volume units, also the ideal reading. Too much modulation results in an over modulated, distorted signal; too little causes problems with signal-to-noise ratio and makes the signal sound muddy or weak. Whichever scale is used, the major task facing a console operator is to keep the needle on the VU meter hovering around the points marked 0 VU or 100 percent modulation. Occasional volume increases into the red are acceptable—indeed, unavoidable—as are infrequent dips into the mud.

Monitor   The monitor is a loudspeaker or headphones that lets the operator hear what's going over the air. The **monitor loudspeaker** (or **air monitor**) is not really a part of the console, although it is connected to the console and operated by console controls. Usually selection controls allow the operator to use the monitor to listen to a number of sources other than what's going over the air. In essence, the monitor is the operator's personal speaker; it does not affect the sound going out over the air.

Amplifier   Before the signal leaves the board, it is usually amplified—boosted—again. The final step therefore involves putting the signal through the **amplifier**.

Review of Console A   The signal from the CD player first passes through the preamp, an internal electrical function of the console. The volume of the pre-amplified signal is controlled by a fader. After the signal has passed through the fader, a button functions as an on–off switch; in this case, the "on" position is referred to as "program." (You'll learn more about the need for these various switches in our discussion of the next console.) Finally, the signal is amplified again. In the case of a radio station that plays only one disc, the **output** of the console is then sent to the hypothetical transmitter. In Figure 2.3, we have diagrammed console A the way a broadcast engineer would do it.

Console A is certainly simple to operate, and it ideally suits the needs of a station that plays just one disc. But it has no flexibility. It allows only the constant repetition of one disc played on the station's only CD player. You could, of course, change discs, but doing so on-air would leave even larger gaps in the program than would starting all over when you get to the end of the disc and quickly going back to the beginning. So let's see how a more advanced console solves the problem.

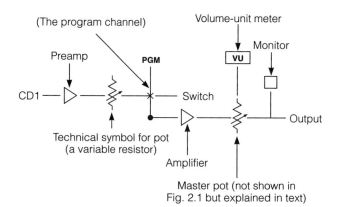

FIGURE 2.3

This engineering diagram shows all of the components in the audio chain for console A. The signals move from the CD through the console components to the output.

Hypothetical Console *B*

The station using hypothetical console *B* has two CD players (see Figure 2.4). This allows the operator to make smooth transitions between selections by having another CD all set to go when one ends. This will eliminate gaps in the program, known in the trade as **dead air**. However, if the goal is to eliminate gaps, the operator must know where the starting point of each CD cut is. There has to be a way to cue the disc—to hear where the first sound in the piece of music starts so that the sound can start immediately after the CD player is started. And as is common in many radio formats, we will **segue** the music; that is, the end of one song and the beginning of another will be overlapped for a second or two.

Console *B* is similar to console *A,* but it has several additions that allow the operator to eliminate gaps and overlap music.

Multiple Input Channels   Having two faders allows the station to use two CD players. This console has two input channels: channel 1 for CD player 1, and channel 2 for CD player 2. CD player 1 and CD player 2 are both sources; that is, each provides an incoming signal. So, aside from the two faders, there will also be two preamps and two program buttons.

The Audition Channel   Don't confuse the audition channel with the input channels on console *B.* The audition channel is a different output from the program channel and provides additional flexibility for the operator. Figure 2.4a shows the switches for both CD players in the audition mode.

Just as the name implies, **audition** allows you to hear a CD, computer, or other source without putting it over the air. The audition channel routes the signal from a source to a speaker in the control room. (There's a recording application, which we will discuss in a moment.) Anything that can be put on program can be played over audition.

Do you notice, in Figure 2.4a, the provision made for selecting the audition channel? The output section in console *B* is really made up of two separate switches. One button turns on the audition channel and one activates the program channel. This is a change from console *A,* which only had a program button that could be turned on and off. Both audition and program can be used independently (see Figure 2.4b).

The Cue Channel   The cue channel serves one of the same purposes as the audition channel: It allows the operator to hear a source without putting it over the air. The operator of console *B* is able, using cue, to find a specific point on a disc before it is played over the station and can therefore cue the disc to start immediately. Cueing often involves determining exactly where to begin the song (some live songs start with applause), so the operator certainly doesn't want to do it over the air. The cue channel plays over a small speaker located within the console. To put the fader in cue, the operator generally selects it by depressing the cue button. Usually, this temporarily disengages the program

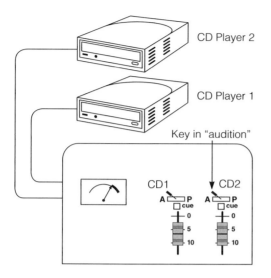

a. Console *B* at a station that uses two CD players (CD1 and CD2).

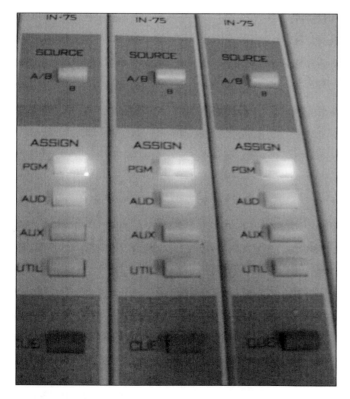

b. Audio console assign switches allow the operator to select program, audition, or other outputs.

SOURCE: Fritz Messere

FIGURE 2.4

channel while the channel is in cue. On older consoles that use knobs instead of faders, you may turn the pot fully counterclockwise to activate the cue channel.

Why, you might wonder, are there two provisions for hearing sources that are not on the air? Cue and audition each have advantages and disadvantages. Cue is very simple to use, as it takes only a push of a button to put the channel into cue. After cueing up a CD, the operator of console B doesn't have to do anything until putting the CD player on air—"potting it up" in radio lingo. But the cue speaker is often tinny and cheap, so if the operator wants to listen to a new piece of music to gauge its suitability for airplay, the cue system is a poor choice.

Audition, on the other hand, routes the signal through a high-quality loud-speaker. Sometimes it is a separate speaker in the control room, though often the audition channel is fed through the same speaker as the program. The operator uses a monitor selector switch (not shown in Figure 2.4a) to determine which channel—program or audition—goes to the speaker. Audition has another very useful capability: If he or she chooses, the operator can play a disc over the air on the program channel while producing a commercial on the audition channel. We explain how this is done later.

Adding the multiple-source channels, the audition channel, and the cue channel to the broadcast engineer's diagram, we have the signal flow of console B, shown in Figure 2.5.

Review of Console B The outputs of two CD players are fed into console B. Each CD player has its own source channel. Because there are two CD players, two source channels, and, of course, two faders, the operator of console B is able to make smooth transitions between CDs, even overlapping the beginning of one with the end of another. More important, the operator of console B can use the audition or cue channel to listen to a source channel without putting it over the air.

As shown in Figure 2.5, the signal flow path for console B starts at the CD players and then proceeds through the appropriate source channels, through the faders and output selectors, and to the audition or program outputs. On this console, the selector buttons let the operator put the signal through either the program or audition channel. Note, too, that the cue channel is activated

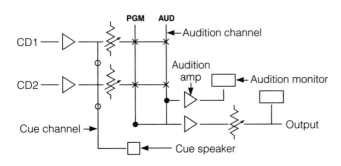

FIGURE 2.5

Engineering diagram of a two-channel console. Compare this with Figure 2.3 and note the added components of an audition channel and cue channel.

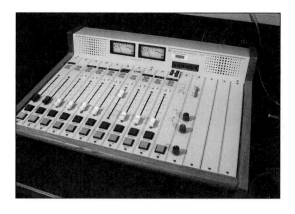

FIGURE 2.6

Small audio consoles like this one are perfect for radio production booths.

SOURCE: Fritz Messere

separately. After the output selector has routed the signal, it goes through an amplifier. The VU meter gauges the loudness of the signal and the signal goes to the transmitter. Figures 2.6 and 2.7 illustrate the locations for these console functions.

Hypothetical Console C

The operator of hypothetical console *C* has a microphone (see Figure 2.8) in the control room and, because of the expanded capabilities of console *B*, can put the microphone over the air and mix it with other sources. The **microphone** is on source channel 1. Beside the microphone, this console has other additions.

The abbreviation *mic*, which is pronounced "mike," is now used widely in the profession (in vendors' literature, in-station printed material, and audio and broadcasting publications). You will see newer consoles with labels "Mic 1," "Mic 2," and so on, and we have used *mic* both as a noun and as an adjective. However, the past and present participles, which are essential in many discussions of radio production, are spelled *miked* and *miking*, respectively. This small inconsistency represents an accommodation to ingrained habits of reading and pronunciation.

Muting System   A special **muting system** cuts the monitor (the loudspeaker that lets the operator know what's going over the air). The muting system is essential when a mic and a speaker are in the same room because, without muting, the mic could pick up the output of the speaker, feed it through the amplification system, pick it up again as it exits the speaker, and so on. The result is known as **feedback**, the same unpleasant phenomenon that occurs when a rock singer gets careless with a microphone too near a speaker. To avoid this result, every time the key switch on the mic channel is opened, the muting system built into a broadcast console will cut the speaker off. We should point out that most audio mixers, as opposed to broadcast consoles, do not have muting circuits. This is one of the differences between consoles built for radio and those meant for

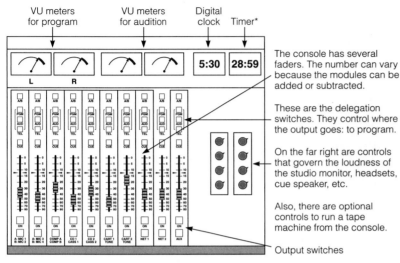

VU meters for program

VU meters for audition

Digital clock

Timer*

The console has several faders. The number can vary because the modules can be added or subtracted.

These are the delegation switches. They control where the output goes: to program.

On the far right are controls that govern the loudness of the studio monitor, headsets, cue speaker, etc.

Also, there are optional controls to run a tape machine from the console.

Output switches

*The timer can keep track of a segment, or how long a particular source plays, or whatever else you program it to do.

a. Functions of a control-room console.

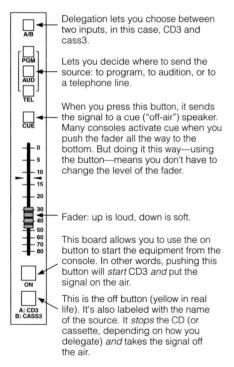

Delegation lets you choose between two inputs, in this case, CD3 and cass3.

Lets you decide where to send the source: to program, to audition, or to a telephone line.

When you press this button, it sends the signal to a cue ("off-air") speaker. Many consoles activate cue when you push the fader all the way to the bottom. But doing it this way—using the button—means you don't have to change the level of the fader.

Fader: up is loud, down is soft.

This board allows you to use the on button to start the equipment from the console. In other words, pushing this button will *start* CD3 *and* put the signal on the air.

This is the off button (yellow in real life). It's also labeled with the name of the source. It *stops* the CD (or cassette, depending on how you delegate) *and* takes the signal off the air.

b. Each audio channel has its own fader. The operator can choose between two inputs and send the signal to program, audition, or other output.

FIGURE 2.7

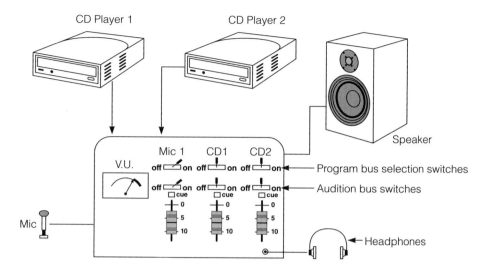

FIGURE 2.8

Console that could be used with two CD players and a microphone.

audio recording or sound reinforcement. The use of a muting circuit, of course, makes necessary the use of the next item: headphones.

Headphones   Headphones form a close seal over the operator's ears, preventing any possibility of feedback. Because the headphones operate when the mic is open, they allow the operator to hear herself or himself speaking into the mic. There's an output for headphones on the console and a pot that controls the headphone volume.

Console *C* also contains a headphone selection button. This allows the operator to hear, for example, the audition channel over the headphones or the cue channel. This feature is very useful if, when the operator is talking over the air, he or she finds that the next program segment hasn't been cued up yet.

Master Fader   This fader controls the entire output of the board. The VU meter actually reads the output of the **master pot**. Many radio production consoles do not have master faders. If they do not, proper output has been pre-adjusted by the engineering staff; the operator is not able to change it. However, many audio mixing consoles have master faders that adjust the relative output from all channels combined.

Review of Console *C*   There are three paths from the equipment in the control room: the two CD players and the mic. In each path, the source channel feeds through a preamp, a fader, a cue channel, a program or audition select button, the console amplifier, and the master pot. Figure 2.9 is an engineering diagram of console *C*.

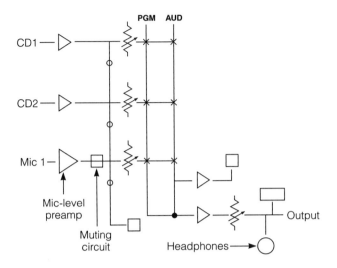

FIGURE 2.9

Signal flow in console C.

Here's one bit of new information: The preamp for a mic is different from the preamp for a CD player. CD players commonly have electronic components built in (these are not shown in Figure 2.9), and the CD player signal is brought into the board at what is known as *line-level*. Other playback devices, such as computers also come into the board at line-level. Mic signals come into the board at a fraction of the level of line-level sources, and the signal goes through a *mic-level* preamp. Because mic-level is lower than line-level, preamps on mic-level channels must raise the level of the signal higher than most preamps for line-level inputs.

The goal of preamps is to bring both the mic- and line-level sources to the same level within the console to simplify the mixing process. It really means that each channel fader on the console will behave similarly without large differences in volume between them.

Hypothetical Console *D*

The radio station using console *D* is linked up with a radio network that supplies a two-minute newscast every hour on the hour. The network feed is brought into the studio via a broadband Internet connection or from a satellite downlink, which the engineer has wired into the board. Another program broadcast on the station using console *D* is a 10-minute telephone talk show, which starts at 30 minutes after the hour.

Now, it certainly doesn't make sense to have two separate channels for signals that are never used at the same time. Console *D* (see Figure 2.10) has an option that allows the operator to choose the network (Net) or the telephone (Tel). Many boards have a specific channel with a set of selection buttons that

---

RADIO RETRO • POTTING DOWN ON THE OLD POT

For many years, almost all broadcast consoles used circular potentiometers, called "pots." When vertical slide faders were developed, they were largely relegated to music recording, where it was important that the engineer be able to look at the pattern of vertical faders to see which channels were high and which were low.

The word *pot* entered radio vocabulary and mutated into a verb, which you may still hear today: "Pot up, the voice is too low," or "pot down, you're distorting."

Circular pots are disappearing because a vertical slide fader is generally more reliable and doesn't require maintenance. The old-style pots had a brush on the back that connected to several contacts arranged like numbers on a clock, and when the contacts or the sensors got dirty, the pot would crackle.

The disappearance of circular pots did not go unnoticed. Many board operators much preferred them to vertical faders because they felt they were a better piece of "human engineering," meaning easier

to use than the more modern vertical design. And there is some truth in this: It's much quicker to twist your wrist than raise a fader, and circular pots let you keep your hands closer to the board for fine adjustment. With a little practice, it was also easy to flip on the switch above the pot and twist it up at the same time.

Perhaps the circular pot will have a resurgence, just like the analog clock face. Many stations were quick to install digital clocks when they first became practicable, and digital clocks were easy to read when doing a time check such as "It's 8:07 under cloudy skies." A combo announcer who is trying to determine when to start a 15-second public service announcement (PSA), a 30-second commercial, and a one-minute weather forecast will often have trouble doing the subtraction when looking at a digital readout. By contrast, old-fashioned second and minute hands are a good human-engineered guide to rationing out time. Therefore, despite advances in technology, many stations still keep an analog-faced clock in view of the announcer.

---

allows you to choose from several possible remote sources you could bring into the console.

Line-Select or A/B Switches   The operator has to be able to decide which signal will be chosen, or routed, to go onto the source channel. Figure 2.11 shows how the **line-select** switches, which permit this, are drawn in the engineer's diagram of console *D*. These switches are often, but not always, directly to the right of the last channel input on the board.

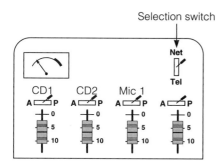

F I G U R E 2.10

Console with an "A" and "B" selector switch.

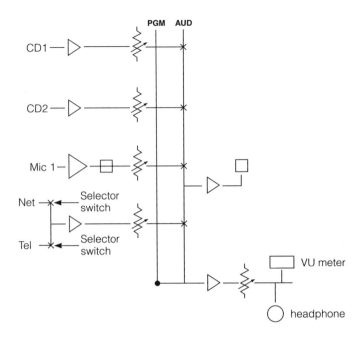

FIGURE 2.11

Signal flow in console *D*.

Review of Console *D* The only new addition to this console is the line-select or A/B switch, which brings a fourth input into the board. This switch allows the operator to select the signal that will go onto the source channel and be governed by the fader.

Summary of the Hypothetical Consoles

The consoles we've illustrated wouldn't be of much use in a modern radio station. Even the relatively sophisticated console *D* doesn't have the flexibility typically needed in a broadcast station, which may use two or more computers, one or more CD players, three mics, two or more **digital cartridge machines**, a telephone input, and a network connection. But the principles illustrated are common to every console. If you understand these principles, you will be able to figure out the operation of any actual radio console.

UNDERSTANDING CONSOLE
FUNCTION: ACTUAL CONSOLES

The radio consoles shown and described in Figures 2.12a and 2.12b allow the operator—who perhaps should now be called a producer—to choose from numerous possible sources. The producer can mix the sources, route them, and either put the combined product over the air or record it for use later.

The console in Figure 2.12a has circular pots, whereas the consoles in Figures 2.12b and 2.12c have vertical or slide faders. In addition to the obvious external features using either pots or faders, these consoles might be analog or digital. Both types of console accomplish the same purpose, using the same basic principles demonstrated in the hypothetical consoles, although their internal workings are quite different.

Analog Consoles

Analog units have the following elements:

- Preamps, which are built into the console and aren't visible.
- Input channels, which allow a number of signal sources to be used and, possibly, mixed together.
- A line selector or routing switch, to determine which of several signals will go onto the source channel.
- Potentiometers (pots)—either the circular pot or the more modern vertical fader.
- A cue channel.
- Selector buttons to route the signal over either the audition channel or the program channel (or both).
- A VU meter to give an objective reading on the loudness of the signal.
- An amplifier, which boosts the output of the console (not visible, because it is built into the console).
- Some miscellaneous controls, which allow the producer to adjust headset volume, choose the source feeding into the headset, or select other convenient functions. An important control is the *monitor volume control*, which you should always use instead of the VU meter when you are adjusting the level at which you choose to listen.

Digital Consoles

Digital consoles function differently from analog units, even though they may look remarkably like traditional units. In a digital console there is no signal path for each channel as we described in our hypothetical consoles. That's because digital signals are made up of streams of numbers (zeroes and ones). However, most digital consoles have the ability to plug analog inputs into the board. (After all, a mic is an analog device.) These analog inputs are first converted to digital signals. Each channel fader on a digital console may modify the intensity and value of the digital input device (for example, a computer's output or a digital cart machine). Usually the output of a digital console will provide both digital and analog outputs.

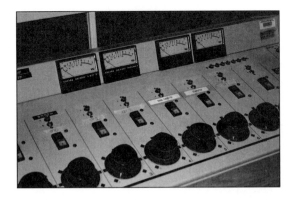

a. Console that uses knob-style potentiometers.

SOURCE: Fritz Messere

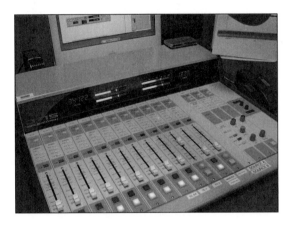

b. Broadcast console that uses slide faders. Notice the A/B selector switch and program/ audition assignment buttons for each channel input.

SOURCE: Fritz Messere

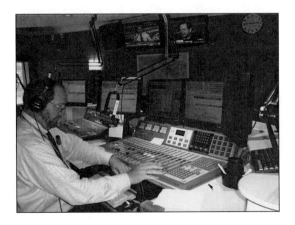

c. On-air console at WCBS-AM in New York. Steve Scott, midday anchor, runs a combo shift from this console.

SOURCE: Philip Benoit

FIGURE 2.12
VU meter readings.

Without getting too complex, you can think of a digital audio console as a fairly flexible hybrid computer workstation with many possible input and output capabilities. Digital consoles range in complexity and features, but they have some features that are fairly standard from model to model.

- Analog-to-digital converters, which allow analog signals to be converted for use within the console.

- Digital-to-analog converters, which allow the digital output of the console to be sent to analog devices such as recorder devices and FM transmitters.

- Selector switches that allow channels to be assigned to different inputs and outputs.

- Faders for each input channel, which, though they function like audio faders, provide control of the data streams for each input.

- A cue channel.

- Digital inputs and outputs to connect to digital sources such as digital cart machines and computers.

- A VU or LED meter to give an objective reading on the loudness of the signal.

- Some miscellaneous controls, which allow the producer to adjust headset volume, choose the source feeding into the headset, or select other convenient functions. An important control is the monitor volume control, which should always be used (rather than the VU meter) when you are adjusting the level at which you choose to listen.

- In many digital consoles, channel "on" and "off" switches that can start and stop external machines such as cart machines.

Regardless of whether you are using analog or digital consoles, they do essentially the same thing, using the principles we showed in our discussion of the hypothetical consoles. Think in terms of those principles, rather than memorizing particular sets of console switches and knobs, and you'll be able to operate any board after a bit of mechanical practice.

Figure 2.13 shows a board in use at a radio station. An adept operator can choose sources and adjust levels while talking into the microphone.

There are many console types other than those pictured in Figures 2.12 and 2.13, but it is not practical to present a catalog of radio consoles here. Don't get hung up on hardware. Rely on a thorough understanding of the principles of console function, and you will be able to operate almost any console.

OPERATION OF THE CONSOLE

An instructor or an experienced operator at your radio station can explain the workings of your particular console to you. Exercises at the end of this chapter will help you build your mechanical skills. Regardless of what equipment is

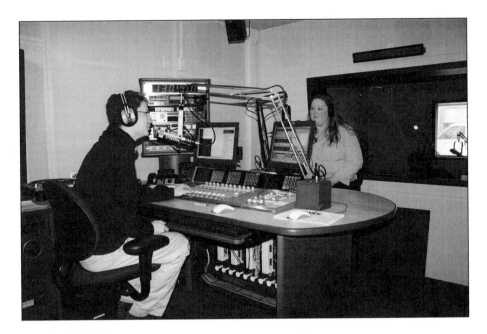

FIGURE 2.13

Main studio at WRVO-FM Public Radio, Oswego, New York.

SOURCE: Fritz Messere

hooked up to the console and regardless of what kind of production is being done, you'll still be doing three basic operations through the board:

- Amplification
- Routing
- Mixing

All these operations are used in the production techniques introduced in later chapters.

At this point, you should primarily be concerned with finding the signals from input sources on the console, riding the levels properly (using the VU meter) to avoid distortion or muddiness, and understanding the signal path. The fine points of production will come later, and your performance will be enhanced with practice.

One other aspect of console operation involves the use of stereo consoles. A stereo signal, as you're probably aware, has two channels (called left and right channels), and a stereo receiver decodes the signal and gives the impression that sound sources are located in certain positions. An FM station generally broadcasts in stereo, but AM stations broadcast in monophonic (mono) sound. We'll discuss stereophonic sound later in Chapter 15. For now, all you need to know is that operating a stereo console is essentially the same as operating the consoles described previously.

Mix-Minus and Phone Modules

Talk shows and audience call-ins are very important for many radio stations, so most modern consoles provide a useful feature that allows the operator to put telephone conversations on the air without getting feedback when the announcer's mic is open. This feature is called *mix-minus*, and here's how it works. Circuitry within the console will sum together all the different signals used *except* the microphone(s) used in the studio. This allows the announcer to talk to telephone guests and hear all the normal program elements without having to worry about feedback through the monitor speakers. This technology greatly simplifies running a call-in radio show.

Phone modules that use mix-minus technology can route the telephone caller to the board's cue channel so the console operator and caller can communicate before the caller is placed on the air. Also, the output of the board's program or audition channels can be sent to the caller while she/he is waiting on hold. Usually these modules have a mono audio input that sends the caller's output to both the left and right channels of the board.

The Virtual Console

Digital "virtual" consoles re-create the look of a standard console while offering some additional features. Software programs such as Adobe Audition, Pro Tools, and others provide great mixing flexibility to advance production. For example, a multitrack program called Audition™ from Adobe Systems creates a virtual console on your monitor (see Figure 2.14).

You can use a mouse to raise or lower the levels of the faders; you can also assign sound sources to different faders or "busses," which are collections of circuits assigned to one fader. While this virtual console would not be used for live radio production, it is enormously flexible for audio production.

Figure 2.15 shows a more complex audio task than we have covered so far in our discussion of consoles. Here a digital workstation is being used in postproduction. A virtual console is being used to produce a specific program segment. The operator is cross-fading among specific portions of three different songs. The software provides the producer with a wide range of control for shortening the musical segments and then mixing them.

Don't worry if you do not understand the purpose of all the different virtual controls. We will explain them in later chapters. But the point here is to show that this mix would be difficult using any of the consoles we've discussed so far in this chapter. The controls on a digital workstation can provide the operator with great flexibility.

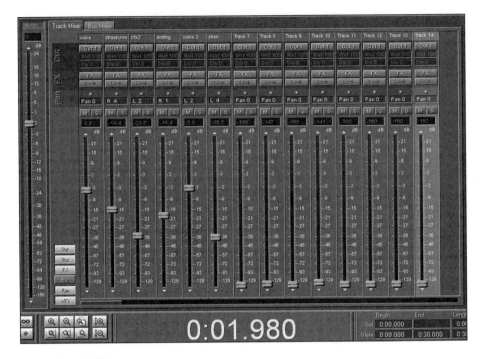

FIGURE 2.14

Adobe Audition's track mixer is a visual representation of an audio console.

SOURCE: Software courtesy of © 2013 Adobe Systems, Inc.

Advantages of the Virtual Console

1. It's easy to assign sources to various faders. In some cases, you can accomplish with the computer what you would actually have to rewire the console inputs to do.

2. The computer remembers your work. Settings can be stored for later recall or changed on the fly, with the computer remembering the settings for each channel.

3. You can try different arrangements to your heart's content. Suppose you have 30 different takes of an announcer's voice-over. You want to hear how they all sound in conjunction with some music that you have previously recorded. With a real console, you would have to run the audio bed through one fader and the voice through another, re-cueing the file each time. With the virtual console, you can stack the different takes of the voice-over and click on each take in sequence. The takes are stored in a digital file, just like documents in a word processor.

4. With a virtual console, special effects are often built into the software, making expensive external hardware unnecessary.

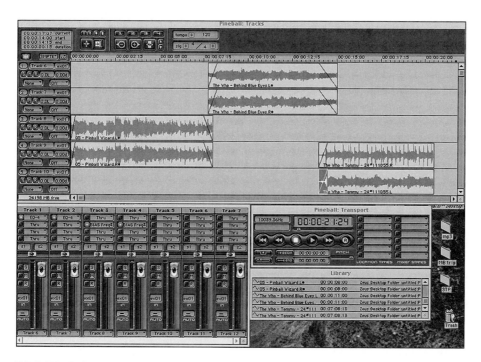

FIGURE 2.15

The virtual console pictured here produces multiple screens showing editing, fades, and transport controls.

SOURCE: Bias, Inc.

Advantages of the Real Console

1. It's still difficult to use your virtual console for actual recording when you need to fade several sources unless you have a *control surface unit* connected to your computer or your program has automation. (The control surface mimics a real console by providing faders to use.) If you have several announcers in the studio, for example, it's really much simpler just to open the announcers' mics on the real console and record, riding their levels as you work.

2. It is much easier to run an airshift with a real console because the real console stays static—that is, it is always there and in the same position and perspective. Remember, too, that if you turn on a sound source and it's too loud—say, a CD comes booming through—it is much quicker to simply turn down a pot or yank down a slider than to use a mouse to find the virtual fader.

    A broad conclusion: The virtual console is much better for doing complicated production of previously recorded segments, such as multitrack work. New virtual studios allow you to access mainframe audio technology. The real console (either digital or analog), on the other hand, is better for fast, simple jobs or putting material out live on-air.

The next steps will help you become familiar with the units that feed signals into the console (Chapter 3), recording and playback units (Chapter 4), and microphones (Chapter 5). First, however, let's wrap up our discussion of console operation by briefly introducing two options that extend the flexibility of the radio console: submixing and patching.

Submixing

A **submixer** is nothing more than a miniature console that combines or "gangs" a group of inputs. The output of the submixer is fed into the radio console. An example will help clarify this. Suppose you have in your studio four talk show guests and one moderator, each with a separate mic. It might not be possible to use five separate pots because your particular console might not have five mic-level inputs, or you might not be able to rearrange existing assignments on the console. The solution? Plug the mics into a submixer (which has several pots and a VU meter so that each mic-level can be adjusted), and run the output of the submixer (which is at line-level) into your console, where it ties up only one pot.

Figure 2.16 shows the Shure SCM810, a unit that can be used as a standalone unit (for example, in an auditorium or as a submixer in a studio). Submixers come in handy during remote recordings or broadcasts, as we explain in later chapters.

Routers and Patchbays

Occasionally you may come upon a situation where the inputs to the console need to be changed. **Patching** allows you to route a signal in a way different from that envisaged when the board was wired together by the station's engineer. There are two ways to change the routing of audio signals. The most common way is to use a **routing switcher** (Figure 2.17a). This is a device that makes connections between the console and its input and output sources at the touch of a button. Many digital consoles now have the ability to route input signals to different channel inputs on the audio board.

Routing switchers can also be used to route the output of a console to a specific input, such as a digital workstation or some other recording device (such as a MiniDisc) for logging purposes. Routing switchers can be very useful

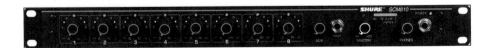

FIGURE 2.16

The Shure SCM810, an eight-channel mixer, can be used by itself or to expand the capability of an audio console.

SOURCE: Shure, Inc.

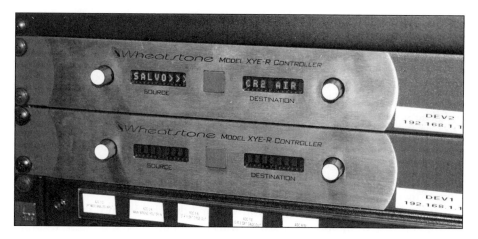

a. Routing switchers act like patchbays. They allow you to choose an audio source and send it to one of a number of different inputs in one or more studios.

SOURCE: Fritz Messere

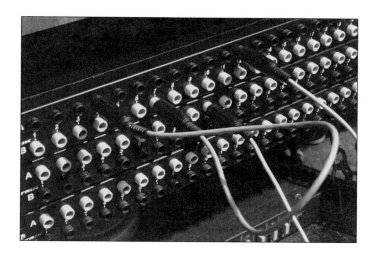

b. Patchbay with
   patchcords connected.

SOURCE: Fritz Messere

FIGURE 2.17

to stations with more than one studio because seldom used inputs, such as a reel-to-reel tape recorder, can be placed in one location but their output can be made available to any studio.

The second way is to use a mechanical **patchbay** (sometimes called a patch panel). Basically, the patchbay (which we'll explain in a moment) performs the same function as an old-time telephone switchboard, using connectors (plugs) to send a signal to a specific source. You, as a radio producer and console operator, will use the routing switcher or patchbay from time to time to make an operation easier or as a short-term emergency measure if something breaks down. For example, let's assume that the output of a computer is normally connected to source channel 3 of a console. Suppose, though, that the computer is broken. Suppose, too, that the only other computer hooked up to the console can't be used because it's on the same pot with a digital cart machine that is in constant use.

The solution would be to patch the output of the working computer into channel 3. This is done by a router assigning the output device to a specific location on the desired audio console. With a patchbay you would use a **patchcord** (see Figure 2.17), which plugs into jacks on the patchbay. Patchcords may be single- or double-pronged, depending on their intended use and the configuration of the bay.

If you come across a patchbay, you will find that the outputs, or sources, are on the top row of the patch locations, with the inputs on the bottom. In other words, you will usually find what comes out of a unit (such as the working computer on the top row) labeled "Comp 2 Out" or something similar. The signal is usually connected to the console on the bottom row, with a label that says something like "Channel 3 In." Close examination of a patchbay will reveal that the outputs and inputs that normally match up are in line vertically. Let's say that compact disc 1 (CD1) normally goes into channel 2. The holes for CD1 will be directly above the holes for channel 2 on the patchbay. This, not surprisingly, is called a **normal connection**. The term is also used as a verb: CD1 *normals through* to channel 2. When you change this arrangement with a patchcord, you are *breaking normal*.

A special jack in the patch panel is called a **multiple**. This allows you to patch one source into the multiple and plug in several patchcords that all carry the same output. That way, you can route one signal to several sources, a practice that is useful on rare occasions, such as when recording a network signal and sending it over the air simultaneously.

As we noted previously, most modern studios use routing switchers; however, if your station uses a patchbay, it is a good idea always to normal a patchbay when you're finished with the studio so that the next person doesn't inherit your special connections.

SUMMARY

After this chapter's discussion, you can probably map out in your head what a typical console does and why it is set up the way it is.

All consoles perform essentially the same functions: amplification, routing, and mixing. Digital consoles frequently can accept both analog and digital inputs.

Among the most significant instruments and controls on the console are the faders (pots), which are simply volume controls; the volume-unit (VU) meters, which give a visual representation of the strength of the signal; and the switches, which turn the faders on and off.

There are three main channels in the typical console: program, audition, and cue. Program goes over the air or to a recording device. Audition is used for private listening through a studio monitor. Cue feeds a signal through a small speaker and is used to find the beginning sounds on records and tapes.

A submixer is a miniature console that allows inputs to be ganged together before being fed into the console.

Patching allows you to reroute the normal signal flow in the console. It is useful for special operations or for emergency use of equipment not wired into the console.

All consoles, regardless of their configuration, operate in much the same way. There is no need to be intimidated by a new console; if you learn the basics, you will be able to run any board, however complex it may appear to be.

APPLICATIONS

SITUATION 1/THE PROBLEM A baseball game, fed from a network, was being aired and would last until 11:30 P.M. At 10:00 P.M., a call came in from the station's general manager: A new commercial had to be made for a client, and it had to go on the air first thing in the morning. Would the operator on duty produce the commercial?

ONE POSSIBLE SOLUTION The operator on duty decided to produce the commercial, which consisted of an announcement read over some up-tempo production music, on the audition channel. To do so, she keyed the control room mic and the CD to the audition channel. She then found the audition output on the patchbay and patched Audition Out into Computer In.

By producing the commercial on audition, she was able to use the same console that was sending the baseball game out on program. As an additional benefit, she was in the control room, not in a separate studio, and therefore was able to check on the game from time to time—not necessarily because she wanted to know the score, but because network feeds can and do run into technical problems, and an inattentive operator can put a half-hour of static over the air. (Most boards have separate VU meters for audition and program.)

SITUATION 2/THE PROBLEM The fader on channel 3 caused a crackling static noise every time it was adjusted. (This happens from time to time, often because the internal workings of the pot are shorted or badly in need of cleaning.) The fader controlled the digital cart machine, and because the operator was in the midst of a show, the problem was becoming critical.

ONE POSSIBLE SOLUTION Before using the cart machine, the operator simply patched its output into a different channel, breaking the normal. Now, the cart machine will be governed by a different fader until repairs can be made to the console. The operator also left a note for the next board operator, explaining the patch.

EXERCISES

1. Perform a combo operation (operate the console and announce) with two
    sound sources like CDs and a mic. The goal is not clean production, just
    board operation.

      Start one CD, and place the machine in play. (Don't worry about hit-
    ting a specific point in the music; that's cueing, which we discuss in the next
    chapter.) Start the second CD after the first one ends, fading it up on the
    console. Try talking over the music, making what you think is a proper
    balance between voice and music. Do a typical disc jockey routine:
    Announce the name of the song just played, introduce the next song, start
    the CD, and bring it up on the board.

2. Make a slip of paper with the name of each piece of equipment that is
    hooked to the console in your radio production studio or lab—for example,
    CD Player 1, Mic 2, Cart 1, CD Player 2, Computer. Toss the slips of paper
    into a hat.

      Put CDs into the CD players and cue up all the other source machines.
    Have someone standing by the mic(s). Your instructor or lab assistant will
    draw a slip of paper out of the hat and announce the names of one or more
    pieces of equipment.

      Your assignment is to quickly start that equipment and pot it up on the
    board. More than one source may be called up at the same time. When a
    mic is called out, you—the operator—are responsible for throwing a cue to
    the person stationed at the mic by pointing at him or her sharply. (This is
    the standard signal for someone to begin speaking.)

      When your instructor calls out "Lose it," you must pot down what's up
    on the board and then turn that piece of equipment off. Give the person at
    the mic a cut signal by drawing a finger across your throat.

      (We'll discuss some other common visual signals used in radio in
    Chapter 7.)

      This drill may seem a little like boot camp. In fact, it is pretty much the
    same approach used to teach soldiers how to operate equipment or assemble
    weapons. You'll find, though, that trying to locate pots and equipment
    under this kind of pressure is a very effective way to learn their operation.

3. Draw a diagram, in the same form as the engineering diagrams shown in this
    chapter, of the console in your studio or radio production lab. Don't worry
    about the details; just try to include the channels and label the sources and
    selection switches.

3

Playback Devices and Console Sources

In the preceding chapter, we spoke about the way an audio signal is routed through a console, but we touched only briefly on the sources that produce that signal.

In this chapter, we describe many of the sources you're likely to encounter in a modern radio station (except for microphones, which we deal with in Chapter 5). During the first 60 years of broadcasting, analog reproducers such as turntables and tape recorders were the primary sources of recorded audio. Compact discs ushered in a digital revolution and CDs started replacing those analog devices in the mid-1980s. As the new century began, almost all prerecorded sources came into the audio console from computer hard drives or network sources. Today it is common for radio stations to mix live local programming with prerecorded materials, so the focus of this chapter is to discuss the three primary inputs for prerecorded audio.

- Prerecorded discs such as CDs and DVDs
- Hard disc units such as cart machines
- Remote inputs such as satellites

While is true that many stations may use other devices such as MiniDiscs or even old analog devices like turntables, we'll focus on the most common input sources. At some time or another you may encounter these older devices and may be required to use them.

Over the past 10 years the compact disc has moved aside as the most common source of music. Today almost all programming is recorded and played back as computer files. The digital revolution has changed broadcasting dramatically.

The field of radio production is constantly changing, and the ongoing development of sophisticated audio production systems continues at an amazing pace, but regardless of the technology, the *result* of creating an effect through the use of production techniques is of greatest importance. You are likely to encounter several different file types when playing back sources, so we'll discuss them briefly here.

DIGITAL AUDIO FILES

Audio playback via a computer or a compact disc or downlinked off a communications satellite may enter the audio console as either a digital or analog signal but increasingly it is likely to be in one or more different digital audio formats. Not all digital files are the same and not all play back on all devices. As an analogy, when creating a word processing document you probably save your work as .doc or .docx files. However, written materials are often distributed in a read-only file format called .PDF files. Audio files also have different formats.

The standard audio format that is the equivalent of a PDF is one used for compact discs. It is called *CD-DA* (compact disc—digital audio) file. This format plays back music with excellent fidelity, but it is not very good for real-time audio editing. The data stored in the CD-DA format uses *uncompressed* audio files that allow storage of between 70 and 80 minutes of sound on a compact disc. The standard CD can reproduce the entire spectrum of audio frequencies with a **dynamic range** (the ratio of the loudest sound compared to the softest sound) nearly equal to live music. All computers can playback standard CD files via their media players like iTunes or Windows Media Player, but most computers do not store or record in this format unless the user is trying to create a compact disc compatible CD or file. Digital audio programs such as *Pro Tools, Adobe Audition, Bias Peak*, and others record using a number of different audio formats. We'll take a look at a couple of digital file formats that you're likely to encounter.

Digital audio workstations generally use the .**WAV** file found on Windows computer systems or the .**AIF** file format found on Macintosh computers. The reasons why there are different file formats are not particularly important to our discussion. WAV files are typically more commonly found in radio, but over the past few years more and more stations have adopted Mac computers, so you're likely to see both. Also, some audio editing programs use a modified version of a .WAV file called the **Broadcast Wave Format** (.**BWF**). The audio recorded in the WAV, BWF, or AIF formats is uncompressed audio, which means that recording and playback quality is excellent. However, the BWF file also has the ability to store some additional data that helps broadcasters provide seamless exchange of audio material among different types of broadcast equipment, such as digital audio workstations and automation systems. Thus, material created in the BWF format can be loaded into software databases that provide radio stations with additional automation capability.

Computers may create and store files in a .WAV or .AIF format, but when you burn files onto CD they are usually burned as standard CD-DA files or as **MP3** (short for MPEG audio layer 3) files. This is because standard CD players cannot playback .WAV or .AIF files. While the standard CD contains about 70 minutes of playback, MP3 files are much smaller so it is possible to get as many as 14 hours of audio on a single disc. Because MP3 files are compressed, they are much smaller than standard CD, .WAV, and .AIF files, so many people use this format to transfer files across computer networks.

How can MP3 record so much more audio on a CD than a standard CD? The answer is simple, although the process is amazingly complex. The MP3 format compresses a music sound file by a factor of 10 or more by using an advanced mathematical modeling technique known as *perceptual noise shaping*. This compression scheme eliminates certain parts of a sound that the human ear cannot readily hear when it is being masked by louder sounds. For example, when an ambulance siren is nearby, that loud siren sound often masks softer sounds around it. Perceptual noise shaping can reduce a 30- or 40-megabyte CD-DA or WAV file into a 3-megabyte MP3 file, allowing the user to store many more music files on a CD-R disc. The size of the MP3 file is a function of the quality level the user selects. The higher the bit rate, the higher the quality of the MP3.

Although the standard audio (CD-DA) compact disc produces a higher-quality sound output than the highest-quality MP3 disc counterpart, you might have a difficult time actually hearing the difference unless you are listening on very high-quality loudspeakers.

Many producers put frequently used sound elements on an audio CD because it is a durable and easily accessible medium (see Figure 3.1a). Also, burning a CD allows a producer to move files to different computers when they are not networked or when the producer is on location.

COMPACT DISCS

In the mid-1980s the compact disc replaced the vinyl record as one of the primary sources of music distribution. Radio stations use compact discs as a source for music and for audio production. The advent of recordable compact discs, which can be recorded at the station, offered exciting possibilities because these media allow archival storage and quick retrieval of legacy sounds specific to the station, such as IDs and commercials. Today most computers will burn CDs.

Compact discs are fairly sturdy media but you should still exercise some caution in handling them. Many experts maintain that most CD "crashes" have been the result of poor handling by production personnel. Despite initial claims to the contrary, CDs are not immune to damage; surface scratches can badly impair playback, and damage to a disc can result in poor audio quality, skipping, or shutdown of the playback.

The compact disc (CD) (see Figure 3.1a) comes in two sizes (both fewer than 5 inches in diameter) and is made of plastic. The information contained on the CD is read by a laser within the CD player (see Figure 3.1b).

A compact disc utilizes digital recording technology and contains one long, continuous stream of data that spirals from the inside toward the

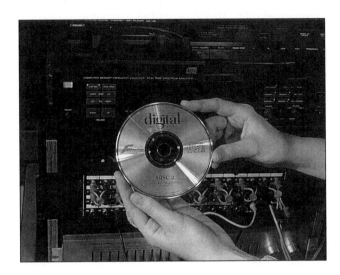

a. Compact disc.
SOURCE: Philip Benoit

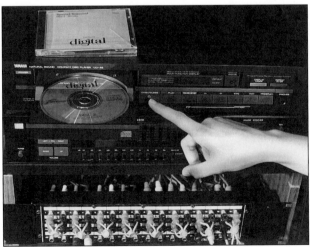

b. Compact disc player.
SOURCE: Philip Benoit

FIGURE 3.1
Elements of a compact disc system.

outer edge. Because the disc itself is not touched physically by a stylus or a pickup device, it is less subject to wear but can be scratched if not handled carefully.

Digital recording means using samples of sound to produce a recording that is stored in computer language—the on-or-off binary code of digital technology (see Figure 3.2). We discuss digital recording later in the book, but for our discussion here the following basic points are important.

1. Digital recordings actually comprise numerically transcribed samples of the original sounds, so in engineering terms, the digital recording is a collection of samples of sounds (although a case could be made that the digital version is a representation of a sound, too).

    These samples are taken with great rapidity. In most cases, digitally processed information is sampled at rates that are slightly higher than two times higher than the highest frequencies humans can hear; this is the **sampling frequency** and is expressed in units called *hertz* (cycles per second, abbreviated *Hz*). One of the sampling frequencies typically used for digital recording, then, would be expressed as 44.1 kHz or 44,1000 cycles per second (*kHz* stands for *kilohertz*, which is a unit of 1,000 cycles per second.) Samples are then coded into the binary digits that give digital recording its name. (See Chapter 4 for additional information on the digital recording process.)

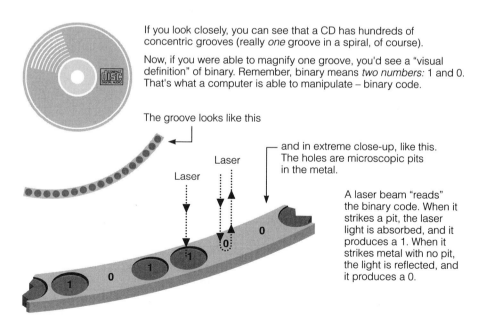

If you look closely, you can see that a CD has hundreds of concentric grooves (really *one* groove in a spiral, of course).

Now, if you were able to magnify one groove, you'd see a "visual definition" of binary. Remember, binary means *two numbers:* 1 and 0. That's what a computer is able to manipulate – binary code.

The groove looks like this

and in extreme close-up, like this. The holes are microscopic pits in the metal.

Laser

Laser

Laser

A laser beam "reads" the binary code. When it strikes a pit, the laser light is absorbed, and it produces a 1. When it strikes metal with no pit, the light is reflected, and it produces a 0.

FIGURE 3.2

Storing binary code on a CD.

2. Digital recording produces a clean-sounding signal. Very little (if any) extraneous noise is introduced into the system during digital recording and playback so there is little or no hiss and no scratchy sound.

3. The digital technology used in CD reproduction produces a different sound than do older analog sources like tapes; many listeners characterize it as "clearer," and unquestionably noise is reduced. You may have never heard some older high-quality analog systems, but some audiophiles claim not to like the digital sound as much as (or better than) analog; some claim that analog sound is "warmer" and more lifelike. Two newer playback technologies, Super Audio CDs and DVD-audio, were introduced. They boasted better frequency response and a wider dynamic range. These audio devices can provide multichannel, surround sound playback while eliminating harsh sound. These technologies have not received widespread consumer acceptance.

In any event, the concept of a "natural" sound is difficult to define. The natural sound of a concert hall, for example, almost always involves some peculiarities of room acoustics, unintended echoes, and various background noises like seat shuffling and coughing. A recording that omits these sounds can hardly be faulted for being unnatural, so we can assume that the goal of audio is not always to reproduce with total realism whatever sounds were originally made.

While CDs are fairly well suited for storing and distributing music or programming material, they are not well suited to broadcast operations. On the plus side, they do not wear out or suffer damage as easily if handled properly. On the minus side, a producer doing a highly formatted music shift would expend a great deal of time trying to switch dozens of CDs in and out of the playback machines.

If a commercial radio station still gets a large amount of music on CDs, it converts music to computer files and plays back those files on the computer instead of changing many CDs. Converting CD tracks to computer sound files makes it easier to automate many of the functions of the radio station. College radio stations are somewhat of an exception to this rule, with jocks often playing a wide assortment of music in a variety of formats.

RECORDABLE CDs AND DVDs

CD recording technology has proliferated in home and broadcast audio (see Figure 3.3). Computer manufacturers have made the ability to record CDs and DVDs a standard feature on most of their computers.

These systems use recordable discs called CD-Rs (CD-write once), CD-RWs (CD-rewriteable) or DVD-Rs and DVD+R (DVD-write once) that have a special photosensitive coating. Digital audio information is recorded on the disc by using a "write" laser to heat up or burn the CD-R coating. When the laser

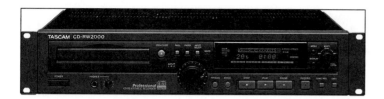

FIGURE 3.3

TASCAM CD-RW 2000 provides many features for recording and producing CDs.
SOURCE: TASCAM, a division of TEAC Corp. of America

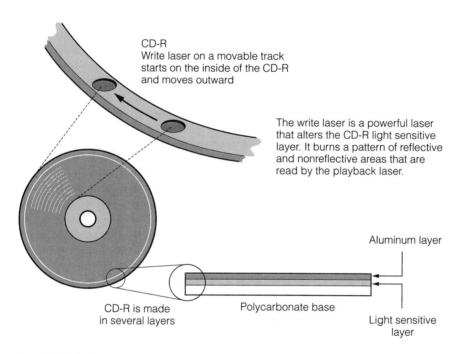

CD-R
Write laser on a movable track starts on the inside of the CD-R and moves outward

The write laser is a powerful laser that alters the CD-R light sensitive layer. It burns a pattern of reflective and nonreflective areas that are read by the playback laser.

Aluminum layer

CD-R is made in several layers

Polycarbonate base

Light sensitive layer

FIGURE 3.4

The write laser is a powerful laser that alters the CD-R light-sensitive layer and burns a pattern of reflective and nonreflective areas that are read by the playback laser.

beam touches the CD-R, it causes the coating to turn opaque (see Figure 3.4). As the data is burned, it sets up microscopic light and dark patterns that either pass or reflect light back into the CD player's *read-laser*. This technology is very common today and it allows for program producers to distribute the material via the standard postal system.

We should note that two different types of recordable media and CD burners exist (see Figure 3.5). CD-R devices record onto a compact disc permanently, whereas CD-RW burners record on a disc that can be rewritten repeatedly. CD-R discs can be played on a standard compact disc player; however, not all CD players will play back CD-RW discs. Thus, CD-RWs are not a

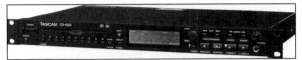

a. Modern broadcast CD players provide a variety of cue, search, and play options for the audio operator. The unit will play both MP3 and WAV files along with standard CDs.

SOURCE: Courtesy of TEAC Corp. of America/Tascam Divisions

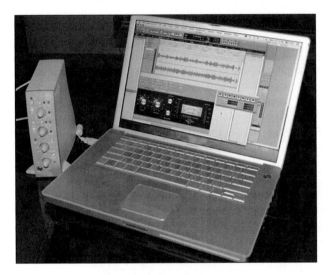

b. Modern computers such as this Mac laptop make it possible to use high-end software anywhere. When the project is finished, the user can burn a CD master right on the same laptop.

SOURCE: Fritz Messere

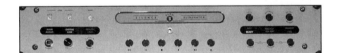

c. Silence Eliminator automatically plays the CD if programming from the station is interrupted. This machine can be programmed to play specific tracks on the CD.

SOURCE: Fritz Messere

FIGURE 3.5

good choice for audio duplication. Note, too, that not all CD-Rs will not play on all broadcast CD players.

CD PLAYERS

CD playback is generally quite simple. You insert the disc into a mechanized drawer, which closes automatically and brings the disc into position for playback. The CD player reads the table of contents (TOC) when the disc is inserted and displays the number of tracks on the CD. When you press play, the laser is guided to the correct portion of the CD. The laser reads the disc from the inside out toward the edge. (The CD file is actually one long spiral track, with the first bits of data being a table of contents file.) Because CDs have several cuts, a selector knob or button on the machine allows you to pick the cut you want to play (selection number 3, for example). Most CD players will display the playing time and total time of the disc in the player. CDs have information only on one side, but that one side can hold more than an hour of program material. (For those who are technically minded, each CD can hold 44,100 samples per second × 2 bytes per sample × 2 channels × 60 seconds/minute × 74 minutes = 783,216,000 bytes of storage information.)

Because CDs can hold more than 60 minutes of content, they are very useful for distributing programming, such as a one-hour music special.

Many radio stations wire the start and stop function into the audio console so that the CD track that has been cued up will fire when the operator presses the "on" or "start" button on the console. This greatly simplifies the tasks for the operator since she will not have to reach to start and stop the CD player. When CDs are automated, the cut numbers may be programmed into a computer. Methods of programming range from a simple computer instruction to play at random without repeating any cuts for a certain time (shuffle mode), to complete program control, cut by cut and hour by hour. Few radio stations use CD automation, however, because most stations want more control over their format and would be unhappy with the dead air between CD cuts (see Figure 3.5c).

Some broadcast backup systems are available that automatically play a CD when the signal from the studio is interrupted. This is an excellent use of CDs since the station can create a prerecorded program that mimics regular programming until engineers can restore normal studio programming.

Today, computer hard drives or digital cart machines, rather than multiple control-room CD players, are the preferred music reproduction method. However, several other playback options, such as MiniDiscs, are still found in many radio stations. These devices are often used as backup machines or to play some special programming. (See Figure 3.5.)

Super Audio CDs, Audio DVDs, and HD Surround Sound Broadcasts

During the 1990s a number of industry leaders were trying to decide what future technology might displace compact discs. Two newer technologies emerged as potential candidates. Super Audio CDs (SACD) and audio DVDs look alike, but they are based on different technologies. Rather than going into a technical discussion about the differences between the two technologies, we would like to focus on their possible uses within the field of audio production.

Super Audio CDs and audio DVDs are capable of much higher frequency response and greater dynamic range than traditional CDs, and these devices are theoretically far superior to MP3s in audio reproduction capability. Perhaps the most interesting difference in these technologies is that unlike regular CDs, they are capable of multichannel surround sound such as Pro Logic II Surround Sound™ and Neural Audio's Surround Sound™. While it is too early to predict whether these technologies will be widely adopted, many stations have already begun broadcasting in HD, which opens the door for surround broadcasting. Some experts say that the automotive environment would be perfect for HD 5.1 radio, but the hitch is that stations that broadcast in 5.1 surround sound cannot use their digital bandwidth for other encoded data services. Internet radio stations can also broadcast in surround sound, and computers running Windows 7 with appropriate hardware can take advantage of this capability. The audience for HD surround radio is very limited as of the update of this edition. Radio stations, whether broadcast or streaming, will have to determine whether an investment in the equipment necessary to broadcast in surround sound will provide the necessary return.

THE DIGITAL CART MACHINE

One of the most popular and useful devices at radio stations is the *digital cart machine*, which actually is not a cart machine at all, but a large hard drive storage system. Some digital cart machines are standalone systems, while others are really computers running a software program that acts like a cart machine. Almost any computer can be programmed to function as a digital cart machine, although standalone devices are often preferred by board operators because they have transport controls and cut buttons for immediate playback. Digital cart machines have the standard record features built into the unit, including some editing capability; however, many stations create promos and commercials in a production studio as opposed to the air studio, so it is possible to use a File Transfer Protocol (FTP) program to load files into the machine from a digital workstation that is connected to the station's internal network.

Most digital cart machines display program elements, such as music cuts, announcements, or commercials, which are in the queue to be played. Some units can store up to 1000 names or titles for tracks and use a "FIND" function to make locating the cuts easier. Often the cart machine is wired to the audio console so that the board operator only needs to push the "on" button on the console to trigger playback of the cart, but in some cases, such as when a computer is programmed to act like a cart machine, the operator starts the segment by using a touch screen or a mouse. Some units feature "hot keys" that allow an operator to assign a specific button to a frequently used audio cut, such as a station ID or stinger. Since the stored cuts can be named and programmed by the board operator, it is easy for a station to make "hot key" assignments match the needs of the station format. So, for example, hourly promos could be named by time slot and day of the week. Such flexibility makes the cart machine an ideal workhorse in an on-air studio environment. Depending on how the cart machine is programmed, it may trigger several sequences in a row. Such a setup is commonly known as *live-assist*.

Digital cart machines can also be used to partially automate a station or to program a computer to provide voice tracking. But the technology allows for human interaction before the fact: the announcer can view the list of music and other cuts and record a voice track that will be replayed later.

MiniDisc

The Sony Corporation introduced the MiniDisc (MD) in 1992 as a replacement for the audio cassette unit (see Figure 3.6). While MiniDiscs have never really been accepted by American consumers, broadcasters have embraced the technology as a logical replacement for the audio cassette machine. This is because several different MiniDisc models were introduced that were compact and easy for reporters to carry around in the field. The sonic characteristics of the MiniDisc are much better than cassettes but are not equal to those of the compact disc or digital workstations. Unlike recordable CDs, MiniDisc technology allows you to record and play back audio tracks quickly. There are even some limited editing capabilities built into the devices, so these factors have led the MiniDisc to be used in news gathering and some field recording.

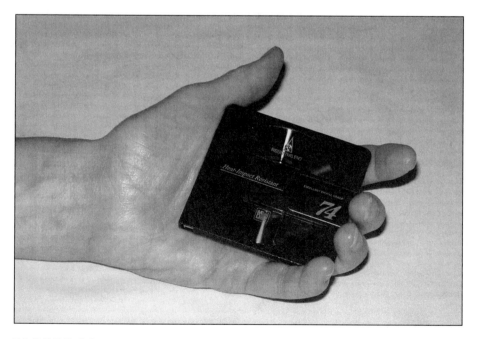

FIGURE 3.6

A MiniDisc, though smaller than a deck of cards, can store as many as 80 minutes of stereo material.

SOURCE: Fritz Messere

RADIO RETRO • TURNTABLES—THE KING OF ANALOG DEVICES

The old-fashioned turntable for LP (long play) vinyl discs is on its way to becoming a museum piece, but don't be surprised if you find one sitting around your radio station or production facility. A few stations still have substantial collections on vinyl, something that makes sense when you remember what a popular format "oldies" is. Usually the turntable is only put to use if there's a need for, let's say, a particular song for a commercial, and that track isn't commonly available on modern media.

There are a couple of things to remember if you're playing back an LP disc on a turntable.

1. LPs are delicate. Hold them with your palms on the edges, or put your fingers on the label and thumb on the edges. Oil from your hands can clog the grooves.
2. Very old broadcast turntables had gears as well as speeds. When you cued up the record (discussed shortly), you usually put the gear in neutral so you could spin the plate on the turntable. There were no markings that say "neutral"—you just had to put the speed control in the middle of the gear-shift. Chances are, though, that you'll be working with a direct-drive turntable where you can choose the correct speed by pressing a button.
3. The disc shown in Figure 3.7 is the size that plays at 33$\frac{1}{3}$ rpm, so that's the speed at which you would set the turntable. Although there are different size discs, such as smaller 45 rpm discs, you will probably never encounter them.
4. Turntables have an on-off switch for starting the motor. This doesn't necessarily put them over the air. You generally back the disc up a quarter turn, start the disc, and then turn up its associated pot on the console.
5. Cueing up discs takes some practice (see Figure 3.7). Put the needle in the groove between cuts, put the turntable pot in cue, slowly spin the plate with your hand, and stop the rotation when you hear the first sound of the cut. Then back up the plate (not just the disc) a quarter turn. When you want the disc to start, press the on button and turn up the pot. Some combo operators like to cue the disc right to the start of the sound, hold the disc by the edge, allowing the plate to spin under the turntable, and then let the disc go when the music is to start. That's called *slipcueing* or *slipstarting*. You can do this

because broadcast turntables have a movable cover on the plate that lets it spin on a disc that's being held still without damaging the disc. It takes some practice but has the advantage that you can just let the record go and start the music at the precise instant you want it to start.

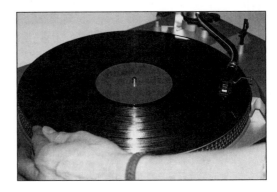

FIGURE 3.7

Vinyl discs have minute vibration patterns cut into the groove walls.
SOURCE: Fritz Messere

We've identified the basic methods of cueing a disc; the choice is pretty much a personal decision. In some cases, slipcueing is handy when you need to make a very tight entrance with music; slipcueing starts the cut immediately without the momentary wait for the turntable to get up to speed. This is very useful for cueing up live concert album cuts because the sound of the audience would create a "wow" if the record were started by other methods. A disadvantage of slipcueing is that it ties up one of your hands during production.

When slipcueing, it's advisable not to fade up the turntable until immediately before you plan to start the cut; this is called **dead-potting**. (Even though your console is likely to have a fader rather than a pot, the term is a carry-over from earlier days of radio.) Otherwise, you may pick up the rumble of the turntable motor and the spinning disc. Starting the turntable with the pot up is known as **hot-potting**. Potting up, or dead-potting the turntable, is generally considered better practice, but with modern, rumble-free turntables, hot-potting seems to be gaining acceptance.

REMOTE INPUTS

Satellite services like ESPN Radio or music services from a variety of suppliers allow radio stations to intermix satellite programming with local programming, or in some cases, completely automate the broadcast service without an operator present. Other remote services may include telephone connections for call-in shows and remote live promotions that the station is doing, such as a store opening or perhaps a local sporting event. In later chapters we discuss how satellite automation works and talk about how to set up remote broadcasts. Here we want to discuss the service as a remote input that you may encounter on the audio console. Remote inputs on the audio console may appear either as analog sources or digital sources.

The telephone has always been one of the essential source components for live radio. Stations frequently use telephone circuits to interview newsmakers, to support local talk shows, or to bring in listeners for live contests or song requests (although frequently the show producer will record contest winners on the audition channel during a musical selection, edit the conversation on a digital cart machine, and then play it back a few moments later). A telephone **hybrid** provides this capability. The hybrid allows the show producer to talk with callers in pre-air and on-air situations and can help simplify the task of screening callers by setting up a queue of people waiting to talk.

A hybrid connects the station console to a standard analog telephone line and can eliminate the cross-talk that would normally be associated with using a standard telephone receiver live on the air. Usually telephone hybrids use some digital processing that separates the announcer's voice from the caller online, providing the listener with a quality experience.

Hybrids are not used for network remotes. Network inputs from satellites provide the station with a live feed from some distant studio connection. On-the-hour newscasts from CBS or ABC Radio or talk radio programming such as ESPN Radio or NASCAR coverage are examples of such live programming.

Programs streamed from a live satellite feed are received from a satellite downlink, usually located somewhere on the station's property. Satellite feeds come into the studio as radio signals that need to be decoded and processed before they are sent to the audio console for broadcast. Because they are usually digital signals, they can be kept as digital signals or converted to analog signals, depending on the capability of the station console. Satellites provide very high-quality stereo sound capability, but they are not the only way stations receive high-quality audio signals. Some stations may use ISDN (integrated services digital network) lines from the telephone company to bring very high-quality audio in from a network or other source where full fidelity is required.

The console operator can use the cue capability of the audio console, discussed in Chapter 2, to listen for pre-cues, but usually the station also has a high-quality studio clock that is synced to geostationary satellite or some other reference source so the operator will be able to ascertain the exact in and out points for remote broadcasts. Satellite services publish billboards about when breaks are scheduled into the program service. These billboards may be on the program service website or sent as an email to the station. The board operator or show producer will need to back-time local segments so as to be ready to pot up the remote source at the appropriate time.

SUMMARY

Both the compact disc and MiniDisc employ a laser beam in place of a mechanical stylus. These systems use the laser to read sound information encoded digitally on a reflective layer. The basic file formats for CDs are CD-DA and MP3. Digital audio workstations used in broadcasting are generally recorded in different computer formats, WAV (or BWF) and AIF.

Compact discs are cued electronically, often by computer. The CD player is capable of locating a particular selection almost instantly. Compact discs offer more nearly distortion-free sound reproduction and are less subject to wear. CDs, though, are not indestructible; they can scratch if handled carelessly. Today recordable compact discs (CD-Rs) are found in many digital audio workstations and computers. MiniDiscs are easier to use for field recording or for logging purposes in broadcast studios.

Super Audio CDs and audio DVDs promise better fidelity and multichannel capability. HD radio has the capability to broadcast multichannel sound, so these discs may find their way into broadcast and Internet studios that provide music in surround sound.

Digital cart machines are essentially hard disc recorders that allow the operator to quickly cue up specific cuts for air use. Some cart machines may be networked to receive files from digital workstations.

A broadcast turntable may still be found in radio stations with large collections of vinyl. Turntables are often found in production booths where the operator needs to make a recording of a track not available digitally.

Remote signals may originate from a satellite program service or from local remote set-ups. For telephone connections, a hybrid is used to help facilitate call-ins. Satellite services are decoded and sent to the console as standard audio signals.

APPLICATIONS

SITUATION 1 / THE PROBLEM A producer at an oldies station was putting together a commercial that called for very tight meshing of 1960s musical elements and wild sound not available on CD. The station format involved fast-paced, extremely closely packed sound elements. Backtracking the disc and potting it up on the board resulted in a tiny but noticeable gap in the sound.

ONE POSSIBLE SOLUTION The producer decided to slipcue the musical elements and wild sound into a computer. By identifying the first sound of the music selection desired, backtracking ever so slightly, and hot-potting the cut, she was able to make a very tight production bed for the spot.

SITUATION 2 / THE PROBLEM The producer of a spot wanted to use a lyric from a popular song. Unfortunately, there was an instrumental introduction leading directly into the beginning of the lyric. The spot really needed that lyric, but the 10-second instrumental before the lyric wasn't appropriate.

ONE POSSIBLE SOLUTION The producer elected to use the pause function on the CD player. He listened to the instrumental introduction and was able to pause the CD player right before the lyrics began. By pressing "play," the CD started instantaneously with the singer's voice. By using this method, the producer avoided hearing any of the instrumental portion of the music.

(*NOTE:* It would be easy to solve both of these problems using a digital audio workstation [DAW], but we haven't discussed computer editing yet.)

EXERCISES

1. Using three discs or CDs, go from one piece of music to another and then to another. Play each disc for 10 or 20 seconds; then fade it down and bring up another.

2. Cross-fade from a vocal to an instrumental; choose an instrumental cut that has a definite ending (rather than just a fade-out). Make the resulting segment exactly 5 minutes long. To do this, you will have to back-time and dead-pot the instrumental. (Back-timing is a technique that allows you to combine two songs or more to make a production piece time out exactly to a specific time. In this case, to make the vocal and instrumental time out to exactly 5 minutes, you would subtract the time of the vocal selection from 5:00 minutes and start the instrumental far enough into its segue so that the combined timing would equal the desired length.)

3. This exercise is strictly a matter of practicing some mechanical movements with a turntable. You may have never cued up a record (disc) before, but practicing some of the basic movements will make the operations much easier. The movements to practice are as follows:

   - Dropping the stylus into the lead grooves on a disc. Keep trying until you can hit all the grooves on an entire side without picking up any of the music.

4

Digital Recording and Recording Devices

M ost material in radio today is prerecorded. Compact discs and music downloads provide the vast majority of music to consumers, although radio stations usually transfer program material to a computer hard disc for actual airplay.

It's quite common to use a CD-R disc burner to record materials during production, particularly when several copies of the material are needed. However, making specific dubs for broadcast purposes is not a new practice. It might interest you to know that as late as the 1950s, many radio stations had vinyl disc-cutting machines for exactly the same purpose.

Ultimately, cutting vinyl discs was impractical because they can't be edited. Vinyl discs were useful primarily for permanent storage of sound. The need for a convenient way to record material that might be used only once or a few times, with further changes possible after recording, led to the development of magnetic recording technology and the use of *audiotape*.

Today, CD burners, hard disk recording, flash and solid-state drive devices, and MiniDiscs have replaced both digital and analog audiotape to a large degree. However, magnetic recording media are alive and well in broadcast studios in digital applications because computer hard drives use magnetic recording technology to store and reproduce data files. Some digital multitracks use magnetic tape to store digital information, and standard analog cassettes are still used for news-gathering and archiving purposes.

Audiotape is often called **magnetic tape** because its magnetic properties allow the storage of sound. Actually, sound isn't stored on the tape. Sound energy is transduced into electrical energy, and those electrical pulses are then transduced into magnetic energy.

This chapter deals with recording technologies commonly found in radio. These technologies are generally divided into two basic types: magnetic and optical. New solid-state technology allows digital file storage on flash cards and new solid-state drives, but we're going to start this chapter with a discussion of magnetic storage. Magnetic tape can store both analog signals and digital information, while optical recording media are used to store digital information only. To understand this process, we'll start by examining how digital recording works. Then we'll look at how signals are stored on magnetic and optical media.

The digital process starts with converting sound into data. Although this technology is fairly complex, we'll keep the explanations as simple as possible. Digital recording technology takes the two components of all audio signals, frequency and loudness, and converts these components into mathematical representations called *samples* and *quantization*. In essence, to make digital recording possible, we need to find a way to represent mathematically the changes of amplitude over time. Harrold Nyquist, a Swedish scientist, developed a theorem for understanding this concept nearly 100 years ago; occasionally you may hear the term *Nyquist rate* in reference to sampling of audio frequencies.

SAMPLING

Sampling is the process of converting analog audio signals into numerical representations. Basically, sampling involves taking a snapshot of the audio wave and breaking it down into very small segments of the signal that can be expressed in a form a computer can use. Computer language uses *binary numbers*, long sequences of 0s and 1s, to represent sound waves that have been sampled. The sampling process is incredibly fast. In fact, one second of audio may be sampled 44,100 times or greater. But let's start with a rudimentary sample that measures an audio signal only twice per second. In broadcasting, these binary numbers will end up representing our audio signals.

This waveform (see Figure 4.1a) is frequently used to represent an audio wave. We call it a *sine wave*. You'll notice that it has a positive side and a negative side. Suppose we wanted to sample this wave at the rate of two samples per second. The two samples for this sine wave would be represented by both the positive and negative parts of the wave, and we could provide some rough digital information, as seen in Figure 4.1b. Unfortunately, this digital sample doesn't provide very much useful information. It simply tells us the signal was on twice: once as a positive signal and once as a negative signal. It doesn't give us much information about the slope of the wave (how quickly the sound approaches its maximum value), for example, so it isn't very useful to us. Just knowing that it goes positive and then negative in one second doesn't really tell us much.

Let's try to sample the same sine wave again using eight samples per second instead of two (see Figure 4.2). This time you can begin to see the representation of the original sine wave because we've increased the sampling rate (number of samples per second) to make the representation more detailed.

Now, imagine using a rate of 24 samples per second (see Figure 4.3) to represent this sine wave. This digital representation looks very similar to the original sine wave. While 24 samples are not fine enough for practical use, we can see what is occurring: As the number of samples increases, so too does the accuracy of the representation of our original sine wave. Imagine how accurate the sample will be when we sample sound at a rate of 44,100 times per second. That's one of the commonly used sampling rates for digital recording. But why?

Humans can hear very low and extremely high frequencies, from a low of about 20 Hz (the lowest notes made on a huge pipe organ) to about 20,000 Hz, the highest overtones of high-pitched instruments (such as a piccolo or a triangle). The sampling frequency for good audio (there's the Nyquist rate again) needs to be about twice the highest frequency humans can hear; 44,100 Hz is a little more than double our hearing capability.

As the samples of the audio signal's waveform are taken, they are converted into binary numbers in a process called **quantization**. The greater the amount of quantization, the better the sonic resolution. As mentioned previously, binary numbers are expressed in zeros and ones. A quantity expressed as a binary number is referred to as a *digital word*. The value of each *binary digit* is called a *bit*. In practical terms, the binary numbers used for high-quality digital audio are fairly large. This ensures that the digital signal is a pretty accurate representation of the original audio signal.

The recording process requires several steps, and we'll take them one at a time. First, as the sound enters the audio circuit, a low-pass filter limits the frequencies to be converted to those humans can hear. Frequencies that exist but are not audible to humans (like a dog whistle) are eliminated at this point. Then, a *sample-and-hold* circuit, used to execute the quantization process, holds the waveform in the computer's memory for a fraction of a second. During this sampling of data, information about both the signal's frequency and its loudness is converted into a series of digital words. Earlier we said that one second of audio would be sampled more than 44,100 times, so you can see that quite a lot of data is being generated in the quantization process. Once the signals are sampled and converted into digital words, they need to be coded into bits. A steady stream of data generated by the coding process now represents the audio.

Next, *error correction* is applied to minimize the potential for problems that may arise while the computer is storing and retrieving the data. A look at the block diagram in Figure 4.4 shows the path the audio signal went through to become bits of information that are ready to be stored in digital form.

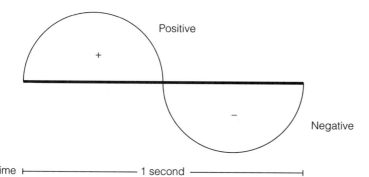

a. This representation of an audio signal is called a sine wave. In this diagram, the sine wave has completed one complete rotation in one second.

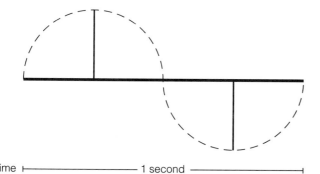

b. The digital representation of our audio signal shows two samples: one positive and one negative.

FIGURE 4.1

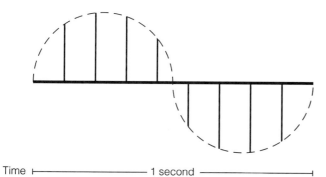

FIGURE 4.2

This digital representation of our sine wave uses eight samples: four positive and four negative.

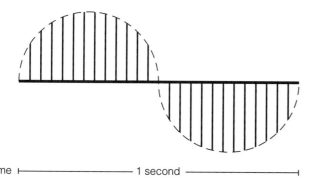

FIGURE 4.3

Digital representation of a sine wave using 24 samples. As the number of samples increases, the digital representation becomes more accurate.

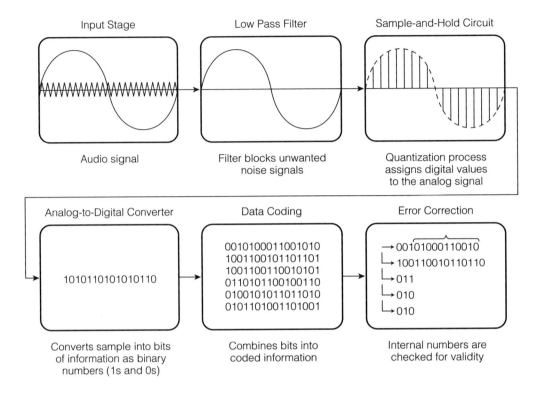

Input Stage

Low Pass Filter

Sample-and-Hold Circuit

Audio signal

Filter blocks unwanted
noise signals

Quantization process
assigns digital values
to the analog signal

Analog-to-Digital Converter

1010110101010110

Data Coding

0010100011001010
1001100101101101
1001100110010101
0110101100100110
0100101011011010
0101101001101001

Error Correction

→ 00101000110010
↳ 100110010110110
↳ 011
↳ 010
↳ 010

Converts sample into bits
of information as binary
numbers (1s and 0s)

Combines bits into
coded information

Internal numbers are
checked for validity

FIGURE 4.4

Block diagram of the digital recording process.

Now that the original audio wave has been converted into usable digital form and coded and error correction has been applied, we can store this information on a computer hard drive or burn it on a CD for use later. Both magnetic hard drives and optical drives (CD and DVD burners) share many basic principles. For example, to store the digital file, we need to *modulate* the digital words, comprising 1s and 0s, as a series of pulses. Hard drives and rewritable optical devices such as CD-RWs can be reused hundreds of times by writing over previous files, but both technologies can fail, resulting in data loss. Newer technology like flash drives store the data in erasable programmable read-only memory chips, but they too are subject to data corruption. So, it's important to create backup files for material that you want to archive permanently.

DISK DRIVE RECORDING

Hard disk drives use iron oxide coating on a spindle, and the record heads lay down a series of magnetic pulses along various tracks on the hard disk. While the principle is just that simple, the actual execution of the process is a bit more complex.

A hard disk drive has one or more self-contained glass disks that have been coated with iron oxide and then polished to an amazingly smooth, high-precision surface. The record/play heads (one for each side) move over the disk without actually touching the surface.

The record/play heads are tiny electromagnets that turn on when the bytes are 1s and turn off when the bytes read 0. When the bytes are 1s, the record heads act like electromagnets and generate tiny electromagnetic waves that flow around the heads. This is called a flux. The recording occurs when the head's flux leaves a magnetic imprint on that sector of the disk. In the recording process, data is saved as a string of **bytes** (*digital words*) in specific locations on the drive. As the information is written onto the hard drive, the computer creates a directory or file that contains the locations where the data is stored. In computer parlance, we call these places on the disk *sectors*.

The recording process is possible because the magnetic domains (the actual size of the iron particles) are extremely small and because the disk spindles rotate at a very high rate of speed, usually 5,400 rpm or 7,200 rpm or higher. Because the magnetic domains are so small, hard disk drives can contain a tremendous amount of data. The read/write heads shuttle back and forth just above the surface of the disk up to 40 or more times per second, and because the disk spindles spin so quickly, it is possible to retrieve data very quickly (see Figure 4.5).

The computer's operating system keeps a directory of where the information is stored on the hard disk. The directory becomes a map of where the data for the *file* is stored. The computer will use the directory to retrieve this information when you want to play it back. If you want to edit the file, the disk drive will write new information about the changes, and the directory will be updated to reflect where this new information is stored on the hard drive. In the playback process, the user can access that information nearly instantaneously by calling up a file name.

The data is transferred from the disk as the play head retrieves the appropriate data and sends it to the computer's random access memory (RAM). When playing back an audio file, the hard drive heads move across the data along a path guided by the hard drive's file directory. Since the data pulses may be spread across different parts of the hard drive, the data is accumulated within the computer in a buffer (called a *cache*) and then transferred to the data registers within the computer. From there the data is converted back into audio pulses by the digital-to-analog (D-to-A) converter within the computer's sound card. Modern disk drives have extremely fast *seek times*, meaning that they can retrieve the data fast enough to allow the computer to accumulate the audio data and play it back as an audio file in real time. However, the system is subject to some problems. For example, as more and more recording and rerecording occurs, hard disks become fragmented because the data for each file is distributed over many different storage sectors of the disk drive. The result can be a hiccupping sound in playback. Defragmenting programs (called disk utilities) are used to rewrite the data files and put them in order on the hard drive.

As disk drives got larger, cheaper, and faster, audio playback via a computer became more of a reality. Today almost all radio stations play back music,

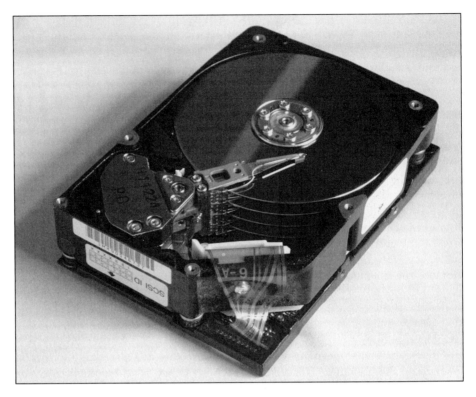

FIGURE 4.5

a. This hard disk drive has four spindles that are coated with iron oxide. Read/write
   heads move above the surface at a very high rate of speed.

SOURCE: Fritz Messere

commercials, and program segments stored on computer hard drives. It's not
unusual to find that a radio station is using six or more disk drives to store all
of its music, commercials, and promos for airplay. Some stations centralize the
music files on a server so the stored program material can be used simultaneously
in different studios. Local computer networks with speeds of 100 MB (megabytes) per second or greater are common, and this is more than adequate for
high-quality stereophonic playback.

Digital Audio Workstations

Software that provides recording and mixing capabilities can turn a computer
into a *digital audio workstation* (DAW). While some manufacturers also make dedicated machines for this purpose, almost any modern computer can function as a
workstation, and new mobile devices like iPhones and iPads have enough computing power and speed to perform audio editing.

Both Mac and PC computers used as digital audio workstations require an interface between the audio hardware and the software. Requirements vary with the desired capability. It is possible to use some audio programs like Adobe Audition, Sound Forge™, and Bias Peak with the standard audio interfaces that come built into the computer, although you will be limited to recording a maximum of two discrete channels at any one time. In order to record more than two channels at one time, more sophisticated audio interfaces are needed. Some programs, like Pro Tools, offer special hardware interfaces and configurations that allow users to record eight or more audio channels simultaneously. These multichannel setups are usually found in recording studios or very sophisticated production studios.

Digital workstations allow a producer to perform editing functions far more easily and expertly than is possible using the rudimentary editing tools on MiniDiscs or old-fashioned analog tape recorders. Digital workstations have several advantages.

The major benefits of this technology are the automatic functions that can be built into the software, making use of the computer's lightning-fast power. For example, by simply adjusting a control that creates a digital cross-fade at the point where you join two sound elements together in an edit, you can make almost any edit virtually undetectable, no matter how tight it is. If you don't like the edit you have made, you can delete it and start all over again with the original sound sources, which remain intact while you experiment with the editing processes.

Once you have a satisfactory edit, you can store it in a file while keeping the original sound sources intact. The sound quality of all materials remains virtually unaffected no matter how much you work with the material or how many versions of a sound file you record.

DIGITAL CART MACHINES AND DIGITAL RECORDERS

Digital cart machines, described in Chapter 3, use the same technology as digital workstations. Indeed, some cart machines are simply software programs that run on standard computers. The internal recording and playback process is exactly the same as that of a digital audio workstation.

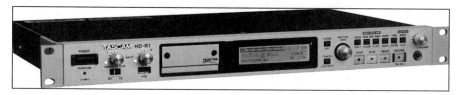

FIGURE 4.5

b. Flash recorders are gaining acceptance in broadcast studios. Flash cards can be moved from one studio to another and files are compatible with most digital audio workstations.

SOURCE: TEAC Corp. of America (TASCAM)

Also making appearances in more and more studios are digital recorders that use flash drives to record and playback.

MAGNETIC TAPE

Magnetic tape is the granddaddy of high-quality music storage, and the principles of operation are not that different from disk drive recording. Multitrack audio recorders are still seen in recording studios, so you may come across them. We'll briefly touch on the theory of recording. **Audiotape** is a strip of material with a thin coating of **iron oxide** (a fancy name for rust) on one surface. The iron oxide particles are in powder form. The particles form a **magnetic flux** when they are exposed to an electromagnetic **field** from the record head (just like in hard drive recording).

The backing of the tape—the material over which the coating is applied—is made of **Mylar™**, a resilient, extremely tough substance that can stretch quite far before it breaks. This isn't necessarily an advantage, because a snapped tape can be repaired, whereas a stretched tape can't. Generally, however, with some care, magnetic tape is a reliable storage medium.

There are many different sizes of magnetic tape used by the broadcasting and music industries (Figure 4.6). They range in width from 2 inches to as small as

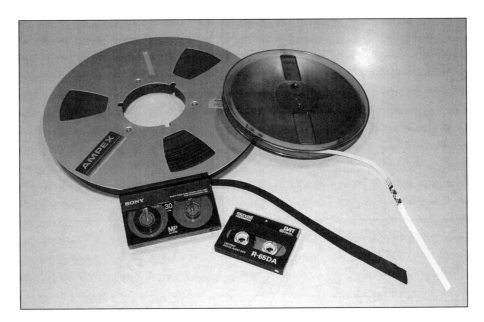

FIGURE 4.6

Reel-to-reel tape shown in 1-inch and ¼-inch sizes. DAT and digital 8-track cassettes are some of the formats available.

SOURCE: Fritz Messere

one-eighth of an inch wide. Some tapes are spooled onto open reels or cassettes. Different-sized tapes serve different purposes. For example, 2-inch and 1-inch-wide tapes are usually found in large recording studios where multiple tracks are a necessity. Broadcasters tended to use quarter-inch tape on stereo (two-track) tape machines and older audio cassettes use tape that's one-eighth of an inch wide. Tapes can be found in either analog or digital formats.

Digital Audiotape

Digital audiotape is the tape corollary of the compact disc: It is recorded using the same kinds of sampling and coding methods described earlier. However, digital audiotape (known as DAT) has an advantage over CDs in that it is readily available for recording as well as for playback, and the tape can be reused over and over again.

Recordable digital audiotape (R-DAT) uses two tracks of digital audiotape on a cassette that is approximately the size of a pack of cards. The tape cassette is loaded into a machine that resembles a videotape recorder. (For an example, see the R-DAT machine shown in Figure 4.7.)

Most machines have a variety of sampling rates, representing the number of times per second that a sound is digitally sampled. R-DAT units typically offer sampling rates of 44.1 kHz, 48 kHz, and (for digital inputs only) 32 kHz.

Workings of the Digital Tape Machine

Like the hard drive we described earlier, the process of magnetic tape recording happens when a tape passes by an electromagnet that arranges the pattern of magnetism in the tiny magnetic particles to correspond to that of the sound message being fed into the recorder.

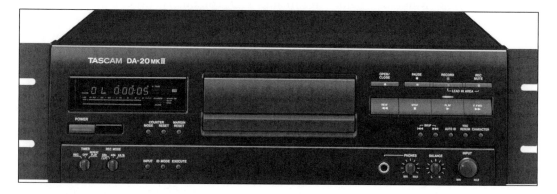

FIGURE 4.7

R-DAT recorder displays cut number and elapsed time on the alphanumeric display.

SOURCE: TEAC Corp. of America (TASCAM)

A **record head** is the electromagnet in the tape machine. The heads in a typical tape recorder perform three functions, but before describing them, let's see where the heads are and how the tape is brought into contact with them.

All tape machines, regardless of their design differences, operate in pretty much the same way. Figure 4.8a is a simplified diagram of the R-DAT tape path. The tape machine draws the tape out of the cassette from the left side of the cassette to the right. The technical names of the left and right components, respectively, are the *supply spool* and *take-up spool*. As tape passes from the **supply spool** to the **take-up spool**, it is drawn across the heads, where a magnetic signal is implanted on the tape or played back from the tape.

The playback process for a DAT machine is almost the reverse of the recording process. Figure 4.9 shows a block diagram of the playback sequence. In the Playback mode, tape is pulled across the head in the same fashion as in the Record mode. This time, however, the heads pick up the magnetic information embedded on tape and send the signal to the demodulator, which reshapes the modulated signals and returns them as pulses of 1s and 0s.

The data is accumulated into memory registers and error correction is applied to the signal, which is then sent to a digital-to-analog converter that reconverts the digital numbers into an analog audio signal. The output is sent first to a sample-and-hold circuit that removes switching pulses from the signal, and then to a low-pass filter that removes extraneous high-frequency noise from the recording.

MINIDISC RECORDING

As we noted in Chapter 3, many broadcasters have used MiniDiscs in news-gathering and as a logging device in the broadcast studio. Originally, the Mini-Disc was thought to be a consumer replacement for audio cassettes. While the technology never caught on in the consumer marketplace, broadcasters began using MiniDiscs before recordable CD computers were common. Today broadcasters will frequently have a MiniDisc recorder in the control room to log live programs or call-in shows to have a record of what was said. However, the future of MiniDiscs does not appear to be very bright. Few manufacturers still manufacture the devices in great quantity, and they are likely to be super-seded by flash recorders in the next few years.

The MiniDisc is a magneto-optical recording device housed in a casing about the size of a floppy disk (see Figure 4.10). MiniDiscs come with different capacities and can store 60, 74, or 80 minutes of stereo audio in a self-contained format. Recorded audio goes through a process similar to that used by other digital media. Like hard drives, the MiniDisc is a random-access medium, which gives it the ability to find and play tracks very quickly.

The audio signal is sampled and coded into digital information, but unlike a digital workstation the MiniDisc compresses the audio signal by a ratio of more than 5 to 1 before it is recorded. The compressed data is in a "lossy" format, meaning that the playback will not mirror the original recording,

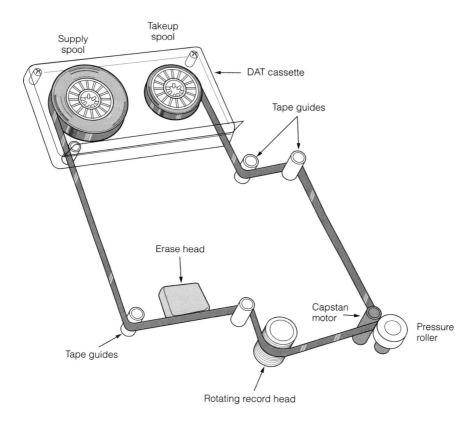

a. Tape is drawn out of the cassette along precision guides, across an erase head, and across the record head. The capstan and roller pull the tape at a constant rate of speed. The tape is wound back into the cassette onto the take-up spool.

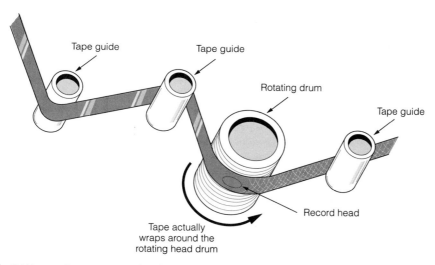

b. DAT recorders use a rotating head drum to increase the ability to record large amounts of data on tape. Tracks are recorded as a series of magnetic pulses.

F I G U R E 4.8

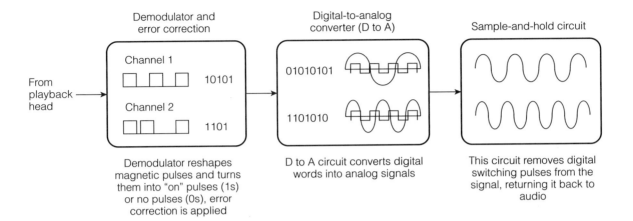

Demodulator and error correction

Channel 1

10101

Channel 2

1101

From playback head

Digital-to-analog converter (D to A)

01010101

1101010

Sample-and-hold circuit

Demodulator reshapes magnetic pulses and turns them into "on" pulses (1s) or no pulses (0s), error correction is applied

D to A circuit converts digital words into analog signals

This circuit removes digital switching pulses from the signal, returning it back to audio

FIGURE 4.9

The demodulation converts the magnetic pulses on tape back into binary information.

even though it may be hard to tell the recording from the original. This compressed signal is then stored on the optical media in a fashion similar to recording a CD-RW.

MiniDiscs can be recorded and reused, and because the material is stored in a digital format, a file directory is updated each time a recording is made. Titles are stored as part of the recorded information. However, unlike CDs, MiniDisc recorders also have some rudimentary built-in editing features. This allows users to identify, edit, and retrieve information very quickly.

MiniDiscs have several features that make them quite attractive for radio stations. First, they do not need to store data in sequential order. The system writes a table of contents (TOC) file that keeps the tracks in order. A total of 255 tracks may

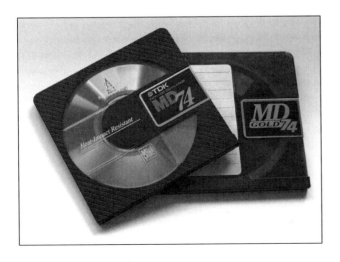

FIGURE 4.10

Although MiniDiscs have been phased out of the consumer electronics market, many broadcast stations still use these devices to log recordings and make air checks. The MiniDisc can be reused over and over again, making them highly affordable. Their small size makes them easily transportable although, as the price of disk storage decreases, it is likely that MiniDiscs will disappear from studios in the next few years.

SOURCE: Fritz Messere

TUNING IN TO TECHNOLOGY • DIGITAL SOUND AND AUDIO COMPRESSION

In Chapter 3 we briefly touched upon the ideal of audio compression in our discussion of MP3 discs. Both MP3 and MiniDisc technologies use audio compression schemes. Generally, the aim of audio compression is to reduce the amount of data required to store or distribute music. This becomes important if a station has an interest in providing a program service over the Internet or if it has a central server for distributing its audio files to production studios. The size of an audio file is determined by the quality of the file (e.g., the bit rate) and the length of the file. Smaller audio files are easier to stream over the Internet and are easier to transfer from computer to computer.

Most uncompressed digital audio files are quite large. For example, an uncompressed one-minute stereo recording made on a program like Digidesign's Pro Tools would need approximately 10 megabytes (MB) of storage on a hard drive. With that setting, the program will sample audio at a rate of 44.1 kHz (kilohertz) per second with a depth of 16-bit quantization. Seventy minutes of music would comprise a 700-MB file, approximately the capacity of a compact disc. Newer high-definition recordings, using 24-bit quantization, for example, would require even more storage space. For comparison, compact discs can hold about 74 minutes of audio.

Both MP3s and MiniDiscs compress audio to create files that are much smaller than their uncompressed counterparts. This allows more files to be stored in a given space, but there is a trade-off in sound quality.

There are many potential ways to compress a data file to make it smaller. Some audio compression systems do not result in any discernable audio quality degradation. Some of these schemes used are known as *lossless* compression because the recorded music quality will be the same as the original. However, these systems tend to reduce the data file's size by only 25 percent, so the compressed files are nearly as large as the original files. They are not practical if the audio files are going to be streamed on the Internet.

The second kind of audio compression system is called *lossy* compression, and there are several different types available. In broadcasting, the most common types of compression are MP3 (MPEG audio layer 3),

used frequently to transfer files over the Internet, and ATRAC (Adaptive Transform Acoustic Coding), used in MiniDiscs.

These systems use psychoacoustic techniques (the study of subjective human perception of sound) to accomplish the goal of retaining quality while creating smaller audio files. Two basic psychoacoustic techniques are used to make the data size smaller. First, as a result of extensive testing, audio engineers have developed ideas about how much change to the music structure can be tolerated by the listener before it becomes noticeable. All sounds have certain harmonics and some are more important than others. The second technique involves analyzing the sound to see which sound frequencies are most important to the listener and which are less important. For example, some frequencies lend clarity to vocals while others add fullness. Once the signal has been analyzed, an algorithm in the recording process will compress the audio file by breaking the audio spectrum into smaller subbands. Then, by reducing the size of certain subbands that are less important to the listener, the audio file can be reduced in size. Taken together, these compression techniques greatly reduce the size of the audio file. Naturally, there is a point of diminishing returns. If too much compression is applied, the sound can become brittle or tinny. But in many cases it is difficult to distinguish the original from the compressed version.

Take a look at the size differences that result from compression. You can see that the difference in file size is very substantial.

- One minute of uncompressed audio = 10 MB
- One minute of compressed audio for MP3 = 0.83 MB
- One minute of compressed audio for ATRAC (MiniDisc) = 1.43 MB

As more and more large audio files need to be streamed or stored, the importance of data compression becomes clear. Radio stations use large computer hard disks to archive important commercials. Jingles, music, and news segments, which also can be stored in a computer, will take up a lot of space. Compression is important as stations cross the digital threshold.

RADIO RETRO • ANALOG TAPE MACHINES

THIS DISCUSSION ABOUT how analog tape machines are used in broadcasting centers on reel-to-reel, cartridge, and cassette recorders and reproducers. While the majority of radio stations have moved to digital gear, there are numerous stations using various pieces of analog gear. We will cover the basic information here.

Figure 4.11 is a simplified diagram of a reel-to-reel tape machine. It bears some similarity to our diagram of the DAT recorder in its layout of controls and operation. All reel-to-reel tape machines, regardless of their design differences, operate in pretty much the same way.

The tape machine draws the tape from the left reel to the right reel. The technical names of the left and right components, respectively, are **supply reel** and **take-up reel**. As tape passes from the supply reel to the take-up reel, it is drawn across the heads, where a signal is implanted on the tape or played back from the tape.

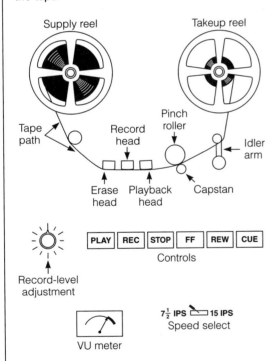

FIGURE 4.11

Basic layout for reel-to-reel tape recorders.

We'll begin with an explanation of the heads and then move on to discussing the movement of the tape in the machine's transport system.

The Heads

Figure 4.12 shows the heads on a tape machine. Reel-to-reel machines have three separate tape heads, each of which performs a distinct function. These heads are called *erase, record*, and *play*. First, the **erase head** scrambles the pattern of the iron oxide particles and obliterates any information previously stored on them. The **record head** produces a magnetic field that arranges the iron oxide particles in a particular order, storing the information on the tape. The **playback head** reads the patterns formed by the arrangement of the iron oxide particles and produces an electrical signal carrying the sound information.

The heads are always arranged in this order (from left to right): erase, record, playback. Since the tape passes the record head immediately before it passes over the playback head, the operator of the tape machine can play back what was just recorded to make sure that there is, indeed, a recording on the tape. Broadcasters used to use this feature to create a slap-back echo as a rudimentary special effect by feeding the playback output of the recorder back into the audio console as a recording was being made.

The Tape Transport Mechanism

Despite differences among models, the goal of all tape machines is the same: to pass a tape across the heads at a constant rate of speed. For the layout of the tape transport mechanism, refer to Figure 4.11. The components of the drive mechanism perform the same functions as they do on a digital audio workstation. The Play, Stop, Fast Forward, and Rewind functions move the tape mechanically in the same way that these controls move the location of playback in an audio file. But unlike a digital workstation, the tape moves mechanically and, depending on the amount of tape, it may take a few minutes to completely move the tape from one location to another.

Tape Machine Controls and Indicators

Although the style of levers and buttons differs from machine to machine, the controls and indicators perform typical functions that are common to most

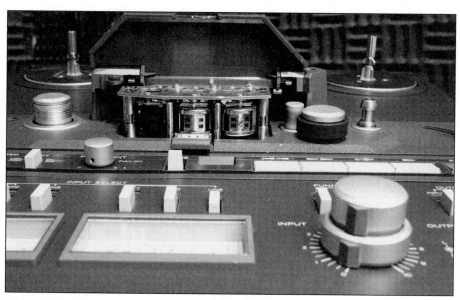

F I G U R E   4.12

Three tape heads (center of photo). Next to the tape heads, the capstan and roller pull the tape across the head at a constant speed.

SOURCE: Fritz Messere

audio machines, from analog reel-to-reel and cassette machines to MiniDiscs and digital workstations.

There are a few controls on tape machines that differ from mechanical machines (see Figure 4.13).

Cue

The Cue control brings the tape into contact with the heads by defeating the tape lifter. It allows you to cue the tape when it's moving in fast forward or rewind. On some machines, the Cue control is also used if the operator wants to hear the sounds on the tape while rocking (moving) the reels by hand, as when editing tape.

Speed Select

This control governs how quickly the tape moves past the heads. The most frequently used speeds on broadcast reel-to-reel tape machines are 7½ and 15 inches per second (IPS). These designations denote the number of inches of tape driven past a given point per

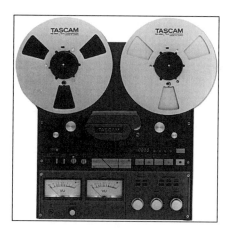

F I G U R E   4.13

This reel-to-reel recorder will accept reels as large as 10½ inches.

SOURCE: TASCAM, TEAC Professional Division, Montebello, CA

second. A seldom-used but sometimes available speed is 3¾ IPS. Note that each speed is exactly double or half the previous speed.

Cueing a Tape

Just as with discs and turntables, you'll need to know where the sound information on a tape begins so that you can put it out over the air or use it in studio production.

Say, for instance, that you have a recording of an interview show. You might thread the tape and fast-forward it with the cue control on until you hear the chattering of sound on the tape—over the console's cue speaker, of course! Then you would wind it to the approximate point at which the sound started, stop the tape machine, and rock the reels by hand until you hear the beginning in cue. Usually, there will be a count-down or cue tone on prerecorded tapes to help the operator.

be recorded. As a result, it is possible to take segments of the MiniDisc recordings and edit or change them. Second, MiniDiscs are fairly rugged and can be used over and over. Third, the basic editing features give MiniDiscs a real advantage over CD-RWs, which are written in sequential order. Finally, MiniDisc files can be accessed randomly (as opposed to sequentially) and are fairly easy to edit and change. Files can be separated or combined easily, too.

SUMMARY

Computer hard disks use magnetic recording technology, which is very important in broadcasting. This is the recording technology used in analog and digital tape recorders. Hard drives have a coating of iron oxide on the disk spindles that can be used to make magnetic representations of the audio signal. The oxide particles align to conform with the signal generated by a magnetic head. In this way, sound information is transduced and stored for later playback.

Digital audio workstations (DAWs) and digital tape provide the highest-quality recording and great flexibility for editing. DVDs, CDs, and MiniDiscs use optical recording systems to burn files onto a light-sensitive medium. Files can be recorded and stored with or without audio compression, which is used to reduce the size of audio files. Some systems, such as MP3s and MiniDiscs, record audio with a slight degradation of sound quality. While 90 percent of all radio stations record material using digital technology, there are still some uses for analog tape recorders or reproducers.

Newer recording devices use solid-state recording technology, such as flash drives, to store materials.

APPLICATIONS

SITUATION 1/THE PROBLEM The producer of a five-minute news program wants the sound of a teletype in the background. He has a sound-effects disc with the teletype sound, but the cut runs for only 30 seconds, and it would be impractical to keep pressing Play to keep the sound going.

ONE POSSIBLE SOLUTION Record the cut on a digital workstation and create loop or record on a MiniDisc several times and use the edit function to combine the audio into one longer track.

SITUATION 2/THE PROBLEM A community bulletin-board segment airs twice every hour at 15 minutes and 45 minutes after the hour. The producer has found a perfect piece of music to introduce the segment, but she notices how inconvenient it is to tie up a CD player twice an hour for 10 seconds of music.

ONE POSSIBLE SOLUTION The producer simply records, or dubs, the first 10 seconds of music from the disc onto a digital cart. The audio file is labeled in the cart machine and it's now very convenient for the console operator to select the file on the cart and plug/play it.

EXERCISES

1. Using a MiniDisc, record someone counting from 1 to 20. Then have someone call out a number between 1 and 20. Your assignment is to cue up the disc as quickly as possible to start at that number. For example, if the number 16 is called out, you'll want to find the part of the track on which the announcer is reading 13 … 14 … 15 … and pause it there. (You will, of course, do this in cue or audition.) Then, bring the MiniDisc up in program and start it. You should hear the cut cleanly start with the number 16. Have several numbers called out until you're proficient at cueing.

2. Decide which type of machine (CD, MiniDisc, DAW, or digital cart) would be best for the following applications, and explain your reasons:

   - The musical opening to a news program.
   - An interview a news reporter will be doing at the site of a demonstration.
   - A 60-second commercial.
   - A half-hour radio drama.
   - A 10-minute interview segment done in the studio.
   - Multiple station identifications. (You might want to try producing sample station IDs on the type of machine you decide is most appropriate.)

5

Microphones and Sound

At many radio stations, you will have little to say about the selection of the microphone that best suits the pickup requirements of the moment. Those who have worked at a variety of radio stations often remark that you will find only a handful of microphone models in most radio stations. All on-air and production studios at a given station will generally have the same model, though another model may be used for remote and news applications. Microphones are designed to serve specific purposes.

Therefore, you don't necessarily need to know all the details of microphone use to do your job in a radio station. A person doing production duties in a small radio station will generally use the mic that happens to be hooked up to the console. A reporter will use whatever mic is handed out before going out on assignment. In many production situations, the simplest of miking techniques and arrangements will be used time and time again.

However, you'll be able to do even a basic production job better with a good working knowledge of microphones. In some cases, a detailed knowledge of microphone use will help you solve a thorny problem. Moreover, in the more advanced areas of radio production, such as recording live music, you must know mic use inside and out.

We offer a realistic explanation of the situation because many newcomers to radio production become somewhat cynical after plowing through explicit details of microphone use and selection in their textbook but never using the knowledge during the class or in their first few jobs. So even though this knowledge might not seem essential right now, it might prove invaluable later.

THE BASICS OF SOUND

The microphone, like many other pieces of equipment that we discussed earlier, is a **transducer**. It changes the energy of the motion of sound into electrical energy. The microphone is the instrument that transforms sound into something that can be used by the record and playback units hooked up to a radio console.

Sound itself is a vibration—a specific motion—of air molecules. What happens is this: A sound source (a cymbal, perhaps) creates changes in air pressure. A sound source causes alternating waves of compression (dense dots) and rarefaction (sparse dots) through the air. When molecules are pushed together, they are said to be in **compression**. Areas of low pressure, where molecules are pulled apart from one another, are called **rarefactions**. To visualize the situation, look at Figure 5.1.

The vibration traveling through the air carries information. The way that the cymbal sounds to our ears is determined by the pattern of vibration. As a matter of fact, the eardrum is a transducer, too. It performs the first step in converting motional energy of vibration into electrical energy in the brain.

The microphone also transduces the motional energy into electrical energy. That energy then might be transduced into electromechanical energy (via storage in a computer file or audiotape), or it might be transduced back into **motional energy** by a **loudspeaker**.

How does a mic do this, and why are certain mics better than others at reproducing certain sounds? To understand these things, let's first explore a bit further the nature of sound itself. This information will come in handy when we try to understand the behavior of sound and the way mics affect its reproduction.

The Elements of Sound

A pure-tone sound is represented by a **sine wave** (see Figure 5.2); you may remember that we used one in Chapter 4 in our sampling example. This is one of the most frequently used symbols in the world of sound, microphones, and radio—and one of the most frequently misunderstood. A sine wave depicting sound is a graphic representation of the rarefactions and compressions of air

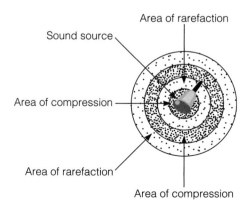

FIGURE 5.1

Compressions and rarefactions.

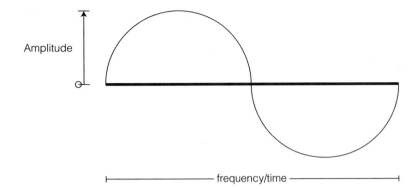

Amplitude

frequency/time

FIGURE 5.2

This sine wave represents a pure tone. As the tone reaches a certain amplitude, its frequency can be measured over time.

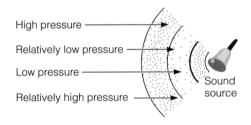

High pressure

Relatively low pressure

Low pressure

Relatively high pressure

Sound source

FIGURE 5.3

Measuring compressions and rarefactions.

molecules. If we were to sample the density of the molecules of a **wave** (pictured in Figure 5.3), we'd find a thick area, then a thinner area, then a very thin area, then an area somewhat thicker, and then a thick area again. A graph of this pattern would look like the one in Figure 5.4a, which is a plot of the sound pattern, not a picture of it. Thus, the sine wave only represents sound. No sine waves emanate from a sound source. The sine wave can be used to analyze several elements of sound.

Cycle   Each time a wave goes through its pattern and returns to its starting point, it has completed one **cycle**. A cycle passes through a complete rotation every 360 degrees. The time it takes for a wave to make a complete cycle is called an *interval*.

A cycle can be measured from any starting point. The plot of a cycle is illustrated in Figure 5.4b. Note that although a sine wave has 360 degrees in a complete rotation, this representation comprises two equal intervals, called *positive* and *negative intervals*. Each interval is 180 degrees long.

Frequency   Frequency is a measure of how often a cycle is repeated in a given period. Formerly, **frequency** was measured in cycles per second (cps). The term *cycles per second* has been replaced by the term **hertz (Hz)**, named in honor of the mathematician Heinrich Hertz, who first demonstrated the existence of radio waves. We will see shortly how frequency plays a role in the nature of sound.

Amplitude   In technical terms, the **amplitude** is the height of the sine wave. Amplitude indicates the volume of the sound. The higher the amplitude, the louder the sound.

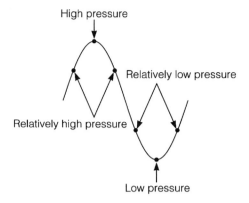

a. Description of what a sine wave represents.

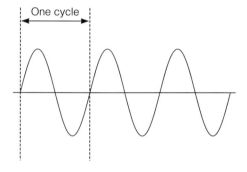

b. One cycle of a sine wave.

FIGURE 5.4
Characteristics of a sine wave.

These elements determine the characteristics of sound, and the sine wave is a visual representation of those characteristics. If nothing else, remember that any sound can be described by one or more sine waves.

The Nature of Sound: Frequency

Why did we say "one or more sine waves"? Sounds consist of combinations of wave patterns or **waveforms**. Although a device called a *tone generator* will produce, by electronic circuitry, a pure wave (when represented on an oscilloscope), most sounds are a combination of many waves of different shapes and frequencies and are called *complex waveforms*.

Frequencies and Your Ears   The human ear can hear very low frequencies from about 35 Hz to extremely high, piercing sounds up to 20,000 Hz. This,

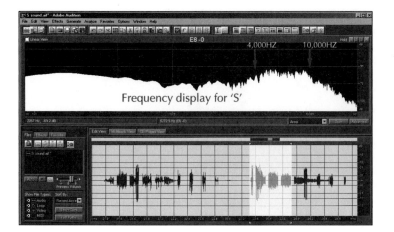

FIGURE 5.5

Pictured here is the display of a male announcer saying the letter S. Notice that the frequency range between 4 kHz and 10 kHz contains a surprising amount of content, which can add sibilance to the sound.

SOURCE: © 2013 Adobe Systems, Inc.

of course, depends on the age and health of the ear's owner. Older people generally don't hear high frequencies as well as young people do. The low end of the scale is a deep bass rumbling; the high end is a thin whine that's barely audible to humans.

How Frequency Shapes Sound   A sound is a combination of various waves— some higher, some lower. The fundamental frequency of an average male voice, for example, is typically around 300 Hz. Consonant sounds such as *t* and *d* are much higher, perhaps in the 1,000-Hz range. Very high, hissy consonants, such as *s*, can be well into the 4,000-Hz range, whereas the *th* in *thin* can approach 6,000 Hz (see Figure 5.5). Other components of the sounds of human speech can range as high as 9,000 Hz.

The higher-frequency sounds, the consonant sounds, lend intelligibility to speech. If high consonant sounds are not reproduced by any of the transducers in the radio production chain, human speech becomes less intelligible. Music that lacks high frequencies sounds muddy and dull; the high frequencies add clarity and vibrancy.

Limiting the range of transduced frequencies affects the tone of speech, too. Older telephones reproduce frequencies from about 300 to 3,000 Hz. The difference between speech over these telephones and speech over a high-quality mic is readily apparent. Various mics reproduce frequencies with varying degrees of effectiveness.

The Nature of Sound: Amplitude

The amplitude of the sine wave represents the volume of the sound. Another way to represent sound volume is by measuring it in *decibels*. A decibel (dB) is a very complex measurement of *relative* sound levels, but you need to remember two essential points about decibels:

1. The higher the decibel reading, the louder the sound. Thus, 20 dB is the sound level of a whisper; 55 dB is loud conversational speech; 75 dB is the

noise level in city traffic; 110 dB is a loud, amplified rock band; and 140 dB is a jet engine at takeoff. (These measurements are expressed in a particular form called *dB SPL*—decibel sound pressure level.)

2. It is believed that an increase or decrease of 1 to 2 dB SPL is the smallest change in sound level a human ear can perceive, but an increase of 6 dB SPL is what the human ear perceives as a doubling of the sound's volume. (Try this out next time you're at an audio board. When a steady sound such as tone moves from −6 up to 0 on a VU meter, does the apparent loudness of the sound seem to double?)

A more detailed explanation is this: You would normally think that when you double the power output of a sound, it would increase proportionally. However, the ear does not hear in a linear fashion. That is, if you were playing a stereo at a level equal to 10 watts of power and you turned it up to a level equal to an output of 15 watts (an addition of 5 watts), you would not perceive the increase as being 1.5 times the original volume. Because it is difficult to measure relative volume by talking about watts, we use a system that measures sound in a way that corresponds to the way the ear appears to hear sound. Hence, the decibel is a very useful tool to measure significant increases or decreases in apparent volume.

Remember the VU meter and the readings on the top scale from Chapter 2? Those volume units correspond to decibels. People often wonder why the VU meter uses 0 dB as the loudest modulation of sound to transmit when common sense suggests that the louder the sound, the higher the dB reading. The answer dates back to the days when radio broadcasts were carried from the network to the affiliate station via telephone wires. Engineers developed a meter that would express changes in relative volume. Actually, it would be very confusing to have a VU meter scale that read, say, from 60 to 120 dB. Therefore, in broadcasting, we have standardized 0 VU to equal a relative sound level that will power our transmitter and/or provide a proper level to our recording devices. Anything less than 100 percent will represent some negative number. This way, we don't have to work with such large decibel numbers.

Remember, the 0 dB reading is relative. A VU meter reading of −3 means that your input is 3 dB lower than the optimum level.

Other Characteristics of Sound

We've pretty well covered the physical properties that make up the nature of sound, but some other areas are also worth considering. **Pitch**, a term commonly used to describe sound, is not the same thing as frequency. Frequency is a physical measurement; pitch is the ear's and mind's subjective interpretation of frequency and loudness, signifying the way we hear a frequency. The human ear just doesn't hear the same way a scientific instrument does. For example, try this experiment. Listen to a siren approaching. As sound gets closer to us, its apparent pitch *rises*, but in actuality the frequency doesn't change!

Duration is a characteristic of sound, too. It refers to the amount of time a sound exists and to the amount of time individual harmonics exist within a complex waveform.

Velocity and distance also play a role in the way we hear sound. Sound is not very fast; it travels through air at only a little more than 1,100 feet per second, or 750 miles per hour. Sound travels at different rates through different media; it travels about four times faster through water, for example. However, it has to vibrate through a medium such as air; there's no sound in a vacuum.

The relative slowness of sound in air can be illustrated by a familiar example. When sitting in the bleachers during a baseball game, you will see the batter complete his swing before you hear the crack of the bat hitting the ball. Because of the slowness of sound, you can perceive echoes (the immediate bounce back of sound) and reverberation (the continued bouncing of sound) in an enclosure with reflective walls. A large room with reflective walls will make the reverberations take longer to *decay*, or die out.

Distance also makes a difference in how loud the sound is when it reaches us. As a sound travels through air, it loses its intensity. When sound travels two times a specified distance, it arrives at only one-quarter of its original intensity. This behavior is said to comply with the inverse square law. This means that the intensity of a sound varies inversely with the square of the distance. For example, as the distance between you and a sound source doubles, the sound intensity will reduce by a factor of 4.

A final characteristic is the sound's quality, or *timbre*. This, again, is a factor in how our ears and mind perceive sound. It has to do with the way harmonics of a sound are combined and with the relative intensities of those harmonics. Those combinations make us perceive a difference between middle C played on a piano and the same note played on a harpsichord.

Summary of the Basics of Sound

Understanding how sound behaves is a prerequisite to learning about microphones, and much of what you need to know concerns how a mic reproduces sound.

Sound is a vibration of molecules in the air, and it consists of rarefactions and compressions. A sine wave is a graphic representation of a sound wave; it is not supposed to be a picture of the wave.

Sound is measured in terms of frequency and amplitude. Frequency, which tells how often in a given period the sound wave makes a complete cycle, is measured in cycles per second, now called *hertz*. Amplitude is the height of the sine wave. It refers to the loudness of the sound and is measured in decibels. Sound travels through air at about 1,100 feet per second.

Characteristics of sound include pitch (the way we perceive frequency), loudness (the way we perceive volume), and quality or timbre (the way we interpret the complex waveforms). Duration refers to how long a sound lasts.

Now that we've prefaced this chapter with an explanation of sound, let's move on to the ways mics work, the various types of mics, and their uses.

THE MICROPHONE: HOW IT WORKS

One of the ways in which a producer selects a microphone and decides on its use is by determining how the microphone reproduces sound and how it colors that sound. (The meaning of this term should become clear shortly.)

Electronics of the Microphone

Sound reproduction is affected by the mechanical and electronic means used within the mic to change the **acoustic** or motional energy of sound—a vibration of molecules in the air—to electrical energy. Certain varieties of microphones are much better adapted to some tasks than are other types. That's why it's important to understand the workings of the three types of microphones most common in radio broadcasting: the **moving coil**, the **ribbon**, and the **condenser**.

Moving Coil   Electricity is formed by moving a conductor through a magnetic field. That's exactly what happens in a generator: Coils of wire are moved through a magnetic field (think of a turbine turning), and electrical current flows through the wires as a result.

That's also what happens in a moving-coil microphone. The diaphragm in a moving-coil mic (see Figure 5.7a) is attached to a coil of wire. The **diaphragm**, a thin membrane, vibrates as it is driven by the sound waves. The coil attached to the diaphragm vibrates, too, and the vibration of this moving coil cuts through the magnetic lines of force produced by the magnets within the microphone. The electrical wave produced carries the imprint of the sound wave by mirroring both the frequency of the acoustical energy and the amplitude of that energy. Moving-coil mics are sometimes referred to as **dynamic mics**.

Ribbon   This type of mic has a thin (usually corrugated) metal ribbon suspended between the poles of a magnet (see Figure 5.7b). The ribbon vibrates in harmony with the sound waves. Technically, the ribbon mic responds to a difference in pressure between the front and back of the ribbon; that's why some people refer to this type of instrument as a **pressure-gradient mic**. Ribbon mics had been becoming less common in radio, but recently new ribbon mic models have been introduced, which suggests that we may see more of them in the studio.

Condenser   A condenser mic operates through the use of an electrical element called a **capacitor**. *Condenser* is actually an old-fashioned name for a capacitor, and it stuck as the name for this type of mic. A capacitor stores an electrical

---

TUNING IN TO TECHNOLOGY • THE SHAPE OF SOUND

"The biggest change brought about by digital technology," says Rodney Belizaire, a recording engineer with WQEV in New York, "is connecting the eye with the ear."

What he means is that the visual depiction of the sound wave as it appears on the computer screen will soon become recognizable to the person doing the editing. You'll never be able to read the waves without knowing what the script is, but if you have even a passing acquaintance with the words, you'll be able to spot them on the screen.

The waveform, often called the *sound envelope*, is nothing more than a graphic representation of the amplitude and frequency of the sound.

Amplitude—which means *strength*—is what you'll be most concerned with when dealing with the visuals on the computer screen. The waveform is higher on the positive and negative side when the sound is louder. (Remember, sound is a system of rarefactions and compressions, which translate electronically to pluses and minuses, respectively.)

Almost all computer programs allow you to determine the time frame over which you view the sound. If you view the words *new on Atlantic* in a frame of one second, the waveform (sound envelope) will look something like the one shown in Figure 5.6a.

Most computer programs allow you to display one second's worth of copy. Many let you get far more precise and hone in on a fraction of a second. What you'll find particularly useful in most standard applications, though, is to display 15, 30, or 60 seconds. That shows you where various sound elements are placed.

Figure 5.6b shows what we mean. This is a commercial for an upcoming CD album release. The narration is interspersed with cuts from the music. The stereo music tracks are on computer tracks 1 and 2.

A sound envelope.

This diagram demonstrates how the waveform reflects the varying amplitude of speech. Below the waveform, we've made letters bigger when in normal speech they are stressed (given greater volume).

You can also see the pause between "new" and "on."

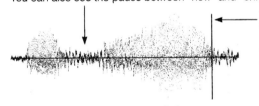

This is a line that sweeps across the waveform when you play it back. It moves in real time — that is, if the whole waveform is a second, it goes from beginning to end in a second. If your screen is set to display 30 seconds, the line will take 30 seconds to move across the waveform.

NEW . . . ON ATLANTIC

FIGURE 5.6
a. A sound envelope.

---

charge. In a condenser mic (see Figure 5.7c), a charge is applied to the side of the condenser known as the *back plate;* as the diaphragm vibrates, it changes the distance between itself and the back plate and changes the amount of charge held by the back plate.

The announcer's voice is on track 3. Where you see the arrows, it means that the computer has been instructed to make a gradual cross-fade—lowering one track while bringing up another. The announcer's track actually starts with the words "New on Atlantic, all your favorite music from…" and then segues into a musical cut from the album, then back to more narration, then another cut, and so on.

You can see, *even without knowing all the copy, how this commercial is constructed*. In later chapters, we'll get into the fine points of editing. For now, just remember that you can see in one simple illustration

how sound, in the digital domain, can be sensed with your ears and your eyes.

Below the waveform, we've made letters bigger when in normal speech they are *stressed* (given greater volume). You can also see the pause between *new* and *on*. This is a line that sweeps across the waveform when you play it back. It moves in real time—that is, if the whole waveform is a second, it goes from beginning to end in a second. If your screen is set to display 30 seconds, the line will take 30 seconds to move across the waveform.

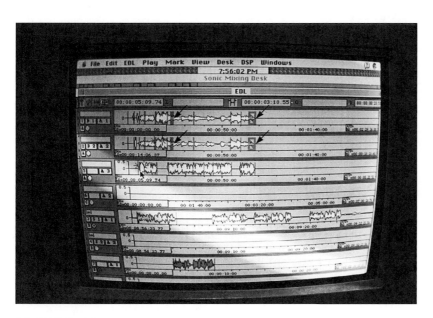

FIGURE 5.6

b. The digital editing process as it appears on a computer screen.

SOURCE: Philip Benoit

Condenser microphones often need a separate power supply to place a charge on the back plate; thus, they may require batteries. Modern condenser mics draw a 24-volt charge from the console, a "phantom" power supply.

Diaphragm   Magnet

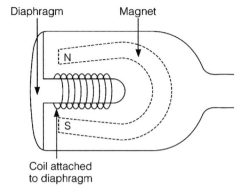

Coil attached
to diaphragm

a. In a moving-coil mic, the thin diaphragm vibrates in response to sound
energy. The attached coil moves
through a magnetic field, generating
an electrical current with a pattern
that corresponds to the pattern of the
original sound.

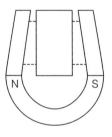

b. In a ribbon mic, sound energy causes vibrations of a metallic
ribbon, which moves through a magnetic field to produce an
electrical current.

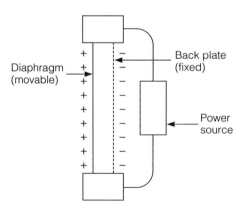

Diaphragm
(movable)

Back plate
(fixed)

Power
source

c. In a condenser mic, sound vibrates the
diaphragm. Movement of the diaphragm varies the electrical pattern on
the back plate.

FIGURE 5.7
The three types of microphone elements.

Pickup (Polar) Patterns of the Microphone

The electronics of a mic also affect the pattern in which it picks up sounds. These patterns, called **pickup patterns** or **polar patterns**, have a major effect on how a particular mic is used. Some mics pick up sounds from all directions, or from the front and back but not the sides, or from the front only. The basic pickup patterns are **omnidirectional, bidirectional**, and **cardioid**. (*Cardioid* is sometimes called *unidirectional*, meaning "one-directional.")

RADIO RETRO • THE KING OF MICROPHONES

If you look on the desks of some talk shows hosts such as David Letterman, you'll see a microphone that is outdated but still a popular icon: the RCA 77DX (see Figure 5.8). The mics are there as props, and several companies still sell nonworking replicas of this symbol of broadcasting.

The 77DX was one of those microphones that inspired loyalty among many announcers and singers. For example, *The New Yorker* recently profiled singer Al Green, who rose to fame with such hits as "Let's Stay Together" and "Love and Happiness." Green's producer credits the unique sound to "old Number 9"— the 77DX that is kept on the shelf and used only for Green. (The studio numbered all its mikes.)

(Another old-fashioned mic, the Shure 55, became known as the "Elvis Mic" because Elvis and his producers were so fond of its sound.)

The 77DX was delicate because of its ribbon element, but a few of them survive today; they impart a warm, rich, and compelling sound that really can't be quantified on a frequency response chart.

It should be noted, though, that the 77DX was not the mic for everyone—because of its delicate ribbon, people who said the letter "P" forcefully made the mic "pop."

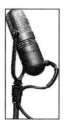

FIGURE 5.8

The legendary RCA 77DX was a modification on an earlier model introduced by RCA in 1932. The 77DX was labeled a "polydirectional" microphone because the user could switch between omnidirectional, bidirectional, and cardioid patterns. The microphone also came in two finishes. The chrome-plated model was usually used in radio but a nonreflective model became a favorite of many television personalities, including CBS legend Edward R. Murrow.

SOURCE: Philip Benoit

Omnidirectional   An omnidirectional mic picks up sounds equally well from all sides, as pictured in Figure 5.9a. To visualize what a pickup pattern is, it's helpful to know how one can be drawn. The mic is placed on a stand, pointed toward a speaker, and twisted in a circle while being kept parallel to the floor. Then the amplitude of the wave it picked up at various poles is measured. As shown in Figure 5.9a, the amplitude is as great at 90 degrees as at 0 degrees (0 being where the mic faces dead-on to the speaker). Remember, the pickup pattern is a *three-dimensional* representation, so mics hear sound from above and below, too. Although we generally assume that the omnidirectional mic picks up sound equally well from all directions, there is a small glitch at 180 degrees, simply because the mass of the microphone gets in the way of the sound waves.

The reason, incidentally, that an omnidirectional mic can be equally sensitive to sounds from all directions is related to the fact that sound is a series of rarefactions and compressions of air molecules. Since the back of the microphone is closed to air, the diaphragm is pulled out by the rarefactions and pushed in by the compressions, regardless of the direction of the sound. The importance of this concept, illustrated in Figures 5.10a and 5.10b, will become apparent shortly.

Bidirectional   The bidirectional mic accepts sound from the front and rear and rejects it from the sides. Its pickup pattern is shown in Figure 5.9b. Notice, too, that the concentric rings indicate sound level in decibels; when the pickup

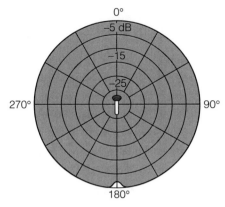

a. Omnidirectional pickup pattern.

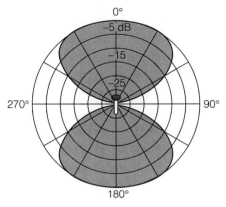

b. Bidirectional pickup pattern.

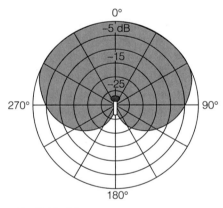

c. Cardioid pickup pattern.

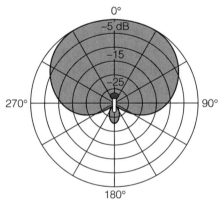

d. Supercardioid pickup pattern.

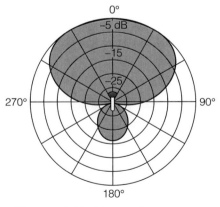

e. Hypercardioid pickup pattern.

FIGURE 5.9

Microphone pickup patterns. Shaded areas represent the shapes of each mic's coverage areas.

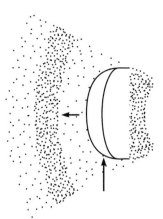 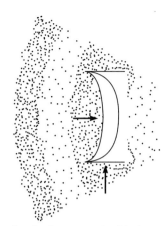

a. Diaphragm pushed out by rarefactions
(low pressure).

b. Diaphragm pushed in by compressions
(high pressure).

FIGURE 5.10

Reaction of a mic's diaphragm to sound. Notice that it makes little difference to the
diaphragm which direction the sound is coming from.

pattern dips toward the center of the circle, it is declining by the number of
decibels indicated on the concentric rings. The bidirectional pattern is typical of
ribbon mics that have the ribbon open to air on both sides.

Cardioid   *Cardioid* means "heart-shaped," as in Figure 5.9c. You can visualize this pattern in three dimensions by imagining that the mic is the stem of
a gigantic apple. Often, the cardioid pattern is called **unidirectional**, meaning that it picks up sound from only one direction. (*Uni* means "one.") Sometimes, the term *directional* is used to indicate the same concept. (For three-
dimensional representations of microphone pickup patterns, see Figures 5.11a
and 5.11b.)

A microphone with a cardioid pattern achieves this directionality by means of
holes called *ports* in the back of the mic. Sound entering these ports is routed through
an acoustic network (see Figure 5.12a) that causes the mic to cancel sound coming
from the rear. In physics terms, the sound waves entering from the rear are *out of phase*
with sound waves entering the front of the mic (see Figure 5.12b). That is, when the
waves are combined, the high points will combine with the low points, and the low
points will combine with the high, thus canceling each other out. This concept of
phase is important in advanced radio production.

The cardioid pattern is a function of sound wave cancellation because of
porting in the mic and is not a result of the particular electronic element in the
mic. Mics with a cardioid pattern can have moving-coil, ribbon, or condenser
elements. Mics with an omnidirectional pattern usually have a moving-coil element but occasionally have a condenser.

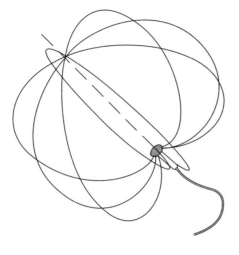

a. Approximation of how the cardioid pickup pattern extends through three dimensions. If you think of the pickup pattern as forming a huge apple, the mic is like the stem.

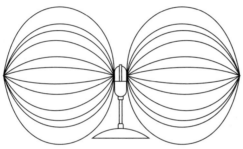

b. Approximation of how the bidirectional pickup pattern extends through three dimensions. It consists of two giant pickup spheres on either side of the mic.

FIGURE 5.11
Three-dimensional representations of pickup patterns.

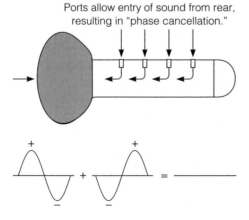

a. Simplified diagram of ports in a mic. The ports let sound enter from the rear and, in effect, cancel itself out.

b. Phase cancellation as a sum of sine waves of opposite amplitudes.

FIGURE 5.12
Mic ports and phase cancellation.

A special version of the cardioid pattern is the **supercardioid** pattern (see Figure 5.9d), which has a tighter curve in front and a lobe in back. The **hyper-cardioid** pattern (see Figure 5.9e) has an even narrower front angle and a bigger rear lobe. Supercardioid and hypercardioid patterns, also called *unidirectional*, are generally used for highly directional applications on booms, such as in television studio work, when it is important to reject unwanted noises.

Frequency Response of Microphones

Different mics respond differently to sound frequencies. There are two compo-nents of **frequency response**: *range* and *shape*.

Range　**Range** simply means the amount of the frequency spectrum a mic can hear. Good mics can hear frequencies all the way up to 20,000 Hz, which is beyond the range of most normal adult ears. A good mic can also hear all sounds equally well, plus or minus about 5 dB, but depending on its design may be more or less directional in picking up sounds from the sides and rear (see Figure 5.13).

Figure 5.14 is a graph of frequency response for a popular studio micro-phone. Notice that several response curves are given. The solid line represents the overall frequency response for the microphone. The higher the line, the bet-ter the mic reproduces the frequency indicated on the bottom line of the graph. This characteristic of the response curve is known as *shape*. Notice that the fre-quency response for this particular microphone is fairly consistent from about 50 Hz all the way out to approximately 15 kHz, until the response falls off below the 5–dB line. This means that the microphone will reproduce all of the frequencies between 50 Hz and 15 kHz equally well.

Shape　The **shape** of the mic response pattern in Figure 5.14 has a bump in the upper frequencies, starting at about 5 kHz. This is because the mic, by its nature,

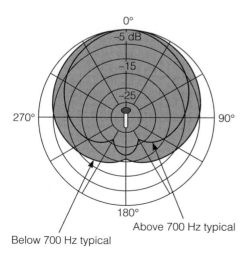

FIGURE 5.13

Graph of a pickup pattern supplied by a microphone manufacturer. Scale: 5 dB per division.

SOURCE: Electro-Voice, Inc., Buchanan, MI.

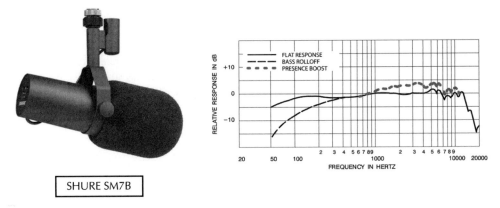

SHURE SM7B

F I G U R E 5.14

The Shure SM7B is a popular studio microphone because it provides excellent vocal reproduction.
SOURCE: Shure Inc.

gives a boost to those frequencies. A mic like this is useful for speech since it powerfully reproduces the frequencies that lend intelligibility to speech. Such modifications of frequencies also add to the coloration of sound, just as a mic lends a sound a certain quality or timbre. There is also a presence boost (designated by the gray dotted line) that can add even more intelligibility to voice by varying the response shape of the mic. The engineer can choose to add presence or keep the response flat. Another switch allows the engineer to roll off bass response, which is useful in noisy environments.

Often, recording engineers miking music set-up will want a mic with a **flat response**—a mic that is capable of responding equally well to all frequencies in the whole audio spectrum. The term **high fidelity** applies well to this characteristic because it means "high accuracy." A mic that responds equally well to all frequencies is high in fidelity; the term also applies to speakers, amplifiers, and so forth.

Cardioid mics tend to boost bass (lower) frequencies as the sound source moves closer to the mic. This is known as a **proximity effect** and is why some announcers who want a deeper sound move in very close to mics with a cardioid pickup pattern.

What does all this mean to you? By understanding the polar patterns of mics and frequency response graphs, you'll be able to avoid various problems. For example, a cardioid mic will reject sounds from the rear and will be useful for console operations, because you do not want to broadcast the clicking of switches and rustling of papers. An omnidirectional mic might be the proper choice for on-the-street news interviews, where you want to pick up surrounding noise to lend authenticity to the situation.

In some cases, a producer might opt for a mic that boosts specific frequencies because, for instance, the high frequencies in speech need a boost for intelligibility. Some mics, such as the Shure MC50, have variable frequency responses; the varying responses are achieved by changing the equalization caps on the mic. Others, such as the Shure KSM44, frequently used as a voice-over mic in broadcasting, can achieve multiple pickup patterns.

Review of Microphone Workings

Microphones are transducers that change the motional energy of sound in the air into electrical energy by means of an electronic element. Three elements are common in radio use: moving coil, ribbon, and condenser.

Some microphones are more sensitive than others are to sounds coming from certain directions. A visual indication of this property is called a *pickup pattern*. The most common pickup patterns in mics designed for radio use are omnidirectional, bidirectional, and cardioid.

Frequency response varies from mic to mic. Because some mics have a broader range than others, they can reproduce a wider range of frequencies. Some mics also tend to boost certain frequency ranges.

PHYSICAL TYPES OF MICROPHONES

We're using a somewhat imprecise phrase when we speak of "physical types" of microphones. This is not a standard term in the industry. It is, however, a good way to classify mics by their intended use. Some of these uses may not usually apply to radio, but we'll show some examples anyway.

Hand Held

Mics meant for hand-held use are, of course, small enough to be easily held. Other characteristics of hand-held mics include durability and the ability to reject handling noise. The Electro-Voice 635A (see Figure 5.15a) is one of the most commonly used hand-held mics in broadcasting because its rugged qualities and good vocal response make it an excellent field microphone.

Studio, Mounted

Mics intended for studio use are usually mounted on a stand or boom. They are generally larger than hand-held mics and more sensitive. The Neumann U-87 (see Figure 5.15b) would be very difficult to use in a hand-held situation, not only because of its shape, but also because this fine mic is so sensitive that it would pick up every bit of handling noise. Some mics, which are small and provide high-quality sound reproduction, can be used in both studio and hand-held situations.

A new generation of studio microphones has been introduced for broadcasting and sound recording. The AKG C-4500B (see Figure 5.15c) has been designed to reduce proximity effect. This mic also features a very low noise level and immunity to overload, making it an ideal choice for digital broadcasting applications.

Headset

Headset mics (see Figure 5.15d) offer hands-free operation and are useful in radio for such tasks as sports play-by-play. These mics also work well for rejecting noise surrounding the announcer.

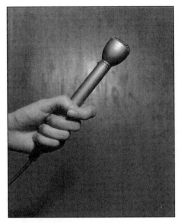

a. The Electro-Voice 635A, an excellent hand-held mic.

SOURCE: Philip Benoit

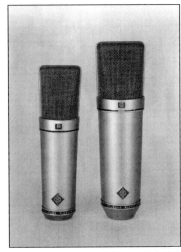

b. Neumann U-87 (left) and U-89 (right) studio mics.

SOURCE: Gotham Audio Corporation, New York, NY

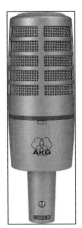

c. The AKG C-4500B has a wide dynamic range, making it ideal for voice-over and music recording.

SOURCE: AKG Acoustics

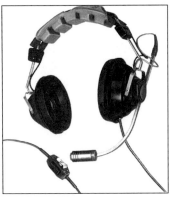

d. Headset mic commonly used for sports broadcasts and other occasions when mic stands would clutter the workspace.

SOURCE: Philip Benoit

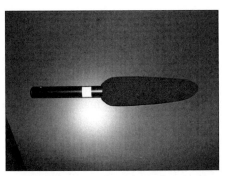

e. Microphones used outdoors frequently have windscreens to reduce wind noice.

SOURCE: Philip Benoit

FIGURE 5.15

Physical types of microphones.

Lavalier

A **lavalier mic** is usually clipped to a person's clothing and is frequently worn by anchors on television news programs. Lavaliers have little application in radio.

Shotgun

Shotgun mics are used for long-range pickup (see Figure 5.15e) in television and film. They have very little use in radio.

We can conclude this discussion of mic types by saying that in radio production you will be using primarily studio and hand-held mics. The way you choose a mic depends not only on type but also on all the factors discussed so far in this chapter.

Some condenser mics allow you to change the pickup capsules. These are called *system mics* because you can change the capsule opening and change the use of the mic from a shotgun to a studio type or even to hand held. This allows a small station to buy one very good microphone system and adapt it to various applications. Unfortunately, most of these condenser mic systems require external or phantom power supplies, and this can detract from their usefulness in certain situations.

Review of Physical Types

The most common mics found in radio are hand held and studio; sometimes headset mics are used for sports applications. There is some overlap: Some mics can be used for studio or hand-held use, and condenser mics of the type called *modular mics* allow you to change the pickup capsule, varying its potential usage.

MICROPHONE SELECTION AND USE

As we mentioned earlier, you may not always have much choice in selecting mics. You'll use what's available. Even then, however, you'll benefit from learning about mics because you'll better understand how to use the one you're given. When you do have a voice in selection, you'll want to make your choice based on these five factors:

1. Type
2. Pickup pattern
3. Element
4. Frequency response
5. Personality

Selection by Mic Type

This is a self-limiting category because you'll generally be using hand-held or studio mics, and the choices are obvious. As we mentioned, some high-quality mics can be used in either application, but beware of using a cardioid mic that has many ports in the stem and back in hand-held situations. You'll change the pickup pattern of the mic if you inadvertently cover the ports with your hand.

Changing the pickup pattern in this manner sometimes happens when pop singers cup a mic too tightly and inadvertently cause feedback: Cutting off the ports changes the cardioid pattern to an omnidirectional pattern and thus picks up the sound from the loudspeakers. Feedback, in this case, happens when sound comes out of a speaker, is picked up by the mic and amplified by the console, is fed through the speaker, is picked up and amplified again, and so on—until the sound is amplified into a loud squeal.

Selection by Pickup Pattern

A news reporter doing a great deal of hand-held interviewing will probably find an omnidirectional pattern more convenient than other patterns because the mic won't have to be moved around as much to keep more than one speaker within the pickup pattern (referred to as being *on-mic*). In studio applications, mics with a cardioid pattern are usually favored because they cancel out extraneous noise. A two-person interview, with guest and moderator facing each other, can be accomplished quite nicely with a bidirectional mic placed between the interviewer and guest, although using two unidirectional mics allows for greater control. For example, if one voice is much more powerful than the other, the volume on one channel can simply be lowered to compensate.

Selection by Element

Certain **elements** do various tasks better than others do (see Table 5.1).

TABLE 5.1   Microphone Element Chart

Element	Advantages	Disadvantages
Moving coil	Relatively inexpensive. Performs well in difficult sound conditions, such as wind. Usually very durable.	The diaphragm has to move a lot of mass, so it can't vibrate as quickly as diaphragms on many condenser models or as some ribbons. This translates into less response to high frequencies.
Ribbon	Very good high-frequency response in many cases. Coloration of sound perceived by many announcers as warm and rich tones. Excellent sensitivity.	Delicate and easily damaged, especially by wind and severe noise overload. Sensitive to popping of such speech sounds as *b* and *p*.
Condenser	The very high-quality condensers have extended high-frequency response, along with what are perceived as bright and crisp highs. Versatility, including, in some cases, the ability to undergo extensive changes in pickup patterns and frequency responses; in some condenser mics, the entire element can be unscrewed and replaced with another. Reasonable durability to mechanical shock (certainly better than ribbon mics).	Susceptible to moisture-related damage. Expensive. Somewhat inconvenient at times because of the need for a separate power supply.

SOURCE: © Cengage Learning 2013

Selection by Frequency Response

There's usually neither the opportunity nor the need to consult a frequency response chart for the intimate details of a mic's sound reproduction. Should you wish to examine a frequency response chart, though, you'll generally find one in the box in which the mic was packed or on the manufacturer's website. Quality mics come with a chart individually prepared for the buyer.

You don't have to read a chart every time you want to pick out a mic, but you should have some general knowledge about range and curve shape.

Range An extremely high-quality mic, with response as high as 20,000 Hz, is useful in music recording because of its "wide" response.

Curve Shape A mic with a bump in the response curve up around the consonant frequencies makes speech more understandable. However, you don't need that speech bump in a mic intended purely for music recording.

Further, some mics have what's called a *bass roll-off* to compensate for the proximity effect. In other words, they deemphasize the bass. A producer who knows that the mic will be used for close-in speech work and wants to negate the proximity effect can activate the bass roll-off control on the mic.

More advanced production may call for a detailed examination of frequency response, but for most purposes, it's enough to know whether a mic has a wide—or very wide—frequency response, whether it emphasizes certain frequencies or has a flat curve, and whether it has adjustable responses.

Selection by Personality

The personality of a mic is a quality that can be difficult to define, but it's a factor nonetheless. Most announcers develop a fondness for a particular mic whose characteristics appeal to the individual. Some announcers like ribbon mics because they add warmth and richness. News reporters often favor a particular moving-coil mic because of its ruggedness and dependability. Recording engineers frequently have high praise for a particular condenser mic that delivers crisp highs when used to record piano music. On the other hand, certain mics may seem temperamental and therefore fall into an announcer's disfavor.

Some announcers don't like ribbon mics because of problems with popping *p*'s and *b*'s. When it comes right down to it, choosing a mic because of its personality is just as valid as selecting one for any other reason.

Adding Up Selection Factors

Once again, you might not be in a position to choose mics for particular tasks. We reiterate that knowing the selection factors may be very valuable in the proper use of the mic you're working with and may someday pay off when you need to choose a mic to deal with a particularly difficult situation.

Although we've tried to avoid the catalog approach to presenting information on microphones, Table 5.2 assembles some of the mics commonly used in

T A B L E 5.2   Microphone Model Chart

Microphone	Element	Description
a. Electro-Voice RE-50 SOURCE: Electro-Voice, Inc.	Moving coil	Omnidirectional; similar to popular 635A; shock resistant; excellent all-purpose mic; internal wind screen; blast filter; rugged.
b. Shure SM-58 SOURCE: Shure Brothers, Inc.	Moving coil	Cardioid; good studio mic; rugged; **pop filter**; most popular stage vocal mic.
c. Shure SM7B SOURCE: Shure Brothers, Inc.	Dynamic	Cardioid; clean and natural vocal reproduction.
d. AKG C-4500B SOURCE: AKG Acoustics	Condenser	Cardioid; frequency response tailored to reduce proximity effect.
e. Neumann U-47 SOURCE: Gotham Audio Corp.	Condenser	Cardioid pickup pattern; excellent voice mic; flat response; warm sound; blast filter; bass roll-off.

(continued)

Microphone	Element	Description	
f. Sony C-37P SOURCE: Sony Corp. of Am.	Condenser	Omnidirectional/ cardioid; four adjustments for bass roll-off; good for voice pickup and musical instruments.	
g. Sennheiser 416 (middle), with 417 and 418 SOURCE: Sennheiser Electronic Corp.	Condenser	Supercardioid; usually boom mounted; flat response; eliminates unwanted ambient sound; excellent for remotes where directionality is desired.	
h. Electro-Voice RE-20 SOURCE: Electro-Voice, Inc.	Moving coil	A high-quality mic; the most popular announcing mic in radio; bass boost with close use; good frequency response; durable.	

SOURCE: © Cengage Learning 2013

radio production and includes some comments on microphone type, pickup pattern, element, frequency response, and personality.

Notes on Microphone Use

Mic use can be extremely simple or extraordinarily complex depending on the situation. Preparing to speak into a studio mic is no more complicated than being sure that you're within the pickup pattern (which will be obvious from listening through the headphones) and not being too close or too far away. It is extremely important that you monitor your voice through headphones whenever possible. Simply monitoring your levels on a VU meter will not tell you if you're popping your *p*'s or speaking off the mic's axis. Make it a rule: Whenever you're ready to switch on the mic, put your headphones on first.

The proper distance for speaking into a studio or hand-held mic ranges from about 6 to 12 inches, though there's no set rule. Actually, the only hard and fast guideline is to work at a reasonable distance based on what sounds correct for a particular speaker and a particular mic. It's good to remember that when you're listening to your voice in a very quiet studio, you may not be hearing yourself the way the general audience will hear you. People in cars and on the go frequently are listening with a good deal of background noise.

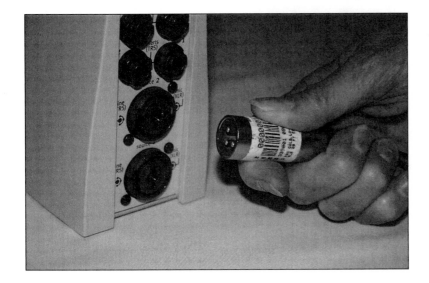

F I G U R E 5.16

XLR connectors. The type being held in the hand is a male. The receptacle is a female. They snap together easily.

SOURCE: Fritz Messere

Setting up several mics in a studio is more complicated than doing a solo airshift. The first thing a producer has to know in this case is how to plug in the mics. Figure 5.16 shows the connectors most commonly used for microphones. The plugs shown, **XLRs**, are the most common. Incidentally, there is a trick to connecting and disconnecting some XLRs. Some connectors have a push-level mounted on the female connector that locks the connectors in place. (You'll feel it snap when you make the connection.) To remove, press the lever and remove the male end by the connector; don't ever pull on the wire.

You'll encounter other connectors on occasion—most often the phone plug connector, a prong about 1¼ inches long, and the mini phone plug, a prong about 1.2 inches long. In some cases, you will need adapters to make one source compatible with another. If you want to plug a mic directly into the record input of a portable MiniDisc recorder, for example, you'll need a female-XLR-to-male-phone-plug adapter.

It's generally best to check with engineering staff about connectors you'll need. The specifications can become quite technical, and a certain level of audio engineering sophistication may be needed to make the connection properly.

Usually mics are placed on floor or table stands. After the mics have been mounted, the next responsibility of the producer in the studio is to place them properly. This task, of course, will vary with the situation. A news interview program may require placement of only one or two mics; a music recording session could require the placement of 20 mics—with five of them placed on the drums alone!

Because of the wide variety of situations, we address mic placement separately in appropriate chapters. For example, we deal with placement of mics for news interview shows in Chapter 13 and placement of mics for music in the section on music recording in Chapter 15.

SUMMARY

Sound is produced by the vibration of air molecules. Sound is a combination of wave patterns consisting of higher and lower frequencies. The intensity of a sound is measured in decibels (dB). Microphones transduce the sound vibrations into electrical current, which can then be fed to a recording device or, through a console, to a broadcast transmitter.

Three basic types of microphones are used in broadcasting: moving coil, also known as *dynamic*, in which sound vibrations cause a coil to move through a magnetic field, thus producing an electric current; ribbon, which features a thin metallic strip suspended between the poles of an electromagnet; and condenser, which discharges current in response to the vibrations of a moving diaphragm.

Microphones have various pickup patterns. Omnidirectional mics pick up sound uniformly from any direction; bidirectional mics pick up sound from the front and rear of the mic but not from the sides; unidirectional or cardioid mics (also known as *directional* mics) pick up sound in front of the mic but not from the sides or rear.

Mics vary in their ability to reproduce sound. The frequency response of a particular mic determines how well it will reproduce a given range of frequencies.

Some mics can be adjusted to vary their frequency response. Selecting a mic depends on finding a mic that has the right pickup pattern, physical characteristics, and personality for the particular job.

APPLICATIONS

SITUATION 1/THE PROBLEM The producer of a 5 o'clock radio program has a touchy problem: The newscaster, Paul Prince, pops his *p*'s badly. What's worse, the station is WPPG (a hypothetical station name) in Pittsburgh, and the name of the show is Public Radio Profiles. Paul sounds terrible when he gives the station identification and introduces himself and the show.

ONE POSSIBLE SOLUTION Short of speech therapy for Paul, the best solution is to exchange the ribbon microphone for a good-quality moving-coil mic, which is exactly what the producer did.

SITUATION 2/THE PROBLEM The sports director of a small station started to do basketball play-by-play from the gym of the local high school. Listeners complained that at times they had trouble understanding her because of the crowd noise and because her voice sounded muddy. The sports director surmised that the omnidirectional mic she had mounted on a table stand just wasn't the right unit for the job.

ONE POSSIBLE SOLUTION Although she didn't have a specialized headset mic, the sports director did have access to a microphone with a cardioid pickup pattern, a durable moving-coil element, and a nice speech bump in the response curve. She replaced the omnidirectional mic with this more suitable unit.

EXERCISES

1. Put a microphone on a stand, and set up the console to record its output. Have someone walk around the mic in a circle while counting or talking. Do this with three different mics: one with an omnidirectional pattern, one with a bidirectional pattern, and one with a cardioid pattern. Play back the tape, and notice the differences in sound pickup.

   Now, using the mic with the cardioid pickup pattern, record yourself reading some copy 16 inches from the mic (speaking directly into it) and then 6 inches from the mic. Notice the proximity effect. If the mic has a bass roll-off switch, experiment with using it, and gauge the effect on the sound.

2. Set up as many different mics as you have available. Have someone read 30 seconds or so of copy into each mic, and record it. (Make sure that person identifies each mic: "I'm reading into the Electro-Voice RE-20, 'Fourscore and seven years ago....'") Play back the tape, and write down (or discuss) your impressions of each version. Give details on why you like or don't like each mic and what characteristics each one has. Make a diligent effort to come up with details. Characteristics of mics aren't always obvious, and it takes close attention to recognize them.

3. Choose mics for the applications in the following bulleted list. You can choose mics from those illustrated in this chapter, or just list the selection factors you'd want for the particular application. For example, a speaker who tends to work very close to the mic and has a deep, overpowering voice probably should not work with a ribbon mic. A moving-coil or condenser mic would be a better choice. The mic should have a bass roll-off control, and it should have a personality that emphasizes brightness and clarity.

   Now, try the same reasoning with the following situations. (There really aren't any right or wrong answers; most are judgment calls.)

   - A speaker with a weak, high, breathy voice
   - Locker room interviews
   - Amateur speakers (guests on an interview show)
   - An announcer who's doing a commercial for a classy restaurant
   - A screaming disc jockey

YOU'RE ON! • TECHNIQUES FOR EFFECTIVE ON-AIR PERFORMANCE: MICROPHONE TECHNIQUE FOR ANNOUNCERS

Here are some tips for sounding your best on-air.

- You can create a more intimate feel by moving closer to the mic. This is especially true with a supersensitive condenser mic, but remember that you will also accentuate mouth noises such as smacking and clicking.

- If you tend to pop your *p*'s and *b*'s, avoid ribbon mics. If you must use one, position yourself so you are speaking across the ribbon, not directly at it. You can't always tell the ribbon orientation from the outside of the mic, so experiment and then learn the correct position for the particular ribbon mic.

- Move back from the mic if you are doing a hard sell approach. You won't overload the element, and the perspective gained by putting a little distance between you and the mic will accentuate the message.

- Move closer to the mic in noisy situations.

- Move back from the mic if you have a deep, powerful voice and tend to sound muffled.

- As a general rule, you'll want to work about 6 inches away from most mics. That's about the length of a dollar bill. Distance will vary, of course, by mic and by circumstance, but 6 inches is a good starting point. (Always wear headphones so you can gauge your vocal quality.)

- Keep the same relative distance from the mic. Don't move in and out unless you have a reason for doing so. (You might, for example, want to create a more intimate effect for one part of the copy.) Beginning announcers often have trouble with this because they move their heads and inadvertently go off-mic or move too close and become muffled.

- Don't grab a mounted mic when it's open. Studio mics often do not have sound dampening for handling, and the audience will hear unwanted noise.

- If you have a problem with popping of plosives, breathiness, or other unwanted speech sounds, try a wind filter. It will block some unwanted noise.

- If you feel you need to deepen your voice, use a cardioid mic and work close to it. But don't get too close or you'll be muffled.

6

Electronic Editing

I n this and the next two chapters, we deal with the mechanics of operating radio production equipment and with the art of *editing*—the process of rearranging, correcting, and assembling the product into a finished whole.

Production, as we've noticed, is something of a nebulous term. Many of us tend to think of radio production as the process of putting together a commercial or assembling a news show. But in truth, any manipulation of sound constitutes production:

- Cutting a small piece out of a long interview for airplay during a newscast is production.
- Making a 30-second commercial is production.
- Running a board while doing a combo operation is production, too—and a very important type of production, because the combo operator reflects the overall sound of the station.

We have divided the basic production chapters along the lines of the three preceding examples. In this chapter, we spell out the basic mechanics of manipulating sound, and we show some of the patterns this manipulation takes. In Chapter 7, we focus on some of the techniques specific to working in the studio and producing segments to be played back on-air at a later date, such as commercials and public service announcements. In Chapter 8, we discuss the techniques used in on-air work.

There is, of course, quite a bit of overlap among the techniques, but we think you'll find this a logical way to go about exploring the nuts and bolts of radio production. Chapter 8 expands on the foregoing ideas and moves on to the subtleties of using radio production techniques to reinforce a message and to create a particular effect, which is the real goal of sitting down at the console in the first place.

THE BASICS OF EDITING AUDIO

Splicing, dubbing, and editing are the basic ways a radio producer manipulates sound. There's a variety of terminology used to describe these basic three functions that audio producers employ. **Splicing** is a term that originally grew up in the early days of the film industry, where an editor physically cut film scenes together to tell a story. Radio adopted the term to refer to physically altering audiotape by cutting it apart and taping it back together again. Today, splicing is done electronically, and newer terminology, reflecting the use of digital workstations, has been added to the list of words to describe editing. Today, we **cut**, **paste**, and **copy** sound files much the same way we use a word processor to manipulate words, sentences, and paragraphs of an essay. Cutting and pasting sounds or sound files electronically is the equivalent of splicing audiotape.

Dubbing is the process of reproducing or transferring a sound file in one form of media to another and is frequently referred to as **extracting** or *ripping* when used in the context of transferring a file from a flash drive or a CD to a computer or digital audio workstation (DAW). We should note that we're going to use the terms *DAW* and *computer or audio workstation* interchangeably in this chapter. The process of making a mirror image of that computer file is called **copying** or **duplicating**. Generally, **mixing** in this situation refers to mixing sound files together into a finished audio production, as opposed to mixing several audio sources together on an audio console.

Editing is a combination of these functions, and more: It can be the process of rearranging, correcting, and assembling sound into a finished product. Editing is a general term that applies to both the physical and electronic rearranging of sound.

Let's try to give these terms some use so they make sense. The following sequence of events shows you the various ways you might manipulate audio on a digital workstation. You've found a section of music on a production CD that you want to use as a musical bed in a commercial. First you would *extract* (rip) the audio from the CD and save it as a sound file so you could manipulate it in your audio workstation. The extraction process takes the audio file from the CD and converts it into a usable file for the audio workstation. Once that is accomplished, you then *edit* the music bed down to a 30-second music piece that you will use under your voice on the commercial. To edit the music bed down to 30 seconds in length, you may have to *cut* and *paste* various small segments of the track together, discarding other segments that don't fit together within your timeframe.

Once you're happy with the musical bed, you **copy** the file and *paste* it into a new file as a track that will match up with the voice track in the spot. Now you're ready to **mix** the voice and music tracks.

Two additional related terms pertaining directly to electronic editing are *destructive* and *nondestructive* editing. Destructive editing, which is a lot like using the cut-and-paste function on a word processor, occurs when a change is made that alters the structure of the sound file. In addition to cutting and pasting, destructive editing may also occur when you make an effects change to the audio file that cannot be undone. For example, adding an echo to a voice track would be considered a destructive change if it was saved and could not be undone.

Nondestructive editing occurs when the original audio components are retained and can be reused if a change in the audio file, such as an edit, does not work out to your satisfaction. Today, most digital audio programs allow the user to perform either destructive or nondestructive audio editing.

The editing process requires some understanding of what you can expect to see on a DAW screen before you begin using it to manipulate sound files.

Looking at the Waveform

A waveform is a visual representation of a sound file. You may have never looked at one closely before, and it might not be immediately obvious to you what you are looking at and what you are looking for. Figure 6.1 illustrates two sound files that demonstrate what the waveform can reveal about the audio track. The first is from a phrase from a Los Lonely Boys song highlighted (see Figure 6.1a). The phrase is made up of four words, "How Far Is Heaven?" The screenshot shows the computer screen for a digital audio software program called Peak Pro.

Look at the two large waveforms pictured in Figure 6.1a. They represent just a few seconds of audio; the peaks represent louder sections, and the valleys represent softer sections of the song. You can see the places in between the words where there is some musical backing and the waveforms are present, but the waveforms are not very large compared with the singing. You'll notice that there really are two primary waveforms. One represents the left channel and the bottom one represents the right channel of audio. The two smaller and denser waveforms above represent the waveform of the entire song along the top of Figure 6.1a. Within the smaller waveform, a narrow box shows the current part of the song displayed by the large waveforms. Note that the larger two waveforms represent a tiny portion of the sound where the group is singing "How Far Is Heaven?" Notice, too, that there appear to be straight, large vertical lines at regular intervals emanating out of the two large waveforms. Those lines represent the loudest portion of the audio, such as percussion instruments like a snare drum or bass drum or bass guitar.

Sound files sometimes have a rhythm or cadence to them. Look at Figure 6.1b. Notice that it is much more difficult to discern the words in the phrase "I guess the change in my pocket wasn't enough" from the song "Forget You" by Gwyneth Paltrow. It is clear that the percussion creates a strong rhythmic element to the song that makes it difficult to "see" the words in this musical phrase. However, if you're editing music that has a regular beat, you can pick out the beats easily by looking for peaks or spikes that occur at regular intervals on the waveform. The spoken word may have a cadence, too, but it is sometimes more difficult to spot. Some sounds will be easy to identify, but some sounds tend to run together. Generally, sounds with a good deal of power are easier to spot. These include consonants such as *d*, *p*, *t*, *z*, and *k*.

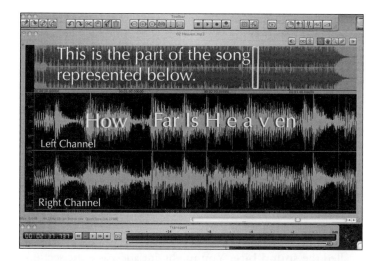

a. The smaller two waveforms on the top of the screen represent the entire sound file. The two larger waveforms are the left and right channels. Note how it is possible to literally see the waveform for "How Far Is Heaven?"

SOURCE: BIAS, Inc.

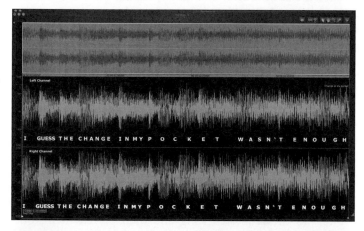

b. With music that has a heavy rhythm or percussive line, it is more difficult to "see" the words in the song. Compare this track with Figure 6.1a where the waveform more closely mimics the words in the song.

SOURCE: BIAS, Inc.

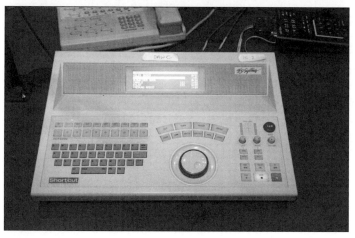

c. Stand-alone workstations like this one are ideal for recording news actualities or listeners' requests.

SOURCE: 360 systems

FIGURE 6.1

Characteristics of a sine wave.

Again, Figure 6.1b shows that the consonant *p* in the word *pocket* stands out easily although the rest of the word is difficult to see as a cohesive waveform. Vowels often lack power and don't create sharp spikes in the waveform. In the waveform in Figure 6.1b, you can see that *I* lacks the same definitive look as the word *in*, where the consonant adds strength to the vowel. The more you practice "reading" a waveform, the more adept you'll become at editing.

Splicing and Editing a Sound File

Electronic editing can be either destructive or nondestructive, and we'll discuss both techniques in this chapter.

The most common reason for cutting a sound file and sticking it back together is to eliminate an unwanted portion of the sound file. You may be recording an interview for an upcoming newscast. In preparing the story you choose to use only a portion of the interview. What you choose to include in the newscast will be called the **sound bite**. You might cut and paste the sections you want to include in the sound file. Alternatively, a producer may choose to rearrange portions of a sound file into a more logical sequence or simply shorten what has been recorded. Often musical beds are edited to meet the time requirements of the spot or program section.

Proficiency at basic editing like this is helpful because it allows you to assemble useful short sound files for newscasts and weathercasts. Today, many stations use a small stand-alone workstation to record actualities from reporters in the field or incoming calls from listeners (Figure 6.1c). For example, stations that broadcast prerecorded segments of people calling in song requests follow this procedure even as the show is in progress. We've all heard people making requests on the radio immediately followed by the song. Chances are that the song request was recorded earlier and edited by the board operator before being played on the air. The board operator then cued up the sound bite and the requested song and then played them, one immediately following the other, to give the impression that the events were occurring at the same time.

Editing can be as simple as these two examples, or may be very involved, such as producing a documentary or commercial that contains dozens of edits. These techniques are part craft but also somewhat like an art form. They definitely involve learning and applying some technical skills, but manipulating sound also requires a good ear and a little patience. We next discuss some of the basics.

The steps in splicing are as follows: marking the first edit point, marking the second edit point, cutting the sound file together (or tape), and pasting the splice. We'll take them in order.

Marking Edit Points

Suppose you have just completed an interview with the mayor, who has told you about an important development in the community. You want to use a brief segment of the interview for an upcoming newscast. You've recorded the interview on a portable solid-state recorder at the mayor's office. Now that you're back at the studio, you need to edit the interview for airing. The first step is to dub (*copy*) the interview into a computer and save it as a sound file. Many portable recorders use SD™ or Compact Disc storage devices, which are easy to pop out of the recorder and into a reader. Importing the file is a relatively easy thing.

There are many different computer recording and editing programs for both PCs and Macs, or your station may own a standalone machine called a digital audio workstation (DAW). They all have the same basic features, although specific, complex features may differ from one brand to another. The edit that is illustrated here was accomplished on Adobe Audition, one of the most popular audio editing software programs.

The recorded interview goes like this:

MAYOR: We have decided to go ahead with construction of a new crosstown expressway from the junction of Interstate 440 to, as you can see right here on the map, Commercial Street, where there will be a major interchange.

While the mayor was talking to you he pointed to a spot on a map in his office, but because the reference to the map is lost on a radio audience, we don't want to include the mayor's mention of it. The task at hand, then, is to cut out the portion of the sound file where the mayor says, "as you can see right here on the map." Because the statement would make much better sense if the reference were eradicated, the logical place to make the first edit point would be the word *to* after Interstate 440:

MAYOR: We have decided to go ahead with the construction of the new crosstown expressway from the junction of Interstate 440 to, ^ (first edit) *as you can see here on the map...*^ (second edit)

We are going to demonstrate how to edit this sound bite using two different editing methods. The first example uses **destructive editing**. Once we complete the edit and save the file, the unwanted portion will be gone forever.

The sound file for the Mayor Hazzard interview is seen in Figure 6.2a. The first **edit point** is where we want to cut the sound file. To do so, we have to find that point exactly, which means that we have to highlight the waveform on the computer screen. Figure 6.2b shows the highlighted portion of the interview that we want to remove.

The computer screen can display a part of or the entire file containing the mayor's interview. Usually, a zoom control allows you to set the width of the sound file. In this case, set the width to display the entire file, which is approximately 16 seconds long. Play the sound file until you reach the approximate first and second edit points; then stop. Did you notice where the unwanted portion seemed to occur? Play the file again until you can find the approximate point where the mayor says "as you can see right here on the map." Play the file again and stop the playback when you reach the first edit point where the mayor says "as." Note where the point is on the waveform. Holding the mouse

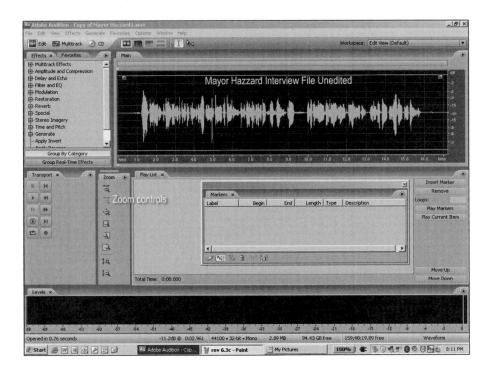

a. Mayor Hazzard waveform before editing. Zoom controls allow the editor to increase or decrease the size of the waveform.

SOURCE: © 2013 Adobe Systems, Inc.

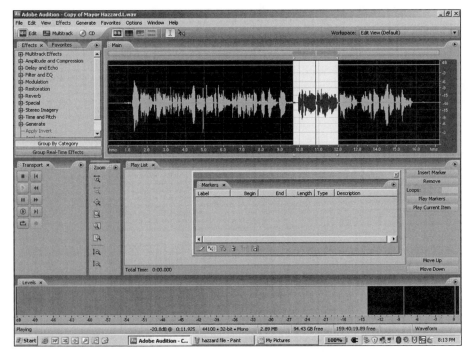

b. The portion of audio "as you can see right here on the map" is highlighted on the waveform.

SOURCE: © 2013 Adobe Systems, Inc.

FIGURE 6.2

button down, drag the pointer across the portion that you think is "as you can see right here on the map." Release the mouse button. (The correct portion of the sound file that needs to be eliminated may be seen in Figure 6.2b.) On most software programs, you can play the section you highlighted by pressing the space bar. (If this does not work, you will need to review the specifics of your audio software.)

Did the highlighted portion encompass the whole phrase "as you can see right here on the map"? Did you highlight too much or too little of the mayor's interview? You can continue to use this technique until you highlight just the portion that you want. Some software programs allow you to set up beginning and ending points, which can be moved separately until you find the correct portion of audio that you want highlighted. By shifting the point slightly one way or the other, you may create a more natural-sounding editing, depending on whether the mayor took a pause or a breath.

Adobe Audition, the program shown in this example, allows you to extend the highlighted portion by dragging the marker at the top of the sound file. Then you can review the new highlighted portion by using the space bar. Some software programs also support a "scrubbing" feature that allows you to shuttle the pointer back and forth over the edit spot. (Check the manual or online help for your system to see what functions your software supports.)

Once you've correctly highlighted the portion to be deleted, you can *Cut* the segment. If you make a mistake, you can use the *Undo* command to restore the deleted portion, change your edit points, and try again. Assuming you got it right the first time, the audio file has been truncated and the unwanted portion has been cut out of the file. The edited file can be saved and is ready for playing during the newscast. However, once you've saved the edit, you may have permanently removed that segment from the mayor's interview.

Nondestructive Editing

Although the destructive method of editing works just fine, you may want to re-edit the interview at some later time and you may not have access to the original file or the deleted portion after you saved the edited interview. Some audio programs won't let you undo an edit easily, especially once you move the cursor to a new location in the sound file. You might also decide, later on, that you chose the wrong edit point. Once you've saved the edited file, you will not be able to undo the edit because you changed the audio file permanently. If this were the master sound file, you'd be out of luck!

Nondestructive editing is a better solution because you can edit the file by marking and choosing certain "regions" within the sound file that you want to play back. To create a region in Adobe Audition, you highlight the portion of the sound file you want and then click *Add* in the Cue control box. First make sure that the Cue List and Playlist windows are added to the screen. (Do this by selecting them in the pull-down menu.)

Try this technique by highlighting the first part of the sound bite (see Figure 6.3a) as shown:

MAYOR: *We have decided to go ahead with construction of a new crosstown expressway from the junction of Interstate 440 to,* as you can see right here on the map, Commercial Street, where there will be a major interchange.

Press *Add* on the Cue box to add this phrase. (Note that you can label and write a description for each cue point to remind you what audio each segment contains.) Now highlight the second portion of the sound bite that we want, starting with *Commercial Street:*

MAYOR: We have decided to go ahead with construction of a new crosstown expressway from the junction of Interstate 440 to, as you can see right here on the map, *Commercial Street, where there will be a major interchange.*

Once this section is highlighted, add the second cue region to the Marker box (Figure 6.3b). Now, to get these cued regions into the playlist, highlight the first region by clicking on it and then click on *Insert Marker* in the Playlist box. Do the same for the second cue region. The two regions will now appear in the Playlist box (Figure 6.3c). When you click on Play Markers, the computer will now play both edit regions, one after the other, effectively editing the file just as if you had permanently cut the unwanted portions out of the original file (see Figure 6.3d).

Nondestructive editing has the advantage of allowing you to change your edit points as many times as you want, without altering the original sound file. Another advantage is that nondestructive editing allows you to play segments of the audio file out of their original order without changing the order of the original waveform. This is the preferred method of computer editing for several reasons. First, it provides a margin of safety that destructive editing cannot provide. Second, because it preserves the original interview, you can reuse or change the sound bite by creating new segments without having to duplicate the file. This allows you to freshen later newscasts more easily. (News stations frequently try to freshen their stories to provide listeners with new perspectives on stories.)

Recording and Editing Talent

Editing news sound bites or interviews for a newscast or sports roundup often requires you to work quickly in order to meet a scheduled newscast or program segment. But recording and editing talent for a commercial, a promotional spot, public service announcement, or some other feature gives you an opportunity to work at a more leisurely pace. In these situations it is good to focus on making the edited work as high in quality as possible. This often means recording the talent using several different takes of the same copy. Good voice talent know how to use their voices to provide different inflections and emphasis on the copy. You may find that a commercial will benefit from a change in reading tempo or that adding emphasis to a particular word

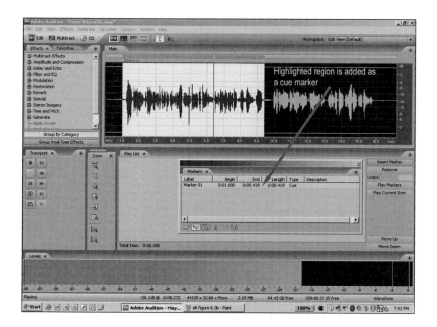

a. The first segment is highlighted and added as a cue marker.
SOURCE: © 2013 Adobe Systems, Inc.

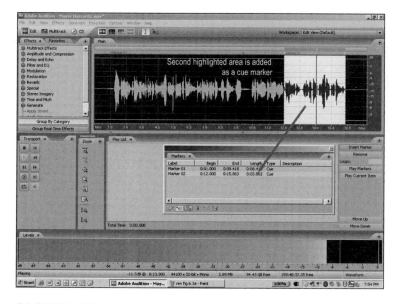

b. The editor has highlighted "Commercial Street, where there will be a major interchange," and has added this segment to the cue list.
SOURCE: © 2013 Adobe Systems, Inc.

FIGURE 6.3

heightens the impact of the spot. Give your talent the opportunity to try several different approaches to interpreting the script. Each separate recording is called a *take*, and talent should provide a *voice slate* for each take with some distinguishing notes such as: "Campbell's Soup, take 1." The next recording

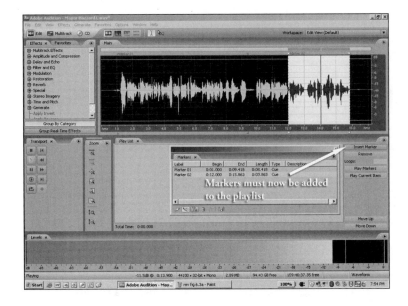

c. Markers must be added to the play list region by clicking on the "Insert Marker" button.
SOURCE: © 2013 Adobe Systems, Inc.

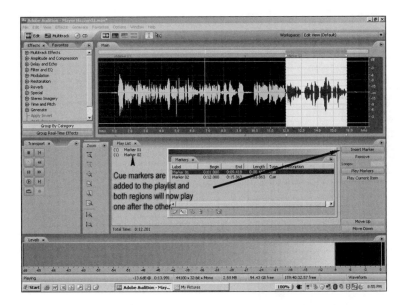

d. By adding cue markers to the play list, you can effectively edit the segments together.
SOURCE: © 2013 Adobe Systems, Inc.

FIGURE 6.3 *(continued)*

would be take 2, and so on. This will provide you with an easy way to identify the different takes.

When recording each separate take, listen carefully for timing, emphasis, inflection, microphone popping, breathing noises, and other possible distractions.

When recording multiple takes, have the talent give a slate for each take separately, or if the talent stops and then wants to start again in the same take, make sure that there is a pause to make editing easier. Frequently experienced editors will take words or phrases from several different takes in order to edit together the strongest possible reading of the script.

Even though we are dealing with editing in this chapter, it is important to point out that a common problem encountered by editors is a change in audio level when recording different voices used in a commercial. Sometimes one reader will be lower in volume or the voice will not be as strong as the other voice. Even small differences in volume or vocal presence can have a marked effect on a commercial's impact. While audio workstations usually have a way for you to lower or raise the audio level of a recorded track, there is not much that can be done to overcome substantive changes in presence in vocal tracks. Therefore, it is vital that you listen carefully to your audio recordings before you release the talent. Care should be taken when selecting microphones, too. As we noted in Chapter 5, using microphones with different pickup patterns or mechanical structures can have markedly different effects on vocal quality. Whenever possible, use the same mics on multiple talent unless you want to create different vocal effects using different microphones.

COPYING, PASTING, AND LOOPING

The same techniques that are used to identify and highlight parts of a voice sound file, which we shortened in our Mayor Hazzard example, can be used to edit music or to create sound "loops" as backgrounds, for sound effects, or for a musical bed. The basic tools of cutting, pasting, and combining can provide you with important skills.

Some production music segments would be perfect for commercials or promotional announcements, but they might not fit into the time frame needed. In many instances, it just would not be appropriate to fade down the music selection because it would sound odd. Most production music produced for broadcasting can be edited. With practice, it is often possible to shorten or lengthen audio segments by isolating and highlighting specific portions and pasting them together.

Figure 6.4a shows an isolated segment from the beginning of "Cochise" by Audioslave. It has been highlighted, and a loop will be created to make the segment longer (see Figure 6.4b). Note the large spikes in the waveform, representing the downbeat of the highlighted segment. Copying and pasting this segment into a new sound file several times produces a longer music bed for your spot.

Most DAWs allow you to create a region within a sound file called a *loop*. Just as the name implies, a loop is useful for taking a small segment of music or a sound effect and making it longer. Drumming or other percussive

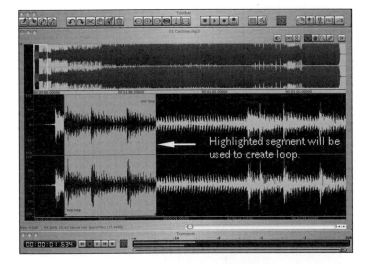

a. The drum portion of this audio track is used to create a loop. The software allows the user to move either the "in" or "out" portion of the highlighted segment.

SOURCE: BIAS, Inc.

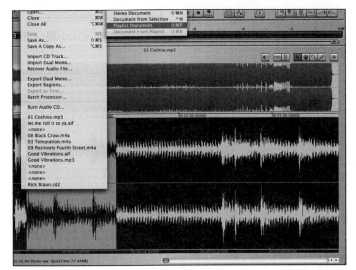

b. Once the segment has been refined, the editor will create a playlist document to make the loop.

SOURCE: BIAS, Inc.

c. The loop created in Figure 6.4a has been pasted into a new playlist document. Each time the loop is pasted into the playlist, the time is extended as a music bed.

SOURCE: BIAS, Inc.

FIGURE 6.4

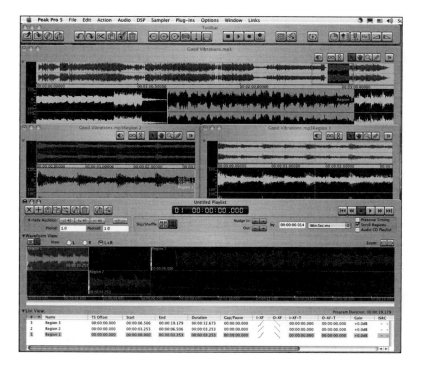

FIGURE 6.5

Three regions have been combined together to create a 20-second bed.

SOURCE: BIAS, Inc.

segments of music frequently make exciting background tracks. Looping makes it possible to repeat these rhythmic phrases, thus creating longer portions that you can use in audio production as a driving background beat or as a fleeting element in a bumper or ID. Loops can be exported into music creation programs such as Apple's Garageband, thus expanding their usability.

To finish the music bed, paste it into a playlist document for the desired time frame needed. Now this playlist document will play the region three times (Figure 6.4c). Note, too, that it is possible to use the cross-fade capabilities of the program to mesh the segments seamlessly.

It is possible to use several different regions to create a shortened version of a song as a musical bed or standalone piece. Figure 6.5 illustrates a playlist of three segments from the song "Good Vibrations." This playlist has combined the segments to form a 20-second version of the piece.

Editing music takes practice and patience, but this is a skill that is definitely worth learning. Music editing gives you great flexibility in radio production.

USING ALTERNATIVE TECHNOLOGIES

Most audio editing today occurs on an audio workstation running one or more of the software packages commonly used by broadcasters and audio recording engineers. But the revolution in mobile computing has created the opportunity

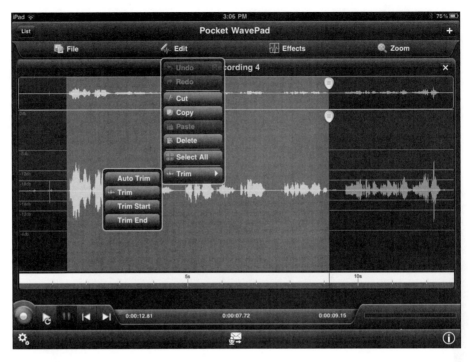

FIGURE 6.6

Today's mobile technology makes it easy for a producer to record and edit sound in the field. Once completed it is possible to send this file via email or a wireless network for broadcast.

SOURCE: Fritz Messere

to record and edit on location and send finished versions of materials back to the station via the Internet or a wireless 3G or 4G network. This new-found flexibility of mobile recording, cloud storage, and fast Internet or wireless networks has made it possible to extend the capability of the radio station.

Devices like the smartphone and the iPad have a number of software packages that allow for editing in the field. Pocket Wavepad allows a user to record and edit full-fidelity .WAV files on an iPad and email the files or upload them to a file transfer protocol (FTP) site so the station can play them back immediately. Figure 6.6 shows both an edited waveform and the options for sending the file to another user.

EDITING WITH A MINIDISC

While most stations use MiniDiscs to archive station broadcasts, some use MiniDiscs as a general-purpose recording device. You will recall from our earlier discussion that MiniDiscs are magneto-optical recording devices that allow

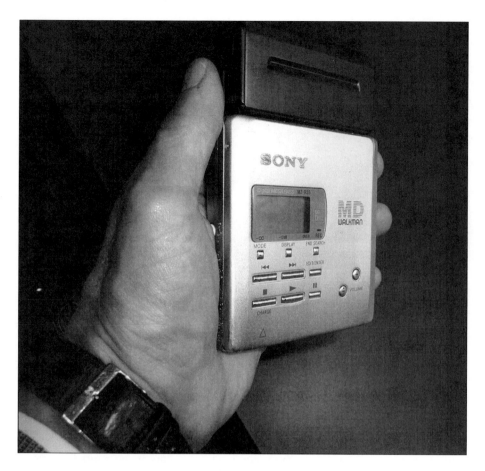

FIGURE 6.7

Handheld MiniDisc recorders can be used for newsgathering.

SOURCE: Philip Benoit

you to record and re-record over the same media. You can use them to record, erase, edit, move, and combine or divide. These editing functions provide some flexibility but are a rather rudimentary editing tool for broadcasters. We present this information because MiniDiscs are used in radio news-gathering operations and it may be necessary, from time to time, to use this editing function (see Figure 6.7).

Remember that we used a portable MiniDisc to record our entire Mayor Hazzard interview originally. If you started with a blank MiniDisc, this would be the first sound file recorded onto the disc. The MiniDisc recorder would automatically number this as cut 1. Now play the interview and practice pressing the Pause control at our edit point.

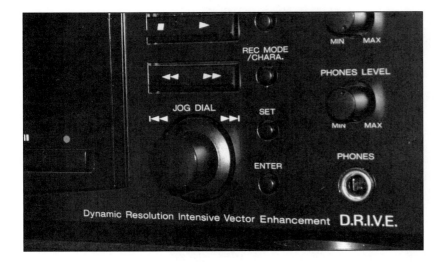

FIGURE 6.8

The jog wheel allows the user to perform basic editing functions on this MiniDisc recorder.

SOURCE: Fritz Messere

MAYOR: We have decided to go ahead with the construction of a new crosstown expressway from the junction of Interstate 440 to <edit point>

After you have the machine paused in the correct location, press Edit on the MiniDisc machine. It will ask you if you want to divide the segment. (Note that on some machines there may be a jog wheel that needs to be turned to display the various editing functions [see Figure 6.8].) Press Set, and the machine will now display *1 <> 2 ? OK* on the alphanumeric display. The MiniDisc recorder is asking you if you want to convert cut 1 into two cuts at the paused location. By pressing Enter you tell the machine to divide the interview into two interview parts that sound like this:

CUT 1: We have decided to go ahead with the construction of a new crosstown expressway from the junction of Interstate 440 to ...

CUT 2: as you can see right here on the map, Commercial Street, where there will be a major interchange.

Now we are going to play cut 2 and press pause at our second edit point, right after the phrase "as you can see right here on the map." Again we are going to press Edit and divide the segments by pressing Set and then Enter. This segment will now be divided between cuts 2 and 3. We now have three different cuts.

CUT 1: We have decided to go ahead with the construction of a new crosstown expressway from the junction of Interstate 440 to ...

CUT 2: as you can see right here on the map …

CUT 3: Commercial Street, where there will be a major interchange.

Finally, we are going to combine cuts 1 and 3 to complete the sound bite. Move the jog wheel until cut 1 is displayed; then press Play and Edit. The machine will now ask you "Divide?" on the alphanumeric display. Rotate the jog wheel until "Combine?" is displayed. Press Set, and the alphanumeric display will display cut 1 and flash cut 2. The machine is asking if you want to combine cut 1 with cut 2. We don't want cut 2; we want cut 3 instead. When you rotate the jog wheel clockwise, cut 3 will replace cut 2 as the second edit segment. By pressing Enter, the machine will edit together cut 1 and cut 3. Our edit is complete. (Note that some MiniDiscs will ask "OK?" before the edit will be executed. Each machine is slightly different, but the procedure is basically the same.) Now play the sound bite and see how your edit sounds.

DUBBING

Obviously, MiniDisc editing is rudimentary in comparison to the features available on a computer workstation, but it can be very useful when a reporter is in the field and needs to make sound bites for airing quickly.

Regardless of whether you use a computer, a MiniDisc, or a digital recorder, you will frequently find yourself copying from one source onto another source. Dubbing is an important tool in your arsenal of production tools.

The dubbing process is done frequently in radio. For example, you might dub a news segment you recorded onto a MiniDisc for archival purposes or for airplay later. When you *dub*, you essentially copy a source in one location to another location or a different medium. The technology that allows you to dub is essentially the same as the technology that allows you to splice and edit. Therefore, when dubbing, it is possible to achieve many of the same goals as we achieved using our editing techniques.

Dubbing from one source to another too many times can cause the quality of the recording to deteriorate, particularly when you are dubbing with an MP3 file or a MiniDisc, where the audio has been compressed, or when you've recorded on analog tape machines such as carts or reel-to-reels. Every new dub of a recording is known as another **generation**. Dubbing too often can result in a loss of quality, including the introduction of artifacts (additional noises) into the recording process.

Advantages of Dubbing

There are some real advantages to the dubbing process, however. Dubbing allows you to overlap elements. If, for example, you want to edit in a piece of music and talk over it, fading the music out, you will have to use either dubbing or more sophisticated features of the DAW. Another plus of dubbing is that it can be accomplished very quickly.

Dubbing may account for some of the editing work you'll do. Stations get most of their music on CDs or from a music service, and they dub this music onto the computer's hard disk for playback. Commercials or jingles often arrive on CDs and need to be dubbed to a computer or digital cart for use on the air. News segments recorded in the field need to be dubbed to a DAW for editing.

Review of Dubbing

Dubbing involves recording program material from one source on another location. It is very useful in editing because it's less work than some other forms of electronic editing; however, dubbing isn't quite as accurate as splicing or importing a file and cutting the beginning and end precisely to time in locating editing points. Dubbing is frequently used when elements are overlapped, especially in music.

SUMMARY

Recorded segments are separated and joined together in two ways: by electronic editing (cutting and pasting information) and by dubbing (electronically copying and reinserting taped material).

Digital audio workstations have greatly improved the process of editing recorded material compared with analog methods. Both dubbing and electronic editing are nondestructive, but DAW technology allows the user to create virtually undetectable edits easily.

The purpose of splicing and editing is usually to eliminate words or phrases, change the order of phrases and dialogue, or shorten or lengthen music beds. Dubbing can accomplish many of the same things, but it is also useful for combining many production elements in a rudimentary fashion.

APPLICATIONS

SITUATION 1/THE PROBLEM A production manager at a local radio station was given the job of producing a commercial for a local political candidate. As part of the commercial, the candidate discussed his views for 40 seconds. However, the candidate had an unfortunate speech pattern: He interjected "uhhhh" many times during his presentation.

ONE POSSIBLE SOLUTION Because it was the producer's job—in this case—to present the candidate in a positive light, the producer dubbed the audio to a sound file and edited all the "uhhhhs" from the politician's remarks. The job took 20 minutes, but the resulting audio sounded smooth and clean.

SITUATION 2/THE PROBLEM The producer of an entertainment show did an interview (on location using a smartphone) with the head of a local theater group. The producer wanted to weave three cuts of the interview into her script.

The script went along the following lines: "And what does Pat Wilbur, head of the Starlight Theater Group, have planned for this season?"... (first cut of interview) ... "But will attendance be better this year than last year's dismal totals?"... (second cut of interview) ... "So how does Pat Wilbur intend to get those attendance figures up?"... (third cut of interview).

What would be the best way to weave those cuts into the script?

ONE POSSIBLE SOLUTION The producer listened to the entire interview several times and made precise notes about where she wanted to cut in and out of the interview.

Because time was short, she decided to dub the three cuts directly onto a MiniDisc, which would be used to play the cuts over the air. (The show was done live.) She put the MiniDisc machine on Record and Pause, played the sound file, and started the MiniDisc in Record as soon as the appropriate section of the interview began, stopping the disc as soon as the desired section of the interview ended. This procedure was repeated for the other two cuts. Thus, there were three cuts sequenced in order on the MiniDisc. Every time the producer wanted to play a cut of the interview, she simply hit the Start button on the machine.

The next cut was cued automatically because the segments were recorded in order.

EXERCISES

1. If you have two or more MiniDiscs available, dub a piece of audio from machine to machine. For example, start with a 10-second music cut dubbed onto a MiniDisc; take that disc and dub from machine 1 to machine 2. Now dub from machine 2 back to machine 1 (putting a new MiniDisc or a clean cart in cart 1). This exercise will accomplish two goals: You'll hear what the effect of successive generations of recording, and you'll better understand the relationship of these machines (for record and playback) to the console.

2. Interview a classmate or colleague using a smartphone or digital recorder. Dub the interview onto your digital workstation, take three cuts from the interview, and weave them into a script similar to the one described in Situation 2 in the Applications section of this chapter. (What you're doing is assembling a series of **voice wraps**.) Don't be too concerned

about the content of the interview or the script; this is just a vehicle for practicing editing techniques. The whole program need not be longer than a minute or so. Once you've completed the editing, you can save the sound file on your workstation or dub the files to a MiniDisc, depending on what your instructor requests.

3. Listen to a half-hour of radio, and identify as many editing structures as you can. Write them down. For example: "Introduction to the 4 o'clock news on WAAA: *establish music, music under, voice up*. This was followed by a *voice wrap* during the first news report."

7

Recorded Program Production

We use the term *recorded program production* to refer loosely to any radio production work that is not done live (over the air). In most cases, the recording is done in preparation for use over the air at a later date.

The basic difference between recorded production and live, on-air production (which we cover in the next chapter) is that on-air production is a one-shot affair; there's only one opportunity to get it right. In recorded studio work, the producer has the freedom to do several retakes of the same production element, to try different blends and mixes, or to scrap the whole project and start over again if it's not working out.

Because of these luxuries, much more complex productions are attempted in recorded work. Whereas mixing a narration, multiple sound effects, and a music bed would be next to impossible all in one take, it becomes a simple matter in the recording studio because the tasks can be attempted one at a time, with the various elements divided into logical steps.

RECORDED VERSUS LIVE, ON-AIR PRODUCTION

How does a radio producer decide whether a production will be done live or put together in advance? There are three elements to consider: complexity, scheduled airtime, and convenience.

Complexity

A production containing many elements must be done in advance. Some commercials are read live, but these are almost always one-voice affairs, with the announcer simply reading copy or **ad-libbing** from a fact sheet.

133

Scheduled Airtime

A talk show that airs at 6:30 A.M. Sunday will be prerecorded in the studio, usually during normal weekday working hours. Trying to get guests to appear live on a crack-of-dawn show is not practical.

On the other hand, newscasts generally are not recorded (and when they are, they're done as close to airtime as possible) because they become outdated as quickly as the news changes.

Convenience

If a production calls for the voice of a specific announcer, is it more convenient to record the announcer or to have him or her come in every time that production is aired? The same rationale applies to the need for repetition of a production. Though the use of music and narration for the introduction of a show might be done live if the program is a one-time affair, prerecording the introduction will be far more convenient if it is to be repeated weekly or daily. The daily sports wrap-up may be live, but the intro and outro, using music and a specific announcer, is probably prerecorded and stored on the digital cart machine.

Along the same lines, pre-producing a piece reduces the chance that an error will be made over the air.

LAYOUT OF A PRODUCTION STUDIO

In a small radio station, the production studio is usually located wherever it fits. Often, it is in the disc library, or in an engineering area, or even in a corner of the manager's office. Today's technology allows you to put a full-sized recording studio in a laptop computer, so the production studio can literally be located almost anywhere. In a somewhat larger station, the basic production studio often looks like the one shown in Figure 7.1.

On the other end of the spectrum is the fully equipped, high-tech production studio (see Figure 7.2a). Another variation of the top-of-the line studio is a set-up with **multitrack** mixing capabilities for recording and remixing original music. Today, many of the digital audio workstation (DAW) programs have multitrack mixing capabilities, and larger stations frequently use these capabilities to record local musical talent. We'll discuss recording and mixing music later in this chapter.

Most medium to large studio set-ups feature a glassed-in area between the main control room and the studio. In large music production studios, the glass divides the performance area of the studio from the control area (see Figure 7.2a). The glass is typically double layered, and the panes are not set parallel to each other or to the studio wall (see Figure 7.2b). This is to prevent internal and external reflections of sound.

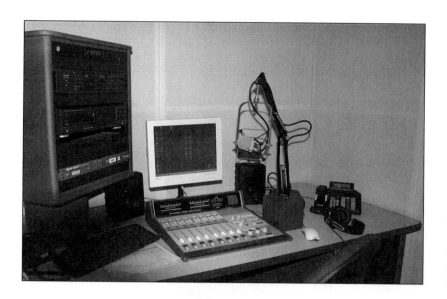

FIGURE 7.1

Basic production studios such as this one may have a minimum of equipment.

SOURCE: Fritz Messere

The most typical radio-station production studio is a one-room set-up, with the equipment usually intended for combo use. Although the studio is intended for off-air production, there generally will be a **hard-wired** link to the main control room so that the output of the production studio can be put live over the air. This arrangement comes in handy when the main control room is out of commission during repairs or other emergencies. The studio may double as an announce booth, used especially by the news department. The news department may also have its own production area, or there may be cubicles set up where news personnel can record or edit stories or tape telephone interviews.

Equipment in the Production Studio

In many cases, the production studio's equipment may virtually duplicate what's in an on-air studio, although there may not be as much of it. In some stations, the production equipment may be hand-me-downs from the on-air control room. The minimum equipment usually includes some sort of console, a computer workstation, a good quality mic, a digital cart, and perhaps a MiniDisc and a CD player. In some markets you may also find cart machines and turntables among the mix of equipment. It may be that the console is nothing more than a portable mixer that the station uses for **remotes**, but it is equally likely today that the production console is a modern digital control surface where the inputs are pulled up on the board from a central location via an Ethernet connection. The point is that there are many different configurations.

As mentioned earlier, a routing switcher may also be a fixture of the production studio. In many cases, the router allows interconnection of different inputs into the production studio with other studios, with the network, or even directly

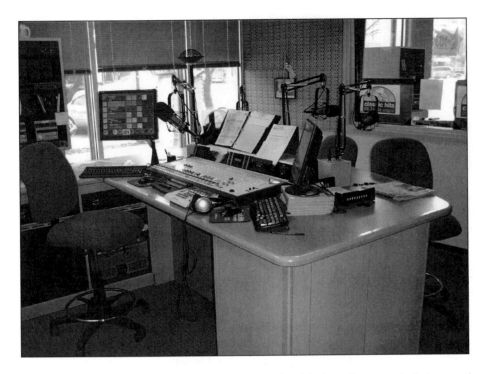

a. Studios at KWIC-FM. Notice that the window on the right has glass mounted at an angle.

SOURCE: Les Glenn—Cumulus Broadcasting

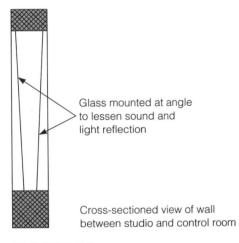

Glass mounted at angle
to lessen sound and
light reflection

Cross-sectioned view of wall
between studio and control room

b. A double layer of glass is used to separate the
control room from the production studio. Air
space between the panes of glass provides
sound insulation from adjacent areas.

FIGURE 7.2

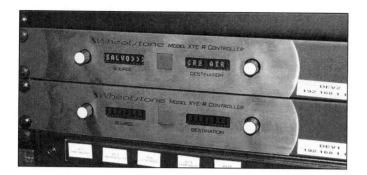

FIGURE 7.3

Routing switchers act like patchbays. They allow you to choose an audio source and send it to one of a number of different inputs in one or more studios.

SOURCE: Fritz Messere

with the transmitter. The input to a channel on the console or its output can be changed at the touch of a button (see Figure 7.3).

In instances where the production studio and an announce booth are adjacent, there is often some sort of talkback system between studios so the engineer can talk with the announcer.

Sound Treatment in the Production Studio

A variety of different commercially available sound-deadening materials (see Figure 7.4) are commonly used to dampen sound reflection in the production studio. In the early days of FM radio, egg cartons were cut up and attached to the walls and provided the same effect.

A carpet is very helpful for deadening sound reflection. On occasion, the carpet is applied to walls to help create an acoustically dead environment. Studios designed for music recording often have hard and soft material surfaces that can be changed. This allows the engineer to choose between a livelier or deader sound environment, depending on the needs of the producer. Generally the announce booth has sound deadening, but that same environment would not be good for recording music.

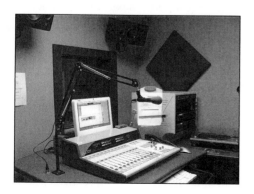

FIGURE 7.4

Sound-deadening material attached to studio walls to reduce unwanted sound reflection.

SOURCE: Philip Benoit

WORKING IN A PRODUCTION STUDIO

Who works in the production studio environment? In some stations, a production manager is in charge of the studio and has the responsibility of overseeing all the station's off-air production. Announcers (jocks) also use production facilities for duties such as voice tracking, promo recording, and commercial spot production. In smaller stations, salespeople often produce their own commercials. Basically, the studio is used by anyone who has to construct a production for later airplay. Today the production studio may also serve to support online programming and services for the station. In this sense, all staff members assigned such duties are producers.

Anyone who undertakes the duties of a producer is responsible for knowing much more about the process of radio than is someone who acts simply as an announcer or a technician. A producer must understand the methods of constructing a **spot** or program. For example, it may be more efficient to break down the production into a number of discrete tasks, such as doing all the music work first and all the narration next, even though that is not the sequence in which the components will appear in the final product.

An analogy from the movie production business is illustrative. Perhaps a certain restaurant is the setting of the last sequence of a movie, and the film begins in the same restaurant. It makes sense for the producer, who has to move around crew, actors, extras, and sets, to shoot the beginning and ending scenes on the same day. (It's not unheard of for the ending of a movie to be shot on the first day of production.) In other words, the pieces or sequences of a movie can be filmed in any order and then edited together in accordance with the script.

You'll find that the same strategy often proves useful in the radio production studio. And, because time demands on a studio are usually high, you'll be able to get in and out much faster if you learn to plan work in **task-oriented sequence**. If, for instance, you have three similar commercials to produce, it may prove useful to do the announcing for all three first and add the music beds and effects to all three next.

Working in task-oriented sequence will become second nature as long as you make an effort to break old thought patterns that require you to work in real-time sequence (doing the beginning first, the middle next, and the ending last). Always structure your tasks according to the most convenient and efficient method for the best use of the production studio available. For example, your voice talent may only have one hour to work with you on a spot. Recording the voice first and adding music or effects, editing for time, and setting the correct levels between sources are things that you can easily accomplish on your own, once you've recorded the voice track. Understanding this principle is what separates a producer from someone who just records a sound file or puts something down on digital cart.

Another factor that will help you develop skill and recognition as a radio producer is an understanding of the basic building blocks of radio and how they relate to studio production. We're talking about music, recorded voice, and sound effects.

RADIO RETRO • THE DEVELOPMENT OF AUDIOTAPE, OR HOW TO SPEND MORE TIME ON THE GOLF COURSE

It has always been a technological challenge to develop a recording medium that captures sound, is easy to use, is reliable, and has the backing of the consumer.

The history of radio recording media demonstrates that complex interplay in an interesting way—and shows how luck and happenstance play a big role in the evolution of media. It also demonstrates that media technologies sometimes find their own way despite the learned predictions of the experts and of even their inventors.

For example, in the mid-1880s Thomas Edison developed one of the versions of the gramophone, which recorded onto wax cylinders. When people told Edison how excited they were that they would be able to use the device to play music in the home, he scoffed. It was a business dictation machine, he told them. No one would want to listen to recorded music at home.

As it happens, people did, but the cylinder was not a very good system. Soon, other inventors began developing the disc, a very practical system where a vibrating needle cut a groove into a disc and the playback unit read those vibrations. Around the turn of the 20th century, several advances were made in disc technology, and the devices became useful not only for recording music, but—a few decades later—for playing it back on air.

Most recorded program production in the 1940s ended up on some sort of disc, often a 16-inch aluminum disc. Bing Crosby, of "White Christmas" fame, didn't want to be tied down to the studio for live broadcast performances. Also, radio network shows were performed twice each night during these times (once for the East and again for the West Coast), so he prodded his technical crew to come up with a good system for recording his show and playing it back. The discs of the time worked, but not all that well. They only held about four minutes of programming on each disc, so you can imagine the possibilities for playback error. Also, the quality just wasn't that good.

Crosby insisted that the crew come up with something better, and he pointed to a new technology that had been developed in Germany: audiotape. While at first skeptical, his producers tried it and it worked. Although it was prone to breakage, tape had much more area on which to store a transduced signal, and it provided better quality.

Legend has it that audiotape came about as the medium of choice for the recording studio because Bing Crosby wanted more time for his golf game. We'll never settle that one, but tape did remain the dominant medium for many years after he popularized it.

For interesting histories regarding the developing of tape recording, see http://www.bext.com/Mullin RPT.pdf.

MUSIC

Music is a very important element in radio production; indeed, it can be argued that for many stations, music is what radio is all about. In any event, it's important for a producer to have an understanding of music. Good producers have the ability to use music to their advantage, to manipulate music to create an effect. Good producers also understand the kinds and varieties of music, and thus can fit productions into the station's overall format. In a production studio setting, you will generally be using segments of music rather than entire cuts.

Sources of Music

The use of music is licensed to a radio station by means of a fee paid to music licensing organizations, the largest of which are the American Society of Composers, Authors and Publishers (**ASCAP**) and Broadcast Music Incorporated (**BMI**). The amount of money paid to these licensing organizations depends mostly on the size of the radio market and the revenue generated by the radio station. Licensing fees cover the performance right to the music (the right to play it on the radio). Stations that stream their programs on the Internet pay a separate fee on a per-song, per-listener basis.

These performance rights do not extend to using a particular piece in a commercial, however; for that use, producers should contact the music publisher for permission to use a specific song for a specific commercial piece, but often specific requirements are not filled very well by the popular music available. Specialized musical selections have been developed to meet these needs. Production music produced for broadcasting usually is available online as a service provided to the station or may come from a broadcast production library on CDs. The company providing the music may charge the station a standard fee for the use of the library or may charge the station based on the number of downloads the station uses.

Various companies sell **production** libraries (see Figure 7.5) as CD sets or music downloads, with each CD reflecting a particular thematic element such as sports jams or urban beats. Stations do not have to worry about performance rights or royalties for this music because the terms of use are set within the contract between the music production company and the radio station. Recorded original music fits the most common production and time requirements of typical stations. For example, **music beds** run exactly 60 or 30 seconds.

Some production packages include vocal selections that can be adapted to fit the needs of commercial production for local merchants. Thus, a 30-second cut might start with a group of vocalists singing: "You'll find it all at the mall." The instrumental background would continue, serving as a bed for the local announcer to fill with copy advertising specialty shops and merchants found at the local mall. The vocal would return, 25 seconds into the cut, to close out the piece with: "Do your shopping where you'll find everything you need!" Often these prerecorded production elements sound corny, so a producer must be judicious in choosing which elements to use.

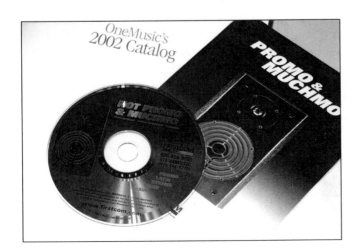

FIGURE 7.5

Specialized music libraries are available for production use.

SOURCE: Fritz Messere

Advertising agencies, which commission the composition of original music for clients, are another source of music. Such music usually takes the form of a jingle, which is incorporated into the client's radio (and sometimes TV) advertising. The beds supplied by ad agencies are very similar to the works furnished by the production library companies, except that the ad agency's musical jingle is specific to one client. (Think about McDonald's and Coke jingles that you've heard.) Some large companies provide their franchises with standardized commercial beds that can be "localized" at the different radio stations.

Specialized production libraries generally are easier to work with than popular music. (You don't have to do as much adaptation of the music, such as telescoping the beginning and end together for one 30-second spot.) Generally the radio station has either purchased the rights to use the music library in its entirety or has agreed to a "*needle drop*" charge for the use of a specific track.

Choosing Music for Production Work

The selection of music can be a formidable task. Music can make or break a production. A commercial, for example, can gain significant impact through the selection of background music that reinforces the message. A poor selection, though, can detract from the message or even be at odds with it. For instance, copy that touts the benefits of a relaxing vacation through the Acme Travel Agency won't be reinforced by heavily rhythmic music. Also, no copy will be helped by an overly familiar selection that draws attention away from the message. Assuming that the station has the performance rights to use music for commercial purposes, even the smallest radio station may have thousands of recordings in its station library. Radio stations often categorize music held in their libraries by type (rock, country, jazz, classical, and so on). Computers make this an easy chore since the software can be manipulated to look for specific genres of music, times of the tracks, types of instrumentation, and so on. If the music is stored on hard drives, it is relatively easy to sort selections and preview the tracks to decide on appropriate music.

Stations that keep CD collections may use a color code or a numerical or alphabetical listing for their music libraries. It is important to understand the broad classifications that stations use so that you can locate music by type quickly and easily. We'll discuss some broad classifications later in this chapter. Using database programs to classify musical selections makes the task of finding different types of music easy. However, there is a very real danger of overusing popular music (assuming you have permission to use the piece). As we indicated, a catchy, popular tune might attract more attention than the message of the commercial so that the listener hears the music, not the message. Conversely, a popular piece of music may be just what is called for in a particular situation. For example, in recent years, some car companies have picked familiar music so as to make a connection between specific songs and the car brand. Often, the car company will negotiate with the music publisher for the exclusive right to use that music. No other commercial can use the same piece of music for any type of automotive advertising.

Many production pieces are chosen by someone who notices that a certain **cut** on the air would be a particularly good piece for production work. Today many pop and urban stations use percussive and rhythmic elements as production beds. Modern audio workstations make it very easy to create loops and segments that can be pieced together to create exciting background elements for production.

In any case, the music must reinforce the message, not distract the user or detract from the content. The style has to fit both the message and the station's format.

Styles of Music

A broad knowledge of music is critical to the radio professional. First, even if your intention is to pursue a career in rock radio, circumstances may dictate a two-year stint at a station with a country or adult contemporary music format even though your first love is modern jazz. Stations with a broad-ranging format, such as the new Jack[1] format, may use a variety of music styles in production, and you need to understand the styles and be able to use them effectively. In addition, modern music produces many **crossovers** from one style into another. Some country music, for example, almost sounds like rock. Being able to recognize elements of various styles will help you categorize music and better use it to achieve effects. Trade magazines and music websites can help you learn more about music and music categories. Here are the characteristics of some of the major styles of music.

Rock   Rock usually features drums and electric guitars. There's generally a distinctive rhythm, which is maintained by bass drum and bass guitar. More avant-garde types of rock music include elaborate electronic effects. The milder rock music selections are commonly used in radio production as music beds. Frequently, snippets of percussive sounds are used repetitively for high-energy commercials.

Country   Today's country genre traces its roots to a combination of Nashville, folk, Appalachian, and Western swing music, but modern country blends elements of pop and rock into its sound. In fact, while it has a diverse heritage, much of the country music repertoire today is orchestrated so that it is virtually indistinguishable from general popular music. The steel guitar was once the cornerstone of country music, but now almost any combination of instruments can be used. Modern country's emphasis on newer music and younger performers have kept it fresh and diverse. In fact, there are several different subgenres within the country field. If you work at a country station, it is important to understand the differences.

---

1. Which basically uses an eclectic and almost random mix of music that does fall into the typical categories thought of as formats

Country music may be used in production to achieve special effects (as a music bed for a rodeo commercial, perhaps) and, of course, is used extensively in production on country-format stations.

Jazz   This style of music can run the gamut from traditional big-band dance music to Dixieland and bebop, and from Latin to bizarre and highly experimental compositions. Jazz generally uses a syncopated rhythm. While jazz is primarily considered an instrumental form, there are notable jazz vocalists who have been very successful. "Cool jazz" is popular and accessible and tends to be good production music.

Jazz has many uses in production and is particularly helpful because so much of it is instrumental. The more experimental types of jazz are less useful, though they can sometimes be selected for effect.

Classical   The term *classical music* is something of a misnomer because *classical* really refers to only one type of music in the spectrum popularly understood as "classical." The classical period is typified by the music of Mozart. The baroque period, which preceded the classical one, is most commonly associated with Bach, who created multiple melodies that interact contrapuntally. (This type of baroque music is referred to as *polyphonic*; its sound can be approximated by the familiar round "Row, Row, Row Your Boat.") The romantic period of music followed the classical period and is characterized by the works of Tchaikovsky and by the later works of Beethoven.

For lack of a better term, *classical* will suffice here, though some people refer to this style as "concert music" or "good music." Light opera and some Broadway music also fall into this category. Classical music occasionally is useful in production as it quickly sets a mood and is generally used to achieve a special effect.

Urban   This music, which is a subgenre of rhythm and blues (R&B), is noted for its heavy bass riffs and highly percussive nature. Urban music has a repetitive beat, making it easy to edit. Rap, urban contemporary, hip-hop, and soul also are considered subgenres of R&B. Urban beds can frequently cut through programming clutter on pop and contemporary stations, but they may not be appropriate for all formats.

General Popular Music   This broad category can encompass many others. The Beatles, *Glee* cast covers, Elton John, and Celine Dion certainly fit into this category, but so do many others. Today females make up a large number of the new generation of pop vocalists. Few instrumentals make the charts or are heard as part of the recurrent playlist. Essentially, today's general popular music tends to be a combination of light rhythmic ballads with melodic overtones rather than orchestral or hard rock. Violins and other bowed strings are mixed in with synthesizers, electric instruments, and percussive instrumentation. Stations with classic hits, oldies, mix, and blended formats will include lower-key rock music selections along with pop in their playlist. In the middle of this group are songs from the 1970s, 1980s, and 1990s. At the other end of the spectrum are the "beautiful-music" sounds of Henry Mancini or Kenny G. Instrumentalists are most frequently heard at Christmas when some stations switch to seasonal programming. Pop music is hard to incorporate as a bed or background since its familiarity tends to make listeners focus on the music and not the script.

Specialty Music   This category includes polkas, waltzes, seasonal music, and marches, which are used in production work when a specific effect is called for.

RECORDED VOICE

Voice, the second major element of production, can be recorded by an announcer running a combo operation or by a producer running the console while one or more announcers speak into a mic or mics.

One common studio production task is the miking of several speakers; for instance, in a roundtable discussion. Here, the microphone techniques we discussed in Chapter 5 are useful, along with some other considerations that we'll discuss shortly. The most important goal of recording voice in a studio production setting, though, is to get a clean recording that accentuates the announcer's voice and delivery. Achieving this goal may involve considerations such as the following:

- Selecting a mic that deemphasizes peculiarities of a performer's speech, such as *p*-popping or excessive **sibilance**.
- Replacing a highly sensitive mic with a less sensitive model to cut down on noise from air conditioning or from the clicking of the speaker's dentures.
- Eliminating table noises (nonprofessional speakers are notorious for table-tapping or clicking pens) by hanging the microphone from a boom rather than attaching it to a table stand.
- Instructing speakers, professional and nonprofessional alike, on positioning and use of the mic. Nonprofessional speakers frequently need to be cautioned about speaking too close to or too far away from the mic.

Duties of these types are common in all production set-ups. Whereas, in some instances, recording voice in the production studio is a simple affair, other situations are complex. Two of the most common difficulties encountered in production work are miking multiple speakers and communicating with speakers when the mics are open.

Miking Multiple Speakers

One typical function of the radio station's production specialist is to set up and record panel discussion shows. With a number of interviewees in the studio, it is tempting to string up mics for everyone who is likely to open his or her mouth.

Most experts agree, however, that the fewer mics you can get away with, the better. An overabundance of mics can cause difficulties in engineering the show (trying to find the right pot to adjust, for example, when you're dealing with six or seven) and in phasing.

It is, however, practical to use two mics when there are two speakers. Perhaps the most common type of interview program involves a single host and a single guest, and recording such a show can be pulled off quite nicely with two cardioid mics, with little overlap of the pickup pattern (see Figure 7.6).

The advantage of this set-up is that the operator is free to control the individual volumes and to maintain a comfortable balance. A bidirectional or omnidirectional mic can be used instead, but the loss in flexibility usually isn't worth the convenience gained from a simpler set-up. However, when there are several speakers, simplicity of mic set-up is indeed a virtue, although care must be taken to ensure that talent speaks at similar voice levels. As we mentioned, phasing problems plague the multiple-mic setup, although new cardioids can be used successfully when the talent speaks close to the microphone (see Figure 7.7).

Also, you need to remember that every time you open a mic, the room tone, or noise present in the studio, increases.

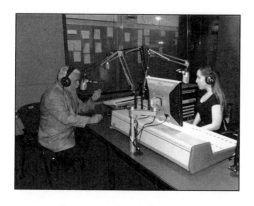

FIGURE 7.6

Simple two-person interview, using cardioid mics.

SOURCE: Philip Benoit

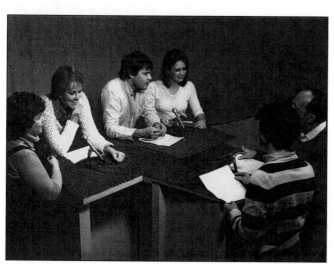

FIGURE 7.7

Layout enabling six speakers to be positioned around three mics. Separation and proper orientation of the mics could, if cardioids were used, prevent overlap of their pickup patterns.

SOURCE: Philip Benoit

To understand phasing problems, let's first recall our discussion of directional mics in Chapter 5. Remember that a **directional mic** cancels sound by means of an acoustic network inside the mic; that is, sounds reach the diaphragm at different times and therefore cancel themselves out. The same effect occurs in the studio: sound arrives at different mics at different times, with just enough difference to throw the phasing off.

This will seem less abstract when you consider that sound does not travel very quickly. Although 1,100 feet per second may seem like a pretty fast clip, note how sound lags behind vision. From the top row of the bleachers, you can easily discern the gap between when the basketball hits the floor during a dribble and when you *hear* it hit the floor. Track runners start when they see the smoke from the starter's pistol rather than waiting for the noise, which they hear a split second later. Now, with sound waves making, let's say, 5,000 cycles per second (5,000 Hz), it's easy to see how a small delay can cause the cycles to be out of phase.

The solution to phasing problems is to avoid, as much as possible, any overlap among the mic pickup patterns. Sometimes this entails putting more than one speaker on a mic so as to avoid overlapping pickup patterns. For example, miking six speakers could be accomplished with three mics, each trained on two speakers so that there's little or no overlap of their pickup patterns.

The concept of phase problems will become crystal clear when you hear an out-of-phase broadcast. In many cases, all that's needed to overcome the problem is some additional separation of the pickup patterns. Moving the mic around will usually solve the problem. Applying a 3-to-1 ratio here is useful (see Figure 7.7). Generally the distance between microphones should be three times that of the distance from the microphone to the speaker. Remember, phase problems are nothing more than the effects of sounds reaching mics at different times and canceling one another out. Remember, too, that even a tiny difference in the times at which sounds reach a mic can cause phasing problems.

One other difficulty of miking multiple talkers is, of course, the matter of sound levels. A speaker who has an overpowering voice generally does not belong on the same mic with someone who habitually whispers. This situation, too, will call for some trial-and-error maneuvering.

Working with nonprofessional speakers creates a secondary problem with setting the level. Although a professional announcer will usually know enough to give you several sentences of speech to let you set the pot at the proper level, amateurs will not. The typical scenario before a panel discussion goes something like this:

PRODUCER: (*or whomever happens to be running the board*): Mr. Smith, could I have a level, please?

SMITH: What?

PRODUCER: A voice level … Could you just talk for me so I can set your mic?

SMITH: What do you want me to say?

PRODUCER: Anything.

SMITH: Hello, hello. Is that enough?

PRODUCER: *(who hasn't even found the fader yet):* No, no, just talk until I tell you to stop.

SMITH: But what am I supposed to say now?

To make matters worse, the level Mr. Smith finally gives the producer has absolutely no relation to the booming voice he will use when the recording starts. Though there's no perfect solution to this problem, one of the least objectionable ways of getting a level from amateur talent is to ask each person to count to 20. Granted, the voice a person uses to count aloud is different from the one used in conversation, but the voice level used by a self-conscious speaker to give a snippet of conversation for the level-taker isn't necessarily what's going to come out during the program either. Asking the talent to count does, at least, eliminate the "What am I going to say?" routine and guarantees several seconds of speech. If there's a rehearsal of the program before airtime, use the rehearsal to set levels.

Communicating with Speakers

One consideration of working in the production studio, especially when recording interview shows, is how to communicate with announcers and guests when mics are open. This isn't nearly as big a problem as it was in the days of live radio— when whole programs, such as variety shows and dramas, were put live over the air—but knowing some simple cues and signals can prevent the inconvenience of having to stop tape to give an instruction. In addition, signals sometimes prove useful when a speaker is going live over the air.

The following hand signals have been around for quite some time, and though you may not have much occasion to use them, they do represent a standard way of communicating in the studio.

You're On   This signal (see Figure 7.8a) consists of a finger pointed directly at the speaker.

Give Me a Level   A chattering motion with the fingers (see Figure 7.8b) indicates that you would like the announcer to give you a voice level.

Kill My Mic   Draw a finger across your throat (see Figure 7.8c). If you're using a headset mic, point to the mic, too.

Wrap Up   This signal is accomplished by a circular ("winding up") motion of the hands (see Figure 7.8d).

Stretch   Make a motion with your hands as though stretching a rubber band (see Figure 7.8e). This tells the person on-mic to keep talking and stretch out the program.

Remember, these signals aren't foolproof, and not everyone knows them. If they are standard in your station, fine. If you work out signals in advance with talent and guests, they may prove useful.

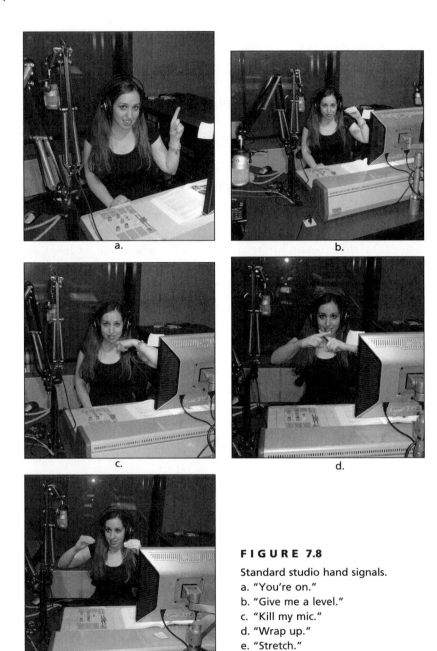

FIGURE 7.8

Standard studio hand signals.
a. "You're on."
b. "Give me a level."
c. "Kill my mic."
d. "Wrap up."
e. "Stretch."

SOURCE: "Philip Benoit" for a, b, c, d and e

SOUND EFFECTS

We have discussed sound effects in various contexts in other chapters. Here we examine how they are used in studio production. Some of the most useful sources of sound effects available to the producer are CD libraries sold by various firms. These discs carry fairly specific entries and list the number of seconds each cut lasts. For example, the entries in the "car horns honking" category might be listed this way:

- 17: Horn honking, Model T Ford, :05
- 18: Horn honking, modern car, :06
- 19: Horns honking, in city traffic, :10

Many of these CDs contain dozens of cuts per disc, so counting them is often difficult. Fortunately, most professional CD players allow you to move to a specific cut on the disc by using a selector knob or a remote control.

Production libraries are also available as computer files, and you can choose a variety of computer file formats, such as WAV, AIFF, or MP3. Sound effects can also be downloaded from various Internet sites, but you need to make sure that you have permission to use the sounds before incorporating them into your productions.

Sometimes you won't be able to find what you need, and a sound effect will have to be created. Most of us are familiar with the standard tricks of the trade for producing sound effects, such as crinkling cellophane to produce the effect of flames crackling. Most of us also know that the results—unless one is an expert— are often less than satisfactory. Many experienced production people who are willing to take the time and effort can custom-make sound effects, but in most radio production, that amount of effort isn't expended.

Most of the sound effects you will have to create yourself will consist of standard background noise, such as the hubbub of a restaurant. Common sense and some experimentation will guide you on this; just be aware that you and the microphone hear differently. Your brain can filter out noise in a restaurant, but the mic is likely to pick up every clink of dishes and scrape of silverware. So, when producing a sound effect, be prepared to try some different mic techniques, and don't hesitate to try various sound levels and to fade different effects in and out to create the sound you want.

COMBINING ELEMENTS IN PRODUCTION

The process of mixing music, voice, and sound effects is, essentially, a matter of feeding signals through the console or manipulating them with an editing process to construct the ultimate product.

A major consideration in combining these elements in a production studio setting is to ensure that the final product comes as close to the original sound as possible (and do it with the smallest possible number of re-recordings of the same segment).

INDUSTRY UPDATE • A SIMPLE AND INEXPENSIVE WAY TO CREATE PROFESSIONAL PODCASTS

Podcasts are useful and powerful tools that schools, businesses, and other organizations can
use to make audio-based information available worldwide.

Coauthor Carl Hausman produces podcasts for clients that include the Institute for Global Ethics, a Maine-based research organization.

Hausman's studio is in a retrofitted closet (Figure 7.9).

Another view of Hausman's studio is shown in Figure 7.10.

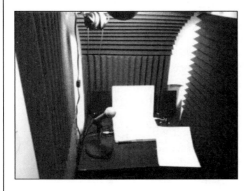

FIGURE 7.9
This studio consists of a laptop computer, a USB mic purchased at a local electronics store, and about $70 worth of acoustic padding purchased at a music store.
SOURCE: Carl Hausman

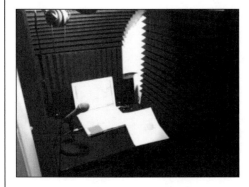

FIGURE 7.10
You can fit a surprising amount of equipment in a small space.
SOURCE: Carl Hausman

The program used for this production is called Audacity. You can download a free version that is amazingly powerful and flexible. Go to http://audacity.sourceforge.net/ to download the program.

There is an excellent online tutorial for Audacity. We won't go through all the steps here, but please note that it's a good idea to save the file before you begin recording (Figure 7.11).

We've named the file "Financial Crisis," the title of the column posted on the website that we will turn into a podcast (Figure 7.12). You can find the column at www.ethicsnewsline.com.

Now, we record the narration, which in this case runs about six and a half minutes. Figure 7.13 shows the end of the narration.

It is a good idea to save as you go along. Now we save the narration (Figure 7.14).

The beauty of online editing is the ability to visualize and easily manipulate the audio. Figure 7.15 shows the opening "three... two... one" countdown. We want to edit it out. With practice, you'll begin to be able to figure out many of the waveform patterns without having to play them back.

Next, we edit out a flub in the narration. When the narrator makes a mistake, he simply marks the time on his script, stops for a second or two, and then begins a "three... two... one" countdown and starts the sentence or paragraph again. The part to be excised is highlighted (Figure 7.16) and cut out.

The narrator had noted the location of the mistake on the script, making the edit easy. The notation is the approximate time of the error. A time printout is located across the top of the display screen.

The fact that the waveform is underneath a readout of the time makes it easy to mark edit points in the script and find them in the waveform (Figure 7.17).

Now the producer wants to insert a music open and a music close. The music has been filed in a separate folder, and it's as simple as moving the mouse to "project" and "important audio" (Figure 7.18).

The narration track is now on top, and the music open, which runs about 15 seconds, is below (Figure 7.19).

The next step is to import the music close, which has also been stored in the appropriate file. You can see the waveform at the bottom of the screen. There is a left and right channel, but the right channel is not visible in this photo because it's below the cut-off point of the monitor. You could see it if you scrolled down (Figure 7.20).

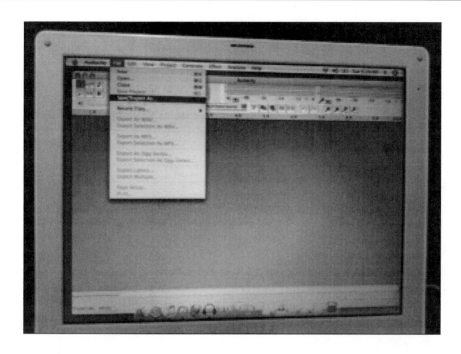

FIGURE 7.11

Saving the file in Audacity.

SOURCE: Carl Hausman

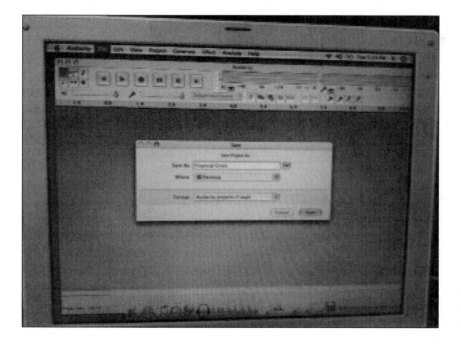

FIGURE 7.12

Naming the file.

SOURCE: Carl Hausman

(continued)

INDUSTRY UPDATE • A SIMPLE AND INEXPENSIVE WAY TO CREATE PROFESSIONAL PODCASTS (Continued)

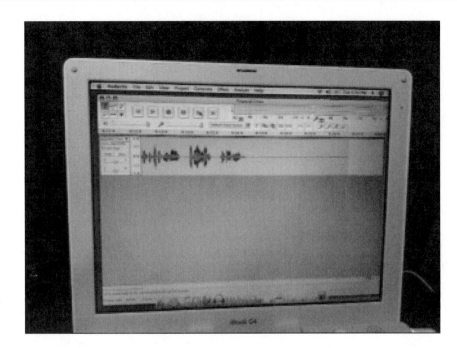

FIGURE 7.13

This is the final few seconds of the narration.

SOURCE: Carl Hausman

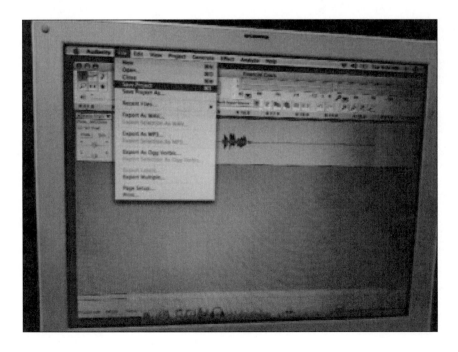

FIGURE 7.14

Saving the narration.

SOURCE: Carl Hausman

(continued)

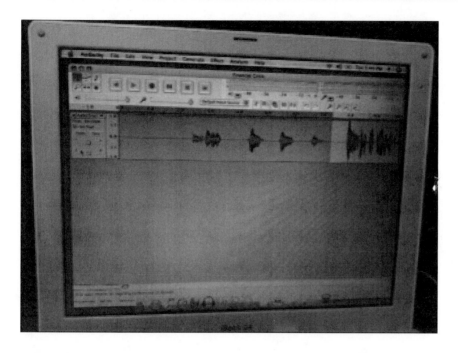

FIGURE 7.15

This is a waveform depiction of "financial crisis…three…two…one."

SOURCE: Carl Hausman

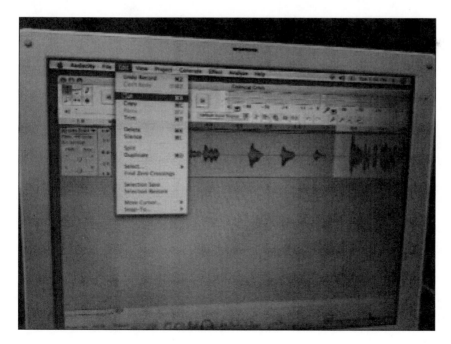

FIGURE 7.16

Cutting out the mistake.

SOURCE: Carl Hausman

(continued)

INDUSTRY UPDATE • A SIMPLE AND INEXPENSIVE WAY TO CREATE PROFESSIONAL PODCASTS (Continued)

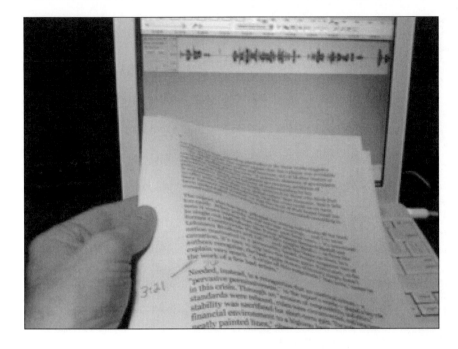

FIGURE 7.17

The location is marked in the script.

SOURCE: Carl Hausman

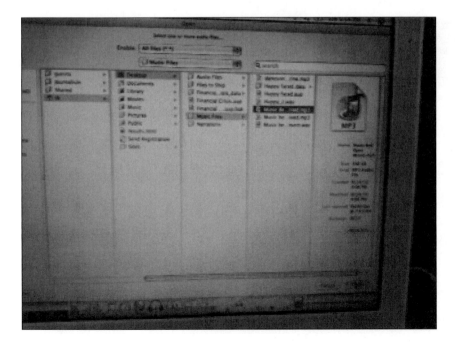

FIGURE 7.18

Importing the music bed open.

SOURCE: Carl Hausman

(continued)

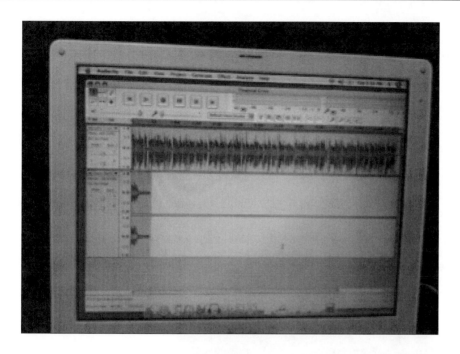

FIGURE 7.19

The narration and the music open are now mixed in the same file, although the start and stop times are not yet correct.

SOURCE: Carl Hausman

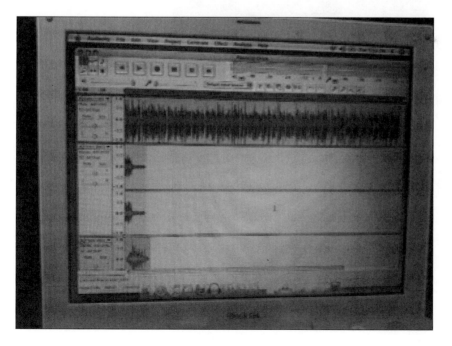

FIGURE 7.20

All three elements—narration, music open, and music close—have been imported and are ready to be moved to their appropriate locations.

SOURCE: Carl Hausman

(continued)

INDUSTRY UPDATE • A SIMPLE AND INEXPENSIVE WAY TO CREATE PROFESSIONAL PODCASTS (Continued)

The rest is easy: We want to piece to open with the music and then have the narration start as the music fades. Figure 7.21 shows a full-file view with the waveforms highly compressed so that six and a half minutes of audio fits into one screen. You can't do precise editing in this view (we will do that in a second) but you can put the elements in rough positions. Note that the outro[2] music bed has been moved to the end. So we have started with music, moved the beginning of the narration over (by using the program's grab tool), and then moved the music outro to the end.

In Figure 7.22, we have zoomed to the "normal" view, where we can do precise editing. As you can see, the music swells and then suddenly fades down. That's where we want the voice narration to start.

Now, the climactic crescendo of the music is positioned to enter as soon as the narration ends (Figure 7.23). Narration is in the top waveform. You can't see the music intro in the second two tracks because it ended several minutes ago.

In order for the file to be made readable by another computer or audio playback device, you would first want to save it as a .WAV file (Figure 7.24). Note that because of copyright restrictions, Audacity does not convert its files directly into mp3 files. However, another free file, iTunes, can easily make the conversion for you.

Finally, convert the file to the highly compressed mp3 format, which is widely used for podcasting. It's as simple as dragging the .WAV file into iTunes (Figure 7.25).

Then, while in iTunes, select the file, go to the "Advanced" tab, and then select "create mp3 version" (Figure 7.26).

You can then email the compressed file, mount it on a website, or upload it to the iTunes. You can visit the iTunes store and listen for free to the podcast used in this example by visiting www.ethicsnewsline.com and clicking on the iTunes tab at the top of the page.

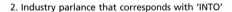

2. Industry parlance that corresponds with 'INTO'

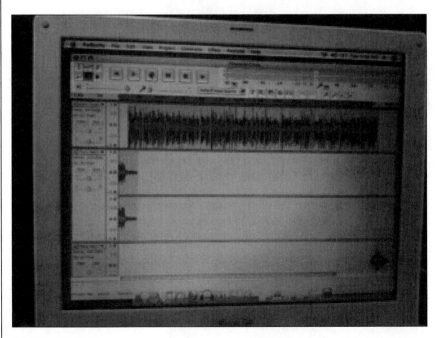

F I G U R E 7.21

The waveforms are moved to their approximate positions.

SOURCE: Carl Hausman

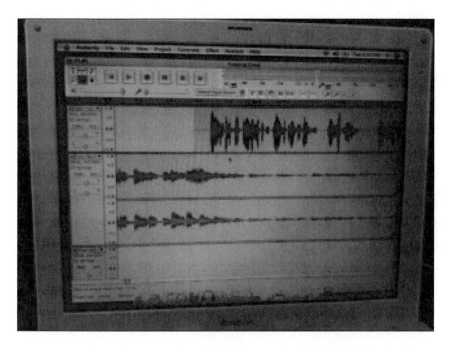

FIGURE 7.22

We've zoomed in so the voice and the climax of the music can be accurately matched.

SOURCE: Carl Hausman

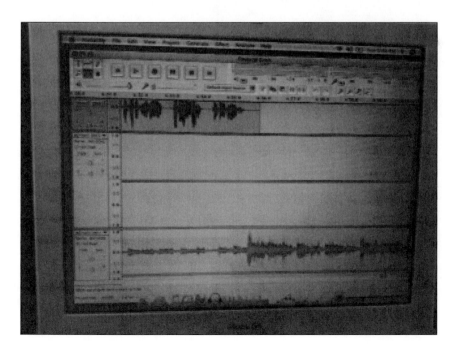

FIGURE 7.23

The music ending is arranged to crescendo after the vocal narration ends.

SOURCE: Carl Hausman

(continued)

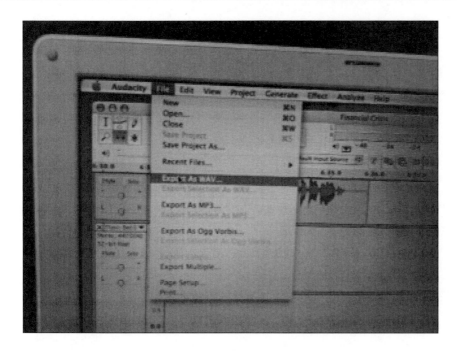

FIGURE 7.24

Save the file as a .WAV file.

SOURCE: Carl Hausman

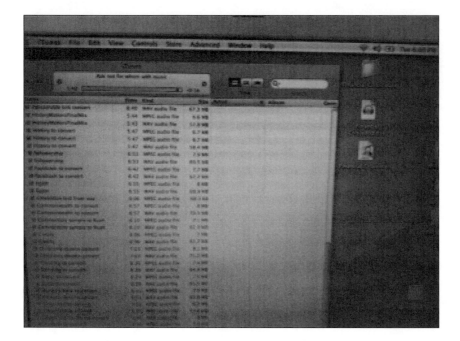

FIGURE 7.25

To convert a .WAV file into an mp3 file, drag it into the iTunes program.

SOURCE: Carl Hausman

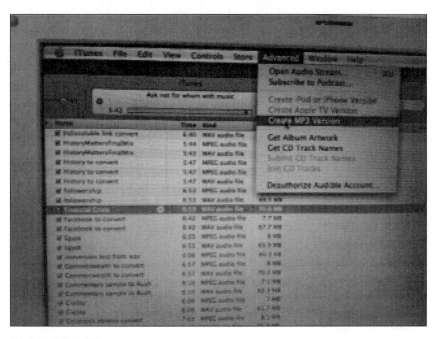

FIGURE 7.26

iTunes can create an mp3 file from a .WAV file in less than a minute.

SOURCE: Carl Hausman

We'll discuss the specifics of various production processes in the appropriate chapters, but this is a good place to point out the ways in which you can efficiently construct production pieces. During production, you will find a number of ways to avoid duplicating your tracks over and over. Most current software programs allow you to separate each element into a single track. Multitrack recording can provide you with great flexibility. The principle is to do as many operations in one step as possible before you mix down to a stereo version; for example, make the whole music bed (with all its tracks) in one step. Some software packages learn the mix as you practice, greatly simplifying the task of creating the proper background.

Another aspect of combining elements in production is to keep an open mind and use as many of the options available to you as possible. Is there an easier way to do things? Think about it, and don't always use the same routine out of force of habit. Use editing and dubbing techniques to their fullest in studio production.

Remember, you can use an edit on a computer software program, stand-alone DAW, digital cart, or MiniDisc for the following:

- Removing flubs from an existing recording
- Inserting questions, answers, or breaks
- Inserting **actuality** sound
- Tightening up and removing lapses in any program

You can make a dub to:

- Play back a sound source in a more convenient format (for example, putting a short selection of music on a digital cart to make it easier to locate)
- Take the place of an edit when you don't want to do destructive edits or cut legacy tape recordings and you're not concerned about adding another generation to the sound source
- Free up a piece of equipment
- Mix two or more sources together

Remember, working in the studio environment will almost always entail striving for excellent quality and efficiency of operation. Although some deviation in quality might be acceptable in live coverage of a news event, something produced in-studio must sound very good, with no lapses in mic technique or production values.

At the same time, remember that nowhere is the "time is money" equation more obvious than in the modern broadcast studio. There may be several people clamoring to use the studio, so doing your work in task-oriented sequence will be most efficient.

SUMMARY

Many programs are recorded in advance because they are too complicated to be assembled live on the air; in addition, program elements such as commercials that will be used over and over are recorded in advance so that the person on air does not have to keep reinventing the wheel to produce them.

Production studios vary widely in size and complexity, from small set-ups in the corner of a room to large operations complete with state-of-the-art equipment.

The most efficient production work is done in task-oriented sequence; that is, production is organized according to the demands of the production schedule. The work is not necessarily produced in final sequential order from start to finish. It may be more convenient, for example, to produce the end of the spot first, then the middle, and finally the beginning.

Music is an important element in recorded program production. It comes from many sources, including the station's standard airplay library and specially licensed production libraries. Sometimes, music is specially recorded for a particular commercial or other spot.

Miking multiple speakers usually involves setting up enough mics and channels so that the console operator can accommodate the natural variance in the power of the individuals' speaking voices.

APPLICATIONS

SITUATION 1/THE PROBLEM The producer was setting up for a show in which she would be running the board for an interview with three guests. The producer had set up one omnidirectional mic. Everything worked fine, but one of the guests happened to have a very, very soft voice.

ONE POSSIBLE SOLUTION Although it is a good choice under other circumstances, the one omnidirectional mic wasn't right for this situation. Instead, the producer set up two cardioids, making sure that the patterns didn't overlap. The two strong-voiced guests were in one pickup pattern; the weak-voiced guest was in the other. Thereafter, the levels could be matched.

SITUATION 2/THE PROBLEM The news director of a small station wanted to use a portion of a large office as an adjunct studio during election coverage. Unfortunately, the room was so lively that it sounded as though candidate interviews were being done in the shower.

ONE POSSIBLE SOLUTION The news director bought some heavy-grade cardboard at the local home-supply store. He made a frame of two-by-fours and used the cardboard as a partition, making the room (in effect) smaller. He also taped some old egg cartons to the wall to help deflect ambient sound and deaden the room noise.

EXERCISES

1. Prepare a commercial for a hypothetical upcoming concert. This very difficult production task is representative of the kind of activity you might be asked to undertake. This particular promo calls for the use of four cuts of a popular singer; although you generally don't use vocals for production work, you'll have no other choice when the assignment is to publicize a performance by a singer. To produce this spot, pick out a vocalist's CD from your personal collection or from your college's or station's production library. Here's the copy you will use to produce the spot:

   APPEARING LIVE AT THE CIVIC CENTER ON JUNE 12, _____ IN PERSON!

   (*first cut up, fade down*)

   JOIN _____ON HIS/HER FIRST TOUR OF _____ (YOUR LOCATION).

   HERE'S THE MUSICAL EVENT YOU'VE BEEN WAITING FOR.

   (*second cut up, fade down*)

   TICKETS ARE $25 AND $15 AND CAN BE PURCHASED FROM SMITH TICKET AGENCY OR AT THE CIVIC CENTER BOX OFFICE.

   (*third cut up, fade down*)

   DON'T MISS THIS CHANCE TO SEE ___ IN CONCERT AT THE CIVIC CENTER, JUNE 12 AT 7 P.M.

   (*close with vocal*)

   Depending on the equipment your school has, you can produce this spot in several different ways. If you have a DAW or computer with multitrack capability, you can dub the music onto different tracks and position them in appropriate places under your voice track. The software within the DAW will allow you to use cross-fading capabilities to make the transitions to music smooth.

2. This time, first prepare the music bed by dubbing the cuts onto an audio track on your digital workstation and then developing a playlist with the appropriate song segments, or use a digital cart machine to edit segments together. You won't be able to cross-fade, so butt the songs together. Now do the commercial by reading copy over the music bed. If your instructor wants, add your voice track to the music track and create a multitrack version of the spot. If not, practice reading the spot live over the music bed.

   There's no right or wrong way to produce this commercial, but trying it using several techniques will give you an idea of the advantages and limitations of each.

8

Live, On-Air Production

One of the surest tests of production ability is to pull an airshift. An airshift usually involves announcing and running the console, although today some radio stations have shifted to fully automated voice-tracked or assisted automation programming from a computer. If it's live, this is the point at which all other production techniques come into play; thus, during the airshift, you are using all of your skills to produce the flow of sound that marks the unique character of your station.

Let's assume that your airshift is live. You will, indeed, use all the skills we have discussed so far. The primary activity in an on-air situation is mixing sound sources through the console. Those sources, of course, go to the transmitter and over the air instead of to a sound file on a computer hard drive. It goes without saying that mistakes are to be avoided at all costs. There are no retakes, and a mistake such as a commercial that doesn't play because of a miscued audio file, which would be a mere nuisance in studio production, is a big problem on the air. For one thing, *dead air* is sloppy. To make matters worse, the commercial will have to be rescheduled (called a *make good*) and, in some cases, an apology given to the angry sponsor, especially if the commercial is tied to a dated event such as a special weekend sale.

An overall consideration of on-air production is the transition from source to source. Even though computers have greatly simplified the process today, this, really, is the essence of on-air performance. Most fast-moving formats center on what's called the *tight board*, meaning that there is hardly any space (in some cases, there is overlap) between sound sources. However, talk stations and many NPR (National Public Radio) stations often use pauses for effect and may not segue one sound with another. Experienced on-air producers develop a rhythm, a sixth sense of timing. Developing that sense is largely a matter of practice, though a thorough understanding of the job at hand will help.

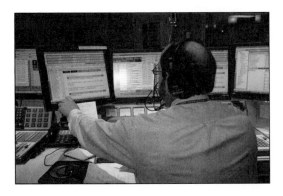

FIGURE 8.1

Today computer automation has helped simplify combo operations. Here, WCBS-AM News Anchor, Steve Scott is able to fire a commercial, a news report, or an actuality by using the mouse or touching the screen or using the broadcast console.

SOURCE: Philip Benoit

TYPICAL AIRSHIFT

On-air production is done by three types of radio station employees: the announcer who runs a board combo, the engineer who runs a board for an announcer, or a board operator at a station that may have automated part of its programming. The set-up used at your station will largely be determined by a combination of station practices and, in some cases, union rules. In general, only the largest markets have a separate engineer running the board for the announcer. Combo operations (see Figure 8.1) greatly outnumber engineer and announcer set-ups, and it is likely that you will be running the board combo in your initial radio jobs.

Today automation systems and computer technology have greatly simplified some of the tasks associated with doing an airshift. We talk more about this later in the chapter, but for the moment, let's assume that your station is not automated.

Duties of the On-Air Producer

An on-air producer—the staff announcer or disc jockey—handles the combo operation. This type of production is complex and stressful, and it usually involves most or all of the following duties:

- Running the console
- Cueing discs and/or recorded media, if music and commercials are not programmed into a computer (on systems that program music and commercials, the on-air talent frequently plays bumpers and stingers and announces live from a digital cart)
- **Riding levels** on sound sources going over the air
- Selecting filler music
- Announcing music, reading commercial copy, providing weather and traffic updates, and, in some cases, reading news
- Recording programs coming in from networks for delayed broadcast

- Answering the telephone

- Monitoring the Emergency Alert System

- Checking for important news, sports, and weather items of local interest, monitoring the news computer, and saving appropriate material for others in the station

- Doing general maintenance, such as filing media, filing commercial logs, dubbing sound files between the DAW and the playback machines (if they're not connected on a network), and sometimes (in very small stations) doing general cleanup

- Taking meter readings if this task is not automated

- Keeping the program log

- Playing back news actualities during newscasts

- Performing off-air production work (sometimes done on the audition channel) when a long program, such as a baseball game or prerecorded show, is airing

- In some cases, assembling and reading the local newscast

If you think these duties can be taxing, you're right. Pulling an airshift can be mentally exhausting. Although listeners might think that playing music and doing a little talking for four hours at a stretch is easy, anyone who's tried it knows that exactly the opposite is true. Audiences want announcers who are bright and cheerful. Filling several hours with interesting talk takes talent and practice.

Emergency Alert System (EAS)   In addition to the hard work involved, acting as an on-air producer involves some potentially critical duties. In times of emergency, for example, the on-air personality must communicate important information to the public in a timely manner. Weather emergencies often call for the on-air operator to relay news and information from local and area authorities.

There are many configurations of emergency systems. Your local authorities may have a system tied in with area stations, be it a radio transmission system or a telephone network. In addition, federal authorities require all stations in the nation to participate in the **Emergency Alert System (EAS)**, a government system established in 1994 that is designed to allow officials to warn the public about emergency situations. The EAS replaced the Emergency Broadcast System (EBS). The old EBS system linked radio stations to the federal government through a "tree" method where large stations would retransmit the alert to regional stations, which would retransmit it to smaller stations, and so forth. This system could only transmit a brief message.

Even though the system was originally designed for notification of national emergencies, broadcasters found that using smaller branches of the tree system allowed transmission of vitally needed weather emergency information. When the new EAS system was designed, officials decided to take advantage of these local capabilities and allow radio stations to customize their emergency inputs.

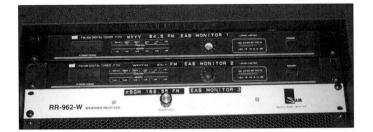

FIGURE 8.2

Emergency broadcast alert monitors. Note that there are separate EAS and weather alert monitors.

SOURCE: Fritz Messere

Now, an EAS alert can trigger several different sources, including weather stations, and the radio operator can receive and rebroadcast highly localized reports (see Figure 8.2).

The EAS monitor in the control room is activated by a *databurst*, which sends a message that can be digitally stored and replayed moments after reception. In the recent past, the vast majority of EAS alerts have involved weather emergencies and natural disasters, such as hurricanes and tornadoes. When Hurricane Katrina struck the Gulf Coast in 2005, radio was able to provide vital disaster relief information to victims while other media such as newspapers and television stations were unable to do so. Following the Katrina disaster, the Federal Emergency Management Agency (FEMA) proposed a new warning system that would integrate the EAS system with a new system called the Integrated Public Alert and Warning System (IPAWS). In 2010, FEMA announced plans to roll out software trials for IPAWS. With this expanded system, the EAS capabilities would expand to include the potential for the President to address the public during a national emergency.

Each radio station must successfully log and receive three EAS alerts per month and transmit alerts three times per month. In addition, a monthly full-scale random test of the system is activated by the federal government. State and local governments may also use EAS to deliver emergency weather information targeted to specific geographic areas.

The federal government, in cooperation with broadcasters, has also instituted the **AMBER** (America's Missing: Broadcast Emergency Response) plan, which uses the alert system to provide information about missing children. When officials confirm a missing child report, an alert is sent via the EAS system. Participating radio stations interrupt programming to provide a description of the abducted child and suspected abductor, and details of the abduction are broadcast to millions of listeners and viewers.

Finally, the Disaster Information Reporting System (DIRS) provides a systematic way to provide information about the status of local infrastructure during times of national and regional disasters. Broadcasters participate in DIRS on a voluntary basis.

Monitoring the EAS system is an important duty for the on-air producer. Each station's equipment is slightly different, and you will receive specific briefings from your station's management. You can learn more about the EAS at its home page: http://www.fcc.gov/pshs/services/eas/. Remember, although

THINK ABOUT IT • ETHICS AND RADIO PROMOTIONS

Promotions can and do get out of hand, and in a particularly tragic case, a Sacramento, California, woman died in January 2007, several hours after participating in a radio station's water-drinking contest.

There was a criminal investigation, but no charges were filed. The woman died of apparent water intoxication after drinking nearly two gallons of water in a contest held at the offices of station KDND.

The stunt involved seeing how long 20 participants who had drunk large amounts of water could wait before going to the bathroom, and the winner would receive a video-game console.

Several days after the death, the radio station fired five on-air personalities and five other staffers who participated in the contest, according to a report from the *Sacramento Bee*. Sacramento television station KOVR reported that the family was planning a civil suit against the station.

According to various press reports, disc jockeys joked about the possibility of people dying from water intoxication and teased the contestant about her bloated stomach. The *San Francisco Chronicle* reported that one disc jockey, who had been told by another jock, "We've got a guy who's just about to die," retorted, "Make sure he signs the release," setting off laughter in the studio.

An excess of water can alter the body's chemistry to such an extent that it can interfere with heartbeat and cause swelling of the brain.[1]

Questions for discussion: Where would you draw the line at a promotion? Do you think the water-drinking promotion was over the top, or was it simply a bizarre and tragic outcome that could have been anticipated? How does this square with reality TV, where all sorts of dangerous stunts are promoted? Is there a double standard?

---

1. Adapted from Ethics Newsline, "Woman Dies after Participating in Radio Station Contest," January 22, 2007, http://www.globalethics.org/newsline/2007/01/22/woman-dies-after-participating-in-radio-station-contest/ (Also available as Lee, Henry K. "Sacramento KDND not culpable in water contest." http://www.sfgate.com/cgi-bin/article.cgi?f=/c/a/2007/04/03/WATER.TMP. Accessed on 11/23/08.)

the duties of an on-air producer may be fun, those duties can also involve enormous responsibility.

Typical Schedule

How are these duties integrated into the working day? We've pieced together what is, from our experience, a fairly standard schedule for the morning and evening announcers at a medium-sized station (see Tables 8.1 and 8.2). We've broken down the duties into on-air and off-air tasks. Both of these schedules reflect the beginning of a typical shift, though there can be infinite variations on the themes presented.

Remember, the announcer is also responsible for introducing the music and must be informative and entertaining in the bargain.

SOUND OF THE STATION

The primary responsibility of the on-air producer is to provide programming that reinforces the format and goals of the station. The identifying characteristics of the radio station are encompassed and expressed in what's known, loosely, as the station's *sound*. The elements of the sound are not only the types of music played. Also dictating the sound are the pace, content, announcing style, and blending of the program sources.

Pace

The schedules shown in Tables 8.1 and 8.2 reflect an hour of programming for a rather slow-paced NPR station. In many of the more frenetic stations, the program elements come fast and furious—a jingle here, a joke there, and then a spot or commercial cluster.

Maintaining a pace means checking yourself to ensure that your on-air segments are not too long (or too short, depending on the station). The delivery, too, will vary according to the pace of the programming at your particular station.

TABLE 8.1   Morning Schedule

Time (A.M.)	On-Air	Off-Air
4:45		Arrives at station, unlocks doors, turns on lights
5:00		Logs into edit and print show rundowns, promos for later programs, national news credits
5:15	Plays updated weather forecast	Prepares first newscast
5:28	Handles live breaks, reads weather, promotes upcoming newscast	Tags show promo
5:33	Live newscast	Enters info into logs
5:35		Starts transmitter readings (6 transmitters)
5:39	Live break, presells upcoming features	Continues transmitter readings
5:40–5:49		Continues transmitter readings
5:49	Live break	Catches up on log entries, answers phone calls, takes some notifications of weather-related school closings (seasonal)

SOURCE: © Cengage Learning 2013

TABLE 8.2   Afternoon Schedule—Programming Primarily Automated

Time (P.M.)	On-Air	Off-Air
3:00–4:00	Monitor station operations	As described below
3:00–3:20		Voice track pre-recorded hour breaks, including weather forecast, underwriters; forward promotion and legal IDs for next three hours
3:20–3:30	Monitor program computer	Monitor changes in weather and respond to weather alerts (such as EAS test, winter weather, and school closings)
3:30–3:45	Monitor program computer	Generate and print out program and underwriting logs, scripts for underwriters; log program events
3:45–4:00	Monitor program computer	Arrange, edit, and produce 3- to 5-minute feature segment to air for next Morning Edition or Weekly Edition

SOURCE: © Cengage Learning 2013

Content

The content of a station is what you say and play. That sounds obvious, but maintaining continuity of content isn't as easy as it might seem. For an on-air producer, continuity of content is maintained by not playing a modern rock song on an easy listening station, or by not using a rapid-fire delivery when you are host of a Saturday night oldies program. Conversely, a hot-hits station wouldn't want the announcer to be too laid-back between two up-tempo selections. DJs usually develop a feel for matching song tempos and announcing.

Here's an important point to remember: Radio is primarily a local media, so often the content of the programming should reflect what is happening in the local community. Your station may have a community bulletin board, but in any event, it is important for you to know what is going on in your community.

Announcing Style

Although the focus of this book is production, on-air operations require a brief discussion of announcing. In combo situations, announcing and production duties are intertwined. The announcer is the producer, and vice versa.

Achieving the proper style of delivery is a matter of matching the style of the station's format. A country music station and a classical music station require different styles of communication. Whereas the country DJ may talk over the music at the beginning of a recording and talk about the artists who performed the music being played, the classical announcer will use a more formal style of delivery, leaving a gap between spoken introductions and the beginning of the recordings being aired. Also, the classical announcer will provide more information on composers than on artists.

To develop the skills that will help you become competent as an announcer, try to get as much practice as possible. If available at your school, take a voice and diction class and a class in oral interpretation. Take every opportunity to read copy in various radio styles, constantly striving for a conversational style. (It's not as easy as it sounds.) One major-market announcer says he developed ad-lib skills by describing the scenery as he drove his car to work each morning. Keep in mind that very few people are naturals at broadcast announcing. Hard work and constant practice are necessary for nearly everyone (see Industry Update on page 171).

Blending the Sound Sources

Some hot-hits stations have almost no on-air silence; in fact, some of these stations frequently combine as many sound sources as possible. The weather, for example, may be read over the instrumental lead-in to music; commercials always have music beds. **Segues** are common; another sound source is always brought up as a piece of music fades. You would not, however, want to blend sound sources this way on an adult-contemporary station, where the format is

---

RADIO RETRO • HELLO EVERYBODY IN RADIOLAND, THIS IS YOUR ANNOUNCER SPEAKING

What is an announcer supposed to sound like? There have been mixed opinions and changing trends on that score since the development of radio. Here's an overview, with a moral at the end.

Early radio announcers were almost all men, and back when radio was still something of an experimental medium, it was thought that a high tenor voice was the best for radio. A sharp, high voice, so the reasoning went, was necessary to pierce the interference and punch through on the radio signal. In opera, it's the male tenors that hit the loudest notes; the operatic tenor speaking voice therefore seemed to be the ideal for radio.

But when radio evolved into a show-business medium, reaching thousands or even millions with the voice of the person on-air, tastes shifted toward announcers who mimicked the popular style of oratory. Orators, people who spoke effectively to large groups, were usually men with booming bass voices. And so the *basso profundo* became the norm in radio, especially in news. The trend carried over to television,

with powerful bass newscasters such as Walter Cronkite dominating the airwaves. Announcers tended to try to sound like Cronkite even if they couldn't, sometimes with comical results.

Equally comical was the sing-song delivery of some disc jockeys. No one knows for sure why that particular style evolved, but one reasonable guess is that it was a vocal delivery that mimicked the highly stylized speech of the master of ceremonies or the vaudeville pitchman.

Today, there is pretty close agreement as to what an announcer is not supposed to sound like: he or she is not supposed to sound like either variety of announcer described above. The artificial voice is passé and sounds ludicrous. Instead, radio managers want people who can communicate on-air, with a style that demonstrates convincing one-to-one communication.

Remember: In radio, you are *talking to one person*. You are not orating, and you are not emceeing a show.

---

much more laid-back. Depending on the station's programming strategy, a country station may use a modified concept of blending sound sources.

Making sure your production values and techniques integrate with the sound of the station is one of the keys to successful on-air production. Following are some other suggestions that may prove helpful.

SUGGESTIONS FOR LIVE, ON-AIR PRODUCTION

We can't address every specific situation because content, formats, and equipment vary widely. But here are some general suggestions for on-air work, along with some cautionary recommendations derived from experience (sometimes unpleasant experience).

Console Operation

You're usually better off zeroing faders as a general rule. However, with the program computer or a digicart, you might want to leave the pot set at the appropriate level. With CD players it's a good idea to zero the fader to avoid cueing over the air. Be extremely careful with faders and selector switches that control the network lines and telephones. They have a habit of being left open when nothing is online. When a signal is fed, it can come as something of a shock to the air person who left the channel open.

INDUSTRY UPDATE • WHAT TO DO ... BUT MORE IMPORTANTLY, WHAT NOT TO DO

When you are running an airshift, you may be entertaining listeners with your patter and engaging them with the rhythm and sequence of what you play.

Or, you may be driving listeners away. Radio program directors worry as much—perhaps more—about people tuning out than people tuning in. Indeed, "tune-out" is a major factor in constructing the format and in choosing (and retaining) talent.

One of the top priorities of a producer who runs a shift and speaks over the air is to keep from irritating listeners. This doesn't necessarily mean *not* being personally disagreeable; some "shock jocks" would actually be an irritant and tune-out factor to listeners if they suddenly became mild mannered.

The point: Tune-out happens when listeners don't get what they expect. If they want to hear the music and the DJ talks over it, they tune out. If they want to hear the DJ talk and he or she doesn't, they tune out.

Avoid the following on-air irritants:

- *Too much hype.* Most staff announcers have toned down their deliveries. Generally, the "in your face" delivery is out of favor in even the hardest-format stations. Delivery today is much more personal.

- *Too much personal banter.* Frequently morning shows feature a female and male combo leading people through the morning commute. Avoid too much personal chatter. While audiences expect some good natured bantering back and forth, make sure that you also focus on the community and the area events.

- *Too many reminders about how much music you are playing.* Interviews with disaffected listeners confirm that when you continually stop the music to tell people how much music you are playing—

TEN HITS IN A ROW!—you irritate the audience. Remember that every time you say "less talk," you must talk to do it. If you are in charge of producing these "sweepers" (announcements about the coming music), bear this in mind!

- *Laughing at your own in-jokes.* Air people sometimes like to convince themselves they are funny by chuckling endlessly with the weather reporter, but this doesn't always seem entertaining to the listener.

- *Stepping on the end of songs.* Listeners may actually want to hear the ending and will resent you talking over it or dumping out of it completely. Research shows listeners are irritated by missing the ends of current hits. On a related note, don't talk over the end of songs that end cold (without fading out).

- *Getting tricky with the call letters.* Radio stations often use "handles," such as "Mix 101," that have no real relation to their call letters. As a result, when stations give the required legal ID (a direct statement of the call letters and place of station location) at the top of the hour, the announcers often try to bury it in a heavily produced montage that touts the station's handle. Listeners get annoyed by this. Just say the call letters, and don't make an enormous production of it.

- *Always talking over the beginning instrumental and butting up to the start of the vocal.* Focus groups say this is an irritant, and it is often perceived as a self-indulgent exercise on the part of the announcer.

- *Insisting that you peg the VU meter with every sound element.* Research shows that listeners are getting tired of ceaseless blasting.

Establishing a Routine

However you choose to run the console, do it consistently. Get into the habit, for example, of always checking to make sure the mic is not up on the console before you say anything. Incidentally, make it a habit never to swear while you're in the radio station. If you make this a personal rule, you'll never let an obscenity slip over the air. The problems engendered by swearing over the air can be pretty serious, and it does happen, so make it part of your routine to banish cuss words from your vocabulary the moment you get near a studio. Mics can be relied on to be open at exactly the wrong time.

One other caution: If your station uses a routing switcher to send inputs to the air console, make sure that you take the time to put all inputs back into their normal states.

Planning in Advance

A good console operator has to be like a good pool player who thinks several shots in advance to avoid getting into the position of not having a good shot. Think the same way in pulling an airshift. If your station does not have music preselected in a computer system, then organize as much music in advance as you can; get as many segments ready as possible. One phone call or other interruption can set you back significantly, and once you're "in the hole," it's hard to climb back out. Spend time each day preplanning your show for the next day. Are there events in the community that you'll want to talk about? Is there an important local sporting event that your listeners would be interested in? Thinking about your upcoming show should be the routine, not the exception.

Being Aware of False Endings

A **false ending** on a song is music that sounds as though it's going to wrap up—but doesn't. The announcer, by this time, has probably started talking and will step all over the real end of the song. This sounds very unprofessional. Checking the time-elapsed feature on a program computer can sometimes help you avoid this problem.

Sometimes commercials suffer from the same problem. You can avoid embarrassment and confusion by clearly labeling program material that has false endings. For example, if your station uses a computer for commercial playback, it may be possible to label the sound file with a way to identify such problems; for example, <Geno's Pizza—false>. Many stations label commercial segments with other endings. For example, if the commercial ends with music fading out, the word *fades* is added to the title; for example, <Geno's pizza—fades>. Most computer programs allow you to view the elapsed time for each program segment on the display. This can be helpful to the operator in determining when a commercial is coming to a close. It makes running a tight board easier, and it also avoids those embarrassing moments of silence known in the trade as *dead air*.

Listening to the Air Monitor

It's a good idea to keep the air monitor playing at a good volume. A low volume from the air monitor won't always allow you to hear, for example, the network line leaking over the air or a computer drive that is skipping. It is also important to monitor the station's broadcast through the off-air or air monitor source. Usually, audio console monitors allow you to choose among program, audition, and off-air sources. Though most experienced producers know this, many inexperienced operators have been surprised to find that the program they thought was being aired without a hitch was not broadcast at all because a patch was thrown or some other technical problem occurred without their realizing it. Why? Because the neophyte operators were listening to the program output of the board instead of to the off-air source. By the same token, keep your headset volume high enough to hear problems when you're announcing.

Clearing Equipment

Don't let CDs, discs, and the like pile up on the equipment; clear them out as soon as possible. If you don't, sometime you will need a playback machine in a hurry, and there won't be one available. If your station is still using an analog cart machine, you'll also be more likely to put a previously played cart on the air accidentally. Clearing the equipment as you go along is one of the best habits you can develop for efficient on-air production.

Planning for the Worst

Nowhere is a mistake more evident than in radio, where an embarrassing silence underscores the fact that the on-air producer has lost control. Today this happens rarely because most program segments are loaded into a computer program and played back one segment after the next. However, no technology is beyond failure, and if your program stops (for whatever reason), you'll need a standby audio source. One way to mitigate this problem when it occurs is to keep emergency material on standby (a one-minute public-service announcement, an extra CD cut, or the like). If your computer crashes, you'll have immediate material to back up your show.

You will also want to prepare for potential engineering difficulties. Learn how to find and run a mic cord in case the control-room combo mic fails and you have to run another one (assuming, of course, no union restrictions bar you from doing this).

WORKING WITH SATELLITE AND NETWORK SERVICES

An increasing amount of radio programming is beamed to the ground by satellite, received by dish antenna, and then rebroadcast over the local station. Such programming ranges from what is still anachronistically referred to as *wire-service* programming, such as news at the top of the hour, to a complete program schedule of music or talk.

News services, along with network feeds, don't enter a station by telephone anymore. While satellite reception of news and network programming has been standard practice for more than three decades, delivery of entire formats by satellite transmission is a relatively new practice, but it has already gained widespread acceptance as the programming has proven successful in many markets.

When a station receives programming via satellite, it is the final step in a series of actions known as the *satellite feed*.

The Satellite Feed

First, the program material is produced at the syndicator's studios and is beamed (in technical terms, **uplinked**) to the satellite. The satellite acts as a relay: It picks up the signal, amplifies it, and rebroadcasts it to the earth. Because of the extremely high position of the satellite, the signal coming to earth covers a wide geographic range, eliminating the need for multiple transmitters to reach remote stations. Satellites can perform this function because they are **geostationary**—parked over the equator in an orbit that is exactly synchronized with the earth's rotation so that the satellite always maintains the same relative position to the ground. Since satellites can retransmit dozens of signals from a variety of broadcast sources simultaneously, many radio program services, such as ABC's 14 radio networks that are carried on the AMC-8 satellite, use this technology as an efficient way to distribute programming to thousands of individual radio stations across the country.

Back on earth, the local station receiving the signal uses a **downlink**—a satellite dish, often located on station property—to bring the signal to a transponder, a device that tunes in the correct channel for the desired program. The output of the transponder is brought into the console as a program input.

Programming via satellite is very sophisticated today. Newer programming technology controls the downlink frequency bands via a Web-based browser. This allows the station to set up the downlink program schedule for the station from anywhere there's an Internet connection. In these interactive systems, the programs are permissioned and labeled for broadcasting using a special authorization key supplied by the programming service. The downlink receiver has a unique identification number that verifies that the station is entitled to downlink the programming. Satellite receivers have built-in hard drives that can store programs for downloading into the station's program computer. Once the program manager logs onto the Web, the browser page displays a series of tabs that identify recorded programs, program notes sent from the programming service, spot-related information, and other pertinent information for the station.

Programming from Satellite

Today, many types of program material are available. Here are some examples.

- *Services that provide complete music/sports programming in various formats.* Such services typically have a carefully constructed format and top-class announcers. One example of a successful program provider is Westwood One, which beams programming to more than 1,400 stations in the United States. Among the diverse programming that Westwood One provides are the following: CNN Radio News, CBS Radio, MTV Radio Network, BET Radio, CMT Radio, Power FM, and sports programming such as NFL and NCAA football. Similarly, Citadel Media provides programming from the

ABC network and many specialized shows such as *ESPN*, *Imus in the Morning*, *The Huckabee Report*, and *Cannon's Countdown* along with specific programming in a variety of formats such as classic hits, classic rock, today's country, and others.

- *Networks that provide specialty programming in part-time or full-time talk and information formats.* These services are enjoying growing popularity on the AM band, where music programming is on the decline, primarily because listeners who enjoy music prefer higher-fidelity FM stations. Such services include national call-in programs and specialized format areas such as *AdviceLine* from Talk Radio Network. One of the most popular weekly call-in shows is *Car Talk* from National Public Radio, which features the comedy antics and automotive advice of Tom and Ray Magliozzi.

  Some networks provide daily programs that fit into the local station's format. Cidadel Media's *Doug McIntyre's Red Eye Radio* covers overnights with a late-night show (1:00 A.M–5:00 A.M Eastern) with a talk radio format. Other services may offer short inserts, such as Westwood One's *Metro Networks* and *Shadow Traffic* program segments that provide news, weather, and sporting information to hundreds of radio stations in the United States.

- *Services that provide short-form programming for integration into member stations' existing formats.* Some of these programs are fairly substantial, such as *CMT's Country Countdown*, which is a weekly 3-hour countdown of the top 30 songs distributed by Westwood One, and Mike Harvey's *SuperGold*, an oldies request show heard on more than 350 stations nationwide every Saturday evening. Others are specials representing a wide variety of interests such as *Hollywood Confidential*, *The Beatles Years*, and *Weekly Country*. Thousands of discrete programs are beamed down to stations, including news-and-information magazine programs, news reports, sports programs, and many business programs.

Online and CD Services

The development of the Internet has created new ways to distribute programming quickly and cost effectively. Today, program providers allow affiliated stations to log on to websites that contain specialized programming tailored to meet the specific needs of many different station formats.

ABC Radio's *ePrep* is a service that provides a wide variety of programmatic material that can be downloaded by the local station using Contemporary Hit Radio (CHR)/Hot Adult Contemporary (AC), Country, News/Talk, International, and Rock formats. Each day, stations can access tour information along with up-to-the-minute music and entertainment news. Preproduced audio clips in an MP3 format provide stations with high-quality interviews and features that can enhance the locally produced show.

When the station programmer logs on, fully indexed pages and all content are summarized, making the addition of specialized programming fairly easy to use.

Other programs are distributed by CDs for airplay. For example, *American Gold with Dick Bartley* is a weekly oldies show distributed either on CD or online. Each week the program supplier provides affiliate stations with the 4-hour show. A cue sheet is provided with the program. Usually these shows provide a low-frequency cue tone that works with the station's automation system to automatically trigger local cut-ins.

How to Use Service Material

An on-air producer has many options in dealing with material downlinked from satellites or the Web, depending on the particular station's format.

Live Broadcast   If the downlinked material is inserted into a locally produced format, the on-air producer treats the transmission as he or she would any other network program. Engineering staff will have wired the output from the satellite transponder into the console. You simply open a console fader at the time—the exact time—the program is due to start. Newscasts, business reports, call-ins, and special music programs can all be broadcast in this fashion.

Delayed Broadcast   Often the material is recorded for later airplay; sometimes this function is automated. For example, large all-news stations typically receive a plethora of news feeds from various services and opt to automate recording machines to save this material. News producers then sort through the feeds at their convenience and edit particularly useful material for inclusion in newscasts. If there is no automation, the on-air personality is often responsible for recording the feed while performing other on-air duties. This usually involves patching the feed into a control-room computer, digital cart, or MiniDisc and then starting the recorder manually.

Program segments are also available from FTP (file transfer protocol) websites and the station simply logs on to the website and downloads a program file containing the correct program. Once the file is downloaded into the station's program computer, it can be scheduled to play at the appropriate time.

Local Insertion   In some cases, the on-air producer receives the complete program by satellite and must insert local programming, which usually accounts for a small but important portion of the broadcast day. Such programming includes local commercials, news, weather, and locally oriented public service programming.

Generally, satellite services will provide local affiliates with clear guidelines for the exact times allocated for local access. One common method is to use a clocklike representation called a *hot-clock* or *pie*, which shows each hour's programming and shows when

1. the service will be broadcasting music and commercials.
2. local affiliates can insert their commercials. Each hour, affiliates might be allowed a maximum of 10 to 12 minutes of commercial time, with 2 to

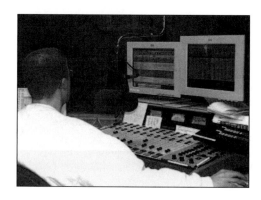

FIGURE 8.3

Corey Anderson at KOGA programming breaks on the NexGen Studio 22 automation system.

SOURCE: Prophet Systems

6 minutes' worth of commercials originating from the network. The remaining time is also allocated for local station identifications, commercial inserts, and promotional announcements.

Some services allow several minutes of optional time during which satellite programming is still delivered, but local affiliates may opt to insert their own material (see Figure 8.3).

Although inserts can be done manually, usually the system is automated. A signal embedded in the satellite feed automatically triggers the station's automated computer system to begin playing a liner, station ID, or commercial cluster.

Automation software usually has its internal clocks synchronized to the 24-hour clock of the satellite to ensure that local cut-ins are precise with no dead air. After the scheduled events are played, a *rejoiner* is played as the local automation system reconnects with the satellite feed. The handoff between the satellite feed and the local announcements occurs seamlessly. Frequently listeners don't know that they are listening to an automated satellite feed. The automation software has built-in capabilities to pause the system so the station can go live for late-breaking news or airing other remote broadcasts. There are many safety features built into the system to account for unexpected eventualities, such as a sporting event running longer than expected.

Satellite networks have devised methods to allow the network announcer to feed, through private lines or via the Internet, local IDs and event announcements. These are played back on cue, allowing virtually complete local customization to the program. (For additional information on computer-based automation, see Chapter 15.)

SUMMARY

On-air production usually refers to running the console live during a broadcast program. When the announcer runs his or her own board, this is known as *running combo*. The duties of an on-air producer are eclectic and usually include such

YOU'RE ON! • TECHNIQUES FOR EFFECTIVE ON-AIR PERFORMANCE: AD-LIBBING

Ad-lib means, literally, to speak "at pleasure." You are saying what comes to your mind rather than what's written on the script. Ad-libbing is a critical skill for radio announcers, and to an extent it is a skill that can be learned and taught.

Here are some principles that can help you ad-lib gracefully.

- *Don't just open your mouth and let the words flow.* You must plan what you are going to say in at least some measure. Inappropriate ad-libs have ruined many a career.

- *Have a well of knowledge from which to draw your material.* It is essential that you are familiar with the music, the artists, and, if you are working in news, with current events. In fact, knowledge of current events is critical to every on-air position because events have a way of working themselves into any format.

- *Use this three-step process:* (1) Plan and encapsulate—sum up what you want to say in a few mental notes, (2) deliver the ad-lib in bite-sized pieces, and (3) keep it short. For example, you might be planning a weather ad-lib. Instead of opening your mouth and letting fly (or inserting foot), break down what you want to say and encapsulate it:

—It's still hot and dry

—but some badly needed rain is on the way.

—It's going to rain all weekend, but right about now most people will welcome a change in weather.

Now you can take a breath and deliver those three ideas in three or four phrases.

- *Remember to keep it short!* Beginning announcers almost always run too long, sometimes painfully long.

- *Before you say anything, think about whether it's appropriate.* Do you want to say something, or just talk? If it's the latter, play another CD cut.

- *Avoid in-jokes.* They seem funny to you and the person in the next room, but they are generally lost on the listener.

- *Practice eliminating pauses and interjections.* Saying "uhhhh" or taking long pauses is annoying. Although everyone needs to collect his or her thoughts from time to time, remember that interjections are more habit than necessity. If you consciously work to eliminate them, you will be surprised at how quickly you can do so.

- *Know the rules.* Beginning announcers are often surprised at how many restrictions and guidelines exist for what will be said on air. Sometimes, station management will go so far as to hand you a Rolodex with lines you are expected to say. Although this is frustrating, there is some reasoning behind it: Station management often has undertaken extensive research to find out what

varied tasks as playing or reading commercials, public service announcements, and news; taking meter readings; operating all control-room equipment; pulling CDs for airplay; and filling in the station *log*—an official FCC (Federal Communications Commission) document.

Operating a console during a live program can be a difficult chore. Some of the operator's responsibilities are to maintain the integrity of the station's sound and to maintain the proper pace, content, and blending of sound sources.

Running the board can be made considerably less complicated if you establish a "safety first" routine: close faders and program switches, recue program segments, and so on. Plan your board operations; think the way a good pool player does, several shots ahead. Above all, be careful around microphones; they have a habit of being left open at inopportune times.

the audience does and does not want to hear. At the same time, remember that in most cases the music, rather than the announcer, is the "star." Find out what management expects you to say and work within the guidelines—at least at the beginning.

- *Know your format.* Ad-libbing requirements vary from station to station and from format to format, but, as an example, here are some principles that are relatively constant:

    Country music requires a good knowledge of the material. It's very difficult to fake. And it is hard to fake liking this music. If you hate country, it's nearly impossible to pull it off. Remember that country music fans are intolerant of announcers who mix up names and facts about the artists. In addition, *never* make fun of the music.

    Adult Contemporary often features the announcer in a "facilitator" role, bringing traffic, weather, school closing info, and so on all together in one place. In general, ad-libs that draw too much attention to the announcer's personality detract from the format, so you may find yourself required to submerge your personality somewhat.

    In Contemporary Hit Radio, Urban Contemporary, or Top 40, there are several types of personalities, including the rock jock, who keeps up a steady patter of information about the artists and the music, and the outrageous jock, who frequently skirts the boundaries of taste by wielding insulting humor. At the extreme is the shock jock, whose reason for being is to annoy people and attract audiences who want to see how far the DJ will go. Be careful if you try to emulate shock jocks, because unless you have the considerable audience and financial clout of Howard Stern, it is unlikely you will find any station management willing to put up with the headaches you cause. Make it a point to back off when your instincts warn that you are approaching the danger zone. But if edgy humor is required, don't back off too much; keep an eye on other humorists and see how they make their jokes work and how they get away with it.

- In news or news-talk, there is no substitute for knowledge. You just can't fake an understanding of the news. When it comes to ad-libbing in this genre, be careful. One misstep could bring on a libel suit. Generally, you should follow the plan, encapsulate strategy, and *stick to what you know*. When ad-libbing news or information, don't speculate. You're much better off saying nothing than giving incorrect information. Also, be careful you don't come off as a know-it-all, especially when interviewing. If you ask a question, make sure you give the guest adequate time to answer the question. Finally, don't speak down to the audience, and be respectful.

Modern satellite feeds allow the on–air producer to interact with a broadcast fed from one central transmission point. In some cases, all the program functions are automated, but sometimes the on–air producer needs to insert local news and weather.

APPLICATIONS

SITUATION 1/THE PROBLEM An announcer's music show ends at 7 o'clock, when she has to hit the network. One problem she's been encountering is that the end of the show has been sloppy: She is always having to pot down the last MUSICAL SELECTION in midsong to hit the net.

ONE POSSIBLE SOLUTION The announcer adopted an upbeat instrumental for her theme song and started the cut, which ran 3 minutes, 20 seconds, at 6:56:40. She didn't put the cut over the air immediately, though: The selection was dead-potted until the previous record ended at around 6:58:10. The announcer then began her *outro* (a colloquial radio term meaning the opposite of *intro*) patter and faded up the dead-potted cut, talking over it.

Because the instrumental—which had a climactic ending—was back-timed to end perfectly, the announcer was able to hit the net cleanly and give a definite ending to her show. (Many announcers who have a standard theme keep it on digital cart or in the program computer.)

EXERCISES

1. Do a mock airshift that includes these elements: three disc cuts, two weather reports, a commercial or public service announcement, and at least 15 seconds of patter. Your airshift should use three styles:

   - Adult contemporary (AC)
   - Fast-paced hot hits or modern rock
   - Laid-back, album-oriented rock

   Don't worry so much about the quality of announcing because that's not the real purpose of this exercise. You should focus on production values. For example, would you talk over the instrumental introduction of a rock cut? How about the ballads for the AC or a country format?

2. Pick three local stations and describe their sound in terms of production values. Listen for things like music and talk overlapping. Does the announcer talk for only a couple of seconds at a time? Conversely, does the announcer spend extended periods in patter? Write down your observations, and discuss how the production values reinforce the sound of the stations.

3. This exercise is done strictly to time. You must fit all the elements into a 10-minute segment:

   - Exactly 1 minute of reading news copy
   - Exactly 30 minutes of commercial copy
   - A CD or musical cut from 2 to 4 minutes long
   - Exactly 1 minute of community calendar listings from the local paper
   - Enough weather to get you through the remaining time

   Dead-pot an instrumental disc while you are reading copy; the music must end exactly when your 10 minutes are up

9

More about the Computer in Radio Production

Today the computer is the essential tool in radio production. At almost all stations it has replaced both tape recorders and analog cart machines, and although it should be remembered that a computer is only one of several tools necessary for radio production, it is probably the most important.

Technological wizardry is not an end in itself; rather, it is a faster and more capable method of manipulating information, creating effects, and controlling various work functions. In this chapter, we address computer technology as it relates to both production and operations. In particular, we focus on applications of the computer to computer-generated effects, computer-assisted editing, on-air production, automation, programming, Web activities, and digital audio broadcasting. In our exploration of computers, we will repeat some material introduced in previous chapters, both for the sake of continuity and so that this chapter can stand alone as an assignment to be read out of numerical order. However, we have tried to keep redundancy to a minimum.

Before zeroing in on the specifics of radio applications, let's briefly review some basics of the computer itself.

COMPUTER BASICS

Today, few areas of modern life have been untouched by the digital revolution and the computer technology that powers it. But sometimes it appears as if those who really understand the workings of the device try to mystify the uninitiated with incomprehensible jargon. (Many of us have trouble understanding simply because the terminology is unfamiliar.) The basics of computer operations are readily understood today. Although particular **hardware** (the computer itself) and **software** (the programs used to make the computer perform particular tasks) vary, whether PCs or Macs, they do the same types of tasks in roughly the same manner. In fact, with today's cloud computing and mobile capabilities, most computer systems work together pretty well. However, in radio PCs have been the preferred machine since they were more easily modified than Mac computers. Today, Macs can run OSX, Windows, and Linux simultaneously, so those differences are becoming less important.

As you already know, computers operate digitally; that is, they work by sequencing large strings of "on" and "off" pulses. The on-and-off code is expressed in digits. (See Chapters 3 and 4, which contain an introduction to digital technology.) The concept of classifying information as "on" or "off" dates to the 1700s. One of the first digital applications was in a Jacquard weaving loom. Paper punched with holes (later replaced by a card) determined the position of a part of the loom. If there was a hole in the card, the loom would perform a certain operation; if there was no hole, the loom would operate differently. The on-or-off principle was used to program the pattern for an entire woven cloth. Later, punch cards were used in a wide variety of applications in manufacturing and calculation. Herman Hollerith used paper punch cards in 1890 for the U.S. Census, starting the data collection revolution.

Speedy calculation—the computer's forte—did not become feasible on a large scale or affordable by consumers until the development of printed circuits and low-cost micro devices, called microprocessors or central processing units (CPUs). Using a process called *photolithography*, a hybrid of photography and engraving, scientists produce a huge variety of different kinds of microelectronics on a chip of a material called *silicon*. Modern CPUs contain millions of transistors strung together on a silicon wafer.

CPUs are the brains of the computer, performing the on-and-off tasks—the manipulation of digits—that constitute the calculation process. The on-and-off function is determined in each instance by the presence or absence of an electrical signal. A system offering these two choices—on and off—is known as a **binary** process; the computer represents information through this binary coding. A sequence of on-and-off pulses is used to denote numbers and letters.

Generally, instructions and information are put into the machine through a keyboard, and the commands and a readout of the information are viewed on a monitor. Today, many modern computers actually have two, four, or more processors, accelerating the computing process and adding functionality to the current generation of software.

The computer stores and retrieves information from a program in **random access memory**, or **RAM**. The other type of memory in the computer is the **read-only memory**, or **ROM**, which is built into the computer at the factory and cannot be changed. ROM usually contains internal instruction sets needed by the computer to start up properly.

The information in RAM, which is usually where the software program is loaded, along with whatever information has been entered from the keyboard, touch screen or sound card, stays there only as long as the computer is turned on, which makes long-term storage in RAM impractical. For this reason, computers are equipped with storage mechanisms, usually in the configuration of a device for writing information on a hard disc. However, many mobile devices and netbooks now use **flash memory**, which functions as RAM and storage together. While flash memory has an advantage over hard drives because it can read and write instantaneously, it is more expensive than standard disc storage.

The computer's strength is its ability to manipulate information. Simple storage is not a particularly compelling reason to use a computer. For example, you might have 2,000 sound effects in the station's library. However, should you desire to find all the sound effects calling for footsteps, your task would be difficult if you had to scroll through a list of every sound effect by hand. However, this search can be accomplished in a few seconds by the computer, which will patiently but quickly check the keywords in the sound file for the words that match with the words you identify.

Such inhuman patience and speed also have many applications in the field of radio. For example, consider how computers now enable a producer to store, organize, and edit a variety of sound files.

COMPUTER-GENERATED EFFECTS

We have already discussed how computers can be used to store and edit sound files, but they have uses beyond these functions. Musicians and independent commercial producers often take advantage of the versatility of programs that use computers to generate original music for commercials and station production. Computers can be connected to a large variety of keyboards and synthesizers using **MIDI** (musical instrument digital interface) technology. Some producers with musical ability use a MIDI controller device (see Figure 9.1) to synchronize the reproduction of sound files created with electronic musical instruments, such as keyboards within audio software such as Adobe Audition, Pro Tools, Cubase, GarageBand, and other music mixing programs.

Many digital sound reinforcement and mixing consoles have MIDI inputs and outputs built into the unit so the console's faders can be turned on or off from within the computer software program. A producer with some musical skills can also use the computer as a MIDI controller in conjunction with a synthesizer (see Figure 9.2). A keyboard linked to a synthesizer can produce a wide variety of sounds. Some synthesizers, for example, produce realistic sounds by combining many different tone and frequency generators together. Each generator is called a *voice*, and synthesizers can use them to produce *virtual instruments*, the sounds of grand pianos, brass, wind, drums, percussion instruments, and so forth. Some synthesizers can produce many sounds simultaneously. A synthesizer that can simultaneously play several voices that sound like different instruments (say, a bass guitar and a piano) and allow you to control those voices separately is called *multitimbral*. Using a multitimbral synthesizer, you can reproduce the sound of a small band or create small sound loops for use in commercial beds.

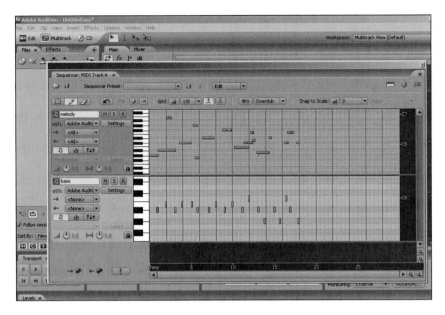

FIGURE 9.1

Adobe Audition contains a powerful sequencer that lets the producer interact with virtual and hardware instruments.

SOURCE: © 2013 Adobe Systems, Inc.

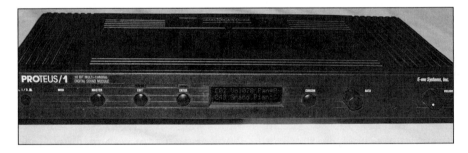

FIGURE 9.2

This MIDI synthesizer is capable of producing the sounds of many different instruments simultaneously.

SOURCE: Fritz Messere

A *sequencer* is a device that enables you to record different channels of MIDI information into some kind of memory device, such as a hard drive. Computers are frequently used as sequencers, and they allow you to record 16 or more channels of information. Although MIDI has many functions that cannot be covered in this broad treatment, here are a few ideas to think about. By using a sequencer, you can control a multitimbral synthesizer or several synthesizers simultaneously.

The sequencer does just what the name implies: It sends a sequence of data to the synthesizers, drum machines, and other devices, instructing them to play a certain note at a certain time, to make it a certain loudness and length, and to make it sound like a particular instrument.

Many firms specialize in providing music and effects software to users of MIDI sequencers; more than one company currently offers loops on CDs. The variety of sounds, coupled with the computer's ability to manipulate each sound and to create music and musical effects, makes the MIDI system an attractive alternative to sound-effects and theme-music libraries on CD, which can cost more than $1,000 per year to license.

COMPUTER-ASSISTED EDITING

As noted in previous chapters, digital technology has replaced the use of razor blades and splicing tape at all but a handful of radio stations. Digital audio work-station (DAW) technology makes it possible to perform sound editing functions with far greater ease and accuracy than ever before. The use of computer hard drive audio recording has essentially eliminated the need for tape as a medium for storing the audio information you will edit.

The typical editing suite uses digital storage of all information on one or more hard drives—music, dialogue, and sound effects. As hardware costs declined, stations moved more and more audio to digital files archived on hard drives. Some stations use a network so that files can be shared between editing suites and control rooms. Many DAW systems are available for both PCs and Macs. A few other systems are proprietary and use their own operating systems. Table 9.1 gives you some examples of popular systems and their uses. Modern laptops and mobile devices make it possible to edit complex audio almost anywhere.

T A B L E 9.1   Editing Software Comparison Chart

Software Package	Platform	Primary Usage	Comments
Adobe Audition 5.0	Mac/PC	Editing and multitrack mixing	Full editing and multitrack capability; very popular with broadcasters
BIAS Peak Pro 6.0	Mac	Editing and mastering	2-track editor—exceptionally fast with real-time effects rendering
SONY Sound Forge 9	PC	Editing and recording	Upgraded multitrack and production software
Digidesign Pro Tools 9.0	Mac/PC	Editing and multitrack mixing	Newly reworked version of the most popular software; a steep learning curve but extremely flexible
BIAS Deck 3.5	Mac	Multitrack mixing	Multitrack companion to Peak; records up to 64 tracks; allows multiple effects
SAW Studio Basic	PC	Editing and multitrack mixing	Scaled-down version of SAW Studio; excellent editing capabilities

In modern digital workstations, the operator uses one of several methods of locating and retrieving the various sources to be edited together so that they can be manipulated. These include highlighting, creating regions, and scrubbing the sound file. The edit can be made and auditioned, and if the edit point proves to be incorrect or some other aspect of the edited playback is unsatisfactory, the points on the waveform can be changed and the edit redone. (See Chapter 6 for a complete description and illustrations.)

As mentioned previously, modern software allows you to use nondestructive editing. There is no risk of losing or damaging the original audio material because the process that takes place on the screen can be reversed without damage to the original sound file. The operator can repeat the process again and again until a satisfactory edit is achieved. Usually the audio material in use during the editing process is stored on the hard drive in a sound file while the edits are stored separately in the computer memory as a *virtual track* or as a *scratch track* (a separate temporary file on the hard drive), so there is no risk of destroying the original through mistakes in editing. Once the edit has been satisfactorily made, the resulting new material will be stored as a new file for eventual use in whatever way is intended.

How can sound be represented on a computer screen? DAW systems create a waveform on the computer screen, as we discussed earlier in this book. When the editor recognizes the portion of the waveform that corresponds to the material to be deleted, the mouse (or other pointing device) is used to delete that portion of the wave pattern. Again, if an error is made, the information can be redisplayed and the process repeated until a good edit is achieved. The edited version of the sound file is stored temporarily by creating a virtual track.

Software technology has made it very easy to eliminate some of the noise that may occur on a recording. An audio waveform representation, sometimes called a **sound envelope**, is much easier to work with and manipulate than you might at first imagine. For example, suppose that in producing a station promo, you begin by playing back a recording of an announcer speaking. Let's assume that the announcer has recorded the words "WRVO Oswego Public Radio." As you play back the sound file, you will see the varying patterns displayed as the words are spoken. Because you can stop, start, or reverse the words, you have the ability to monitor how the waveform changes with the spoken words. (The same can be accomplished in dealing with music.)

We've specifically recorded noise at the beginning of a sound file for demonstration purposes. By looking at the sound pattern on the computer screen, you can easily identify the noise as the pattern that hovers around center line. It has a small but constant waveform. (See Figure 9.5.) The waveform of some electronically produced noise is different in character from that of natural sound. In many cases, it has only a positive or negative waveform, and for reasons that are beyond the scope of this chapter, the pattern often falls visually on only one side of the center line. To edit out the noise, the producer can simply select the portion of the sound pattern that represents the noise and instruct the computer to delete that pattern.

In some instances it is not possible to simply delete the noise as we have done here. Software packages such as BIAS's SoundSoap can remove pops, clicks, and audio hum from recordings. SoundSoap has a *Learn Noise* feature that automatically eliminates not only intermittent sounds but also background noise such as air conditioning. Another useful feature is called *Preserve Voice*. Using this feature, the software automatically removes extraneous sound outside the human voice range. SoundSoap can be used as a standalone program or as a plug-in application within audio editing programs. Other programs that offer similar functions are available for audio workstations, and most do a reasonable job of removing unwanted audio. But the best idea is to always strive for recording the highest quality audio in the first place.

The steps in a typical digital editing sequence are illustrated and described below. There is a pause and some noise before the announcer begins. He or she has already read the copy "WRVO Oswego Public Radio."

Suppose that you want to remove the word *public* and make the ID simply "WRVO Oswego Radio." Here's one way to approach the task. The directions below reflect the commands found in ProTools. (This sound file was edited in ProTools 9 HD.)

1. Move the mouse pointer to the part of the wave that indicates the extraneous noise before the announcer says the call letters WRVO. By using the Scrubber tool, it is possible to scrub back and forth through the waveform to hear the section in real time. This will help you to determine the exact beginning and end of the unwanted section. Once the exact section is located, switch from the Scrubber tool to the Selector tool to highlight the unwanted portion of audio. Using the Delete key removes the unwanted noise (see Figure 9.6a).

2. Next we're going to remove the word *public* from the audio file. Mark the waveform that corresponds to the word *public* using the same technique (see Figure 9.6a). Using the Cut function from the edit menu removes the unwanted word (see Figure 9.6b). ProTools is a complex program and provides the user with a number of ways to control edits. These functions include *Shuffle*, *Spot*, *Slip*, and *Grid*. For example, using editing controls in the Grid mode allows the editor to remove audio sections while maintaining spaces between edited regions (see Figure 9.6c). In the Shuffle mode, the sound file closes over the highlighted area of the unwanted word. These editing modes provide the user with control over how each edit is handled.

3. Depending on your needs, you could manipulate the computer to eliminate the word *public* and splice *WRVO* and *radio* together. If there is too much or too little space between the words, you can call up the previous menu and rework the edit. Since we are in the Grid mode, we are going to highlight the word *radio* (see Figure 9.6c) and combine it with the station's call letters (see Figure 9.6d).

INDUSTRY UPDATE • CREATING PRODUCTION BEDS • SONICFIRE PRO AND GARAGEBAND

SonicFire Pro 5 is one of several computer-based programs that allow a producer to create royalty-free music or sound effect beds for radio commercials or audio tracks for video segments. It runs on either the Mac or PC platform and uses the power of a computer to facilitate logical transitions between pre-recorded music segments. SonicFire Pro is able to build custom audio beds of specified length. While the program is best suited to video applications, it does provide radio producers with the ability to create a wide range of customized musical beds without needing any musical training.

In the *Express Track* mode, a producer can search for specific categories of music by style, mood (instrumentation), intensity, or some other feature. The music segments come in either stereo or multitrack selections and can be purchased directly off the Web. Once a multitrack version is selected, *Express Track* can compute all the possible musical arrangements available for that piece (see Fig. 9.3). The variations in style or

mood often reflect additions to or subtractions from the full arrangement of the piece. A very useful feature in the multitrack mode is to select the dialog version in mood settings, and this creates a piece that is tailored to be used under voice.

The producer can also select any time segment and the program automatically develops a version to the precise time needed. By varying the relative proportion of the different music layers, you customize the overall mix. For example, it is possible to specify a 13-second theme with rhythm and brass and have the software program develop this bed for immediate use. If the music is good but the timing is wrong, you can (for example) specify a 14.5- or 15-second theme with rhythm, and the computer will immediately produce the new variation requested. When looking for the right type of music within a specific time parameter, this is a very useful feature. The key to making this software work is to use the power of the software to adjust the parameters of the musical choice. Suppose

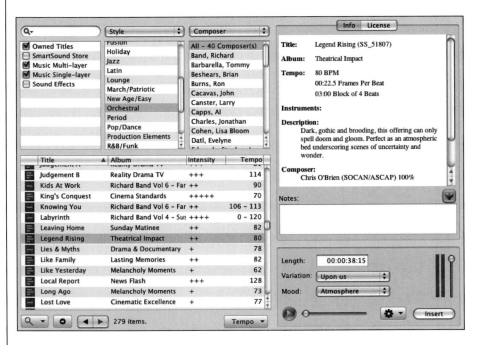

FIGURE 9.3

Software programs like SonicFire Pro provide producers with the ability to create royalty-free music beds that meet specific tempo, time, and thematic production requirements.

SOURCE: SmartSound

that SmartSound created a bed that timed out right but had too many components. Using the *mix* feature of the program, a producer can modify it by adjusting all the audio levels of the instruments in the piece. Dozens of libraries containing different kinds of music are available, but a producer can use Express Track Web and preview individual selections online. Once the right piece is found, purchasing that one or many tracks is pretty simple. Using different discs allows you to change your beds by using different genres or styles of music as well as changing the mood, tempo, or theme. For example, some discs focus on acoustic themes, others contain orchestral music or Latin rock, and still others provide sound effects that allow the user to mix sound elements together while specifying parameters such as bed length, tempo, and style.

The output can be saved as either a WAV or an AIFF file, so the music bed can be easily imported into any standard digital audio software program.

In 2004 Apple Computer introduced GarageBand, an inexpensive music recording and creation software package, which allows a producer to develop music soundtracks using pre-recorded digital instruments and MIDI music loops. However, in addition to using pre-recorded loops, this application also lets you record up to eight music tracks, as you would with multitrack recording software, or you can import music files into the program. This capability gives you great flexibility. In addition to the ability to record vocal tracks and

other special instrumentation along with the MIDI track for commercial use, you can import already created musical beds and then add voice tracks or sound effects tracks over the music. The GarageBand screen looks like other multitrack set-ups with audio level and panning features, but the tracks can either be recorded directly or pulled in from the music libraries that come with the software. Interestingly, the latest version of GarageBand includes jingles and special production tools such as ducking, a process that dynamically reduces the volume level of musical beds under voice tracks. These new capabilities may enhance the production sophistication of small radio stations and production houses. Additional loops packages (see Figure 9.4) and websites with new samples extend the number and kinds of instruments and rhythms available, making it possible to develop unique beds for particular clients.

The advantage of creating custom mixes for commercial clients is obvious.

Frequently custom music is scored, arranged, and produced by small audio production houses. If the station has a client who is unwilling to pay for original music scoring but wants a special sound, software packages such as SonicFire Pro and GarageBand may provide a low-cost alternative to hiring musicians to create original music scores. Producers with some basic musical knowledge can create fairly advanced production tracks for their clients.

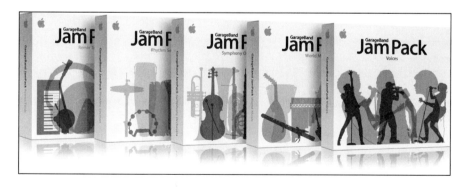

FIGURE 9.4

GarageBand allows a producer to create music beds using digital recordings of real instruments or MIDI notes in a multitrack environment.

SOURCE: Apple Computer

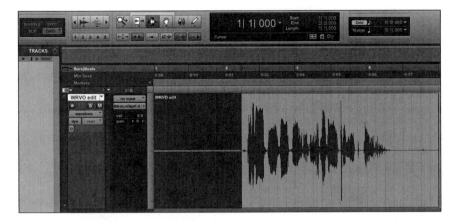

FIGURE 9.5

The smaller repetitive waveform represents noises before the larger waveform, which represents a vocal waveform.
SOURCE: Digidesign, Inc.

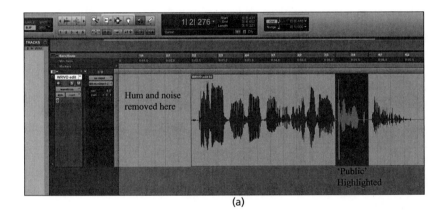

Hum and noise removed here

'Public' Highlighted

(a)

a. This waveform represents an announcer saying "WRVO Oswego Public Radio." We removed the extraneous noise before the announcer speaks, and highlighted the word "public."

SOURCE: Digidesign, Inc.

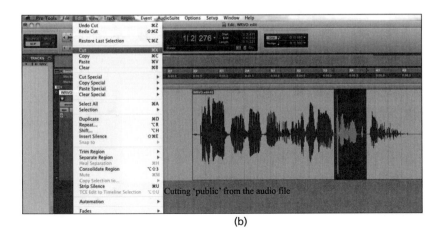

Cutting 'public' from the audio file

(b)

b. The word "public" has been highlighted in this recording. By selecting Cut from the edit menu, we will remove the highlighted segment.

SOURCE: Digidesign, Inc.

FIGURE 9.6

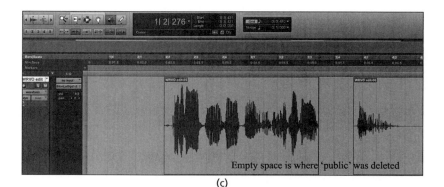

c. The empty space between the two waveforms is where we deleted the word "public."

SOURCE: Digidesign, Inc.

(c)

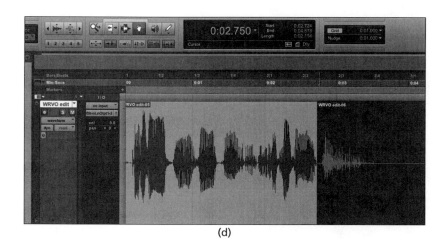

d. We've combined the two sections, completing our edit.

SOURCE: Digidesign, Inc.

(d)

FIGURE 9.6 (continued)

4. Your options don't end here. You could add reverb to the words, mix music beneath them, equalize the voice track, or speed up or slow down the pace of the words. Using the time shift ability in ProTools, the ID has been shortened from 2.1 seconds to 2.0 seconds (see Figures 9.7a and 9.7b).

Today's audio workstations can do basic and advanced editing, plus much more. While Macintosh computers seem to be favorites of musicians and music producers who use MIDI programs to interface with computers and synthesizers, many broadcasters prefer Windows-based systems that can be integrated with other broadcast equipment that works in the PC environment.

In addition, many systems are being integrated into networks, allowing files to be shared among different workstations in the broadcast or production complex.

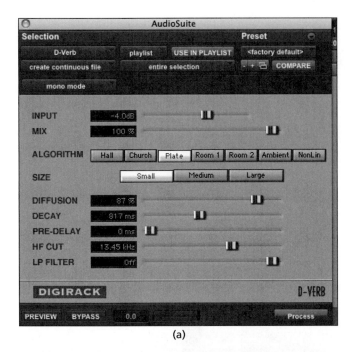

(a)

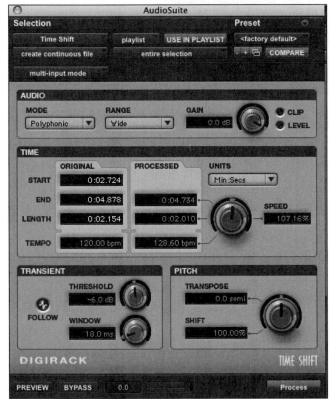

(b)

FIGURE 9.7

Software capabilities of modern digital workstations simplify the process of adding effects, such as reverberation and changing the actual timing of the recorded segment Figure a and b.

SOURCE: Digidesign

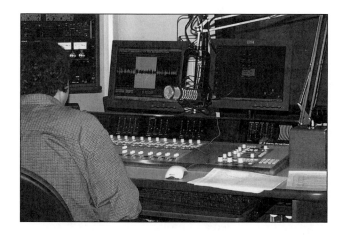

FIGURE 9.8

The editor in this production booth has called up the digital audio workstation as an input on this digital console.

SOURCE: Fritz Messere

The traditional radio console, incidentally, is becoming smarter thanks to digital and networking technology. One trend is to connect audio consoles as part of a larger network that shares input and output resources. In essence, a smart bridge connects all inputs and outputs and then routes those signals to various audio console surfaces as users call them up. For example, a CD unit may be called up in one studio while another person working in a production studio calls up a sound file from another input gear from the audio router. The actual mixing and switching is accomplished within the central audio processor, but the person working in the studio is actually controlling the mix (see Figure 9.8). Since the technology for routing signals and processing is all housed within the central audio processor, a simple CAT 5 cable can be used to connect audio console control surfaces. TCP/IP networking connectivity allows digital consoles to talk with computers running specific software and with digital workstations. This greatly simplifies both the wiring and operations for radio stations.

Some digital consoles use computer software to recall particular settings. For instance, you might have a particular set-up for leading into the news. Some digital boards allow you to store and name the switch and fader settings for each operator's task. All this can be programmed into the board's memory, with the correct levels coming up each time. The ability to set up these new audio consoles to meet the needs of specific users is a real advantage.

Digital consoles and audio workstations have many applications in off-air production, too. An edit can be rehearsed many times, with settings corrected until the result is perfectly tuned on the DAW. If the system is networked, that sound file will be immediately available to the on-air producer in a different studio.

COMPUTERS IN AUTOMATION
AND SATELLITE SERVICES

Probably the most immediate and visible application of computer technology to radio is in the area of automation and live-assist automation. Many radio stations have adopted some form of **automation** to help with the broadcast day.

Automation refers to using technology to allow a process to run with a minimum or absence of on-site human labor. A related concept, **live assist** refers to the use of automatically sequenced commands to help the person running the console execute a series of tasks.

A brief history of radio-station automation will help you understand the current role of computerized automation technology. Automation first came of age in the late 1950s and early 1960s via what now appear to be cumbersome methods of automatically cueing sound sources. The development of the cart machine and its eventual widespread use in the 1960s greatly enhanced the promise of automation. Because the broadcast cart was a continuous loop device, it could recue itself and be loaded into various mechanical devices capable of transporting and playing one or more carts.

In the early to mid-1970s, cartridge **carousels** became extremely popular. The carousel was a circular device that rotated and brought the carts into contact with the playback device. Usually, the carousels were synchronized with reel-to-reel tapes (supplied by a program syndicator), which had to be changed by hand every few hours.

Automation appeared to be the answer to the problems faced by many stations, large and small. It drastically cut back on personnel costs and generally provided high-quality program material. The prerecorded voices of the announcers were of the highest quality, and the music was carefully selected according to ostensibly well-researched criteria.

However, station owners found that automation, the apparent answer to any station's financial woes, could actually drive listeners away. Audiences soon tired of the transparently canned format of many of the syndicated programs offered for automated systems. Many stations brought back live announcers for the entire

---

RADIO RETRO • EARLY AUTOMATION—RADIO IN A CAN

Today, an entire radio station can be run through an off-the-shelf computer, but back in the early 1970s, there were no off-the-shelf computers. Many radio station owners, though, were willing to try crude computer technology because they could see the economic benefits of running a station with little person-power.

Often it was the FM station that was automated, and the AM disc jockey would have to tend the computer and the automation system in his or her spare time. One popular method of automation involved three large reel-to-reel tape recorders and two cartridge carousels. The computer was programmed to play content from reel 1, then commercials from cart 1 and cart 2, then two songs from reel 2, followed by another commercial stop set, and so on.

There were problems with this setup. First, it wasn't always reliable, and when the automation went

bad, it was comical (unless you were the person tending the automation). It wasn't all that unusual to hear a commercial, two songs, and "The Star Spangled Banner" from the station sign-on playing all at once—or hear nothing at all.

The biggest problem, however, was the sequence itself. It was obviously "canned." A generic-voiced announcer would back-announce the songs incessantly ("You just heard Captain and Tennille with 'Muskrat Love,' and before that, the BeeGees with …"), and because of the limited supply of tapes, listeners who spent a lot of time with the station became able to predict what the next song would be.

Still, these formats were instrumental in establishing FM radio as a prime provider of music. In the 1970s, FM radios were not as common as today, and it took listeners some convincing to get them to listen to the FM bands, even if their favorite music was there.

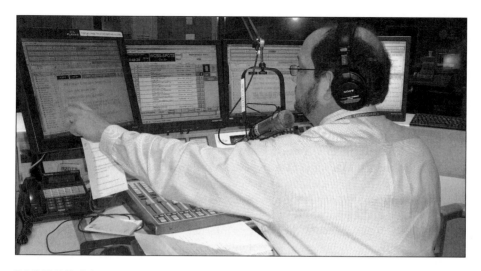

FIGURE 9.9

Here, WCBS Anchor Steve Scott runs an entire combo operation from an array of computer screens within easy reach and touch. He can fire program elements by touching the screen, by using his mouse, or by a button on the console. Note that literally all communication within the station is at his fingertips: wire copy, e-mail, memos, audio files, and the Web page.

SOURCE: Philip Benoit

schedule or for certain high-listener periods and used automation for slow times such as overnight shifts.

Just when automation appeared to be on its way out, computer technology brought it back to the forefront of radio operations. Modern automation uses the power and sophistication of current technology to accomplish tasks that were difficult or impossible to do with older-generation systems that involved complex hardware and mechanical relays. Today's automation systems provide partial or complete on-air control of programming by using a wide variety of software products (see Figure 9.9). While much of the program material on automated systems may come from one or more computer hard drives, automation software can provide the board operator complete control over all source inputs.

Functions such as organizing playlists of music or announcements, inserting voice tracks, and keeping program logs are easy for computers, and they can even interface with satellite-delivered programming. For example, in stations where programming is received by satellite, the computer system senses subaudible cue tones that are fed along with program material. The tone is separated from the program signal and fed to the satellite interface hardware. Such tones then activate local program elements, which are integrated into the satellite-fed programming.

Here are some examples of what cutting-edge automation and software technology can do:

■ A satellite feed beams down current music in a tightly controlled format. The music is back-announced by a highly professional announcer located at the system headquarters in a major market. As a music sweep is about to end, the satellite beams down a subaudible tone (usually 25 or 35 Hz), which activates a computer or cart machine at the local station airing the satellite-fed program. The announcement says, "You're listening to [local station's call letters]." Then the satellite feed takes over again, with the announcer saying, "That was [name of song and artist]." The seamless integration of local and satellite elements adds to the production value of the programming.

The automation system has customized the satellite broadcast service, ensuring that the automation doesn't sound canned. Certain automation systems even have a method for the announcer to feed local announcements, such as upcoming community events, to the particular market. These sound files could be prerecorded by the announcer and sent to the local station as WAV or MP3 files via the Internet. The file is sent via the Web, downloaded into the station's program computer, and called up by the automation system at the appropriate time.

- A radio newsroom features a central server networked with computers in several different studios. Reporters and editors can tie into the news system and exchange information with one another as well as access network and wire-service news feeds. Nobody has to run back and forth trying to find copy; it's all instantly accessible. TCP/IP technology is used to connect consoles together, greatly simplifying automation and wiring.

- News and public-service programming, however, has benefited from improvements in mobile technology. Reporters in the field carrying smartphones like an iPhone or Android can record interviews or breaking news. Using a software app, the reporter can edit sound bites in the field and transfer that sound file back to the studio. He or she simply connects to a network (possibly via a wireless hotspot) or sends the file via a 3G or 4G network and transfers the file back to the station. Once downloaded into the station's program computer, it's ready to be integrated into a local newscast or newsbreak. Of course, mobile technology has made it possible to initiate a breaking news report from nearly anywhere in the world today.

- Computerization provides greater control over the output of the board. Some new systems provide for separate equalization (EQ) and dynamics processing (compression) for every fader. (These and other advanced capabilities are discussed in Chapter 15.) This allows a station to tailor the audio for each channel rather than just for the output of the console. Such capabilities allows stations to better match the sounds from satellite or other external inputs with those of the local studio.

- Automation systems are now commonplace in many radio markets, large and small. In most automation systems, commercials, songs, and voice tracks can be stored, sorted, and logged by the system. This is possible because the system stores all audio files on one or more hard drives. Once a file is placed on the computer's hard drive, it can be cataloged and searched easily because the programs maintain a database of each program element. Such digital systems also control the sequencing of program events so the program director can shuffle music sweeps, vary spotsets, and cross-fade in and out of jingles. When searching for specific program elements, such as music, it is possible to search by song title, musical category, or length. This flexibility allows the user to search the music database in multiple ways.

- Systems like Wide Orbit Automation allow stations to use talent in remote cities to voice track. When the program director finishes creating a music log, the software sends the beginning and end of the song before and after the voice track to the remote announcer and then emails that announcer to let her know the shift is ready for voice tracking. When the jock records a voice track, it is automatically sent back to the station for airing.

Many automation systems allow the program elements to be coordinated between a satellite source and locally programmed **stopsets** so that the transition is undetectable to the listener. A common problem with previous satellite automation systems involved difficulties in varying the program elements to fit the periods allocated for local inserts, such as commercials, IDs, and information reports, without sounding canned. Modern automation systems take care of such problems because they have the ability to automatically select different local intros and promos as network programming changes. When a program element is missing because of an error, backup announcements of the correct length can be automatically substituted so that the gap is not noticeable to listeners. The system has the ability to allow announcers to provide voice tracks from the studio or from remote locations via the Internet. Automation systems can even automatically insert Emergency Alert System (EAS) broadcast alerts into the playlist.

Today's computer systems can be linked to traffic (scheduling) and logging functions so that a time-linked record is kept of all program elements that are aired. Billing can be done automatically with verification of the time at which a client's commercial ran, and all program elements are logged.

For example, Smarts Broadcast Systems has a radio billing and traffic system that generates daily logs for the station. Program material such as spots and jingles can be assigned into particular stopsets or fixed in station break positions. Commercials can be set for ROS (run of schedule), for specific day parts, or in fixed positions within the broadcast day. The software will automatically generate standard co-op tear sheets and billing information for the sales staff.

In the area of traditional station-based music programming, digital systems are capable of generating music playlists for various periods such as a day or a month at a time. Music can be categorized by artist and style of music and automatically scheduled to play only in **day parts** that are appropriate to each selection. A station using a tight playlist during drive time could add more variety to the music mix during midday or evening hours. If the radio station is part of a broadcast group where several stations broadcast from the same facility, a server-based music system would allow several stations access to the same music library simultaneously.

Although some would argue that automation is not in the best interests of the industry as a whole—because jobs are often lost as a result of the expanding use of technology—automation does offer certain advantages to radio employees and to listeners. For employees, live-assist automation makes things easier on the person who runs the console. Now he or she may have to push only one button to trigger a sequence of five or six events. Computer-driven systems make it possible for many time-consuming tasks to be accomplished by touching a button or (in a touch screen system) by touching an appropriate part of the video monitor.

Because new technologies have made it easier for announcers to do their own production work, there has been a perceptible trend toward requiring announcers to run combo, even in large markets. For example, a number of CBS-owned and-operated stations are requiring talent to work combo as a money-saving measure.

What benefits does automation offer the listener? Points can be made on many sides of the issue, but many people enjoy listening to top-quality programming supplemented, thanks to computer control, with local inserts. Even small markets can have top-quality music formatting and announcing coupled with locally originated material. Today's automation software even allows a group owner to run the same music on two different stations in different parts of the country with separate breaks programs for the particular market.

On the other hand, many listeners find that stations with tightly controlled program elements become monotonous over time. And it is often obvious when two stations in nearby markets share talent and playlists.

Job descriptions and duties performed by radio personnel have been changing as a result of automation. Some small-market personnel originally assigned to spinning discs (the same music available anywhere in the country) have had their job focus changed to sales, local news, or community service when the station has changed to automated services. Unfortunately, in many markets, announcing staff rosters have simply been cut back or eliminated and music so tightly controlled that the station's sound has become bland.

COMPUTERS IN THE PROGRAMMING FUNCTION

Although the word *programming* has many meanings in the context of radio production and operations, the activities comprehended by one specific definition—the process of planning and documenting the material aired over the station—have been greatly speeded up and enhanced by computer technology. In the previous sections of this chapter, we've mentioned examples of how programming and production are melding to deliver sophisticated production. Scheduling music, commercials, and other program elements is extremely time-consuming and complex. However, the situation is eased considerably by specialized software. Natural Broadcast Systems, for example, features a traffic and scheduling system that can do the following:

- Keep track of all program elements and provide a printout (log)
- Make a record of all commercial availabilities
- Ensure that commercials for directly competing products (two airlines, for example) are not scheduled within a certain time of each other

EMERGING ETHICAL ISSUES IN ONLINE MEDIA

About a year ago I was asked to give a talk to a group of professionals who work in various online media, including radio, about emerging issues in online ethics. I was skeptical about whether the topic was too abstract to be of interest to communication practitioners, but I was wrong—I received a lot of feedback from professional advertising and public relations people telling me that indeed these issues were surfacing in their worlds.

Here are seven emerging ethical problems, leveraged by digital technology that may soon blink on your radar:

1. Digital records can live forever, requiring proactive ethical decisions about their lifespan. As an example, think about the huge difference in impact of the digitization of a newspaper's archives, which makes for a profoundly different ethical issue than the mere existence of some old paper copies in the storage room. There are hundreds of new dilemmas that could spring from this premise: For example, if Prisoner X is cleared of his crime by a DNA test after spending 5 years in jail, do we go back and correct all of the stories in the archive? Or make annotations to the old stories? Or remove the stories altogether? Even videos become immortal once they are cast around the Internet. A bad television commercial will be reincarnated on You Tube and other video-posting services, as will bad Karaoke recorded with a cell phone.

2. The speed of digital communication exponentially increases the chance for error. Speed—and the expectation of speed in the age of the eternally hot connection—not only causes error but magnifies it. Add to that the pressure-cooker effect of digital communication, which affects almost everyone in every line of work. Think about how the acceleration of your working life due to the demands of your email and your Blackberry affects your performance and your state of mind.

3. Data are dangerous when unsecured, creating an ethical obligation to play it safe. Several high-profile incidents have demonstrated that plain old slipshod handling can precipitate information-age debacles. Companies have left sensitive data unsecured, unencrypted, in a cab, or on a lost laptop. This problem doesn't relate only to keepers of vast databases: Think about the possible consequences related to answering one of your emails if you hit the Reply to All button when you meant to reply only to the sender.

4. We're all engaged in cross-cultural ethics. The cliché about digital communications shrinking the world became a sudden reality in recent months when the fact that major U.S. Internet firms censor their content to gain entrée to the vast Chinese market showed up on Congress's radar screen. By whose rules do we play when engaged in international communication?

5. We are what we link to. Online news publications, in particular, face ethical dilemmas related to linking. You may choose not to show a violent incident, or something that is patently offensive, but can you compromise by linking to it? It's a problem that has little ethical precedent and needs some hard thought and discussion.

6. Search results are presumed to be honest and impartial, but are they? This is a complex question. Some sites' search engines elevate certain results because they are paid to do so by advertisers seeking prominent placement. Most of the major independent search engines don't have "pay to place" search results, but that doesn't guarantee that their results can't be cooked from the other end by webmasters using various tricks to score higher in the rankings. There's a slippery slope between healthy self-promotion and dishonest skewing of search results.

7. Technology enables rampant plagiarism. The Internet is the world's greatest copy machine, and the problem of ownership of ideas is incredibly complex. If you are preparing a print ad, how far can you go in copying a design element? Is cutting and pasting a report from a mosaic of many sources still plagiarism?

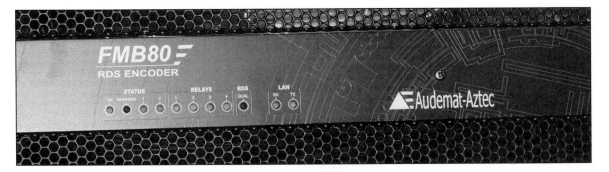

FIGURE 9.10

RDS encoders can be used to display call letters and song titles. They also can be used to identify radio station formats and provide traffic report information.

SOURCE: Fritz Messere

- Provide salespeople with a way to program a flight of spots immediately and to let the sponsor know the airdates
- Automatically generate bills for spots aired
- Allow sales management to compare records of individual salespeople and to use projections (quotas) for each salesperson

The possibilities for computer use in all areas of radio—special effects, editing, on-air production, automation, and programming—are virtually limitless. For example, Radio Data System (RDS) encoders now provide song titles and call letters to radios equipped with RDS displays (see Figure 9.10). Even the most devoted apostles of high-tech, however, are quick to warn that gadgetry is not an end in itself. The computer can perform work faster and can make it easier, but it cannot make good radio. Good radio is made by the skill of the producer and is played out in the brain of the listener. Radio, after all, is center stage in the theater of the mind—and imagination will never be supplanted by gimmickry.

Interactive Media and Radio Programming

The explosion in the use of mobile devices and specific applications (apps) that work on a variety of these devices has created opportunities for radio stations to distinguish their services from all the other mobile radio and audio services. For example, *Iheartradio.com* provides the listener with a high-quality streaming service. As of this writing, more than 750 station choices were available via this service. Entering the local zip code brings up stations nearest to the listener, but one can also search by artist, bringing up specific stations dedicated to that artist and music of that genre. AOL Radio online provides live feeds with defined formats along with CBS radio stations from around the country. Pandora provides the listener with a radio programming service based on individual music preferences defined by the listener.

With so many choices, one might question how local radio stations could compete against the many choices available. Some radio stations are using their HD channels to provide specific format programming. Other stations have adopted interactive services that provide their listeners with more direct contact and connections with the stations and with station listeners. iPhone, iPad, Android, and other mobile platforms allow listeners to connect directly to stations regardless of whether the listeners are in the service area or at some distant location.

In the past year, new services have emerged that give listeners greater access to the announcer, to the music played, and to other listeners of the station. One such software provider, Local Media, allows listeners the opportunity to have a live chat with the DJ through Facebook, Twitter, Instant Messenger, or a mobile device app that runs on either iPhones or Android platforms. On the Facebook page or on the application, a "Wall" provides the jock with a central location to receive and respond to listener feedback that gets aggregated from the different possible communication channels. The jock can choose to publish some messages to a public feed available to all listeners, or she can communicate to listeners individually. These new services help connect the listener to the station and can build loyalty among listeners over time.

SUMMARY

The modern computer uses hardware (the system itself) and software (the programs) to accomplish its goal. The computer can perform many functions at incredible speed while offering great flexibility.

One particularly useful function of the computer in radio is to create effects, including music, using a MIDI (musical instrument digital interface) synthesizer or music development software that uses previously recorded MIDI sound loops. You don't have to be a skilled musician to use these packages; the programs for creating music are user friendly.

Digital audio workstations have replaced analog recording devices. Digital workstations provide the radio producer with great flexibility in recording and editing. In computer-assisted editing, the information is stored digitally and manipulated through visual representations on a computer screen.

Perhaps the most visible impact of computer technology in radio is in automation and live-assist programming. Automated gear can be incredibly flexible, and live-assist can allow an operator to handle many complex tasks by clicking a mouse or, in some cases, just by touching the computer screen.

Computers have an important role in the programming function. Today, even small stations use computers to generate logs and schedule program elements.

Online services and mobile applications are adding capabilities to radio stations and options for listeners.

APPLICATIONS

SITUATION 1/THE PROBLEM A producer wanted to put together a station promo package featuring a chorus chanting the station's call letters. Unfortunately, only two announcers were on duty, and volunteers for a chorus were nowhere to be found.

ONE POSSIBLE SOLUTION Using a DAW with multitrack capability and sound-processing equipment, the producer laid down two voices in digital storage, changed the characteristics of the voices slightly, then laid them down again on new tracks, repeating the process until he had what sounded like a chorus of more than a dozen voices.

SITUATION 2/THE PROBLEM The production manager of a station that was inter-faced with a satellite service did all of her production on a digital editing unit. Her most recent effort needed some work: A voice-only commercial cut to fill a 60-second hole ran only 58 seconds. There was no time to call the announcer back in to recut the spot.

ONE POSSIBLE SOLUTION One aspect of digital storage is the ability, in some hard-ware, to speed up or slow down the playback. Slowing down a playback exces-sively would have distorted the voice, but stretching it by 1.5 seconds was hardly noticeable—much less noticeable, certainly, than 2 seconds of dead air on an all-hit music station.

EXERCISES

1. If the appropriate equipment is available, record the following effects. The content is not the central issue; what is important is to note how manipula-tion of the sound changes the effect produced. Produce and record the following:

   - A series of notes or tones of steady pitch, with a fast attack followed by a diminution of volume
   - A series of notes of steady pitch, where the tone builds up to a crescendo at the end
   - A series of notes of steady pitch, with no change in volume—just an abrupt on-and-off attack
   - A series of notes in which the pitch changes rapidly or warbles
   - A hissing noise similar to the white noise of a running shower or the static of snowy television.

2. Again, if the equipment is available, draw representations of the waveform (envelope) pictured on the screen for each production in Exercise 1. (Do this to the best of your artistic ability, but remember that drawing skill is not the point here.) Show the drawings to, and then play the sounds for, someone who is not familiar with this exercise, and see if he or she can match the pictures with the sounds.

3. The following is a pen-and-pencil exercise for those who do not have access to computerized equipment. Write a paper (your instructor will specify length and format) focusing on whether, in your opinion, the technological revolution in radio has had a good influence or a bad one on the medium. For example, do you feel that technology is replacing the human touch in radio? Do you believe that it is better to have live announcers on most radio stations or is voice tracking an acceptable substitute? Do you feel that the types of technology available are improving radio, freeing people to be more creative? Regardless of your viewpoint, present your case using information from this chapter, information you have gathered in other classes and through research, and the following supplemental data sources:

    a. Facts gathered from trade journals. *Broadcasting and Cable, Electronic Media,* and others will probably be the most helpful ones. These publications are widely available in libraries or online.

    b. An interview with a local veteran of radio, preferably an on-air personality.

10

Achieving an Effect

If you'll permit us to stretch a point a bit, think of Chapters 6, 7, 8, and 9 as an art lesson in which you learned the basic brushstrokes. It's now time to explore ways to create light, shadow, substance, and mood.

As a radio producer, you will be called on to create a variety of effects using the basic skills we explained previously. Producing an effect calls for more than a learned-by-rote recall of mechanics. It involves imagination, experimentation, and a certain amount of trial and error.

This is not to say that producing an effect is entirely a seat-of-the-pants affair. Specific techniques must be mastered, and technical expertise must be matched with creativity. This chapter serves as a bridge between the first nine chapters, which dealt with techniques and mechanics, and the chapters that follow, on radio drama and on dramatic elements in radio production, commercial production, and news and public-affairs production. This chapter also reviews many of the elements discussed earlier and touches on some of the aspects to be dealt with later. The mix of elements is important because the marriage of technology and art—the ability to create an effect—is the heart of radio production.

WHAT IS AN EFFECT?

When we refer to the overall mood, impact, and appeal of a radio production, we use the term *effect*. We don't mean a specific sound effect (such as the screeching of a car's brakes).

Modern communication theory points out that getting a message across depends on more than the validity of the message. Reaching people with a message also involves pulling their emotional strings—creating a mood of excitement, perhaps, or a feeling of identification. These emotional activators can often be turned on and off by means of radio production techniques.

A commercial to spur ticket sales for a football team, for instance, would certainly seek to create a mood of excitement: the sound of a kickoff, followed by the roar of the crowd, supported with upbeat, vibrant music. To create this example, the producer would have to know how to dub in sound effects, either taking them from a sound effects collection played back on a hard drive or a CD, downloaded from the Internet (assuming you have rights to use the effect), or recording the desired sound at a game, using basic microphone techniques. All production techniques, of course, hinge on properly mixing and routing the signals through a console and recording them on a digital workstation or other equipment. The producer uses production skills to assemble and form the structure of the commercial, but an understanding of creating an effect is necessary to produce the subtle message, the nuances, responsible for the impact and drama of the message.

KINDS OF EFFECT

The focus of the message—and the effect you want to create—won't always be the same, even in quite similar situations. Assume, for example, that the radio station's sales manager, who needs a commercial for a restaurant, wants your help in creating an effective 30-second spot.

Soft music, you say? The sound of tinkling glasses, coupled with some low conversation and a mellow-voiced announcer? Perhaps. If the restaurant is an elegant one (or tries to be), your choice of soft music would be correct. However, restaurants are as different as people. Could it be a sports bar? Then the background might need a livelier piece and louder conversation. In this case, the announcer would have a full delivery. Digging a little deeper, you may discover that this particular client's restaurant has an ethnic flair; if so, might a Latin piece or other specialty selection be more effective? Perhaps this is a fast-food establishment. You, the producer, would most likely seek to convey a sense of fast action; thus upbeat, quick-tempo music would be the logical choice.

Music, like any other production element, must support the theme. You will be wise to etch this principle deeply within your thinking because straying from the overall theme is the most common mistake of the novice radio producer. Every production element must support the theme or it will detract from the message.

HOW PRODUCTION ELEMENTS SUPPORT A THEME

The upbeat music in our fast-food restaurant commercial conveys a specific impression: speed, excitement, and vibrancy. This production element supports the theme of a message for a fast-food establishment; it would certainly detract from a commercial for an elegant restaurant. Think of how McDonald's uses the same musical phrases in a variety of ways to support its message. McDonald's might be advertising breakfast specials or its specialty coffees, and while the music tempo might vary, the theme reinforces the fact that it's a McDonald's commercial.

Such themes aren't always so readily apparent. There's no obvious guideline on how to produce a commercial for a personal computer, for example. In fact, the approach eventually adopted might evolve after months of sophisticated market research aimed at discovering what approaches trigger the emotions of typical computer buyers. Obviously, such intricate planning won't be left up to the producer.

On many occasions, the sales manager and the client know exactly what mood and effect they want. It will be up to you to achieve that effect and to choose production elements that support the theme. There are many production elements other than music and sound effects, but let's focus on those two for the time being. Later in this chapter, we'll discuss sound quality, voice quality, and so on and explore their proper use. The production elements of music and sound effects can support a theme and bolster the message in many ways. Here are some brief examples illustrating how these elements fit into the overall scheme of things.

Creating Excitement

Producers of soft-drink commercials depend on the capacity of radio production to create excitement and to make their product appeal to a market that seeks thrills, activity, and youthful enjoyment of life. The music chosen—apart from the lyrics, which tout the benefits of the beverage—must support this mood of excitement.

Think, too, of the music you've heard at the introduction of sports play-by-play programs. Was the music a leisurely, sentimental ballad? Of course not. It was up-tempo, hard-driving music that implied that the program to follow was going to be a fast-moving, exciting event.

Creating Immediate Identification

What does the sound of a stopwatch ticking conjure in your mind? If you're like millions of other Americans, you will think immediately of the CBS News program *60 Minutes*. And that's exactly what the producers would like you to think.

Why? Because the familiar stopwatch theme is one element that immediately distinguishes *60 Minutes* from its competition and creates a certain amount of loyalty among viewers and listeners. In any medium, that is the name of the game. The sponsor of a commercial wants that commercial to stand out; the producer of a talk show wants listeners to distinguish that show from the competition and wants it to have some sort of tag they can identify with.

An important point: Whatever production element is chosen for the task of creating immediate identification, it must support the overall message. The sound of cannons firing, for example, would certainly attract attention, but it wouldn't do much to demonstrate that the upcoming news program is going to be important and dignified. In fact, such confusion within the message would detract from the identification factor; listeners probably wouldn't mentally link the news show and the signature cannon shots.

Evoking an Emotion

What does the sound of automobile horns blaring mean to you? Chances are it evokes the feelings you experienced the last time you sat, hot and frustrated, in a traffic jam. The producer of a commercial for an airline trip to a Caribbean island could use this factor effectively. Sound effects are one of the most effective tools for evoking an emotion. In fact, sometimes a couple of seconds of sound effects can save several lines of dialogue, making the commercial copy less pedantic.

Summary of Effects

The goal of radio production is to achieve an effect. The goal of achieving an effect is to be able to reach a certain group with a message. In many cases, the group and the message may be spelled out for you by an advertising manager or the client who wants you to produce a commercial. We offer a more complete discussion in Chapter 12.

When reporting to the producer of a news or sports program, you will be asked to use production elements that support the show's theme and create listener identification. As we discussed in Chapter 1, the producer in modern radio is responsible for reinforcing the station's particular sound—the quality that distinguishes it from its competitors up and down the dial.

Remember, you may be responsible for production in a variety of different jobs at various radio stations. You may be an announcer who produces commercials and public service announcements after your airshift. (The airshift is also, of course, a product of radio production.) Maybe you work at a station group and must produce commercials that will be heard on several stations in the same market. You may be a news reporter responsible for piecing together a half hour's worth of news items and integrating them into an overall theme. Your job in the sales department at a small station may involve hands-on production. You may be the program director, in charge of ensuring that everything that goes out over the air strengthens the format, the station's "sound." Regardless of the job title, you will be using the basic production equipment and techniques described in the preceding chapters to achieve the effects discussed so far in this chapter. And as we've seen, you will be using various production elements.

HOW A PRODUCER USES PRODUCTION ELEMENTS

We have briefly touched on how the production elements of music and sound effects are used to create an effect. Other elements can serve the same purpose. We now examine each element and show how and why it creates an effect.

Music

The observation that music reaches deep into the human psyche won't surprise you. Music has moved people to march to war and has waltzed couples into matrimony. Music of all types is instantly available to the radio producer. The sources from which you will draw music include these:

- Your station's general airplay music library. The station has paid a fee to various licensing agencies for use of the music, and you may be able to use some of these discs in your productions.

- Certain types of production CDs for which you must pay per **needle drop**—that is, whenever a cut from one of these discs is dubbed for use in a production. This situation is more common at recording studios that are not affiliated with a radio station and do not pay a licensing fee for general airplay music.

- Music beds supplied by a national advertiser for use by locally affiliated merchants or businesses. For example, a lawnmower manufacturer might supply to its distributors a commercial in which the company's jingle is included at the beginning and end of a 30-second spot, with a 15-second hole of background music—a bed—over which an announcer would read copy for the local merchant's store. (More on this in Chapter 12.) These cooperative, or *co-op*, advertising materials come in a wide range of structures.

- Original music composed specifically for a certain purpose, such as the type of jingle music used in beds; jingles produced locally for businesses; and music composed for use in themes of shows or productions. You may, from time to time, become involved in the recording of such music, or maybe your station generates its own beds using one of the software programs discussed in Chapter 9. (We examine that aspect of radio production in Chapter 15.)

Music is such an evocative tool that it is used in a great many radio production tasks; unfortunately, it is also frequently misused and overused. Here are some brief rules of thumb to help you, the producer, use music properly in the aesthetic context.

Do use music

- When you can find a logical reason to do so. Use music to create a mood and reinforce a theme.

- When the music has a logical purpose and fits into the format of your station. A hard-rock music background for a public service announcement will not complement the sound of a station playing an adult contemporary format. As we discussed in Chapter 1, the producer must respect the integrity of the station's format.

Do not use music

- Strictly as a reflex. Many times you'll be better off without it. Suppose, for instance, that every other station in town uses a brief musical opening (sometimes called a **stinger**) for newscasts. Do you, as a producer, feel compelled to do the same? No, of course not; a "cold" opening can certainly be effective, and in this case, will set you apart from the competition.

- Indiscriminately. This warning applies specifically to the novice radio producer who is tempted to use currently popular music within announcements or other productions, whether or not it serves to reinforce the message. With current music, the listener often tunes out the message.

A final note: Be cautious of using vocals as background for a produced announcement. Although lyrics that proclaim something to the effect of "I'll be your friend forever, just give me a call ..." might tempt the producer of a public service announcement for a community health agency, mixing vocals with a voice-over can make both the lyrics and the announcer unintelligible. Cross-fading and other technical operations, however, can sometimes mitigate the problem.

Sound Effects

The example of blaring car horns used in an advertisement for a Caribbean vacation shows the value of appropriate sound effects. (Note the word *appropriate*.) A sound effect is generally considered to be any sound element other than music or speech. Sound effects (SFX) can come from the following:

- Special sound effects libraries, CDs, or audio files the radio station purchases and buys the rights to use. Sound effects libraries are usually on CD or downloaded from an Internet site. Software packages of sound effects are available, too.

- Sound effects recorded by the producer. This practice sounds simpler than it really is. The old-time radio trick of crackling cellophane to simulate the sound of flames often sounds exactly like crackling cellophane. A door slamming, as another example, won't always sound like a door slamming. With certain microphone placements and certain doors, it can sound like a gunshot instead. Recording your own sound effects will take some experimenting, both with producing the sound and with placing the microphone to record it.

Regardless of how a sound effect is produced, its appropriate use can add to the message. Inappropriate use can make the message seem hackneyed, amateurish, and off the mark.

There are two good reasons for using sound effects.

Do use sound effects

- To save time and words. A vacation-oriented commercial might start with a blast of wintry wind to reinforce the message. Use of the sound effect has saved the producer some verbiage; there's no need for an announcer to say: "Don't you hate winter and the latest stretch of miserable weather?" The sound effect, lasting only a second or two, has created the desired image.

- To inject drama. Audiences have come to expect a bit of drama in all media. A bit of drama that reinforces your message can grab the attention of your target listeners. Can you picture, for example, the kind of audience and the kind of message that would be matched up in a commercial that features the sound effect of a baby crying? A sports car engine roaring? A rocket taking off?

Do not use sound effects

- Just because they are there. The producer should not even consider using a sound effect in the absence of a definite need and purpose for that effect. Keep in mind that overuse of sound effects is one of the most common mistakes made by newcomers to radio production. You will mark yourself as an amateur by falling into this trap.

Sound effects are an excellent production tool, but if they're used just for the sake of using them, they are inappropriate and can detract from the message. Use a sound effect when it's logical and serves a purpose. For example, if your commercial takes place in a car, the producer would probably want the sound of a car motor to be in the background all the way through the spot. Other times sound effects need to take a primary role in the commercial; consider, for example, the need to have the sound effect of a phone ringing where the script calls for a person to answer the phone. Today, with cell phones and different ringtones, you need to consider matching the ring to the appropriate character answering the phone. Chapters 11 and 12, on radio drama and commercial production, respectively, expand on the ways sound effects communicate a message effectively.

Coloration of Sound

Coloration of sound is a nebulous quality that cannot always be singled out. This production element is difficult to define. However, you will understand it when you hear it. Eventually you, too, will use sound coloration techniques to produce an effect in your own production work.

Some examples may be helpful. Compare the overall sound quality of a friendly, up-tempo DJ on an adult contemporary radio program to that of a sedate news and public affairs interviewer on a public radio station with a more leisurely format. You know there's a difference even though you can't quite articulate it.

One reason the up-tempo DJ maintains such an intense sound is the electronic *compression* and contouring of the signal; this is done quite scientifically, we might add, and it involves boosting the volume of softer sounds and using some frequency equalization so that the entire presentation has a specific presence (and so that, the program director hopes, the signal will stand out more than the signals of competing stations do when the listener scans up or down the dial). Heavy compression would not be appropriate in a slower-paced talk show because the electronics would insist on boosting the periods of silence between questions and answers, creating an annoying "pumping" effect.

Compression is just one example of a process by which sound is altered to achieve coloration. A mild **echo** is often electronically applied; we cover this effect more thoroughly in Chapter 15. FM stations, which transmit high-resolution signals, often favor high-quality microphones that reproduce a wide spectrum of sounds, including breath and mouth noises of the announcer, making the voice seem very close up and intimate.

Microphones can have a powerful effect on the coloration of sound. As you might remember from the discussion of sound quality (or timbre) in Chapter 5, the way sound patterns are reproduced affects the way we perceive those patterns. Often, the coloration is actually a desirable type of **distortion**. We present examples of sound coloration in Chapters 11, 12, and 14, which deal with drama, commercials, and remote and sports production, respectively. We discuss some technical methods of achieving coloration in Chapter 15. A radio producer should be prepared to confront the coloration concept. Don't be surprised when the program director asks you to produce a brighter sound or requests a promotional spot with a more personal feel.

Timing and Pace

Whether you are producing a music program, a news show, or a commercial, timing and pace will directly affect the mood and the message. This production element is one of the most critical aspects of the entire spectrum of radio production. Yet timing and pace have some effects you might not, at first thought, be aware of. Try this comparison:

- Listen to a commercial for securities or other investments. (Such commercials are quite common on radio talk shows, especially talk shows dealing with business issues.) Note the very slow, deliberate pacing. Why? Because we've developed a negative image of fast talkers. The announcer who sells us major investments must be someone who sounds knowledgeable and trustworthy.

- Contrast the foregoing approach with soft-drink commercials. Trust, here, is really not a factor. An image of a lifestyle is being sold, and that image generally represents a youthful and fast-moving crowd. Commercials for soft drinks include music with modern themes, frequently sung by pop artists of the day.

We cite these examples in the hope that you will develop a critical ear when it comes to determining the timing and pace of your own work. Keep in mind, always, that the pace creates an effect and must reinforce the message. Also remember that sometimes a new idea is successful precisely because it breaks with programming conventions.

Walter Winchell, the legendary broadcaster whose radio career peaked in the Depression era, entered radio after experience as a newspaper gossip columnist. Initially, he was given little chance of success because radio announcers at the time were expected to have a slow, mellifluous delivery. Winchell, however, broke the rules with a rapid-fire, staccato delivery: "Good evening,

Mr. and Mrs. America, and all the ships at sea, let's go to press ... Flash! ..."
His delivery was breathless, punctuated with the dit-dit-dit of a telegraph key,
and it accomplished exactly what he wanted. It implied that Winchell had a
fast-moving program, figuratively grabbing the listener by the lapels and
shouting, "Wait 'til you hear this!" His timing and pace reinforced Winchell's
message.

Another veteran broadcaster, Paul Harvey, was an acknowledged master of
timing, and his technique will help us make an important distinction. Harvey
kept up a varied, energetic pace, but he also captivated his audience by use of the
well-timed punch line, usually preceded by a dramatic pause. "And the man
woke up the next morning to find," Harvey might say, "that he'd been spraying
the annoying mosquito not with insecticide ... [pause] ... but with [agonizing
pause] ... a can ... of blue spray paint!" You can hear some of Harvey's legendary
broadcasts on YouTube.

Timing and pace are also major elements in the production of a music program. In many laid-back, album-oriented rock stations, the whole format is built
around low-key timing and pace. Compare that with the frenetic, nonstop
approach of the fast-talking-contemporary hits station. Both are trying to project
an image.

Voice Quality

This production element doesn't necessarily imply a qualitative difference
between good and bad voices. *Voice quality* is the overall image that an announcer's voice projects. Often, a producer chooses the announcer to be used for a
particular production. Sometimes the producer is assigned a particular task and
must use a designated voice (or his or her own voice) to maximum effect, perhaps making some subtle changes in delivery.

In any event, matching a proper voice and delivery to the message at hand is
the important element here. Many aspects of selection and delivery are reasonably obvious. A news moderator's voice calls for a measure of authority. A spot
designed to convince young people to shop at a particular store might well benefit from a young voice and an intimate, chummy delivery. Think of other
examples. Do advertisements for women's medicines often feature a sympathetic
female voice? Why?

Another aspect of voice quality is the lack of distraction. Voices used on
the air, it's generally agreed, should not have defects (we're not just referring
to pathological speech defects here) that will detract from the message. One of
the most common distractions is improper breathing by the announcer.
Overly breathy voices, except when they are a well-known novelty, sound
amateurish. Often, inexperienced announcers can be heard gasping for air
between phrases. Such gasping sounds might not be apparent in everyday
speech, but a mic can be merciless. The cure for this is to maintain generous
breath support—a good tankful of air—instead of trying to talk until all your
breath is expended. Plan where to take breaths; breathe at natural pauses in
the copy. Advertising copy should be read with meaning. Don't just read
until you can't read any more.

The Sound of Words

A radio producer is often responsible for writing the copy that is read on the air. We address specific copy techniques in the next section and in the appropriate chapters (notably in Chapters 12 and 13, which discuss commercials and news), but one point must be considered here: writing for the ear.

Words can evoke moods. Note how the words *dine* and *eat* create different moods. So do *invest* and *buy*. The physical sound of the words also has an effect. *Businesses* is not a great word for the ear because the three *s* sounds make the word hissy and unattractive. Doesn't *firms* sound better?

Copywriting

Here are three general principles of copywriting:

1. Remember that you're writing for the ear, not the eye. Use active verbs whenever possible. Long sentences and intricate constructions have no place in radio. Keep your sentences short and conversational. Avoid references such as "the latter option." (The listener can't refer to the copy and decide which is the former and which is the latter.)

2. Remember that your writing must be *read*. That sounds obvious, but it isn't. It takes practice to write in a rhythm that can be read easily by someone else. Be particularly careful about your use of commas and dashes; incorrect usage can make the copy virtually unreadable.

3. Pay close attention to technical format. Each station has a more-or-less standard way of writing copy. Some stations, for example, use all-capital letters for anything to be read over the air. Most stations use various abbreviations, such as SFX for sound effects. The technicalities vary from station to station, so be sure you follow local form. Otherwise, the copy you produce can be very difficult for an announcer to decipher.

In summary, production elements are features that are useful in creating an effect and reinforcing a message. Many are obvious; some require a bit of thought. All have an impact on how a radio production will affect an audience.

Production elements also blend into one total package. Most radio productions contain a variety of elements. In judging various elements, you, the producer, must always determine whether they make sense within the context of the message. Does this sound effect get the point across? Will the music make the message stronger, or will it be a distraction? Does the announcer's voice convey the right message? Do the words convey the full message? Are the words written for the ear? The key to successful production is making sure these decisions are not left to chance.

USING ELEMENTS OF SOUND TO
ACHIEVE AN EFFECT

Until now, our discussion has been largely theoretical. At this point, we consider exactly how the production techniques you've learned from preceding chapters come into play. The job of a producer usually involves being half artist and half

INDUSTRY UPDATE • ACHIEVING AN EFFECT AND THE BOTTOM LINE: PRODUCTION PROMOTION

"On top of events; active, forceful; the source for news and information." Is there any doubt that this is the ultimate description of an all-news radio station?

Getting that image across through the vehicle of the production studio is the job of Bill Tynan, director of creative services for WCBS-AM, an all-news station in New York City (see Figure 10.1). The station nominated him for an A.I.R. award for best production/creative services producer in 2005. He calls many of his promos

"proof of performance" pieces, meaning that they show the listener that he or she made the best choice in tuning into WCBS.

A favorite technique is to edit together snippets from coverage of a news story and have an on-air promo ready the next day. Tynan's promos, for example, have featured breathless reporters giving on-scene reports juxtaposed with announcer copy that reinforces the idea that WCBS was there. One word of caution, though, is applicable to almost all

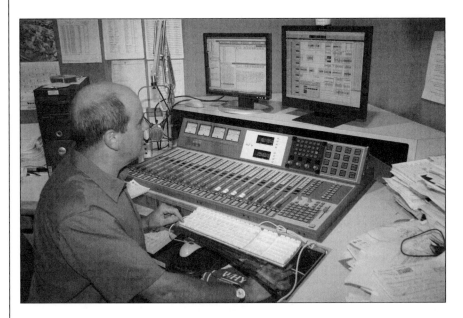

FIGURE 10.1
Bill Tynan, director of creative services for WCBS-AM in New York City, producing a promo.
SOURCE: Carl Hausman

technician. You will use highly sophisticated electronic equipment to translate what you want to do into the technical form of a finished product, something that can easily be played back over the air.

Problems in production often arise when the producer thinks he or she is too much of an artist to bother with the technical side of things. Similarly, production values suffer when a producer enamored with complex gadgetry forgets that he or she is in the business of communicating. A musician must know how to blow a horn and finger the valves properly, but must also have the artistic ability to play notes that convey meaning. Although machines can be programmed to play production and promotion operations. "Don't be too self-congratulatory," Tynan says. "You don't want to come across sounding like 'Gee, wasn't it wonderful there was a disaster and we were there first.'" Tynan notes that the computer vastly simplifies his particular type of production work. During a typical promotion piece, he might have to cross-fade seven or eight cuts. BC (before computers), he would have had to dub those cuts to cart, do three cross-fades onto another cart, and then cross-fade those carts for the final mix. Tynan notes that his field has seen an enormous amount of change in the past few years, and most recently that change has centered on the introduction of multimedia to the website. He writes on his portion of the WCBS website: "Seeing how WCBS has evolved from traditional over-the-air broadcasting to the amazing service we now provide online is very exciting for me. There's just so much audio and video on our website available on demand that it's changing the whole dynamic of how people use the radio station. It's a far cry from the days I spent as a kid listening on a hand-held transistor radio (or the old tube radio in the kitchen, where I listened for school closings with my mom). But the station's role remains essentially the same ... to be a vital source of information for people whenever they need it. To have played a role in that mission, and to have worked with such dedicated people over the years has been an honor indeed."[1]

Now, he can simply load the cuts into the computer, call them up, put them where he wants them, and program the cross-fades. Figure 10.2 shows an example of one of his scripts.

1. Bill Tynan, WCBS Newsradio 880, New York, August 20, 2007, www.wcbs880.com/pages/11278.php?contentType=4&contentId=107442 (accessed July 5, 2008).

"A PROPANE TRUCK SLAMS INTO AN OVERPASS IN WHITE PLAINS SHATTERING THE CALM OF NIGHT!"

MAN: "Trees were on fire, people were screaming, you thought the end of the world was coming!"

"THE WCBS TEAM WAS THERE IN THE WEE HOURS OF THE MORNING TO BRING YOU COMPLETE COVERAGE!"

LAMB: "A fireball swept up from I-287, igniting houses ..."

JEFF: "Neighbours thought a bomb had gone off when the exploding truck lit up the early morning sky ..."

SCHLD: "A lot of these people are very happy and lucky to be alive ..."

QUINN: "It was a nightmare for residents, now it's a nightmare for commuters ..."

BUSCH: "Pick up the southbound New York State Thruway; that's moving very well ..."

TOM K: "Seriously consider Metro-North if you're gonna be coming down there ..."

"FOR THE LATEST ON ROADWAY REPAIRS AND ALTERNATE ROUTES, STAY WITH WCBS NEWSRADIO 880!"

WCBS-AM

FIGURE 10.2

A script for a promo at an all-news station.
SOURCE: Courtesy of WCBS-AM.

trumpets, they generally don't do a very good job. With that in mind, let's see how someone who is a radio producer, rather than just someone who knows how to run the equipment, performs some simple operations.

RECORDING A VOICE

You have learned the chain of events that allows you to record a voice on a digital audio workstation (DAW), or perhaps on a Mini Disc, or a digital cart machine. Now, start thinking like a producer. You want to record a two-person news interview program (one moderator and a guest). Let's start with the fundamental needs: Will you use the same type of mic used for recording classical music? Do you need the same type of quality and pickup pattern? What about the effect of the equipment on the participants? Although the conveniently located studio mic suspended from a boom can do the job, will this large instrument hanging in midair between the moderator and the guest have an intimidating effect? You bet it will.

People unfamiliar with radio generally regard the microphone with the same distrust as they would a dentist's drill. As a producer, you must take this into account. You are likely to find that the best results are achieved with two mics mounted inconspicuously on table stands. You can also use two good-quality lavaliers, although they may not be found in the typical radio studio. There's more to selecting a microphone than addressing the technical considerations we discussed in Chapter 5. See if you can come up with some other examples.

Recording Music

You've progressed to the point of being able to cue a sound file or a CD, make it play, and route the signal through the console and into a computer workstation, digital cart machine, or some other recording device. Now, let's imagine an actual production.

You have been assigned the task of cutting a 30-second public service announcement (PSA) for a local community health hotline. The music you want to use contains some lyrics and some entirely instrumental portions.

The lyric you want to use is "I'll be your friend forever, just give me a call …" But you can't just run the song under the announcement for two reasons:

1. There are more lyrics following the ones you want to use at the beginning of the spot, and they will make your reading of the script unintelligible.

2. You want the spot to end with a musical climax. To be precise, you want to use the instrumental climax that just happens to be at the end of this 3-minute piece of music.

How would a producer working combo approach this dilemma? If you have the time or if the editing is not complex, the best solution will be to pick out the appropriate music segments using a digital computer workstation. You can easily highlight regions and place them into a playlist on programs such as Adobe Audition (see Figure 10.3) or Bias Peak Pro. The software will allow you to create a smooth transition to fade out one portion of your music while you fade up another. Editing the musical bed will provide you with the smoothest and best-sounding background. Now you can record your voice and musical bed onto a second machine, such as a Mini Disc or a digital cart.

Another better solution would be to use the highlighted cuts and paste them in the multitrack area using computer software. Then you could record your voice and align the tracks perfectly using the many capabilities of the DAW. This solution would allow you to use the amplitude and cross-fade capabilities of the software. Such production takes a little more time initially but can provide a more polished final product.

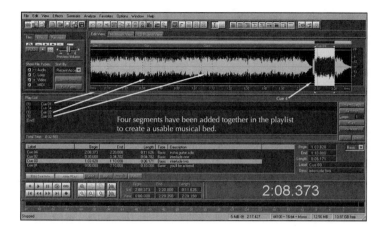

FIGURE 10.3

Four segments from this song have been pulled into a playlist to create a musical bed. This is easily accomplished by highlighting the desired regions and adding them into the playlist area.

SOURCE: © 2013 Adobe Systems, Inc.

If you don't have a digital workstation available, there are alternate ways to create a useful musical bed. One possible strategy is to record the final 25 seconds of the song onto a Mini Disc or some other recording medium.

Because you know (by reading the time on the CD or by timing the piece yourself) that the cut is exactly 2:30 long, you simply start the CD and the timer simultaneously and start recording when the timer reaches 2:05. You have determined that the opening lyric takes about 9 seconds (and you have timed the copy you will be reading). At this point, you can recue the Mini Disc and follow this sequence:

- Start the CD and fade it up on the console. (Of course, you've already taken levels and know how high to put the volume.)

- Start the timer as the CD begins playing.

- Record the first 5 seconds of the lyric.

- Start the Mini Disc with the fader down 5 seconds into the CD before you open the mic. Remember, you have four more seconds before the lyric will finish. The spot is now set to finish exactly when you want it to: 30 seconds from the beginning of the spot.

- Open the mic and read the copy.

- When the important line of lyrics ends, begin to fade the CD under your voice (a process called *ducking*) and read your copy. While reading the copy, execute a cross-fade. That is, fade up the Mini Disc as you fade down the CD. Done gradually, and underneath the cover of your voice, the cross-fade may not be detectable. Remember, at this point, the music should not overpower your voice.

- Be sure to use headphones to monitor your mic level relative to the music level.

- When you have finished reading your copy, bring up the music to the correct level on the VU meter to finish the spot.

You've created a perfectly timed spot that includes the beginning and end you want. All the production elements reinforce the message and create an effect. In particular, the music reinforces the message. The result is a package that puts the point across, with all the production elements enhancing the message. (Incidentally, you can make this PSA in several possible ways. Another way of doing things that might prove easier is to record 40 seconds of the song on a digital cart. That way you won't have to start the disc during the spot; however, you will have to keep accurate time before the spot begins.)

The point of this discussion is to illustrate the fact that there are several possible solutions to most production problems. Depending on the amount of time you have and the equipment available to you, as a producer you'll frequently be called upon to determine the best way to create a spot or program segment.

SUMMARY

The ultimate goal of radio production is to achieve an effect—to create an image in the mind of the listener and communicate a message.

Production elements in a piece of production support a central theme to achieve an effect. For example, upbeat music in a restaurant commercial conveys vibrancy and excitement. Production elements are also used as signatures to create immediate identification in the minds of listeners.

Music is a common production element used to achieve an effect. Music is best used when it explicitly contributes to the communication of an idea. Using music just for the sake of having it is often distracting and counterproductive. Likewise, sound effects must be used judiciously. Sound effects can be very effective when their use is logical and supports the central theme. When they are used just because they are available, sound effects become pure gimmickry.

Coloration of sound, another contributing factor in achieving an effect, refers to the technical ways sound is manipulated. Other contributors to achieving an effect are timing and pace, voice quality, and the sound of individual words.

APPLICATIONS

SITUATION 1/THE PROBLEM The producer was given a tough and very important assignment: Produce a commercial for men's cologne. The talent—a woman—seemed to read the copy correctly, but the client didn't like the spot even though he couldn't spell out what didn't ring true about it. His only comment was, "It doesn't sound like she's talking to me."

ONE POSSIBLE SOLUTION After giving it some thought, the producer changed microphones. Using a higher-quality mic with a cardioid pickup pattern, he instructed the talent to move in closer. The result: greater presence and a more intimate feel for the commercial.

SITUATION 2/THE PROBLEM The producer at an FM station was in charge of preparing a PSA calling for air-pollution abatement. According to the script, the announcer was to read copy outdoors with birds chirping in the background.

But when this was tried, the portable equipment didn't produce very good quality: The birds, which really were chirping in the park where the spot was taped, were barely audible on the final product.

ONE POSSIBLE SOLUTION Realizing that the way things sound to the ear is not necessarily how they sound to the microphone, the producer recorded only the birds on one tape. This gave her the option of varying the volume when she mixed the announcer and the background sound effects through the console.

The announcer's voice track presented another problem. It sounded terrible when recorded on the portable equipment, whose quality just couldn't match the studio mics. This lack of quality would be sorely apparent when the spot was played on air. But recording the announcer's copy in the studio made the whole spot sound phony. It sounded, not like an announcer standing outdoors, but like a studio recording mixed with sound effects.

The producer remembered what she had learned about the physics of sound and realized that the problems stemmed from the fact that the microphone was in a very lively part of the studio, near several bare walls. Some experimentation resulted in the relocation of the microphone to a dead area. Without the sound bouncing off the walls, the sound was flatter, and the listener could much more readily imagine that the entire spot had been recorded outdoors.

Now the producer was finding that she could achieve the effect she wanted, within the technical restrictions of the equipment. One problem remained, however. Although the bird noises she'd recorded in the park worked well for the background, they weren't of sufficiently high quality to be brought up full, as she had wanted to do in the beginning of the spot. She felt the production needed to open with a couple of seconds of solid sound effects, which would then fade down under the announcer.

She solved this problem by finding the appropriate sound effect in the station's sound effects library. The only entry she could find ("Bird Calls") would not have been appropriate for the background of the entire spot, but it was perfect for an attention-getting opening. To create the whole package, she used the birdcall from the CD and cross-faded it to the ambient sound she had recorded.

The ultimate result was a high-quality PSA that achieved the desired effect.

EXERCISES

1. Construct a script for a 60-second PSA. For this exercise, be sure to include the following:
   - One sound effect
   - A music bed
   - Narration

   Be sure that everything in your PSA has a purpose. Nothing must seem to be thrown in for its own sake.

2. Under the supervision of your instructor, produce the PSA.

3. If a production music library is available to you, have class members select music they feel is appropriate for the following:

    ■   The opening of a news program

    ■   Background for a beer commercial

    ■   Background for a fashion show

    Discuss these selections, and discuss class members' impressions of the three scenarios. (Conceptions of a good beer commercial, for instance, will vary from person to person.) Note the difference in class members' conceptions of both the scenarios and the proper selection of music.

4. Cast celebrities for voice-over parts in the following hypothetical radio productions. (Remember, the celebrities will be heard and not seen.) Write down your choices and your reasons for making them.

    ■   A commercial for aspirin

    ■   A commercial for an elegant restaurant

    ■   A PSA for saving wildlife

    ■   The part of an insane murderer in a radio drama

    ■   A commercial for high-priced, somewhat frivolous women's accessories

    Discuss your reasoning with class members and your instructor. During your discussions, try to state as directly as possible what it is about each celebrity's voice that would create the proper effects and get the various messages across.

11

Drama and Dramatic Elements in Radio Production

The purpose of this chapter is not to demonstrate what is almost an obsolete art form, but rather to introduce the principles of radio drama that are present in other forms of radio production.

This very short chapter contains only one exercise. Instead of the usual complement of exercises, we have provided a full-length radio drama in Appendix B. Production of the drama can serve as a class project; merely reading it will give you insight into the structure of drama and dramatic elements. If time doesn't permit (production of a radio drama is a big project), the exercise at the end of this chapter will suffice.

Radio drama per se is no longer very common in America, and that's unfortunate.

Old-time radio drama, as its devotees can attest, involved the audience in a way that television cannot. A radio drama creates images in the mind that can furnish a much more vivid picture than can be produced by even the most sophisticated television production company.

Radio drama is also an excellent way to learn the mechanics of editing, mic placement, recording voices, and mixing. You'll find the production of the drama provided in Appendix B to be exceptionally challenging but quite instructional as well. Radio drama techniques can be adapted for inserting dramatic elements into commercials and, in limited applications, into news and public-affairs programs. That's the essential focus of this chapter.

THE STRUCTURE OF DRAMA

A *drama* is a composition that tells a story through action and dialogue. It generally involves a conflict: person versus person or person versus society or nature. A drama, in its broadest form, has a plot; usually, the plot has a beginning, middle, and end. A drama includes dramatic techniques, such as suspense and exposition. Let's review this description and see how each term relates to radio drama and to dramatic elements in radio production.

Action

Because radio is not a visual medium, action must be portrayed through sound. Try this: Close your eyes and imagine what sounds would be needed to convey what was happening at a boxing match. Action in a prizefight would be dramatized on radio with the ringing of the bell, the roar of the crowd, and the smacking of gloves.

Dialogue

The dialogue could provide a description of the fight. Spoken words are very important in radio drama. Words provide most of the information and meaning in a scene, and they describe most of the action. The prizefight scene, for example, could be fleshed out with dialogue from a ring announcer or conversation in a fighter's corner.

Plot

The plot is the storyline. All action and dialogue must advance the plot; that is, each scene of action or dialogue must move the plot along and reinforce the message.

Beginning, Middle, and End

Drama usually has a sequence of events and a conclusion. Although dramatic elements within radio production don't always have a complete beginning, middle, and end sequence, there almost always is some sort of resolution in which the problem is solved. In dramatic terms, this is known as the *denouement*, which is the resolution of a conflict.

Conflict

Conflict in drama doesn't always have to be a struggle between two people. Conflict can consist of a person's struggle to overcome back pain or a depressed mood, a type of conflict that is portrayed frequently in radio commercials. (Resolution, of course, would come from the sponsor's pain remedy.)

Suspense

Suspense is what compels us to keep listening. To achieve suspense, plot writers refrain from providing conflict and resolution at the same time. Will Mrs. Smith's back pain be cured? We usually have to wait through about 20 seconds of product pitch to find the answer.

Exposition

Details must be revealed in a logical and realistic fashion. The process of imparting information is known as *exposition*, and it's an important part of all types of drama.

Think about it: Gracefully giving the audience all the information it needs to understand an unfolding scene is a very difficult task. In plays written centuries ago, a popular form of exposition consisted of having two maids, through supposedly casual conversation, set the scene while dusting the master's house. This type of exposition, a clumsy recitation of facts, came to be known *as feather-duster exposition*, and modern writers usually avoid it.

More graceful exposition techniques might involve a short dramatic scene. Let's say the producer of a radio commercial wants to set a scene that supports a family's need to buy a home computer to help a child with math homework. Would it serve the client's purposes to have mother and father—in the role of the maids mentioned above—discuss Junior's poor report card? Perhaps, but the scene could be set more effectively and quickly with, for example, a short classroom scene, where Junior demonstrates his lack of mathematical acumen by botching a problem at the chalkboard. Or, perhaps we might hear Junior talking to himself about solving the problem in front of the class. Drama can take many forms.

DRAMATIC ELEMENTS IN COMMERCIAL PRODUCTION

Even though you may find little occasion to produce the kind of full-scale drama included in Appendix B, you will certainly have the opportunity to incorporate dramatic elements in commercials you produce.

"Oh, my head is killing me!" How often have you heard that line, or one similar to it, in an advertisement for a headache remedy? It's the start of a common drama—a slice of life, so to speak—that can be played out effectively. Note how much more effective it is to use the dramatic scene than to have the announcer prattle on about the fact that Mrs. Smith has a headache. Drama, in effect, serves two purposes in a radio commercial: to capture attention and to compress time.

Capturing Attention

All of us are interested in how life unfolds. Why else do reality programs, and other similar dramatic forms, draw such rapt interest? In the radio commercial, a dramatic scene engages the listener and drives home a point. For example, a comedic scene featuring some incompetent mechanics attracts the listener and

(PHIL WHISTLING "DECK THE HALLS." SOUND EFFECTS OF PAPER RUSTLING AND BOX BEING SMASHED ABOUT ON TABLE ... SOUND EFFECT CARRIES THROUGHOUT.)

LEW:	HEY ... WHAT ARE YOU DOING?
PHIL:	I AM BUSILY WRAPPING A WONDERFUL CHRISTMAS GIFT IN A DECORATIVE FASHION. HOW DO YOU LIKE THE LITTLE ... OOPS, I CUT A LITTLE HOLE IN THE TABLECLOTH THERE. OH WELL ... I'LL PUT A VASE THERE AND NO ONE WILL NOTICE.
LEW:	LOOK, YOU'RE WASTING YOUR TIME WITH THAT MESS. IF YOU WOULD JUST ...
PHIL (INTERRUPTS):	WAIT. PUT YOUR FINGER RIGHT THERE AND HOLD IT. THEN WHEN I SAY "LET GO," TAKE IT AWAY REAL FAST. OK ... LET GO. (SOUND OF VIOLENT RUMPLING OF PAPER AND SMASHING OF BOX. GIFT ENDS UP ON FLOOR.)
LEW:	LOOK ... INSTEAD OF GOING THROUGH ALL THAT, WHY DON'T YOU TAKE YOUR GIFTS TO COUNTY SAVINGS BANK?
PHIL:	COUNTY SAVINGS WANTS MY GIFTS?
LEW:	THEY'LL WRAP THEM FOR YOU. FREE. THEN YOU CAN PICK THEM UP IN TIME FOR CHRISTMAS ... ALL NEATLY WRAPPED.
PHIL:	THEY'LL DO THAT FOR ME?
LEW:	YOU AND ANYONE ELSE WHO BRINGS IN THEIR GIFTS BEFORE DECEMBER 16TH.
PHIL:	YOU DON'T SAY? HEY, YOU DON'T SUPPOSE THEY KNOW HOW TO MAKE A NICE SCOTCH TAPE BOW DO YOU? I WAS JUST ABOUT TO ... (FADE OUT)

F I G U R E   11.1

Script for a commercial that uses dramatic elements to attract attention.

SOURCE: © Cengage Learning 2013

sets the stage for the upcoming spiel that tells why Joe's Garage does a better job than the bunglers depicted in the commercial. Note how the commercial reproduced in Figure 11.1 uses a similar dramatic scene to attract attention.

Compressing Time

Which approach seems more effective from a radio producer's point of view?

1. John works at a newspaper; he is a reporter, and the pressure is very intense. Right now he's working under a tight deadline. The pressure gets to him sometimes and results in heartburn and an upset stomach.

2. SFX (sound effects): KEYBOARD TYPING, OFFICE COMMOTION.

VOICE: John, deadline for the fire story is in 5 minutes!

JOHN: Boy, this pressure really gets to me sometimes ... heartburn, acid indigestion ...

Notice that scene 2 would take about half the time needed for scene 1. Similarly, a sound effect of clapping thunder and pouring rain takes much less time

(OPEN WITH SOUND EFFECT OF CAR BEING DRIVEN DOWN ROAD)

WIFE: IT'S SO HARD TO SHOP FOR A HOME IN SUCH A SHORT AMOUNT OF
               TIME.

HUSBAND: YOU'RE RIGHT. AND WE REALLY HAVE TO FINISH BY TOMORROW ...
               OR WE HAVE TO COME BACK ANOTHER TIME.

WIFE: (SIGHS)

ANNOUNCER: YOU DON'T HAVE TO GO THROUGH ALL THAT AT JOHN HOLMES
               REALTY AT 143 WEST SECOND STREET. AT JOHN HOLMES REALTY,
               WE DON'T RUN YOU ALL OVER TO LOOK AT EVERYTHING THERE IS
               FOR SALE ... WHAT WE DO IS SIT YOU DOWN IN OUR COMFORTABLE
               LOUNGE AND LET YOU LOOK OVER OUR ILLUSTRATED GUIDE TO
               HOMES ON THE MARKET. YOU PICK THE HOMES THAT FIT YOUR
               NEEDS AND PRICE RANGE, AND THEN WE'LL GIVE YOU A TOUR
               USING OUR MODERN VIDEOTAPE EQUIPMENT. SO IF YOU FIND
               THAT YOU DON'T LIKE THE WALLPAPER, YOU'LL KNOW IT BEFORE
               DRIVING THERE. WHEN YOU SEE THE HOME YOU'D LIKE TO GO AND
               LOOK AT, WE'LL TAKE YOU THERE FOR A CLOSE LOOK. IT'S A
               SIMPLE PROCESS TO BUY A HOME AT JOHN HOLMES REALTY.
               COME AND SEE US AND WE'LL SHOW YOU.

FIGURE 11.2

Script for a commercial that uses dramatic techniques to compress time.

SOURCE: © Cengage Learning 2013

than announcer's copy telling how bad the storm is. Figure 11.2 shows a commercial that compresses its premise by using dramatic elements. In Chapter 12, we deal with the concepts of attracting attention and compressing time, as well as with other facets of radio commercial production.

DRAMATIC ELEMENTS IN NEWS PRODUCTION

The goal of drama is to tell an interesting story in a compelling way. The goal of news is not so different. Although a news producer must be extremely careful not to mislead listeners or to falsify information for the sake of dramatic impact, judicious use of dramatic elements is certainly acceptable. Documentaries usually contain some dramatic elements; a story on beachfront pollution, for example, can be enhanced with the plaintive call of seagulls.

Contrast, an important facet of drama, is also used as a dramatic element in documentary production. Thus, a politician's claim that tax revenues are insufficient could be juxtaposed against a city official's contention that most of the city budget is squandered on salaries for no-show employees or in other wasteful ways. Playing the two cuts back to back, without comment, increases the dramatic value and makes a point that no amount of narration could. Music is also an important element of documentary production, though it is rarely if ever used in hard news production, except in newscast openings.

Remember that narration of news, public affairs, and documentaries can use dramatic elements, too. Don't be afraid to try new ideas in news production.

Dramatic elements, as long as they are tasteful and not deceptive, can significantly freshen up what might otherwise be a stale area of radio production. News producers doing long-form reporting frequently record *wild sound* to accompany the actual story narration or interview. The sound of police and fire trucks racing to a scene, for example, can be cut into a news report to give it extra impact.

TECHNICAL CONSIDERATIONS OF RADIO DRAMA

The most immediate consideration in producing radio drama or inserting a dramatic element is to create the illusion of place and movement. By *place*, we mean the location of the actors; by *movement*, we mean their physical movement through space.

Giving the Illusion of Place

Acoustic characteristics are important in determining place. For example, would you believe that a lively, reverberating sound was coming from someone on a beach, even with seashore sound effects in the background? No, it wouldn't be convincing (just as the lively studio made the outdoor scene in the Applications section of Chapter 10 sound unnatural).

Would you believe that someone was shouting from across the lawn if the actor was miked 3 inches from his mouth? Would an intimate conversation sound natural if it was being picked up by a mic several feet across the room?

The proper illusion of place is determined by mic technique. The producer will have to move actors farther from or closer to the mic to achieve the proper effect or may need to change the placement of the mic. If it doesn't sound convincing to you, it won't convince the audience.

Giving the Illusion of Movement

Radio drama often entails movement of the actors, so it's important that the mic set-up give the illusion of movement. A script element that requires an actor to leave the room and slam the door, for example, will have to sound believable. As we suggested earlier, actually having an actor slam the studio door may not give the effect desired because the mic doesn't hear the way ears do. A better approach might be to have the actor take small steps, moving just a few feet away from the mic. The door slam can be dubbed in or done live by a studio assistant, if it sounds believable. In any event, there must be an illusion of movement within the scene, and the movement must be played to the mic to achieve a realistic sound.

Making the Background a Fabric of Believability

The sounds we hear (or ignore) as everyday background noise would be far too intrusive for a radio drama. That's because in real life we focus our attention on certain sounds and exclude other sounds from our attention. In radio drama, it is very important to plan the background sound effects to create a fabric of believability. If we need to move through busy streets, the sound effects must take us from one location to another. Often, the inexperienced producer mistakenly sequences sounds one after another instead of weaving and blending them together. Have the sounds move in and out of perspective. This weaving of sound is accomplished with preplanning and careful execution of audio levels. It is a vital element of dramatic believability.

The proper perspective is a function of more than just loudness (or, in the case of stereo drama, of spatial position). Perspective also includes the way a character would hear sound. A movie sound effect best exemplifies this. In a boxing film, the sound of the blows is far different when the view of the camera (perspective) represents the person being hit. The blows are often portrayed, visually and aurally, in slow motion as crashing, catastrophic explosions. When the camera serves as the observer, the blows are not portrayed so dramatically.

Mic Techniques to Achieve Illusions
of Place and Movement

Creating illusion of place is largely a function of the physical shape and construction of the studio, but, as we mentioned earlier, the distance of the actors from the mic plays a major role. The ideal set-up for a radio drama in which actors must deal with place and movement is to suspend the mic from a boom (see Figure 11.3) and group the actors around it. This protects the actors from tripping over wires and bumping into floor stands.

An omnidirectional mic is best, although bidirectional patterns can be used. A high degree of presence is usually felt to be a desirable attribute in radio drama, so a sensitive condenser mic might be a wise choice. A variety of technical

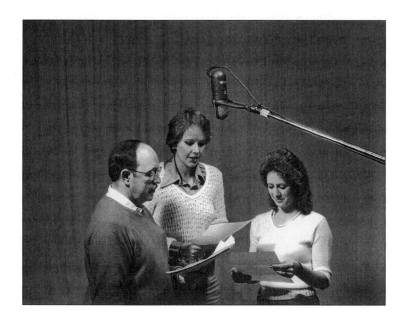

FIGURE 11.3

Actors grouped around a boommounted mic.

SOURCE: Philip Benoit

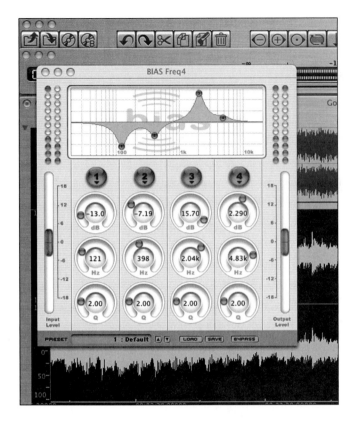

FIGURE 11.4

Using the four-band equalizer built into the software, it is possible to create a realistic telephone effect for any regular sound file.

SOURCE: BIAS, Inc.

devices can come in handy for creating a variety of illusions, but they don't necessarily have to be elaborate. A two-board clapper, for example, makes a convincing gunshot and is always ready to go off with a little help from another person in the studio.

Today's software makes it possible to accomplish many effects that previously had to be done manually or with special equipment. Figure 11.4 shows how equalization makes it possible to create a telephone effect (as if someone was calling in from a telephone). Many special effects can be created using special features in DAW software.

Sound Design

Drama production, from conception to completion, is a long process and must be planned with the final product visualized at every stage. Always keep in mind that dramatic elements in radio are an illusion. They don't just happen; they have to be created. A certain amount of technical skill and planning is a necessity for the producer who wants the listener to believe in that illusion. The process of developing a preproduction idea of what the production will sound like is called *sound design*. If your commercial will benefit from some dramatic elements, planning them in advance will be useful.

SUMMARY

Although radio drama as a distinct art form is long past its prime, drama and dramatic elements are common tools in a wide range of radio production tasks. Many successful commercials are actually miniature dramas or comedies. A dramatic element generally has the traditional structures of drama: action; dialogue; plot; a beginning, middle, and end; conflict; suspense; and exposition. Dramatic elements can attract attention, and they can compress time by expressing many thoughts in a small dramatic scene. Dramatic elements have some place in news production, though it is essential that they not be used to mislead the listener.

Among the radio producer's major considerations are creating the illusion of place, giving the illusion of movement, and making the background a fabric of believability. Achieving illusions of place and movement can be accomplished through mic techniques.

APPLICATIONS

SITUATION 1/THE PROBLEM A producer was given the assignment of producing a 15-minute documentary on the effects of government loan programs on local farmers. It soon became apparent that the collection of interviews she intended to gather would prove to be extremely dull. One interview in particular, a question-and-answer session with a farmer and the farmer's accountant, promised to be deadly.

ONE POSSIBLE SOLUTION To liven things up, the producer took two steps. First, the narration was done not in the studio but on-site at a local farm; background audio lent a dramatic texture. Second, instead of questioning the farmer and accountant, the producer convinced them to talk with each other, dramatizing a frank discussion of how the government's loan policies had affected the farmer's operation. The goal was to listen in on a conversation between the farmer and the accountant, not to question them.

SITUATION 2/THE PROBLEM A producer at a New England radio station was given the task of developing commercials for a glove manufacturer and retailer. Previous ads had featured nothing but announcer's copy extolling the toughness and warmth of the gloves; those commercials did not appear to be effective. The sponsor's instructions were, "Give me something with a little more zip."

ONE POSSIBLE SOLUTION In search of that elusive "zip," the producer came across evidence that the gloves really were tough. The fishermen who operated in the Atlantic coastal waters favored them almost exclusively. The producer took a portable recording device out onto the fishing boats and interviewed some of the fishermen wearing the gloves. The fishermen (who were compensated for their endorsement) spoke of how tough their job was on gloves and how a good pair of gloves made life on a fishing boat a lot easier. One fisherman also described an incident in which his gloves had helped him weather a brutal storm. With the ambient noise and some dubbed-in sound effects, the producer was able to use the dramatic scenes to produce a compelling commercial that met the client's needs.

EXERCISE

Create a 60-second spot that tells the story of your first day in college. Consider telling the listener about first-day encounters such as registration, dining-hall eating, finding your classroom, meeting a friend or roommate, getting lost on campus, and discovering third- and fourth-year students. Do this using only sound effects and music. (*Hint*: Voice can be used as a sound effect when we don't hear any particular person speaking.)

12

Commercial Production

Commercial production, as far as managers and owners are concerned, is at the core of radio's main purpose: to make a profit. Like it or not, that's how commercial stations survive. It is critical that commercials, which are the tangible result of the sales effort, be done well and stand out from the clutter. As a producer of radio commercials, you will have three responsibilities:

1. To produce commercials that stimulate sales,
2. To produce commercials that please the client, and
3. To produce commercials that fit your station's sound.

Point 3 is more important than you might suspect, because whatever your station's sound might be, it assuredly is not "all commercial." In other words, listeners tune in to hear a particular type of music, or news/talk, or the ball game. Commercials are often regarded as clutter by the listener, and a message that seems both tedious and out of place will be doubly objectionable.

That's why the latest trend in radio advertising is to do more with less. In fact, in 2005 the giant radio chain Clear Channel began promoting 30-second commercials, as opposed to 60-second ones, with the slogan "less is more." The goal is to cut clutter—and the onus is now on the producer to make the point of the commercial more quickly while keeping the listener's attention through a stopset.

The producer of a commercial (who can be anyone at the station—a sales manager, an announcer, or a production manager) must translate the goals of keeping attention and cutting clutter into a radio production that will not only work with the audience, but also please the client. In addition, today's radio producer faces unique challenges in crafting commercials for the virtually unknown territory of podcast sales.

In this chapter, we address all the elements that make up a commercial, including general sales appeal, content, and production values. It's important to have a well-rounded view of the commercial, because most radio professionals will deal with commercial production at a variety of levels at different points in their careers. Keep in mind that your function in putting together a radio commercial will include any or all of the following:

- Writing the script or putting the concept together
- Narrating the commercial
- Doing the hands-on production work
- Convincing the client that your approach is the proper one

The last duty is a common bugaboo of the commercial production field; the producer is often caught in the middle between the salesperson and the client and must act as the final arbiter of what is effective and what constitutes good production.

You may have a great deal of responsibility in determining what elements and production values will make the commercial effective. This is likely to be especially true if you function in both sales and production capacities, which is common in first broadcasting jobs (and sometimes is the only way to make a decent income).

WHAT MAKES A COMMERCIAL EFFECTIVE?

We are convinced, after more than a half century of involvement with broadcast advertising, that there are no hard-and-fast rules for determining a commercial's effectiveness. In fact, rules that occasionally get handed down from on high are often proved wrong. Several years ago, top advertising agencies determined that humor was not an effective way to help sell a product; as proof, they pointed to large firms whose very entertaining commercials didn't move the products. But then a funny thing happened: Humorous commercials began to be the crux of very successful ad campaigns, and they are commonplace today in all formats.

Even though there are no firm rules, we feel that the most important principle of radio advertising is that commercials, like programming, must engage the audience's attention and not be an irritant, because radio listeners, especially in cars, have a new station only a push of a button away. This is pretty much what happened in the evolution of television. Twenty years ago and more, there were fewer choices and fewer remote controls. The theory at the time was that an irritating television commercial could be effective because it made the viewer remember. Several years ago a successful TV campaign admonished people because they had "ring around the collar." It was irritating but it worked. The important thing about "ring around the collar"—or any other commercial for that matter—is that it engages attention and appeals to a fundamental human drive. Consider that the dreaded ring was always discovered in a public and often posh environment, such as a cruise ship. (Never while hubby was playing touch football, though.) There was always a scene of the poor housewife squirming in humiliation as her husband's ring around the collar was loudly pointed out.

However, it's unlikely that an irritant spot would be as effective on modern TV; this is a lesson radio has learned, sometimes painfully. So what *does* work in radio? There are no magic formulas for producing effective commercials; even the major advertising agencies, backed with millions of dollars for research, bomb sometimes. Conversely, commercials that fly in the face of research and established practice have done spectacularly well at times.

Although you generally won't be able to research the effectiveness of the commercials you produce (except for getting feedback from local merchants), you can take advantage of the basic appeals that appear again and again in broadcast advertising by including the elements of effective commercials in your productions.

ELEMENTS OF EFFECTIVE RADIO ADVERTISING

Essentially, a radio commercial has to be effective in terms of sound. There's no picture, so the sound must compensate. That's not necessarily a disadvantage. A picture in the mind can be infinitely more persuasive than a picture on the screen or in a print ad.

Writer and producer Stan Freberg demonstrated this attribute quite effectively in a well-known promotional spot produced for the Radio Advertising Bureau. He created an imaginary scene, complete with sound effects, in which he drained Lake Michigan, filled it with hot chocolate, added a mountain of whipped cream, and had the Royal Canadian Air Force drop a 10-ton maraschino cherry on top. Freberg then challenged potential advertisers to "try that on television." (Can you imagine the sound effects Freberg would have used?)

The point is that all the imagination of the listener is brought to bear on the message through the use of music and simple dramatic techniques—many of them the same ones we outlined in the previous chapter. Bill Burton of the Detroit Radio Advertising Group puts it this way: "Radio is an ideal sales vehicle to stretch the imagination as well as the mind. What better medium to sell the great aromas of perfume, shaving lotion, warm vegetable soup for lunch or the smell of turkey and ham cooking—there is no way you could convert these wonderful aromas to picture or film, but the visualization in the mind can be overwhelming. All great radio takes place in your mind. The characters and situations you identify with, the taste, smells, emotions, all come to life through the power of your imagination."[1] Remember, too, that radio advertising can and

---

1. http://radiodetroit.com/resources/creativity.html

should be geared toward a target audience. One of the great advantages of radio is that its audiences are usually clearly defined. Want to advertise acne medicine? Buy some time in the evening hours of the local hot hits station. An advertiser with a Mercedes-Benz dealership would be wise to check out an all-news station. The beer company advertising directly to its potential customers certainly will buy some time on the local station that carries the baseball games.

You, the radio producer, can take advantage of both elements of radio advertising—the ability to create mental pictures and the targeting of advertising—to create effective commercials. This means that you must think in terms of radio. It sounds obvious, but it's not. For one thing, the producer of radio commercials is often at odds with the client. This is because many merchants have the idea that the only effective commercial consists of an announcer reading as many store items and prices as can be crammed into a 30-second spot. We're not overstating the case. If you are in charge of at least some of a commercial's creative concept (this is often so, especially if you are involved in the sale), this is a situation you will probably experience time and time again.

The producer dealing with such a client faces a ticklish situation. The easy way out is to give the client what he or she wants, which might not be particularly effective, meaning that the account could soon be lost. Alternatively, the producer can lobby for a more enlightened approach, which could conceivably produce much better results and bring about an increase in advertising. However, keep in mind that even the most cleverly constructed commercial can fall flat.

In the long run, you and the client will both be better off by shying away from the approach of listing the entire contents of the client's store. Here are two examples of how Lew O'Donnell and Phil Benoit, who once owned an advertising agency, handled the problem. We're not saying that these are the best approaches or the only approaches; they're simply alternatives that were effective.

A Shoe Store Advertisement

A local merchant had, for years, run back-to-school ads listing 10 or 11 brands of children's shoes and their respective prices. Results were middling. Although the shoe store owner initially opposed the idea, a radio campaign was developed in which the nostalgic excitement of back-to-school time was re-created in the minds of the parents (see Figure 12.1).

A Car Dealership Advertisement

Another merchant, the owner of a car dealership, was convinced to alter his advertising from a recitation of cars and prices to an approach that encouraged potential customers to browse on Sunday. The script (see Figure 12.2) also conveyed a low-key attitude.

Notice how major advertisers avoid the listing approach. Grocery store chains, for example, may note one or two specials, but the thrust of the commercial is,

ANNOUNCER: REMEMBER THE EXCITEMENT OF GOING BACK TO SCHOOL WHEN YOU WERE A KID? THERE WAS THE SLIGHT SADNESS THAT SUMMER WAS OVER, BUT THERE WAS ALSO THE SENSE OF ANTICIPATION … NEW BEGINNINGS AND A FEELING OF GOOD TIMES AHEAD FOR THE NEW SCHOOL YEAR.

ALONG WITH THAT SENSE OF EXCITEMENT CAME THE TIME WHEN YOU WENT SHOPPING FOR NEW CLOTHES. THEY ALWAYS HAD A SPECIAL KIND OF "NEW" SMELL TO THEM. AND WHEN YOU SMELL IT TODAY, YOU PROBABLY THINK OF GOING BACK TO SCHOOL.

BEST OF ALL, THOUGH, WAS GETTING NEW SHOES. YOUR OLD RELIABLES HAD JUST ABOUT MADE IT THROUGH THE PAST YEAR. AND NOW IT WAS TIME TO GET THOSE BRAND NEW ONES THAT WOULD GET YOU OFF TO A GOOD START.

WELL, VONA SHOES, 122 WEST SECOND STREET, IS THE PLACE THAT CAN BUILD SIMILAR MEMORIES FOR YOUR CHILD. AND WHILE THEY'RE AT IT THEY'LL SEE TO IT THAT YOUR CHILD GETS QUALITY AND A GOOD FIT. THE TOP BRAND NAMES IN CHILDREN'S FOOTWEAR IN VONA'S EXTENSIVE INVENTORY MEANS THAT YOU'LL FIND THE SIZE YOU NEED AND YOU'LL GET VALUE.

THAT'S IMPORTANT FOR YOU. BUT FOR YOUR CHILD, THERE WILL BE EXCITEMENT AND THE FUN OF GOING TO BUY SHOES FOR BACK TO SCHOOL.

A TIME FILLED WITH SIGNIFICANCE IN A YOUNG LIFE.

VONA SHOES … WHERE THEY UNDERSTAND YOU.

FIGURE 12.1

Script of a commercial that uses an appeal to nostalgia to persuade its audience.
SOURCE: © Cengage Learning 2013

"Our stores are friendly and convenient, offering the largest selection at the best prices." Much of this message can be communicated through dramatic technique or through music. However, almost any approach will be better than the crammed-in list. For one thing, a radio listener might not even comprehend a list of products and prices, even though a list is effective in a newspaper ad. Second, a list of products and prices doesn't exploit the strengths of radio advertising.

What does exploit radio advertising's strong points? Essentially, any ad that creates mental images and proves a benefit to the consumer. That benefit may be tangible (saving money) or perceived (avoiding the humiliation of ring around the collar).

A Humorous Pizza Commercial

Humor and the personal approach of radio can captivate an audience, drawing listeners into a scene played out in the theater of the mind. A little sarcastic humor, if it's not overdone, can engage listeners who are using radio as an escape from their commuting. An interesting example is shown in the two scripts that

ANNOUNCER: SHOPPING FOR A CAR IS AN IMPORTANT PROCESS. ONE THAT TAKES TIME AND THOUGHT. YOU LOOK AND YOU TALK … YOU DEAL AND YOU DECIDE. BUT THERE ARE TIMES WHEN YOU WOULD LIKE TO BE ALL ALONE AT A CAR DEALER'S LOT AND JUST TAKE YOUR TIME TO LOOK OVER THE SELECTION OF CARS WITHOUT TALKING TO A SALESPERSON.

WELL, AT BURRITT CHEVROLET ON BRIDGE STREET IN OSWEGO, WE UNDERSTAND THAT NEED. SO HERE'S A SUGGESTION. COME ON SUNDAY. ALL OUR CARS ARE ON THE LOT … AND THERE'S NO ONE THERE. YOU CAN BROWSE TO YOUR HEART'S CONTENT.

OF COURSE, ONCE YOU'VE HAD A CHANCE TO LOOK OVER OUR FINE SELECTION OF BRAND NEW CHEVROLETS AND OUR GREAT A-1 USED CARS, YOU'LL PROBABLY WANT TO COME BACK FOR A TEST DRIVE.

THAT'S WHERE OUR SALESPEOPLE CAN COME IN HANDY. THEY'RE AROUND THE OTHER SIX DAYS OF THE WEEK, AND THEY'LL BE HAPPY TO SET YOU UP WITH A TEST DRIVE. THEN THEY'LL WORK WITH YOU TO COME UP WITH THE BEST DEAL AROUND ON THAT CHEVY OR USED CAR.

SO PLEASE … BE OUR GUEST. VISIT BURRITT CHEVROLET ON WEST BRIDGE STREET, OSWEGO. DO IT ON SUNDAY AT YOUR OWN PACE. THEN COME BACK ON MONDAY, OR TUESDAY OR ANY OTHER DAY, AND FIND OUT WHY WE'RE THE "DEALIN'EST" GUYS IN TOWN.

FIGURE 12.2

Script of a commercial that tries to lessen the pressure of the car-buying process.
SOURCE: © Cengage Learning 2013

link together in Figures 12.3a and 12.3b. These humorous pizza commercial scripts are offered through a pizza marketing association to local clients. You can hear how they sound by clicking on the MP3 file at http://www.pmq.com/mag/2001summer/marendt.shtml.

PRACTICAL APPROACHES TO RADIO COMMERCIALS

In this section we discuss the specific appeals radio advertising can make, as well as the nuts-and-bolts construction of a radio commercial. We provide a rather cold-blooded listing of some of the emotional triggers that are frequently used in advertising. These appeals aren't usually discussed in this manner, but if they are to be used, you should recognize them for what they are. Although there's no universal agreement about the effectiveness of all these appeals, because advertising is an area of few cut-and-dried truisms, we believe that the following appeals represent motives used in modern advertising.

We refer to a number of well-known television commercials to illustrate the appeals, because spots aired on network television will be familiar to almost all

Pizza spot #1

SFX (Sound Effects): NOISY RESTAURANT, VIDEO GAMES, KIDS YELLING

VOICE 1: HELLO, SIR, WELCOME TO PINKY'S PIZZA PLAYHOUSE!

VOICE 2: YES, UH, HI. I'D LIKE TO GET A TABLE AND HAVE SOME PIZZA PLEASE.

VOICE 1: OKAY! WHO'S THE BIRTHDAY BOY?

VOICE 2: IT'S NOT A BIRTHDAY … JUST ME. I JUST WANT TO GET SOME PIZZA.

VOICE 1: OKAY, HERE'S YOUR PARTY HAT!

VOICE 2: PARTY HAT? WAIT … DON'T YOU HAVE A QUIET LITTLE TABLE SOMEPLACE? MAYBE IN THE BACK-(GETS CUT OFF)

VOICE 1: OH SURE! RIGHT BY THE PINKY'S FUNTOWN BAND! BOFFO! SHOW THIS GENTLEMAN TO TABLE 67 PLEASE!

BOFFO: SURE THING BOSS! (HONKAHONKA)

VOICE 2: (TRAILING OFF INTO RESTAURANT): WAIT … HOLD IT … I JUST WANTED A NICE QUIET DINNER …

ANNOUNCER: LOOKING FOR A GREAT PIZZA PLACE WITH A RELAXED ATMOSPHERE? TRY LUIGI'S PIZZERIA. FANTASTIC PIZZA AND PASTA, GREAT SALADS, AND YOUR FAVORITE IMPORTED AND DOMESTIC BEERS, ALL IN A COMFORTABLE SETTING. WE'RE OPEN 11 AM TILL 11 PM SEVEN DAYS A WEEK. PLUS WE OFFER A COZY LITTLE LUNCH BUFFET MONDAY THRU FRIDAY.

SFX: (BACK TO PINKY'S)

VOICE 2 (PITIFULLY): BOFFO, IS MY PIZZA READY YET?

BOFFO: ALMOST SIR. BUT FIRST, LET'S ALL SING ALONG WITH THE PINKY'S FUNTOWN BAND!

VOICE 2: GROAN!

ANNCR: FOR THE BEST PIZZA AND QUIET DINING, COME BY LUIGI'S PIZZERIA ON OAK STREET. AND WE PROMISE, NO CLOWNS.

F I G U R E 12.3

a. Pizza spot number 1.

readers; radio commercials are usually done on a local or regional basis and would therefore be less useful for this discussion.

Each of these commercials is aimed at an individual. Too often we tend to think of our audience as a group of listeners, but actually our audience is made up of individuals. Think about when you listen to radio. You listen, perhaps, in your car on the way to work or with a mp3 player or iPod at the beach. Commercials should always address an individual and get him or her involved in the

---

Pizza spot #2

SFX: QUIET RESTAURANT

HOSTESS: HELLO, WELCOME TO LUIGI'S PIZZERIA.

VOICE 2: YES, UH, HI, I'D LIKE TO GET A TABLE AND HAVE SOME PIZZA PLEASE.

HOSTESS: OKAY! RIGHT THIS WAY.

VOICE 2: WAIT, THERE AREN'T ANY CLOWNS BACK THERE I HOPE.

HOSTESS: CLOWNS? I'M NOT SURE I UNDERSTA ...

VOICE 2: AND YOU'RE NOT GONNA MAKE ME WEAR ANY SILLY HATS ARE YOU?

HOSTESS (SEEN THIS BEFORE): AHH, NO SIR. NO PARTY HATS, NO CLOWNS, NO WAITERS NAMED BOFFO.

VOICE 2: HEY, HOW DID YOU KNOW ...?

HOSTESS: YOU WENT TO PINKY'S PIZZA PLAYHOUSE, DIDN'T YOU SIR?

ANNOUNCER: LOOKING FOR A GREAT PIZZA PLACE WITH A RELAXED ATMO- SPHERE? TRY LUIGI'S PIZZERIA. FANTASTIC PIZZA AND PASTA, GREAT SALADS, AND YOUR FAVORITE IMPORTED AND DOMESTIC BEERS, ALL IN A COMFORTABLE SETTING. WE'RE OPEN 11 AM TILL 11 PM SEVEN DAYS A WEEK. PLUS WE OFFER A COZY LITTLE LUNCH BUFFET MONDAY THRU FRIDAY.

SFX: (BACK TO LUIGI'S)

HOSTESS: HOW IS EVERYTHING, SIR?

VOICE 2: MMMMM. THIS IS GREAT PIZZA ... BUT WHO'S THAT GUY WITH THE ORANGE HAIR I KEEP SEEING? HE'S NOT A CLOWN IS HE?

HOSTESS: NO. THAT'S JUST MARVIN THE BUSBOY. HE ALWAYS LOOKS LIKE THAT.

ANNCR: FOR THE BEST PIZZA AND QUIET DINING, COME BY LUIGI'S PIZZERIA ON OAK STREET. AND WE PROMISE: NO CLOWNS.

F I G U R E   12.3 (continued)

b. Pizza spot number 2.

SOURCE: Reprinted by permission of Dick Marendi

message. This is far more effective and appealing than the stereotypical "Hey, all of you out there in radioland" approach. While it's hard to believe in light of what goes on the air in most radio markets, at one time radio was considered such a "personal" medium that advertisers were reluctant to feature certain products, as described in the Radio Retro in this chapter.

Appeal to Personal Fulfillment   The Army's promise to help you "be all that you can be" typifies this appeal, which offers a subtle promise that the sponsor's

---

RADIO RETRO • YOU CAN'T SELL THAT ON THE AIR

In the early days of radio, producers and advertisers really weren't sure what the medium was for. Was it a music box? Was it a companion? Was it a source of information? And what would be the most appropriate way to sell a product or service, given that radio was totally different from other entertainment in that it came to you rather than you going to it, as you would go to a film or a concert? The radio sat in the living room and was almost like a part of your family.

WEAF was AT&T's flagship station in the 1920s, and it struggled with the problem of what to do about advertising. The prevailing model of early radio, where advertisers paid for a half-hour of entertainment, was ineffective. But some powerful members of the public, including Secretary of Commerce Herbert Hoover, who would later become president, bristled at the idea that important events on radio would be "sandwiched" between patent-medicine ads. WEAF experimented with distinct commercials for products—as opposed to sponsorship of an entire program—but warily drew up a list of things sponsors couldn't do. No hard sell, no samples, no mention of store locations, and no embarrassing products. A commercial for toothpaste was refused because the manager of WEAF felt it was too "personal" a topic to be mentioned on the air.[2]

---

2. For an interesting history of advertising in radio, see the excerpt from Erik Barnouw, *The Sponsor: Notes on Modern Potentates* (New Brunswick, NJ: Transaction Publishers, 2004) at http://social.chass.ncsu.edu/~wiley/courses/comtech/sponsor.html.

---

product can help you be the person you always knew you could be. A credit card firm, for example, devotes a commercial to a woman in a college classroom, fulfilling her personal ambitions because, apparently, she was able to charge her tuition bills. Although we might quarrel with the approach of the credit-card commercial, isn't it more effective than reciting a list of all the places where a credit card can be used (even though it might be everywhere you want to be)?

Appeal to Authority   Don't we all want a person who knows how to take us by the hand, figuratively, and tell us about a product? Notice how former senator Robert Dole used the authority appeal in encouraging men to seek treatment for sexual dysfunction.

Appeal to the Bandwagon Effect   "More and more people every day are discovering..." appeals to a desire to get in on a trend. This is a powerful human emotion. Be in with the desirable people! Use the same products as the "in" crowd! Do you recognize several major advertising appeals that stem from this approach?

Appeal to Fear of Rejection   This is subtly different from the bandwagon effect because it illustrates the negative aspects of not being on the bandwagon. Commercials dealing with personal hygiene products are, without a doubt, the ultimate exploiters of the fear of rejection appeal. Note how people turn away from the poor unfortunates with bad breath, dandruff, and so on. You don't want to wind up like them, do you?

Appeal to Sexual Success   This appeal can be as blatant as a well-known commercial that implied that a certain brand of toothpaste would whiten your teeth, making your smile more attractive. This category overlaps a number of other appeals, including personal fulfillment and fear of rejection. In many cases, this message is so obvious as to be offensive to some. Consider the stockings commercials featuring someone who is ostensibly a career woman—but people just can't stop looking at her legs.

Appeal to Reinforcement of Listener's Ego   "You know that this product is better because you're an intelligent person" is a common approach. In effect, the commercial gives the listener a chance to use the product or service and prove that he or she is, indeed, as smart as the commercial maintains. Various stock trading companies use this approach in their advertising.

Appeal to Prestige   "Don't you deserve a [fill in name of car]?" Were it not for an innate need for prestige, items such as luxury cars and designer clothes probably wouldn't sell at all. The appeal to prestige hits that sensitive nerve that prods us to prove, through our cars, clothes, and club memberships, that we're a little better than other people.

Appeal to Value and Quality   This appeal cuts across several categories, including prestige and reinforcement of ego, but the effect of this approach is to convince the listener that the product or service is worth the price. Car commercials often state that the consumer can save money in the long run by buying a high-quality car that will hold up. Other commercials touting brand-name products use the same appeal. Sometimes direct comparisons are used.

Appeals to Other Emotional Triggers   Nostalgia, family ties, guilt, loyalty, tradition, and even simple acquisitiveness all play roles in reaching listeners.

Execution of Radio Commercials

Various techniques for reinforcing the appeal of a commercial make the message effective. Most of these techniques have been covered in other parts of this book, but here we deal with some of the specific applications to radio commercial production.

Music in Radio Commercials   Music is very effective in establishing a commercial's mood or an overall set of conditions—perhaps even the attitude of a person acting out a dramatic element. For example, music that features other singers joining in is a strong motivator for the bandwagon effect. A commercial that appeals to nostalgia can quickly set the scene by using old songs. In this case, music becomes a sort of shorthand way of communicating a message. For example, it's far more efficient to set the stage with some dance-band music than to load up the precious time with spoken copy designed to indicate the time frame.

Music, then, is very helpful to the commercial producer in creating a mood and reinforcing a message. However, music is not always a favorable attribute in a commercial. As we already noted, popular songs can be overused. To make matters worse, a currently popular song may detract from the message because listeners tune into the song and ignore the thrust of the commercial.

Music for commercials can come from sources other than the station's air-play library. To review, music can be obtained from the following:

- *Generic commercial music libraries*, which can be purchased as a collection or downloaded from the Internet. These collections feature music themes for a wide variety of applications. This type of production music is often useful, but it can become repetitive. Music production companies constantly update their offerings to keep the packages fresh and current with music trends.

   Some older musical packages included songs with lyrics that tend to be on the corny side, such as "You'll find it at the mall." Moreover, once a lyric becomes associated with one retailer, it loses its usefulness for other applications.

- *Jingles from a national advertiser's ad agency.* When large manufacturers provide a contribution to local merchants' advertising budgets, the result is known as cooperative, or *co-op*, advertising. The same types of jingles are used by large organizations that have local franchises. Most of this prepared music comes in a form known as a donut, whose "hole" is filled in by the local merchant's copy. Figure 12.4 shows an example of a script for a donut co-op ad. Many national manufacturers provide both the copy and the jingle. The local retailer inserts his or her own local address or store information in the donut.

RADIO SCRIPT

JOAN MAYER

30 SECONDS

CO-OP

USE WITH TAPE CUT #2

MUSIC OPEN: (10 SECONDS)

FADE MUSIC UNDER

ANNOUNCER: THAT'S RIGHT, THERE IS NO BETTER WAY TO GET INTO SPRING THIS YEAR THAN TO BUY YOURSELF A COMPLETE COORDINATED SUIT AND SHOES OUTFIT BY JOAN MAYER. YOU'LL FIND A WIDE SELECTION RIGHT NOW AT _____.

A JOAN MAYER OUTFIT MAKES IT EASY TO SAY "I'M READY," READY FOR SPRING. THE WIDE SELECTION OF TWO-PIECE SUITS IN LIGHTWEIGHT DACRON WITH COLORS TO MATCH AND COORDINATE WITH OUR QUALITY BRAND OF SPRING FOOTWEAR MEANS THAT YOU'LL HAVE NO TROUBLE FINDING THE OUTFIT OR OUTFITS THAT MAKE YOU LOOK YOUR SMARTEST FOR SPRING. SO STOP IN SOON AT _____ AND MAKE YOUR SELECTIONS FROM OUR SELECTIONS.

MUSIC UP: (5 SECONDS)

F I G U R E 12.4

Script of a commercial that uses a donut.

SOURCE: © Cengage Learning 2013

- *Original music produced locally.* Local advertisers or advertising agencies often engage recording studios to compose original music for radio advertising. This usually isn't as difficult or as expensive as you might think, and some locally produced music can brighten a spot considerably. Some radio stations use musically talented staffers and freelancers to produce musical spots in-house. In the use of any music, the producer will generally follow the guidelines expressed in Chapter 6; the editing structures (blending music and voice) are used extensively in the production of commercials.

Voice in Radio Commercials   The producer's role in dealing with vocal execution in commercials often extends to doing the actual announcing or choosing an announcer. The producer is also responsible for ensuring that the correct phrasing is used. Although guidance in announcing skills is beyond the scope of this book, it is important for the producer to know that anyone who reads copy must stress key words. The meaning must be clear; if the goal of the commercial is to express value, the word *value* must receive its proper stress.

Technology has had an impact on commercial production. Today, a producer can bypass the large recording studio. The Industry Update in this chapter describes how it's possible to produce commercials in the comfort of your home.

Today, the announcer must be believable. In the most basic terms, someone portraying a senior diplomat should not sound like a 21-year-old. Another aspect of believability is consistency of the message: Does the announcer extolling the virtues of the friendly neighborhood bank sound friendly? Remember that booming bass tones don't make an announcer's delivery believable. In today's radio, the communicator, who communicates with an audience rather than orating at them, is supplanting the announcer.

Another aspect of choosing an announcer is the compatibility of the announcer's voice and delivery with the approach of the message. For example,

- The *hard-sell* approach requires an announcer with an authoritative, strong voice (but not necessarily a deep one).

- The *sincere* approach calls for an announcer who is casual and does not have the disc jockey type of artificial delivery. An announcer with the sing-song artificiality commonly found in contemporary hit radio (CHR) would be an extremely poor choice for a commercial requiring sincerity, such as a spot for a bank.

- The *whimsical* approach often borders on the comedic. This approach (remember Lake Michigan being filled with hot chocolate?) requires an announcer with a good deal of flexibility and acting ability. An offbeat voice often fills the bill quite well. An affected, booming, announcerish voice does not work well in this type of commercial unless the commercial is a parody of affected, booming announcers.

- Any *dramatized* element in a commercial requires an announcer with acting ability. Proficient announcers are not necessarily good actors, so careful screening must be done when casting a commercial that contains dramatic scenes.

The major point here is that in order to take advantage of the different approaches available in radio advertising, the producer must be able to match the proper style of delivery to the message.

SUGGESTIONS FOR PRODUCING EFFECTIVE COMMERCIALS

The basics of producing good commercials are closely tied to the basics of any good radio production: a clear message and clean production. The elements we

---

INDUSTRY UPDATE • THE HOME SOUND STUDIO: TECHNOLOGY MAKES BIG-TIME SOUND AVAILABLE TO SMALL PRODUCTION AGENCIES

When Jay Flannery was interviewed for this Industry Update section in the previous edition (circa 2005), he estimated that someone could set up a professional-quality home radio/recording studio for less than $20,000.

Not much more than three years later, he estimated that the price could be about half that. Of course, the truly amazing thing about technology is that 15 years ago a studio of similar quality would have set you back more than $100,000.

Flannery is president of Class A Communications in Liverpool, New York. A veteran of the Syracuse, New York, radio market, Flannery is one of thousands of independent producers who have set up shop in their homes, using personal computers as their production engine. Flannery produces a variety of products, from liners to commercials and instructional tapes.

The newest aspect of his business is producing commercials and liners for web-cast radio programs. For his commercial work, he frequently interacts with other home-based freelancers, such as voice talent; one of his frequent co-workers is a woman who lives in Texas, and all their interaction takes place online. Flannery writes the commercials, which often contain one male voice and one female voice. She records her lines; Flannery records his; and he edits both voices together digitally.

While the equipment involved is not cheap by any means, Flannery notes that in the world of start-up businesses the entire studio is less than a florist, for example, might pay for a truck. While he is reluctant to recommend any specific equipment because digital gear evolves so quickly, he does observe that anyone getting involved in home-based radio production should do the following:

- Buy the fastest computer you can afford with the biggest hard drive possible. Hard drives are a bargain in any event, he notes, because storage prices have plummeted in the past few years.

- Use your audio editing computer exclusively for production work. Other programs can interfere with storage and processing.

- Get the best sound card that you can afford. (A sound card is the digital circuit board that processes audio.) The sound cards that come as standard equipment with the computer are rarely of sufficient quality for pro-style production work. Do your homework! Different cards work better with varying systems.

- Consider going all-digital. Analog equipment, such as mixing consoles, will work fine, but digital consoles will give an added boost to quality and convenience.

- Get audio-editing programs that suit your needs. You don't have to spend a fortune, and some of the high-end programs, while excellent, may be more than you need. You will also want a program that creates PDF files because you'll spend a lot of time exchanging scripts by email. Also, consider a program that will allow you to make your own music. It's not as complex as you might expect. Anyone with a rudimentary knowledge of a keyboard can pick out notes, layer them using music-editing software, and produce a good-sounding bed.

What about the challenges of working in a home environment? A good mic cancels out a lot of extraneous noise, and while Flannery says he occasionally has to re-record a segment because of a dog barking or the doorbell ringing, it's less of a problem than you might expect. With careful planning, he says, you can find a quiet spot and a quiet time to record in almost any home or apartment.

spell out in this chapter will help you define the message and structure it properly. Here are some specific suggestions concerning the specialized case of radio commercial production.

Know Your Audience

Some commercials fail because the message does not reach the intended audience. Make sure that your script addresses its target audience and conveys the message in a clear fashion. If your commercial makes a claim, try to identify what aspect of the product or service fulfills the claim.

Avoid Gimmicks

For some reason, producers and local merchants seem to fall in love with echoes, sound effects, and so forth. A commercial that depends on gimmicks often has its essential message weakened. In addition, producing all your commercials with gimmicks becomes repetitive. Although electronic effects and sound effects certainly have a place in commercial production, be sure, before you use them, that they reinforce the message and have a direct bearing on the commercial itself.

Summarize the Thrust

You should be able to summarize the thrust of a commercial in a few words: "The clerks in this store are very knowledgeable about their wares," or "This bank is friendly and wants to give you personal attention." Commercials that stress the benefit of a product or service tend to work best in radio. The shotgun approach—mentioning every possible benefit of a product or service—usually doesn't work very well in a radio commercial, primarily because of the listener's short attention span and because time is limited. If the message seems scattered or fuzzy, rewrite the commercial. Remember that if you're attempting to use a 15- or 30-second ad to reduce clutter, your approach must be surgical.

Note how the copy in Figure 12.5—30 seconds' worth—manages to crisply and clearly hit on all the main points of the product, a high-quality piece of jewelry. Note, too, that many of the concepts are abstract; it's not like selling a piece of hardware. There are no wasted words in this copy.

Don't Blast the Listener

Some producers have become enamored with the idea that louder is better, and they take considerable pains to make sure that every sound element peaks the VU. There's no question that you should strive for bright technical quality, but excessive loudness and abrasiveness can often detract from the message.

Read the Spot to the Client or, Better Yet, Play a Good Demo

If you're in the position of writing the spot and getting approval from the client, you can wind up with a better product by reading the script to the client rather

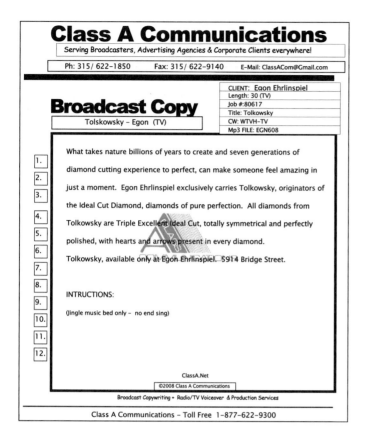

Class A Communications

Serving Broadcasters, Advertising Agencies & Corporate Clients everywhere!

| Ph: 315/ 622-1850 | Fax: 315/ 622-9140 | E-Mail: ClassACom@Gmail.com |

Broadcast Copy

| Tolskowsky – Egon (TV) |

CLIENT: Egon Ehrlinspiel
Length: 30 (TV)
Job #:80617
Title: Tolkowsky
CW: WTVH–TV
Mp3 FILE: EGN608

1.
2.
3.
4.
5.
6.
7.
8.
9.
10.
11.
12.

What takes nature billions of years to create and seven generations of

diamond cutting experience to perfect, can make someone feel amazing in

just a moment. Egon Ehrlinspiel exclusively carries Tolkowsky, originators of

the Ideal Cut Diamond, diamonds of pure perfection. All diamonds from

Tolkowsky are Triple Excellent Ideal Cut, totally symmetrical and perfectly

polished, with hearts and arrows present in every diamond.

Tolkowsky, available only at Egon Ehrlinspiel. 5914 Bridge Street.

INTRUCTIONS:

(Jingle music bed only – no end sing)

ClassA.Net
©2008 Class A Communications
Broadcast Copywriting + Radio/TV Voiceover & Production Services

Class A Communications - Toll Free 1–877–622–9300

FIGURE 12.5

A 30-second script for high-quality jewelry.

than handing over a piece of paper. Why? Because people tend to pick at words instead of grasping the whole concept. They also tend to overestimate drastically the amount of copy that can be squeezed into a given time frame. Reading your spot aloud leaves no doubt in the client's mind that it is, indeed, 30 seconds' worth of copy. By reading the spot aloud to the client, you project the thrust of the commercial as it should be presented, and you don't get involved in a 10-minute argument about the choice of a particular word.

If you have a good-quality, roughed-out spot recorded, by all means play it to the client. However, if it's very rough, playing audio will be counterproductive.

Don't Force Humor

If there's any doubt about whether a spot is funny, it's probably not. Nothing falls as flat as a failed attempt at humor. Also, be realistic about whether a significant part of your listenership will find the joke offensive. You can't please everyone, and there are some people who are chronically offended by almost all humor, but remember that people from different backgrounds than you will have strikingly different sensibilities.

Radio copywriting is on an economy kick—not related to saving money, but words. In order to keep radio an engaging medium, program managers have of late been cutting commercial clutter. Long commercials, essentially 60-second spots, are being pared back to 30. Anything that detracts from the core message is being surgically removed.

In addition to reducing commercial annoyances, many in the communication industry believe that attention spans of all media consumers are getting shorter. Evidence for this is anecdotal and probably difficult to back up with scientific precision, but intuitively many of us think that with people of all ages becoming used to the rhythm of Web surfing, text messaging, and email exchanges, the days of the leisurely message are over.

Even in long-form narrations there is a consistent drive for economy of words, which is probably not a bad goal regardless of time constraints.

The purpose of this section is to provide guidance on how to get the most verbal bang for the buck in writing for the ear; how to express the maximum in the minimum number of words.

1. Look for powerful words that communicate a lot in a short time. Try to avoid modifiers whenever possible. For example, instead of writing, "The range of loan options is really confusing," try "bewildering." Instead of "totally out of patience" use "exasperated."

2. Always look to avoid needless modification. Instead of "it was all right for the most part," write "adequate."

3. Be sure to stay with one topic. The radio copywriting website MaverickStrategy.com advises that when writing a commercial you need to relentlessly hone in on one feature and deliver benefit after benefit. The analogy: If you are personally trying to sell someone a couch, you wouldn't interrupt to sell him drapes.

4. Be specific. Use focused words. Don't say "save a lot," say "save hundreds of dollars."

5. Appeal to all senses. One of the challenges of radio is to overcome the fact that it only works through the sense of hearing. It's up to the copywriter to paint a visual picture that communicates the message quickly and cleanly. Lowell Christensen president of the radio production company Spot-Works, offers this example:

   I remember when I was a kid growing up on the farm. It was a blistering hot day on the bald prairies. The sky was clear blue and you could see the heat waves floating on the horizon. Out comes mom with a tall glass of ice cold lemonade. Beads of condensation had formed around the outside of the glass ... lemonade never tasted so good. I just painted a picture in your mind. Did you picture the blue sky? Did

Achieve High Technical Quality

Strive for the best possible technical quality in your commercials. The piece has to be a 30-second gem, and it must sparkle. It's a good idea to save copies of all commercials in the event of hard drive or cart failure; otherwise, you'll have to reproduce the whole spot. Incidentally, always save hard-to-reproduce production elements, such as jingles or elaborately created sound effects, in case you want to re-cut the commercial with a new slant while retaining some of the original production elements. If your commercial was produced on a computer workstation, save the playlist (also called an edit list) as well as the raw sound files.

Don't Overuse a Particular Piece of Music

There's a tendency to seize on a piece of music that works well for production purposes and to use it constantly. Resist this. If you use music from your station's you see the heat waves in the distance? Did you imagine the beads of moisture on the outside of the glass? That's the power of radio.

Steps 3 and 4 go hand in hand. Telling a story is painting a picture in the listeners' mind using emotional experiences they can relate to.

This is such a vital point that one thing needs to be made clear: Telling a story does not necessarily mean that every commercial needs to start with "Once upon a time...". Telling a story can be as simple as the sound of a car that won't start, howling wind in the background, and the chattering of teeth. Anyone with an unreliable car will relate to that scenario and think about how annoying it is to have that happen. Then, tie in the sales message: "A tune-up at Al's Auto will prevent..." etc.[3]

6. Be careful of loading too much information into a spot. More is less. The ear can only grasp so much.

7. Remember that stories are effective ways to communicate a lot with a little. A quick scenario—let's say, a dramatization of someone struggling with a disorganized loan officer—can communicate an idea much more quickly than straight persuasive copy. Think about how various stories have become so important in our culture that they communicate reams just through their basic plot lines: Dr. Jeckyll and Mr. Hyde (people are complex and have different sides to their personalities, Romeo and Juliet (sometimes people's backgrounds make a relationship impossible), or The Wizard of Oz (some people need external valuation such as medals or diplomas to make themselves feel worthwhile). So tell a story.

8. Consider straight reads with bullet points. A straight read from the announcer is returning as a favorite among clients because it not only conveys the personality of the host but cuts through much of the highly produced clutter found on the airwaves. If your announcer is a good ad-libber, consider having him or her ad-lib from five or six bullet points. This way the main thrust is capsulized (assuming the announcer is skilled) and delivered with brevity and impact.

9. Do not try to force words down the listener's ear with accelerated copy. Be sure that whomever is going to read the spot does not have to rush. Speeded-up copy hardly ever sounds genuine, has an unfortunate connotation with "fast talkers," and generally backfires.

10. Edit, edit, edit. Don't be satisfied with the first draft, nor necessarily the fifth. Work on your copy until it is concise and polished. Even if you're not the one reading it, be sure to read it aloud to make sure it flows, it's clear, and all unnecessary words have been excised.

----

3. http://radioproductionservices.com/radio_copywriting.html

airplay library, keep alert for new selections that would lend themselves to production work.

An index of the music beds used for various productions is sometimes a good way to ensure that a particular piece does not get overused. Tape an index card to the back of a CD case, and list the spots and dates you used certain cuts. (Imagine how embarrassing it would be to find that you and another producer had recently used the same cut for two different banking commercials.)

Keep the Message Simple

Too many ideas in one commercial, as we've discussed, can muddy the whole concept of the spot. Keep the message focused.

Avoid These Five Common Mistakes in Commercials

In general, steer clear of what we call the Big Five mistakes of commercial production, some of which we have already touched on. To summarize, avoid the following:

1. *Lack of focus.* The listener must be given a simple message that doesn't wander from idea to idea.

2. *Poor technical quality.* This includes commercials that are too loud, too soft, badly mixed, or badly produced. Take pains to re-cut or re-dub a commercial when it doesn't sound as good on the air as it sounded in production.

3. *Lack of completeness.* As we pointed out in Chapter 11, a message is more effective if it has a beginning, a middle, and an end. A commercial that just sort of peters out, ending without a satisfying conclusion, loses some of its impact.

4. *The assembly-line approach.* We all develop certain working habits, but when a producer makes several commercials that sound the same, there's a serious problem. The commercials will lose impact, and clients—who, after all, have ears, too—will complain. Make an effort to vary your approach from time to time. Use different announcers and production music. Don't use the same special effects on commercials for different clients. If you are able, try going out of your market for announcers. There are many voice-over artists who will record your copy at a reasonable fee and email you the file.

5. *Fear of experimentation.* Don't shy away from trying a new approach just because it hasn't been done before in your station or your city. You may make mistakes, but never allowing yourself the freedom to experiment limits both your creative potential and the potential benefits to your advertising clients.

Radio advertising offers a viable outlet for your creativity—an outlet that will permit your creativity to be strongly appreciated. And although advertising can sometimes be a pretty cold dollars-and-cents affair, radio advertising producers have shown that creative advertising, done honestly and in good taste, can be effective.

PRODUCTION APPLICATIONS IN STATION PROMOTION

Closely related to commercial production done for a station's advertising clients is the production that a station creates for its own promotional efforts. Known in the industry as *station promotion*, this is an area that has recently assumed greater importance than ever because competition for the attention of radio audiences has never been keener.

First, our society is saturated with a wide variety of media forms. Each does its best to get audiences to spend time consuming the information or entertainment it offers. Second, every radio station on the air faces stiff competition for listener attention and loyalty within its market and medium and from alternative listening devices such as car CD players, iPods, and so forth. Unless a station succeeds in attracting the attention of a significant number of listeners, the revenue it generates from advertising will fall off, and the station will ultimately fail. Even in public broadcasting, audiences are critical. Listeners are a major source of financial support, and major underwriters of programming are reluctant to support programming that doesn't attract enough listeners.

The bottom line is that stations can't rely anymore on their programming alone to ensure an adequate base of listeners and, hence, advertisers. Promotion is a major tool in generating the listener interest that produces loyalty to a station's programming. Production is a key element in creating promotional vehicles that help stations build their identity and create excitement and interest among listeners.

There is a fundamental difference between the kinds of production techniques used for commercial production and the work done for station promotion. As we mentioned earlier, it is generally wise to avoid the use of gimmicks in commercial production. The idea is not to have the production techniques call attention to themselves. Rather, you want to focus audience attention on the sponsor's message.

In promotion, however, the elements of production are more central to the success of the effort. The heavy use of such effects as staccato repetition, reverberation, sound effects, sound coloration through **flanging** (shifting the pitch of recorded elements), and the punch that is added by the skillful blending of many different and often unusual sound elements is what attracts the attention of the audience. In many instances, the copy used in promotional spots may be virtually nonexistent. The only words in some promotional spots are in single spoken lines (known as *liners*) that function as a slogan. The line "More music, less talk," for example, might be the only copy used. This might be followed by the station call letters or another kind of identifying name followed by some reference to the station's spot on the radio dial. The phrase "Hot 106," for example, might be followed by a musical jingle.

The key to making such spots effective is the way the elements are blended and the effect produced by the overall sound of the spot. You might, for example, start the spot with a sound effect created electronically, add flanging to the announcer's delivery, and insert the sound of drumming between the voice-over and the jingle. All this might be recorded over a music bed from a production music library that has been "time compressed" so that it ends just as the jingle begins. The whole thing might be under 10 seconds in length when it is ready to air.

It is difficult to recommend specific techniques that might be employed in promotional production situations because the field is open to so much experimentation and creativity. The key to becoming a successful producer of promotional production is to become well versed in the kinds of audio effects that can be produced within the capabilities of your studio equipment. The availability of digital workstations with multitrack capability and access to good libraries of sound effects and production music can be enormously beneficial. Increasingly, digital audio workstations are broadening the creative possibilities for promotional production considerably with software plug-ins that allow the producer to modify the sounds in unusual ways.

Whether you operate with state-of-the-art technology or the modest equipment and facilities that still characterize many fine radio stations, your creativity as a producer can be the major ingredient in production for station promotion. Listen to as many different stations as you can. Whenever you have the opportunity, ask producers how certain effects are created. Perfect your production skills. Lastly, experiment and keep on learning.

Promotional production that is skillfully integrated into the on-air schedule can significantly help you create the identifying elements that together make up the sound of the station. No other area in the field of production offers more creative challenges and rewards to radio producers.

SUMMARY

Producers of commercials must meet a number of goals, including producing commercials that stimulate sales, producing commercials that please the client, and producing commercials that fit their station's sound. Many elements help make a commercial effective. Often, those elements run deeper than you might at first imagine. For example, it is not enough simply to run lists of merchandise and prices in a radio ad. Radio requires entry into the theater of the mind.

Many appeals are involved in radio advertising, including appeals to personal fulfillment, to authority, to the bandwagon effect, to fear of rejection, to sexual success, to reinforcement of the listener's ego, to prestige, to value and quality, and to other emotional triggers.

Music is an important tool in radio production, but it is helpful only when it reinforces the central theme of the spot. The voice of the announcer obviously plays a critical role. It is not enough, however, that the announcer has a good voice; he or she must also have a voice that is appropriate to the particular spot.

Commercials should have a narrow thrust; that is, you should be able to summarize the commercial in a sentence. If it is too complex for capsulation, it is too complex to be a radio commercial. Simplify it.

Production for station promotion focuses on creating excitement among listeners that helps attract them to the station and that helps distinguish your station from its competitors. The key to success in production for station promotion is an extensive knowledge of audio production techniques and creativity in their use.

APPLICATIONS

SITUATION 1/THE PROBLEM The production director of a radio station was putting together a commercial for an ice cream parlor. The client insisted on copy that touted the old-fashioned atmosphere of the store; the copy included a physical description of the ice cream parlor and a dissertation on old-fashioned value. As it stood, the commercial was flat, talky, and unfocused.

ONE POSSIBLE SOLUTION About 15 seconds of the copy was deleted, and a bed of Gay Nineties music was substituted. The banjo and piano music, which was bright and cheerful in addition to conveying a sense of period, augmented the message, which could then be clarified and refined.

SITUATION 2/THE PROBLEM A local bank, one of the station's largest customers, had become extremely unhappy with the lack of results from its radio advertising. The commercials, which were elaborately produced with music and narration by the station's morning personality, a young woman, stressed the honesty and dependability of the bank and its people. However, the message didn't seem to get across.

ONE POSSIBLE SOLUTION The music and fast-paced delivery were scrapped, and new commercials were cut. The new spots featured the voice of the station manager, a woman in her late fifties, who stressed, in a conversational, low-key tone, that the bank and its people were honest, dependable, and an asset to the community. As a result of this change, the production values supported the message.

EXERCISES

1. Replace the following announcer's copy with a shorter dramatic scene or sound effects sequence. Your goal is to shorten the message, focus it clearly, and give it greater impact. This assignment can be done either as a hands-on production exercise or as a mental exercise, with the solution scripted out.

   "Rolling Hills Apartment Complex is more than a place to live. It's a place to enjoy—there are tennis courts, a swimming pool, and a golf course. You can enjoy all these facilities, and families with children are welcome. Everyone can have a lot of fun at Rolling Hills."

   (*Hint*: How could sound effects work here?)

   (*Hint*: How about a dramatized scene of happy residents?)

   (*Hint*: What should the voice sound like?)

2. A bank has come to you with a desire for commercials to entice more young professional customers. Write a 60-second commercial that meets this need. One hook might be a young doctor saying that she doesn't have time to manage her money thoughtfully and that the people at the bank are a great help. Could sound effects or dramatic elements help clarify this message? If time and lab facilities are available, produce the spot.

3. Write a treatment (a description of the approach and production elements) for each of the following situations. Tell why you think each will be effective.

   a. A shoe store wants to reach blue-collar workers with a message about its tough work boots.

YOU'RE ON! • FITTING YOUR COPY INTO THE ALLOTTED TIME—HOW ANNOUNCERS CAN READ TO TIME

A great deal of recorded program production involves laying voice into a commercial, public service announcement, or promo, and that task almost always involves working within rigid time constraints. A 30-second spot has to be exactly 30 seconds, and a 10-second announcer's lead-in to the start of a vocal has to be equally precise. Some commercials, for example, come with a "hole" in the middle where the local announcer inserts copy. This is not as difficult as it seems. Here are some techniques for developing your own internal clock.

■ First, recognize that this skill comes with experience. Keep practicing.

■ Develop a familiarity with music and music phrasing. Listen critically to music, or take a music appreciation course, and you'll be able to identify things like key changes and the distinction between a trumpet and a French horn solo. This will be helpful because you'll find that music beds now are laden with cues. You'll be able to rehearse your copy and note that you have to finish the first narration when the key changes, and finish the whole reading about two seconds after the trumpets enter.

■ Learn to time yourself in 10-second intervals. If you can accurately gauge 10 seconds, timing 30 or 60 seconds will take care of itself. Practice with copy and a stopwatch. Count how many words you typically read in 10 seconds.

■ Mark your copy with time cues. Write hints to yourself on the copy.

■ Learn how to compress copy. There is often too much copy and too little time to read it. This is a problem particularly in local commercials, where merchants may want an absurd amount of detail squeezed into 30 seconds. You and your sales-people can educate them, but it's a safe bet that you will be spending much of your career trying to compress 45 seconds worth of copy into 30 seconds. This isn't easy, but there are a couple of tricks you can use:

■ Keep all the elements of the copy in proportion. Think of it this way: When an orchestra speeds up a piece of music, it speeds up everything … the quarter notes, the half notes, the rests, and so forth. They remain proportional. You must do the same thing with your copy; don't change the phrasing or eliminate natural breaks between words or phrases. Speed up everything. Don't alter the melody and rhythm of your voice.

■ Read ahead in your script. Reading ahead allows you to speed up the copy but retain its natural cadence. When you read the same word aloud that your eyes are hitting in the copy, you become a reading machine and sound like one. By contrast, when you read a few words or a sentence ahead in the copy, you are reciting phrases and will be communicating, not repeating words. It takes practice, but it's not as difficult as it seems.

b. A drugstore has a new line of cosmetics for men. The store's manager wants to reach young adult males and convince them that it's all right to use cosmetics. (Would a well-known local athlete be a good choice to pitch cosmetics?)

c. A hardware store wants to attract apartment dwellers rather than just homeowners. (What products at a hardware store would be of interest to apartment dwellers, and why should they go to a hardware store to buy them instead of to a department store?)

13

News Production

News production is a critical portion of the work done in a typical radio station. For one thing, news is a very visible part of many stations' product, so the production values stand out clearly. Because news is aired frequently on most radio stations, particularly on the AM band, the news producer is called on to do news production and to change production values at a quicker pace.

It isn't always possible to change the content of a news story every hour or half-hour, but it is possible to change the production or editing structure. For example, the news producer may decide to eliminate an *actuality* (a recorded audio segment) used at 8:00 A.M. and instead read the quote as part of the news story at 9:00 A.M. The producer might also elect to use two actualities within a story instead of one and re-cut the news story for the next hour.

The hectic pace of news requires that you be able to do the work quickly. In addition, you must do the work well: The radio network news may play immediately before or after the local report, and the producer must offer production that doesn't suffer by comparison.

When starting out in radio, expect to wear many hats. Virtually everyone involved in radio has, at some time, been required to do and understand news production. Air personalities in smaller stations are often expected to be able to come up with acceptable newscasts; even salespeople can be called on to discuss the newscast in detail.

Regardless of your particular role in preparing news programming, the important thing for you to remember is that radio is a medium of sound. More and better sound doesn't necessarily guarantee a good newscast, but it does add to radio's impact and appeal.

What do we mean by "more and better sound"? Essentially, the goal of radio news programming is to offer something more than an announcer reading the copy. Additional sound elements—such as an interview conducted with the subject of the story; a live, on-the-scene report from a radio station staffer; or the noise of a riot taking place—add to the variety and maximize the impact.

These attributes relate to the strengths of radio and the qualities radio news can stress. Radio is unsurpassed for timeliness and portability—getting the story on the air quickly, anytime and anywhere. This was no more evident than in the Hurricane Katrina disaster. For many thousands of people in the disaster area without power, small portable radios were their only links to news and information. Radio is also a personal medium, a one-on-one method of communication, and as such, can effectively relate the human-interest values in a story. Further, the personal medium of radio can bring a listener into proximity to a story, directly on the picket line or at the scene of the fire. Sound sources can help a great deal in this regard.

Again, sound sources do not make the newscast. Good journalistic principles must be followed, and the voice and delivery of the on-air person must be appropriate. The news producer—whether he or she is the actual gatherer and reader of news or the executive in charge of the station's overall news effort—is responsible for a wide variety of duties. The total gamut of these duties (which may be split among several people) involves news gathering, news writing, assembling the elements of a newscast (including stories and sound elements), and news reading and reporting.

Let's now take a look at these duties and examine how production plays a role in their execution.

NEWS GATHERING

One limitation of radio news is that the newsperson is often tied to the studio. In smaller stations especially, the news director may be the only newsperson. Although a good reporter will make every effort to get out into the field, at least to make rounds at the police station, city hall, and so forth, much news gathering must be done from the studio. In larger stations, street reporters do on-the-spot news gathering.

In either event, news gathering consists of obtaining facts from which stories are written. It consists of collecting *actualities*, the recorded segments of news events or news makers. An **actuality** can be an interview segment or a recording of the **wild sound** resulting from an event, such as a funeral march or the wailing of fire sirens. Although the terminology varies across the country, wild sound or an interview actuality is often referred to as a **sound bite**; however, that term is more widely used in TV than in radio. *Sound bite* generally refers to an interview segment. News gathering for radio also involves a great deal of recording from the telephone.

In smaller stations, much of the news gathering is done by perusing the local paper. Although it's not generally admitted, many local newscasts involve the announcer reading directly out of the paper. Sometimes the listener can even hear the pages being turned! More often, though, stories are rewritten. In small and even medium-sized markets, the radio newsperson won't have many sources at all other than the newspaper, though over reliance on the paper must be avoided. For one thing, papers are wrong on occasion, and when the paper is wrong, you are wrong. In addition, most newspapers are quite sensitive about the reuse of their material by another profit-making organization. Many newspapers are copyrighted and could take legal action against a station that makes a wholesale appropriation of their material.

Another drawback of relying too heavily on the newspaper is that radio news is expected to be "up to the minute," whereas newspapers are generally several hours out of date by the time they reach the reader. It's important for a radio news staff to develop its own system of news gathering (sources, calls to the police, and so on) because listeners generally aren't tolerant of old news, which has about as much appeal as yesterday's newspaper.

NEWS WRITING

Words—their order, their meaning, and their rhythm—can be considered to be a production value. The style of writing influences the sound, and writing does, of course, put the whole package together. Writing also involves the way sound elements are assembled.

Although a treatise on news writing is beyond the scope of this book, it is important for a news producer to remember that what is written must sound right when it is read aloud and must be conversational. Stilted, ponderous writing has no place in radio. Be aware that the listeners have only one opportunity to understand what is being said; they cannot look back, as they can with a newspaper article. Clarity is critical.

Another difference between newspaper and radio writing (and another reason for not reading from the newspaper) is that newspapers use the **inverse pyramid** writing style, in which the important who, what, where, when, and why are listed in the first few sentences. Its advantages in the print media notwithstanding, this format is generally both confusing and boring to the listener. Radio news demands shorter sentences and active verb tenses, and this style of writing is really quite different from newspaper journalism. To repeat a popular and worthwhile phrase, radio writing is written for the ear, not the eye.

For example, a newspaper **lead** might read, "Twenty-four-year-old John Smith, of 91-B Mechanic St. in Centerville, was killed in an accident today near the Jefferson Street on-ramp to I-100, when his car collided with a truck that was traveling the wrong way on the ramp, police said." That sentence (which is not extremely long as newspaper leads go) would be confusing to listeners, who would be better served by, "A local man died today when his car collided with a truck police say was heading the wrong way on an expressway off-ramp." Now, the details can be presented in ear-pleasing, bite-sized fashion.

Sentences in broadcast news writing should be kept short (a maximum of 20 to 25 words). Attribution is usually put first. In other words, "State Police Captain David Smith said today that there is no word on the fate of the missing hunter," rather than, "There is no word on the fate of the missing hunter, said Captain David Smith of the state police."

Proficiency in news writing will come from journalism courses and on-the-job training, so we won't expand on it here except to remind you that if you are not adept at using computers you must learn. Today's newsroom requires use of a variety of programs, both for writing and editing, and it's essential that you become a quick study because these systems are not always standardized. Many radio stations simply won't hire news people who can't type reasonably well; in any event, typing is a skill that will come in handy in almost any broadcast career.

NEWS ASSEMBLY

An important responsibility of a news producer is to fit the pieces of the newscast together and decide what will go on the air. (We're talking here about a newscast, though we examine other facets of radio news production later in this chapter, along with more specific details of newscast structure.) The assembly process can involve both choosing stories and story order and choosing the sound elements.

Choosing Stories and Story Order

What goes on the air? What goes on the air first? Often, the responsibility for answering these two questions will fall on you, and you will need a sense of news judgment. Running a story first makes it, in effect, the lead story and imbues it with additional importance. Although news judgment is a subject better addressed in journalism classes, the radio news producer must be aware that it is often necessary to shuffle news stories from hour to hour to provide variety in the news. A story is often pushed up in the rotation simply because it is new. The time element is an important consideration because radio is a medium that thrives on timeliness—radio can provide news more quickly than any other medium can.

Choosing Sound Elements

Next, you may select an actuality and integrate it into the copy. In addition to the actuality and wild sound described earlier, you will often have access to reports filed by journalists in the field. These reports usually come in the forms of **voice reports**, or **voicers**, and **voice-actuality** reports.

Voice Reports These straight news items are reported by a journalist and signed off in a fashion such as "This is Jane Roberts reporting for WXXX News." Voice news reports usually run between 30 and 90 seconds, though there's no hard-and-fast rule.

Voicers A voicer is a short report delivered by a reporter in the field, generally recorded in one take and featuring a standard closing, such as "Bob Smith, WXXX News".

Voice-Actuality Reports A voice-actuality report is constructed in the manner of a voice wrap, the editing and production structure explained in Chapter 6. A voice actuality is simply a report from a journalist with an actuality segment inserted. It is signed off in the same way as a voice report.

A QUICK PRIMER ON RADIO NEWS WRITING

One of the more common complaints we hear from those in a position to hire radio news personnel is that the applicants simply lack writing ability. We urge you to take as many courses as you can on broadcast news writing. For now, it will be to your advantage to acquaint yourself with the basic principles in this news primer. Because production equipment is used by almost everyone now, the line between producer and reporter is blurred. It's safe to say that if you want to go into radio news, you must know how to write, and today, the need for writers is greater than ever.

To start with, remember this essential fact: The writing style you use for broadcast will not be the same style you use for written reports, term papers, newspaper copy, or anything meant to make a direct path from paper to eye to brain. Broadcast copy makes a path from eye to mouth to ear, so it must be different in style, punctuation, and sentence structure.

Don't try to write broadcast copy using the same punctuation and sentence structure you'd use in a term paper or business report, or you'll wind up with unreadable copy. Conversely, don't use broadcast style to write your reports or papers. The work will come back disfigured by red scrawls scolding you: *Incomplete sentence! Poor sentence structure! Paragraphs too short! Ideas not fully developed! Do not use contractions!*

The first thing you should remember about broadcast news writing is that you're not exactly writing. You're committing speech to paper. You are telling a story, a story that will be spoken. You must use words and phrases that can be spoken naturally, and you must relay the story in the form we're used to hearing people use when they tell a story.

For example, suppose you just received a letter informing you that you've won a full scholarship to Harvard Law School. You pick up the phone to call your father. After, "Hello, Dad," would you use the following words?

"After four years of diligent work, my efforts were rewarded. I received a letter from Harvard Law School today. 'We are pleased to inform you that you have been awarded a full scholarship covering all tuition, fees, and room and board,' the letter said."

We doubt it. No one speaks that way—not even the professors at Harvard Law School. More than likely, the conversation would sound like this:

"I'm going to Harvard Law School ... for free! The hardest four years of my life finally paid off. *A full scholarship*! The letter I got today says the scholarship covers tuition, fees, and room and board."

What we've seen, of course, is another comparison between print style and broadcast style. It is obvious that the first example, although lucid in print, is absolutely unreadable if you try to say it out loud. The first example does not tell a story conversationally; the second does. With that in mind, let's see how broadcast stories are "told" on paper.

Script Conventions for Radio

What we'll do here is "build" a radio story from top to bottom to illustrate the way a radio script is put on paper. The goal of this section is not so much to demonstrate techniques of writing, as such, but rather how the standard story is constructed and scripted. Stations vary widely in their particular script formats, but most are variations on the following theme. So, to follow the chain of events from the very beginning, we'll start with the paper and keyboard, then begin working at the very top of the script page and work our way down the page to the ending.

Paper and Print

Even with the spread of computers into radio newsrooms, hard copy will probably always be part of the news writing process. Many smaller radio newsrooms are not yet computerized and may never be. The investment simply cannot be translated to the bottom line. Instead, you may type your story into a word processor and then print it out to be read on the air. (In small markets, integrated audio-text programs may not even be on the horizon.)

This is not entirely a function of economics. Modern news computer systems perform many functions that are not needed in a small radio newsroom, such as calling up graphics or listing the dozens of events found in a half-hour newscast (see Figure 13.1). Although news software is becoming popular in medium and large radio stations, in smaller stations most copy winds up on paper anyway. Even the bravest newscaster reading from a computer-driven prompting device would be reluctant to go on-air without hard copy clutched in his or her hand in case of a computer crash.

So because broadcast news writing still involves words on a page, remember that those words have to be easily readable. That means a lot of white space on the page, as few corrections as possible, clearly made corrections when they are necessary, and a large, clear type. Many stations use a special large typeface such as Executive or Orator.

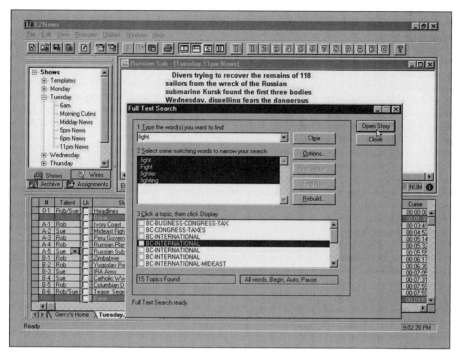

FIGURE 13.1

Computerized news packages are found in medium- and large-market stations. These programs perform many advanced features, such as performing full-text word searches.
SOURCE: Automated Data Systems

It's very hard to read copy that is crammed tightly on the page, so most radio and TV stations triple-space their copy. Some stations double-space, but triple-spacing is more the norm. Triple-spaced copy is more easily readable than double- or single-spaced, and it leaves room for last-minute corrections to be penciled in. Wide side-to-side margins are also helpful.

SOME NEWSCASTERS FIND COPY WRITTEN IN ALL CAPS TO BE MORE READABLE. THAT MAY BE SIMPLY BECAUSE THEY ARE USED TO SEEING COPY TYPED THAT WAY; IT'S SOMETHING OF A TRADITION IN NEWS WRITING. THERE IS NO UNIVERSAL STANDARD; SOME STATIONS USE ALL CAPS, AND SOME USE STANDARD UPPERCASE AND LOWERCASE. AT LAST CHECK, Associated Press (AP) RADIO AND REUTERS, THE TWO MAJOR WIRE SERVICES, AND ALL THE TELEVISION NETWORKS USE UPPERCASE AND LOWERCASE. WHAT'S YOUR OPINION?

The choice will usually be made for you because you're obligated to follow whatever system is used in your particular newsroom. If you have a choice, we would suggest uppercase and lowercase, a format that appears to be the growing trend in broadcast copywriting. Although some announcers contend that copy written in all caps is more readable, most of us are used to seeing uppercase and lowercase English in almost every other written work. Furthermore, writing in uppercase and lowercase makes it easier to determine whether a word is a proper name.

"THE FIRE IN OVERLAND, OHIO" can cause a second of doubt and hesitation for an anchor who might wonder if "Overland" is a town or if the writer is trying to make some distinction between "over land" and "over sea." "The fire in Overland, Ohio" can't cause such confusion.

One last word about paper and typing: In radio, there is often no need for multiple copies of the script, since computers allow copies to be stored electronically and called up at will. Having two copies of the script for radio is usually enough. Remember that it's usually a good idea not to overwrite previous versions of a story because you'll need a record of what was actually broadcast.

The modern radio newsroom is increasingly a modern-looking place, though, with paper rapidly disappearing (though it remains a handy, portable, and durable technology). More often than not, the radio newsroom in larger markets is a multimedia center, with banks of televisions and computers. (See Figure 13.2.) Because many radio stations are integrating media on their websites, the modern radio workstation may include video-editing software. In fact, it is not unusual for radio reporters to use video cameras and take the audio for the radio newscast and use the video for posting on the website.

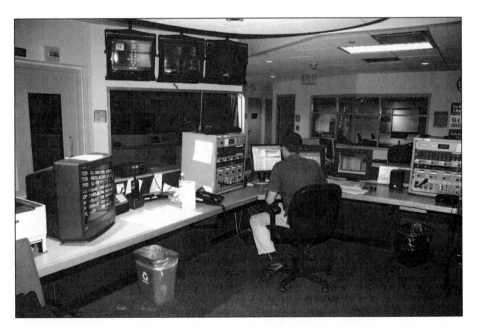

F I G U R E 13.2

Modern newsrooms will include a variety of news sources as well as computer and editing equipment.

SOURCE: Fritz Messere

Many large stations use a system called ENPS (Electronic News Production System), a software package designed by the AP. ENPS gathers news from a variety of sources, allows news people to share copy, audio, and video, and facilitates editing in a variety of media, including publishing directly to the Web. According to the AP, about 700 newsrooms in 58 countries use ENPS today.

The Header

Most broadcast news departments require writers to put some basic information right at the top of the page: the slug, which is a very brief description, usually just a keyword that identifies the story; the writer's name or initials; and the date. The exact location of these entries varies from newsroom to newsroom. Some departments put the three slug items on separate lines, flush against the left margin:

NURSES
HAUSMAN
9/17

or across the top line:

NURSES   HAUSMAN   9/17

The header provides a means of quickly identifying the story itself and finding who wrote it, in case something about the story is questioned or another reporter needs additional information and must talk with the writer. The date is essential for a number of reasons, including the fact that scripts are kept for archival purposes, and you'll need to know when the events described happened when referring to the archives. For example, this story concerns a nursing shortage at a city hospital and features an actuality from the hospital administrator as she addressed the city council. If you do a follow-up story next month, or next year, you'll need to know when the meeting took place.

A second important reason for including the date is that all scripts look pretty much the same, and you need a reliable way to tell an old story from a new story. *Always* double-check the dates of local and wire-service copy before you read it. (A sad-but-true story illustrates the reasoning behind this warning. A janitor once found a two-year-old piece of wire copy behind a desk he had moved when waxing the floor. He put the paper with the rest of the pile on the desk—that day's news copy, of course—and it was read on the air. The story referred to a bill being vetoed by a president who was no longer in office.)

A very good idea that is put into practice in some radio newsrooms is to mark, on the script, the time of the newscast during which the story was read. You can handwrite or type this at the end of the header. Since most radio news stories are rewritten during the day, keeping track of the newscast time will clue you in as to how the story has evolved through several rewrites and will also save confusion if a listener or management has a question about the story "on the 7:30 A.M. newscast" and you need to figure out what version went over the air. So your final header might look like this:

NURSES	HAUSMAN	9/17 7:30 A

We recommend this format.

The Story

Now comes the body of the story. Drop down two triple-spaced lines and begin writing.

NURSES	HAUSMAN	9/17 7:30 A

The administrator of City Hospital says the nursing staff is in critical condition.

Jane Smith appeared before the City Council last night to warn that a severe shortage of nurses is causing a health-care crisis. Smith says almost a third of the nursing positions at City Hospital are currently unfilled. And, she says, everyone suffers because of the shortage.

Tape Cues

An actuality from Ms. Smith is in a computer sound file or recorded on some kind of equipment (e.g., digital cart machine, MiniDisc, analog cart). But you need to indicate certain information about the sound file. The reader of the script needs to know three things:

1. That there *is* a sound file (or a tape) and it should run at this point in the story. The script should contain an advisory listing the name of the file (or tape)—the title with which it is labeled. In this case, it would most likely be "Smith." ("Smith" would be written as the sound file name. If there are two cuts from Ms. Smith, the files would be labeled "Smith 1" and "Smith 2.") Modern news software shows the actuality within the script and includes the title of the actuality as well as the time and outcue.

2. The time of the sound file (actuality). This is important so that the newscaster can be ready to start reading at the appropriate time— obviously, when the recorded segment ends. If it's a long actuality, say, 20 seconds, the newscaster may elect to use those 20 seconds to perform some last-minute emergency chore, such as quickly proofreading the upcoming story.

3. The outcue. An *outcue* is a written transcription of the final words spoken on the tape. This is the newscaster's cue to begin reading the rest of the story.

It is also helpful, but not always necessary, to know the incue for the actuality. This immediately reassures the newscaster that the correct sound bite is being played and, conversely, warns the newscaster if the wrong file has been "fired," giving him or her the opportunity to cut the file quickly and avoid a prolonged period of embarrassment.

Inserting the actuality advisory into the script is sometimes done this way:

NURSES	HAUSMAN	9/17 7:30 A

The administrator of City Hospital says the nursing staff is in critical condition.

Jane Smith appeared before the City Council last night to warn that a severe shortage of nurses is causing a health-care crisis. Smith says almost a third of the nursing positions at City Hospital are currently unfilled. And, she says, everyone suffers because of the shortage.

AUDIO: SMITH RUNS: 20

INCUE: "LAST NIGHT WE HAD...

OUTCUE: "... CAN'T GO ON MUCH LONGER."

There are myriad variations on methods of indicating audio cues, but most involve a recognizable combination of the items shown.

One not so common but very effective method is to print out the entire actuality on the script. This way, if the sound bite does not roll, the newscaster can simply read the quote as if nothing had happened, ad-libbing the "she saids" as appropriate. A complete transcription of the actuality would look like this when incorporated into the script:

NURSES	HAUSMAN	9/17 7:30 A

The administrator of City Hospital says the nursing staff is in critical condition.

Jane Smith appeared before the City Council last night to warn that a severe shortage of nurses is causing a health-care crisis. Smith says almost a third of the nursing positions at City Hospital are currently unfilled. And, she says, everyone suffers because of the shortage.

AUDIO: SMITH RUNS: 20

"LAST NIGHT WE HAD ONE ELDERLY GENTLEMAN WAIT AN EXTRA HOUR AND A HALF FOR HIS PAIN MEDICATION. WE JUST COULDN'T GET TO HIM. WE WERE STACKED UP WITH

THREE EMERGENCY CASES AND WERE SHORT FIVE NURSES ON THE SURGICAL FLOOR. I'M AFRAID, REALLY AFRAID THAT THE NEXT TIME THIS HAPPENS IT'S GOING TO BE WORSE THAN LEAVING AN OLD MAN IN PAIN. HE JUST MIGHT DIE WAITING ... AND I LITERALLY THINK THE STRESS IS KILLING THE NURSES. THIS CAN'T GO ON MUCH LONGER."

Some major news organizations, such as network radio news centers, transcribe all actualities used during the newscast. They usually don't do this on the script, but rather on a separate form that includes other information about the actuality. The transcription is available to the newscaster (kept in a separate pile from the script) in order to serve as an emergency paraphrase in case the actuality fails to play. This practice is becoming increasingly rare because news software can provide the reader with the transcript of the actuality.

Story Tags

The final step is to conclude the story with a sentence or two, known as a *tag*. It is generally considered poor form to simply end with an actuality and go to the next story. Doing that confuses the listeners and makes the story seem oddly incomplete. Besides, in this case, there is still more detail begging to be written. We know there's a nursing shortage, and we know that the administrator is complaining about it, but why is there a shortage, and is anything going to be done about this situation?

So here's how those questions might be answered and the story concluded:

NURSES	HAUSMAN	9/17 7:30 A

The administrator of City Hospital says the nursing staff is in critical condition.

Jane Smith appeared before the City Council last night to warn that a severe shortage of nurses is causing a health-care crisis. Smith says almost a third of the nursing positions at City Hospital are currently unfilled. And, she says, everyone suffers because of the shortage.

AUDIO: SMITH RUNS: 20

INCUE: "LAST NIGHT WE HAD...

OUTCUE: "... CAN'T GO ON MUCH LONGER."

City Hospital administrator Smith says she simply can't attract nurses because of what she calls a double whammy. She says there is a statewide shortage of nurses... and claims that City Hospital cannot compete for those nurses because of poor working conditions and lower-than-average salaries.

City Council chairman Arthur Lake says he'll establish a task force to look into the option of hiring an outside firm to recruit nurses from other cities.

###

Here are some points about the script worth discussing.

1. The ### at the end indicates that the story has ended. In other words, it shows the reader that there is no second page. Most radio stories do not run longer than one page, but when they do it is imperative to indicate that there is more copy to follow. Some news writers put "(more)" (without quotation marks) at the bottom of the page. Others draw an arrow indicating that the story is continued. If the story on which we're now working were on two pages, it might be so indicated in this manner:

NURSES PAGE 2 OF 2 HAUSMAN 9/17 7:30 A

The administrator of City Hospital says the nursing staff is in critical condition.

Jane Smith appeared before the City Council last night to warn that a severe shortage of nurses is causing a health-care crisis. Smith says almost a third of the nursing positions at City Hospital are currently unfilled. And, she says, everyone suffers because of the shortage.

TAPE: SMITH RUNS: 20

INCUE: "LAST NIGHT WE HAD…"

OUTCUE: "… CAN'T GO ON MUCH LONGER."

City Hospital administrator Smith says she simply can't attract nurses because of what she calls a double whammy. She says there is a statewide shortage of nurses … and claims that City Hospital cannot compete for those nurses because of poor working conditions and lower-than-average salaries.

NURSES PAGE 1 OF 2 HAUSMAN 9/17 7:30 A

City Council chairman Arthur Lake says he'll establish a task force to look into the option of hiring an outside firm to recruit nurses from other cities.

###

2. If you must split a story into two pages, never break a sentence. Always end a page with a complete sentence.

3. Notice that we re-identified the speaker in a slightly abbreviated form after the actuality ran. Making a second reference after the actuality helps clarify the story in the listener's mind. Radio listeners are often distracted or for some other reason miss part of a story; perhaps they just drove through a

tunnel or only now tuned in to the station. In any event, using a shortened second reference after the actuality gently reminds the listener who has just spoken and keeps the listener on track.

Some news organizations ask the writer of the story to time the script. The running time, including the actuality, is frequently written in the upper right-hand corner. You can approximate the script time by reading the copy out loud or counting lines. Line-counting depends on your personal type font size and margin set-up and is generally less accurate than reading aloud. Many news software programs will, as previously mentioned, time the story based on the newscaster's typical reading speed.

Lead-In to Voice Reports

It is quite common for this type of story—a report on a city council meeting—to be filed by a field reporter, recorded in its entirety, and left for the morning newscaster. The story will generally be protected and concluded with the station's standard outcue. A standard outcue is what reporters are instructed to say at the conclusion of their piece, such as "Mike Michaels reporting from City Hall for WXXX News."

Mike Michaels's report, a voice actuality (sometimes called a VA or a wraparound), might read like this:

City Hospital administrator Jane Smith warned the City Council that a severe shortage of nurses is causing a health-care crisis. Smith says almost a third of the nursing positions at City Hospital are currently unfilled. And, she says, everyone suffers because of the shortage.

"LAST NIGHT WE HAD ONE ELDERLY GENTLEMAN WAIT AN EXTRA HOUR AND A HALF FOR HIS PAIN MEDICATION. WE JUST COULDN'T GET TO HIM. WE WERE STACKED UP WITH THREE EMERGENCY CASES AND WERE SHORT FIVE NURSES ON THE SURGICAL FLOOR. I'M AFRAID, REALLY AFRAID, THAT THE NEXT TIME THIS HAPPENS IT'S GOING TO BE WORSE THAN LEAVING AN OLD MAN IN PAIN. HE JUST MIGHT DIE WAITING … AND I LITERALLY THINK THE STRESS IS KILLING THE NURSES. THIS CAN'T GO ON MUCH LONGER."

City Hospital administrator Smith says she simply can't attract nurses because of what she calls a double whammy. She says there is a statewide shortage of nurses … and claims that City Hospital cannot compete for those nurses because of poor working conditions and lower-than-average salaries.

City Council chairman Arthur Lake says he'll establish a task force to look into the option of hiring an outside firm to recruit nurses from other cities. This is Mike Michaels reporting from City Hall for WXXX News.

###

You will frequently write scripted intros for a voice report or voice actuality. The intro may be a simple handoff to the piece, but often it is used to update the story, making it more current by reporting on the status of protected items in the recorded piece. For example:

NURSES MICHAELS VA INTRO PAGE 1 OF 2 HAUSMAN 9/17

City officials are meeting today to start looking for solutions to what's been called a health-care crisis in the making. Council president Arthur Lake is holding a meeting with the City Hospital administrator at this hour. Lake and the City Council got an earful about the situation at last night's meeting, and Mike Michaels was there.

AUDIO: MICHAELS

RUNS 58

OUT: SOC

MICHAELS REPORTED THAT CITY HOSPITAL ADMINIS-TRATOR JANE SMITH WARNED THE COUNCILORS THAT A NURSING SHORTAGE AT THE HOSPITAL IS JEOPARDIZING PATIENT CARE AND CAUSING ENORMOUS STRESS AMONG THE NURSES. THE CITY COUNCIL IS GOING TO SET UP A TASK FORCE TO INVESTIGATE NEW METHODS OF RECRUIT-ING NURSES.

You'll note several points relating to the intro.

1. The time element (last night) is written in the intro and not the VA. Therefore, the VA could be used in the 11:00 P.M. report and the 7:30 A.M. report. The actuality won't spoil because it's been intelligently protected. The intro can be adjusted to compensate for the time element.

2. The intro does not repeat Mike Michaels's first sentence. It sounds very awkward to have the same words repeated.
"Mike Michaels says there's a health-care crisis brewing at City Hospital."
Michaels Audio: "There's a health-care crisis brewing at City Hospital. Last night ..."

3. However, the introduction does make a declarative statement about the news event. This is usually considered much better practice than simply saying, "Now, Mike Michaels has a report about the nursing shortage at City Hospital."

4. In addition to the information you would expect (the time, the name of the sound file or cut number, and the fact that it ends with a standard outcue), this introduction includes a brief summary of the

story. Writing this kind of intro takes time, a commodity in short supply in broadcast journalism, so many newsrooms don't follow this practice. But it is highly recommended. If the actuality doesn't run, the newscaster can simply read the summary—and no one listening will be the wiser. (Another alternative is to have Mike Michaels leave a copy of his script handy, assuming the report was fully scripted and not partially ad-libbed. You can cover by ad-libbing from Michaels's script.)

Punctuation

Some broadcast news writers use a mark called an ellipsis (...) to indicate the pauses in a story.

> More bad news from the State House today ... state taxes are on their way up again.

The jury is out on whether ellipses are the right form of punctuation for broadcast news. (Although *ellipsis* is the technical term for the three dots, most people in the news business just call them *dots*. Actually, *dots* is probably more correct because the term *ellipses* can imply, if you use the literal sense of the term, that something is missing from the printed material. That is the true technical use of an ellipsis. But that's not why ellipses are used in broadcast news writing.)

Some news writers like using dots. Mike Ludlum, former executive director of news for CBS radio stations and the former news director of all-news radio stations in New York and Boston, finds them useful. "Dots work very well to show the flow of the writing," he says, "and to indicate effective pauses and emphases."

But Ludlum also notes that many news anchors prefer incomplete sentences with periods to reproduce the conversational style so often used in broadcast news writing.

> More bad news from the State House today. Taxes are on their way up again.

In summary: Either technique is fine. Use what's standard in your department or station. Dashes are all right, too, and are especially useful for setting off a clause in the middle of a sentence.

> A long day—and a soggy one—for runners in the Marine Corps Marathon.

Commas are used pretty much as they are in standard print writing: to separate clauses and items in a list. There are elaborate and highly specific formulas for comma use in standard written English, but for broadcast news writing it's probably best just to use a comma where you would normally pause when speaking out loud. Which of the following two examples rolls off the tongue more easily?

> The officers who saved the woman from the fire have been identified as Tom Roberts Melvin Hastings and Bob Griffith, all of the 14th precinct.

Actually, this sentence is a bit long. Let's use dots to break out another phrase and make the sentence more readable.

> The officers who saved the woman from the fire have been identified as Tom Roberts, Melvin Hastings, and Bob Griffith ... all of the 14th precinct.

The use of an apostrophe for forming contractions is also the subject of some debate—not about the apostrophe, but about the contraction—although most news writers use contractions freely because they make the phrases more conversational. As a general rule, contractions are fine—recommended, in fact—*except* when there's a possibility of misunderstanding.

You'll note that the previous sentence includes *there's*, and this sentence uses the contraction *you'll*. If spoken aloud, there would be no question that the writer meant *there is* and *you will*. But be careful with *can't*.

> The school board president says she can't grant the wage increase sought by union clerical workers.

This is a particularly difficult sentence in which to read *can't* and have it clearly understood. The word might easily be misunderstood as *can*, which will obviously change the meaning and probably anger or perplex some members of the audience. Better to use *can not*. Spell it out as two words, just for emphasis. It's even better to recast the whole sentence so that you can avoid the can–can't problem altogether.

> The school board president says there's absolutely no way she can grant the wage increase sought by union clerical workers.

Words

Some words and sentences sound stilted when read aloud. Others are tongue-twisters that may cause the newscaster to stumble, hiss, or pop. The formula is simple: If you can't comfortably read it out loud, or if it sounds unnatural when spoken, don't write it on paper.

> A giant pall hangs over Washington as the House writhes in internecine party warfare.

Nobody uses "giant pall" in conversation except, perhaps, for newspaper headline writers. Very few people can say "House writhes" without stumbling or spitting, so don't write it. "Internecine" is a word best saved for your master's thesis. Few people know what it means, and even those who do would find it inappropriate for news copy.

Jargon and Technical Words

Along the same lines, be wary of technical terms or jargon. You may know what a CAT scanner is, but many in the audience won't. Saying that CAT is an acronym for computerized axial tomography won't help since few people know what that term means. So define it in lay language.

> Riverdale Memorial Hospital has filed for funding to buy a CAT scanner, a multimillion-dollar machine that visualizes the inside of the human body without using X-rays.

Slang is acceptable in some situations, but be sure, if you use a slang term, that it's a word that people understand, it does not make your English sound substandard, and it is not offensive.

Active versus Passive

Broadcast news writing is usually more effective, direct, and understandable when it is in the active voice rather than the passive voice. A sentence is in the active voice when the subject performs the action.

> Mayor Leavitt delivered the report.

A sentence is in the passive voice when the subject of the sentence is acted on via the object, using a word such as *by*. (This is an informal definition specific to our example and not grammatically correct in all cases.)

> The report was delivered by Mayor Leavitt.

In general, attempt to keep your writing in the active voice. An occasional use of the passive voice is acceptable. On occasion, the passive voice is preferable for variety, but the active voice generally carries the story forward with more vigor. In fact, you can use quite a lot of simple, active-voice subject-verb-object sentences in broadcast news writing. When all else fails, stick to the basics, especially in a confusing story laden with heavy detail. Subject-verb-object constructions are easy to write and easy to understand.

"Says" and the Use of Present Tense

The word *says* is part of two common scripting conventions. One is to use the present tense whenever possible. If you look back over the radio script slugged NURSES, you'll see *says* used several times. *Says* is generally a better choice for broadcast copy than *said* because it is in the present tense—and radio and television are "now" media. However, be aware that there is something of an inherent inaccuracy in using the present-tense *says*, because what someone said yesterday is not necessarily what someone says today. Use *says* under most circumstances, but if you are quoting a controversial statement or a statement pegged to a particular time, use *said*.

Senator Smith says his opponent is a fraud and a liar.

You'd better pin that down to a time and place because Senator Smith might not be saying that today, especially if he has recently heard from his opponent's lawyer.

Senator Smith—in a speech last night before the West Side Veterans of Foreign Wars annual banquet—said his opponent is a fraud and a liar.

Also use *said* if the statement is placed in time or space, regardless of whether it is controversial.

As he stood before the Memorial Day crowd, the mayor said that the threat of nuclear war must be eliminated—forever.

There is another problem with *says* or *said*. We get tired of writing it. We *assume* that people get tired of hearing it, but there is some debate about whether anyone in the audience really notices. So we hunt for alternatives.

Note that in one section of the radio script, we used *claims* instead of *says* or *said*.

She says there is a statewide shortage of nurses … and claims that City Hospital cannot compete for those nurses because of poor working conditions and lower-than-average salaries.

Claims is an entirely different word from *says*. It implies a degree of skepticism—which is probably warranted in this case. As a reporter, I would feel a slight discomfort in using *says* in the clause that alleges that City Hospital has poor working conditions because the statement is just that—an allegation. *Claim* implies that this is an unproven statement made by a person or group; however, *claim* can lend an unintended air of suspicion.

State College President Martin Gold claims enrollments are up this year.

Is there some suspicion that he's lying? If so, *claims* is all right, but if not, it adds an unintended twist of skepticism to the story. Stick with *says* most of the time. Although it is tempting to use *claims*, *declares*, *pronounces*, and so on, *says* is usually your best option.

One more consideration about verb tenses is important. Even though *says* is an example of the basic principle of keeping broadcast copy in the present tense, don't shift tenses so that they create a silly sentence or distort reality.

A man is dead this afternoon after committing suicide this morning.

That's a real example that, though not misleading, sounds just plain idiotic. But here's another real example.

A Bronx woman is shot to death … and police continue their manhunt.

This one *was* misleading because the woman was shot a full day before the story aired. The lead might induce people who heard yesterday's news to believe that another Bronx woman was shot. So when something important happened, please don't get cute with the tenses. Just say that it happened and tell when it happened.

Numbers and Abbreviations

Some characters that are perfectly plain in written English are jarring to the newscaster who has to read them aloud. Numbers, symbols, and abbreviations may be tongue-twisting or might take a split second to decode mentally, so news writers have developed specific conventions to deal with them.

Numbers

Usually, you can simply round off large numbers. A city budget of "almost fifty million dollars" is reasonably accurate if the figure is $49,887,211.12. You can also round off distances. "A 200-mile trip" is all right even if you know it is really 202.5 miles. But don't round off specific statements of important fact where the number really makes a difference. You would not, for example, round off mortality figures in an airline disaster (unless the numbers were estimates, in which case you should say they are estimates).

Spell out numbers from one to ten, and use numerals after that. The same scheme is handy for ordinal numbers, except most writers use numerals after eleven: first, fifth, eleventh, 12th, 20th, and so on. Ages are usually given before the name: "19-year-old Mark Smith." By the way, it's usually best to use the numeral when indicating ages, including those below 13. Use "4-year-old" and not "four-year-old."

Symbols and Abbreviations

Symbols and abbreviations are usually distracting in copy meant to be read aloud. For example, the $ symbol is best left out; write "five hundred dollars." Parentheses are rarely if ever used. Spell out "percent." Quotation marks are hardly ever used since broadcast quotes are paraphrased or orally attributed.

Abbreviations can cause news anchors to stop in the midst of reading news copy if the abbreviations are unfamiliar to them, so be careful. Be *especially* careful if you are writing copy to be read by people new to your area. TPK may be a standard abbreviation for "turnpike" in your city, but an out-of-towner may have no clue of what it means.

Short of Mr., Mrs., Ms., and Dr., you're well-advised to spell out everything.

Names

Broadcast news writers generally do not use middle initials. However, there is a notable exception: If you are reporting that a man named Frank Jones died in a traffic accident, it's best to give as much information as possible, including the middle initial and the complete address. Why? Because there may be dozens of Frank Joneses in a major city—even in a medium-sized city—and reporting the death of Frank Jones could very well panic the friends and family of Frank A. Jones, Frank B. Jones, Frank C. Jones, and others.

Again, remember that the conventions mentioned here are not universal. Don't think that a script differing from the specifications outlined in this chapter is "wrong" or, for that matter, that what you have read here is "right." Every station's script format has idiosyncrasies and variations.

So use whatever format is common in your department or station, but be prepared to adapt to different ways of doing things when you move on. That, of course, will be hardly any trouble at all because you've learned the basic principles. As for the technicalities, they can be picked up in an afternoon.[1]

NEWS READING AND REPORTING

In small stations, the role of producer is combined with the roles of reporter and news reader. Again, the broad topics of news reading and filing reports are beyond the scope of radio production as discussed in this book, but it's important to remember that they do play a role. Inflection and tone are as eloquent as the choice of words. Pace of the delivery certainly is a production value. Another production value is the quality and style of the ad-lib type of report filed by journalists in the field, which may involve using the telephone or two-way radio. As a news producer, you should be aware that this kind of ad-lib report is done with some frequency in radio news and is the kind of thing radio does better than any other medium.

Many radio stations have used timeliness to their advantage by calling themselves "news leaders" or "the news authority" in the community. Such slogans need to be backed up with good coverage and accurate reporting, but time and again, radio has demonstrated its ability to go live at a moment's notice. Often, this can be done with a simple phone call. Anyone who has ever listened to NPR's *All Things Considered* or CBC Canada's *As It Happens* knows of radio's superior ability to cover breaking stories immediately.

Gathering, writing, assembling, reading, and reporting the news are the basic tasks that constitute the structure of news programming. These tasks can be integrated into various types of programs, which, for the sake of discussion, we group into public-affairs programming, newscasts, and talk shows. (Talk shows are often a part of public-affairs programming, but they are different enough to merit separate discussion.)

---

1. Portions of Primer on Newswriting were adapted from Carl Hausman's book *Crafting the News for Electronic Media: Writing, Reporting and Producing* (Belmont, CA: Wadsworth, 1992).

NEWS AND PUBLIC-AFFAIRS PROGRAMMING

Although it has no precise definition, **public-affairs programming** differs from news in that it is less immediate. Public-affairs programming is usually directed toward a specific topic, which is examined at greater length than is possible in a news report. The role of a producer in public affairs can involve selecting the topic for discussion or examination, choosing guests, making all the organizational arrangements, and even setting up the mics.

The mainstay of public-affairs programming is the interview or talk show, which we discuss in detail shortly. Public service announcements are also the public-affairs producer's responsibility.

Public service announcements, known as PSAs, are generally short announcements, similar in structure to commercials, which are provided at no charge on behalf of nonprofit organizations. PSAs are usually 30 or 60 seconds long, have the same structure as commercials, and can be approached with the production techniques we described in Chapter 11.

One purpose of the PSA is to draw attention to a message. You wouldn't want to tamper with a newscast by adding music or staged dialogue, but the PSA can certainly benefit from attention to production details.

NEWSCASTS

In radio, the newscast is often a 3- to 5-minute program inserted into the music programming of the station. In most cases, the station offers the newscasts on the hour or on the half-hour, though the local news may follow the network news and may therefore be presented starting two, three, four, or five minutes after the hour, depending on when the station breaks away from the network newscast. (Radio networks structure the newscasts so that local affiliates can break away gracefully at various points.)

The newscasts produced locally are usually put together in a newsroom, which contains a variety of equipment to facilitate construction of the newscast. The equipment in a typical newsroom includes means for recording from the telephone, a vital part of radio news gathering (though some stations choose not to use telephone interviews). There is usually a computer or MiniDisc in the newsroom for recording audio and editing, and a wire-service computer as well. In some cases, the newscast is done directly from the newsroom, so the newsroom might also house a mic and console or small mixer.

The content and structure of the newscast vary greatly among stations. Following are some of the typical mixtures and arrangements.

Exclusively Local News

Many stations carry network newscasts and devote their news staffs entirely to local news. News staffs typically gather, write, assemble, and read the newscast over the air. The local news in such stations usually includes two or more pieces of actuality. Much of the local news coverage is written based on articles from the local newspaper. If staff size permits, local meetings are covered (usually in the evening), and a voicer is left for the morning reporter.

Local News with Wire Copy

Many stations integrate international, national, and state copy into locally originated newscasts. By and large, radio stations get their state, national, and international news from wire services, most notably AP, CNN, and Reuters. There are other news services, many available as Internet services or email, and some are syndicated through the postal mail.

Although today their transmissions are via satellite, the name *wire services* is still used, a reminder that all news was once fed over telegraph and telephone wires. The wire services offer special feeds to broadcast outlets—feeds that differ from the service given to newspapers. Essentially, the stories are shorter and written in broadcast style. The stories are often constructed in such a fashion that they can be updated quickly, with new information plugged in. The wire services specify where the new information is to be inserted.

The offerings of wire services include extensive news summaries, which are fed at predetermined times during the day; briefer summaries, which provide a couple of minutes' worth of copy; headline summaries; stock reports; agricultural news; commentaries and feature pieces; sports; and weather.

Wire services also feed special features that relate to current news items. A newsperson can use these features, which are fed well in advance of an upcoming event, to bolster a station's coverage of a major news story, such as a political convention. Wire-service material is slugged (a **slug** is a brief identifying or clarifying phrase) with the time of transmission, along with other relevant facts (see Figure 13.3).

Wire services provide what's known as a *state split*; that is, the circuits of the services are turned over to state bureaus, and state news is fed to the appropriate stations. Much of the news is gathered by local stations affiliated with the wire service and phoned in to the wire services. Traffic fatalities, for example, are almost always phoned in by local affiliates. The weather is also delivered in a split. Several forecasts are fed, and the local newsperson picks out the appropriate forecast. (A local forecast might be slugged, for example, SEVEN WESTERN COUNTIES.)

Wire services are very useful, and they provide material that a local station couldn't easily obtain anywhere else. Unfortunately, the excellent job done by wire services, combined with the fact that many radio stations are badly understaffed, leads to the rip-and-read syndrome, wherein the newscast consists of the announcer reading 2 minutes of whatever's available. This phrase is a holdover from the time when wire-service feeds were printed out on paper on a teletype machine. The board operator would run into the newsroom and rip the copy off the wire about a minute before he or she had to read it over the air.

In small stations, the rip-and-read approach to news often results in a newscast's being read by a staff announcer rather than by a full-time

AP V0901 RD INT—2ND MORNING DRIVE NEWSWATCH 12–15 6:54A
ENGINE PROBLEMS CITED IN CRASHES ... BAD SIGNS IN BASEBALL ... TAX
CUT COMING

(MORRISVILLE, NORTH CAROLINA)—ONE ENGINE APPARENTLY QUIT ON THAT
AMERICAN EAGLE COMMUTER PLANE THAT CRASHED TUESDAY IN NORTH
CAROLINA. OFFICIALS SAY THE FLIGHT RECORDER CAPTURES THE CREW TALKING
ABOUT A "FLAMEOUT" AND ABORTING THE LANDING. FIFTEEN PEOPLE DIED IN
THE CRASH.

(FRESNO, CALIFORNIA)—WITNESSES SAY BOTH ENGINES WERE OUT WHEN A LEAR-
JET CRASHED INTO A FRESNO, CALIFORNIA, NEIGHBORHOOD YESTERDAY. OFFICIALS
SAY BOTH CREWMEN DIED IN THE CRASH AND AT LEAST 15 PEOPLE ON THE
GROUND WERE HURT. THE PLANE HAD BEEN TAKING PART IN A NATIONAL GUARD
WAR GAME.

(NEW YORK)—A NEW POLL INDICATES ALMOST SIX IN TEN AMERICANS ARE WILLING
TO PAY MORE TAXES, FOR JOBS AND TRAINING, TO HELP PEOPLE GET OFF WELFARE.
THE SAME NEW YORK TIMES–C–B–S NEWS POLL FINDS STRONG SUPPORT FOR LAWS
REQUIRING WELFARE RECIPIENTS TO WORK.

(RYE BROOK, NEW YORK)—THE TWO SIDES IN THE BASEBALL STRIKE ARE HARDEN-
ING THEIR POSITIONS. TALKS BROKE OFF YESTERDAY, AND TODAY OWNERS MEET
IN CHICAGO, WHERE THEY'RE EXPECTED TO IMPOSE A SALARY CAP. THE PLAYERS
VOW TO FIGHT THAT MOVE IN THE COURTS.

(WASHINGTON)—JIMMY CARTER SAYS HE'LL TRY TO END THE BOSNIAN WAR, IF
BOSNIAN SERBS MAKE GOOD ON SOME PROMISED CONCESSIONS. HIS ANNOUNCE-
MENT FOLLOWS MEETINGS WITH BOSNIAN SERB OFFICIALS IN GEORGIA. THE WHITE
HOUSE SAYS CARTER IS WELCOME TO TRY, BUT NOT AS A REPRESENTATIVE OF
THE U–S.

(BRUSSELS, BELGIUM)—NATO'S DEFENSE MINISTERS ARE RENEWING THEIR SUPPORT
FOR U–N PEACEKEEPERS IN BOSNIA. CLOSING OUT MEETINGS IN BELGIUM, LEADERS
SAY THEY'VE TOLD THEIR GENERALS TO FIND WAYS TO BACK UP THE PEACE-
KEEPERS. BUT PLANS ARE ALSO BEING MADE FOR EVACUATION IF IT BECOMES
NECESSARY.

(WASHINGTON)—AUTHORITIES SAY A FEDERAL GRAND JURY HAS BEGUN CALLING
WITNESSES TO SEE IF THERE'S ANY CONNECTION AMONG ATTACKS ON ABORTION
PROVIDERS AROUND THE COUNTRY. AN ABORTION RIGHTS ACTIVIST SAYS IT'S
ABOUT TIME. BUT AN ANTI-ABORTION LEADER CALLS THE PROBE A "WITCH HUNT."

(UNITED NATIONS)—UNICEF SAYS IT'S WINNING THE BATTLE AGAINST CHILDHOOD
DISEASES. THE AGENCY SAYS (M) MILLIONS OF CHILDREN HAVE BEEN SAVED UNDER
A COMPREHENSIVE MEDICAL CAMPAIGN LAUNCHED IN 1990. IT SAYS PNEUMONIA
AND MALNUTRITION REMAIN MAJOR KILLERS.

F I G U R E 13.3

Sample of wire-service copy.

SOURCE: © Cengage Learning 2013

newsperson. The notion that it's an acceptable practice to simply rip-and-read is one rejected by most journalists, and the newscast often sounds exactly like what it is: a half-hearted and somewhat sloppy approach to a station's news commitment.

If you use wire-service material in your newscasts—and you almost certainly will at some stage in your radio career—proofread the copy in advance. Keep an eye out for state and regional stories that directly affect your community. Sloppy rip-and-read newscasters often overlook state and regional stories that might relate, for instance, to the health of a local industry or to a current or former local resident.

Wire services provide such an excellent resource that many people involved in radio news production often overlook some important working principles. Here are some brief suggestions on using wire services effectively in radio news production.

Acquaint Yourself with the Schedules and Workings of the Service   Very often, the schedule of transmissions isn't posted; if that's the case, track it down and learn it. The wire services provide working manuals, pronunciation guides, and other descriptive literature that can be very helpful but that often don't filter down to the news staff. Asking for and reading through support material will be beneficial. The AP also publishes a useful style guide that is a key reference source for all broadcast journalists.

Check Copy for Typos and Pronunciation Problems   When you are reading on the air is the wrong time to puzzle over a typo. Typos do happen on wire-service feeds. You may even encounter garbled material. Don't take a chance on stumbling through an unfamiliar name or word. Use a dictionary if you're in doubt, and ask someone at the station for advice on how to pronounce names of local people and communities.

Wire services generally provide pronunciation guides for difficult-to-pronounce words. Learn to use these guides, and you may save yourself and your station some embarrassment.

Always Verify the Time of Transmission of a Story   If you print your news in hardcopy, one piece of paper looks just like another. That's why it is important to check through copy to make sure that an old and dated story doesn't get included in copy scheduled to go on the air. Monitor your printed wire copy to be sure an update on your story has not been sent.

News with Wire Copy and Network Audio

In addition to newscasts, some wire services and networks provide voicers, actualities, and voice actualities to affiliated stations. This kind of arrangement allows you to be creative, provides more flexibility in sound, and gives the newscast a professional sound. Correspondents report the news from all over the world, and actualities from breaking news stories are fed as soon as they are gathered.

A wire service, such as AP, will feed a description known as a **billboard**. The billboard describes the piece; tells its length; and states whether it is a voicer, a voice actuality, or an actuality. The individual pieces are counted down ("Rolling in three … two … one … In Washington today, there was …") so that the person in the newsroom can start the record machine at the proper time or can edit out the countdown cue on the computer.

Remember, the audio service is a different entity from the wire-service copy, which comes in via a satellite feed to a computer. The audio service is an extra. This type of product is also available from private organizations seeking to provide news features free in return for the publicity. Colleges and universities often run such services as a part of their public-relations operations (see Figure 13.4). News services using RSS (rich site summary) technology can provide updated information directly to users who subscribe to the service.

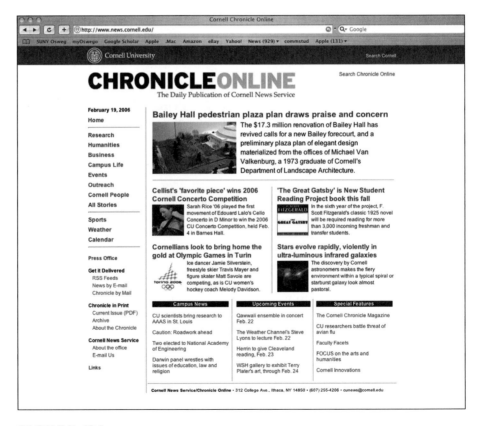

FIGURE 13.4

Promotional websites such as this one can prove useful in developing story ideas.

SOURCE: Courtesy of Cornell University

TALK SHOWS

Talk programs can run the gamut from news-oriented, issue-focused, community-affairs programs to celebrity interviews. Often, though, they come under the jurisdiction of the news or public-affairs department.

Most often, the talk show is prerecorded and features a host and one or more guests discussing a prearranged topic. The two most common forms are the one-on-one show and the panel discussion. A popular variant is the call-in show.

In the *one-on-one talk show*, an interviewer and a guest discuss a topic. The interviewer often runs her or his own board, with the guest on a separate mic in the same studio. Sometimes an engineer runs the board.

The *panel discussion* features a moderator and several participants. Here, proper miking and a good moderator become major considerations. Aside from following the mic techniques outlined in this book, you can deal with the problem of miking a panel discussion by keeping the number of interviewees as small as possible. Some panel discussions on radio are truly awful because they are impossible to follow. A clamor of disembodied voices makes things very tough on the listener.

It's important, in a multiperson discussion, that the producer or moderator identify each speaker frequently during the program and avoid, whenever possible, having two or more people speak simultaneously. (This happens more often than you might think.)

The *call-in show* is a talk program designed to include the listening audience, and it's very popular on local news/talk stations. Often it is presented around a previously announced topic of discussion, but sometimes listeners call in and speak about whatever is on their minds. What's on listeners' minds is not always suitable for airing, however, so a delay system is often used. That is, the program is recorded live and fed back over the air several seconds later. Producers of call-in shows often screen calls in advance, weeding out cranks, and clarifying the topic with the callers. A board operator handles the delay system, monitoring the signal that goes out after the delay.

SPECIAL EVENTS

The news and public-affairs producer often is responsible for special events production. We cover many of the technical aspects in Chapter 14. Keep in mind that you may be called on to cover a wide variety of events, such as store openings, county fairs, and press conferences.

PRODUCTION TECHNIQUES FOR
NEWS AND PUBLIC AFFAIRS

Certain techniques are most appropriate in particular types of productions. In this section, we discuss some of the techniques that are particularly relevant to news and public-affairs programming and that are not covered elsewhere in the book.

Interviewing

Although a complete discussion of interviewing would be more appropriate in a performance course, certain principles relate directly to production. Interviewing is actually a news production technique because the way a question is phrased will determine the product that results. Here are some suggestions.

Ask Simple and Direct Questions   Try to put yourself in the place of the listener and determine what the listener would like to ask. For example, in questioning the spokesperson for a utility that is raising its rates, be sure to ask how much the rate hike will cost an individual listener. It is also important to phrase the question so that it is not vague or overwhelming; that way, the answer you get is less likely to be evasive or too long.

Invite Bite-Sized Answers, but Don't Ask Yes-or-No Questions   A plain *yes* or *no* will not provide you with much actuality. On the other hand, questions that invite ponderous answers are bad because the answers can be too unwieldy to edit. Here's an example:

Do ask: How much more will a homeowner be paying in property taxes after revaluation?

Don't ask: What impact will revaluation have on homeowners in the area, and how do they and the city council feel about the situation?

Ask Follow-Up Questions   On a talk show, it's important to pursue a line of questioning if an interesting conversation develops. Formulate questions on the basis of previous answers. Don't fall into the trap of coming into the interview with a list of prepared questions and sticking to it no matter what. This practice is a common mistake, resulting in an interview that will appear to the interested listener to be almost laughably bad. The listener isn't tensely clinging to a list of questions; he or she may be genuinely interested in the responses obtained and probably wants to hear an intelligent follow-up.

Fill Listeners In   This is very important in a radio talk show because statistics tell us that listeners tune in for a shorter time than do television viewers. The producer or moderator should frequently mention the names of the guests and identify the topic.

Story and Actuality Editing

Knowledge of editing is essential for newscasts. Editing allows you to inject some variety because you can take different pieces of interview segments, rearrange these actualities, and rewrite the stories around them. In addition to offering variety, editing the actualities allows you to shape the story to be told in the quickest and most succinct way possible.

One of the biggest challenges for beginning news producers is how to create a story and edit an actuality from a news interview. What part of the audio should be used on-air? Which part should serve as information that will be written into a news story? Although there are no hard-and-fast rules, it may help to remember that fact usually is better written into the story, whereas reaction and comment are better used in actuality. For example, the listener is less interested in hearing a politician recite by how many votes he or she won than in hearing the politician's reactions to winning and her plans for after the election.

Using Sound Sources in Radio News Production

The use of sound sources as background in radio news production is often overlooked. Sound bites can really dress up a news story. Traffic noise, for example, can be a helpful adjunct to a story about highway construction. If you've been assigned to do a live, on-the-scene voice report, it is generally helpful to have local noise in the background because it will make the story more immediate for the listener. If you're covering a fire, for example, wouldn't it be much more effective to have the noise of the fire engines and roaring flames in the background? Oddly, some news reporters (accustomed to studio conditions) seek a quiet place to voice their report.

Think of sound elements that can be used in your radio reports (without, of course, being overdramatic or misleading). Plan in advance for the sound bites you want to pick up.

Using the Telephone to Maximum Benefit

At one time, it was a common practice among radio news reporters to feed tape over the telephone by using a pair of alligator clips connected to a tape recorder and to a telephone. This could be done quickly from a remote location. Today, it is increasingly difficult, however, to find public phones with mouthpiece connections that detach easily. A better solution is to use a flash recorder, such as the Tascam DR-07 portable digital recorder (see Figure 13.5), which can record a digital file that is transferred to a computer and then sent to the station via a wi-fi network connection.

The widespread availability of cellular telephones holds considerable promise for radio news professionals in the field. This technology offers many advantages. An important one is that because you can easily use your cellular phone from virtually anywhere, you don't have to search frantically for a phone when you want to get a story back to the studio. Headsets are available for nearly all models of cellphones, and the audio quality of newer digital cellular phones is also far superior to that of wire-connected phones. Some cellular phones are capable of being connected to tape recorders and MiniDiscs, though in some models this can void the warranty on the phone. Perhaps the most significant advantage of cellular telephones, however, is that they allow you to report live directly from the scene of a news story.

The telephone, of course, is also a news-gathering tool—in fact, one of the most important news-gathering tools. Although you can't always get celebrities to come to the studio or grant an in-person interview, it's surprising how amenable they can be to a phone call. A routine story, even a state story taken from

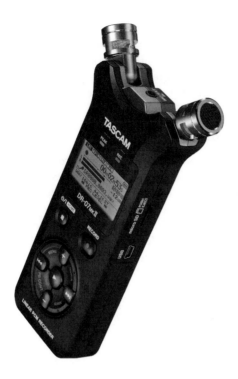

FIGURE 13.5

Modern flash recorders provide reporters with high quality recording than can be edited on laptops and sent back to the station via a wireless network or 3G phone card.

SOURCE: Courtesy of Teac Corp. of America/Tascam Division

the wire service, can be given added importance by carefully done telephone interviews.

Recording from the phone is a common practice in radio and definitely should be exploited by a news producer. You must inform all parties that a recording is being made. Check with your news director for guidance on legal and procedural policies concerning telephone recording at your particular station.

Using Modern News-Gathering Technology

Although the industry is in a state of flux concerning the role of computerized technology in the newsroom, modern gear is making inroads into radio operations. Here are some points to consider.

Digital editing (described fully in Chapters 6 and 9) is the standard practice in the modern newsroom, and the versatility of the equipment promises improved newscasts. The newsroom of today depends on digitally stored sound and computer-generated readouts of audio information rather than on carts, cassettes, and grease pencils. If the radio station uses a server-based filing system, as soon as a reporter saves an audio file onto the server it can be played back in the control room. Networking has helped simplify the process involved in getting actualities on the air once they've been edited and saved.

Computer systems run the gamut from plain word processors to integrated packages that edit and play audio. Word processing has gained wider acceptance in radio news, although a few stations still use standard typewriters. The primary advantage of word processing is, of course, the speed with which corrections and additions can be made. Furthermore, many news-oriented set-ups allow more than one staffer to have access to a story. The most sophisticated of these systems allow wire-service material to be fed directly into centralized computer systems that many different staff members can access through the use of networked PCs. This aspect of computer use in radio news operations is gaining increasing acceptance in many medium-sized radio newsrooms.

Modern news software captures wire-service material and feeds it into a computer so it can be used by a number of different people at the same time. A writer can work on an update of the story for the next hour while another writer edits the copy for the anchor currently on the air. Locally generated stories can also be handled in this way. These systems allow many functions to be performed by various staff members (see Figure 13.6).

If, for example, news developments take place in a story that is about to be aired, a writer can quickly update the story and flash it immediately to a screen in

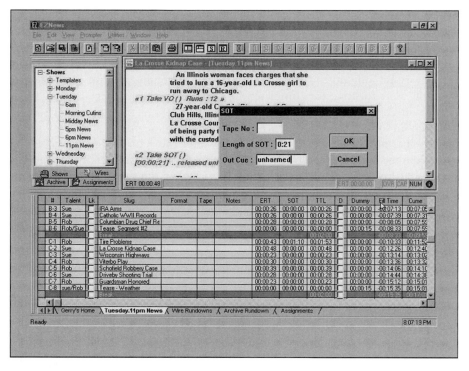

F I G U R E   13.6

News software makes it easy for a producer to update and rearrange the stories in a newscast.

SOURCE: Automated Data Systems

the on-air studio. The on-air news reader can then delete the original version of the story and substitute the updated version by reading it directly from the screen. Updated headlines can be written and immediately related to the anchorperson while he or she is on the air. Bulletins can also be handled in this way. File stories can be forwarded to the station's Webmaster, simplifying the process of updating news stories on the station's Web page.

Modern transmission gear has had a major effect on radio news-gathering practices, and technology's influence continues to grow. Today's radio reporter is often equipped with a portable transmitter for feeding live reports back to the station; major stations have a series of boosters located throughout the city to ensure quality transmission. Cellular telephones have also made it possible for smaller stations to report live from the scene of a breaking story. Satellite feeds have had a noticeable effect on news and public-affairs programming. Modern news and information formats allow local breakaways, which create the appearance of an integrated news program.

Making the Newscast a Cohesive, Unified Whole

The elements should follow logically, and the pace and style of delivery should be varied to reflect story content. This sounds obvious, but many newscasters don't alter their deliveries relative to the story. Thus, the piece on the polar bear cubs born at the zoo is delivered in the same style as the report of the two-fatality auto wreck. Avoid a joking style in general, and be particularly wary of light-hearted readings of serious stories.

In essence, the newscast is an entire story, and though the individual elements vary in content, the items should follow gracefully. Within the newscast, you will want to strive for completeness; don't leave the listener hanging, waiting for an answer that never comes. On a related note, don't leave actualities hanging; in other words, don't play an interview segment and then move directly into another story. Have some copy after the actuality, even if it simply identifies the speaker. Incidentally, it is always a good idea to identify the speaker of an actuality before and after it's played. One of the radio news producer's primary responsibilities is to avoid confusing the listener.

Responsibility is a word often repeated in radio newsrooms. Providing the news is a heavy responsibility, and it's important not to forget that. News people don't have to be stuffed shirts, but they do have to realize that they're in a serious business. Of course, even though it's serious, it can also be fun. News—and in particular radio news—is one of the fastest moving and most exciting of all professions.

SUMMARY

Radio news people have a great advantage over their competitors in other media because radio is relatively simple and immediate and stories can be gathered and relayed with great speed. Broadcast news writing has its own style. Sentences are shorter than in newspaper stories, and attribution comes first in a sentence.

Wire services provide valuable news and information that can be integrated into a station's news effort. However, it is important for a news producer to avoid the temptation to "rip and read." Interviewing skills are essential to the radio newsperson. Among the most important points to remember when conducting interviews are to ask follow-up questions, ask simple and direct questions, and ask questions that invite concise responses. Yes-or-no questions, though, are best avoided.

Don't be afraid to use sound sources in radio news production. As long as they are not used to distort the facts, sounds of crowds chanting, fire engines racing, and the like are appropriate and enormously evocative.

Don't forget that the telephone is one of your most useful tools. You can record an interview from the telephone, and you can feed recorded stories back to the station with the phone.

Modern news processing systems can capture wire-service material on a computer and allow many different staff members to work on stories simultaneously. Such systems allow for rapid updating of stories and instant airing of new developments.

APPLICATIONS

SITUATION 1/THE PROBLEM A news reporter was assigned to cover a potentially violent job action at a local plant. Arriving on the scene, she found that picketers had been instructed not to talk to the press and police would not let her pass police lines to do an interview. The obvious approach was to read her notes into the microphone, but that seemed a particularly dull way to cover the story.

ONE POSSIBLE SOLUTION The reporter placed herself as close to the police lines as possible and voiced her report with chanting and other wild sounds in the background. Later, a scuffle broke out, and she recorded wild noise from that altercation and edited it into another report, which she produced back at the station.

SITUATION 2/THE PROBLEM The news producer on duty Sunday afternoon found that there was nothing going on—and he had a half-hour newscast coming up in 2 hours. The only items available were feature stories in the local paper, but another organization's feature stories are not easily rewritten and adapted to a local radio newscast.

ONE POSSIBLE SOLUTION One state story fed by the wire service dealt with the governor's plans for improving the quality of public education in the state. It was a substantial and interesting story but had no local angle. The news producer checked through his files of telephone numbers and called the following individuals:

- the principal of a local high school,
- the head of the local teachers' union, and
- a student at a local state college.

He asked for their reactions to the governor's proposals and recorded the actuality off the phone. Now he had a good lead story for the upcoming newscast.

YOU'RE ON! • TECHNIQUES FOR EFFECTIVE ON-AIR PERFORMANCE

Interviewing for Radio News

Asking a question and getting a straight answer is a more complicated process than you might expect. Interviewees frequently have vested interests and seek to answer questions in a circuitous way. Although an answer might not be an abrupt departure from the path of truth, it could involve a trip down a more scenic byway. Sometimes interviewees will tell you an outright lie, flatly refuse to answer a question, or evade an issue. Journalists in radio and other media have developed a variety of specialized techniques for extracting information when confronted with these circumstances.

Good journalistic interviewing is a three-part process. The experienced questioner uses the following approach:

- Assess the motivations of the person being questioned, because those motivations play a strong role in determining the ambience of the interview and the type of information that will be provided.

- Determine the appropriate structure for the interview.

- Use specially structured questions to evoke a meaningful response. Sometimes these questions lead directly to the point. Other times, they are open-ended "discovery" questions designed to get and keep the interviewee talking.

Note that these are generalized categories, not prescriptions. Many journalists have their own styles, and this chapter doesn't purport to inform you of the "only" way to do interviews. However, these methods are good starting points.

Motivations of Interviewees

Why does someone talk with a reporter in the first place? It's an important question because the character of the information you receive is determined, in part, by the circumstances that brought you into contact with the interviewee. Those circumstances include the interviewee's professional obligation, desire for personal or professional gain, inadvertent entry into the public eye, and desire to confess or divulge information.

Professional Obligation

Some people are compelled to speak with the news media because it is their job to do so. Police departments, for example, have designated public-affairs officers. The military often calls the person with that duty a public information officer or PIO. Public-relations professionals for profit-making and nonprofit organizations are also compelled (to an extent) to speak with the media; after all, that is a function explicit in the job description.

A person bound by professional responsibility to speak with a reporter may do so with some reluctance depending on the circumstance. For example, police departments are required to furnish certain facts to the media, but there is no law requiring them to do so enthusiastically or to provide you with additional facts that will make the story complete. Although police departments will generally dispense information to the press over the phone, the officers involved often find it a bothersome chore and sometimes "forget" to inform reporters of major incidents.

When a public relations (PR) representative is compelled to speak with a journalist purely because of professional obligation, he or she may frequently provide incomplete data. No PR person, for example, will welcome an inquiry about toxic wastes found on the company's property. It is likely that you will receive perfunctory answers and that the PR representative will not volunteer potentially damaging information. Remember, there are very few cases where anyone is *obligated* to give you a complete story. No law says a PR representative has to spill his or her guts just because a reporter is on the phone.

So, when someone gives you information because he or she is under a professional obligation, remember that what you receive may be perfunctory in nature, may be incomplete because the person answering your questions will probably feel no motivation to lead you to the heart of the story, or may be intentionally misleading if your inquiry involves a negative angle.

Personal or Professional Gain

Some interviewees appear before cameras and mics for the sole purpose of promoting their organization, their product, or themselves. There is nothing inherently wrong in this. However, a journalist has an obligation to present the information in a balanced manner and to ensure that the facts aired are a matter of legitimate public interest—and not just a free advertisement for the person being interviewed.

Public-relations people will usually adopt a markedly different attitude when speaking with a journalist about a subject promising personal or professional gain, as opposed to those circumstances where they grudgingly deal with the media to fulfill a professional obligation concerning a story they don't particularly want publicized.

Public-relations professionals can be solicitous and charming and will often provide you with valuable information. For example, good PR people (who often were reporters themselves before entering the much more profitable field of public relations) know what reporters need and in what form they need it. For example, on a day when there is a major confrontation in the Middle East, public-relations representatives from major universities across the nation are likely to be on the phones to major news media, attempting to line up interviews with the universities' Middle Eastern affairs experts. Such an arrangement can benefit everyone. The reporter, who was scrambling to come up with an angle and an analysis, has an expert dumped in his or her lap. The university receives nationwide publicity and, so the theory goes, gains credibility in the eyes of potential students and their families.

But remember that information provided to you under such circumstances may not always be top quality. To continue the example of the university and the Middle East, remember that the PR executive is under pressure to place faculty on news programs and may provide you with an "expert" who is less qualified than someone you could have sought out on your own.

This, of course, is not a broadside against PR people. They simply have a job to do, and everyone wants to be presented in a favorable light. Representatives of almost all businesses feel their organizations will benefit financially from favorable publicity. Politicians, for obvious reasons, want good publicity. But even though information provided to you for personal or professional gain is not necessarily duplicitous, remember that such material is not provided merely for the sake of giving you information.

Inadvertent Entry into the Public Eye
Some people become caught up in events simply because of happenstance. They witness a tragic accident or come home from work to find their home burned to the ground. Crime victims, too, are unintentionally thrust into public scrutiny.

Such sources of interviews are under no obligation to provide you with information. Nor will they carry the ideological baggage of the political candidate who provides information for his or her personal benefit, so they are not likely to provide you with information that supports their particular agenda. But veteran journalists know that people thrust into the public eye nevertheless do present two credibility problems: First, they often are inexperienced witnesses. Second, they are frequently reluctant to provide information.

Sift and weigh information like a historian when you deal with an "inexpert witness's" evaluation of an event. Historians who chronicle battles, for example, sometimes use a colloquial phrase called "the corporal on the battlefield syndrome." This refers to problems often inherent in an account provided by someone who viewed an event from a limited perspective. The corporal, for example, may exaggerate the fierceness of the fighting because it was his first taste of combat. He also could overestimate his unit's role in winning the battle, basing his estimation on the justifiable exhilaration felt by a group of soldiers who fought shoulder-to-shoulder in a life-or-death situation.

Desire to Confess or Divulge Information
Many people come forth with material because they simply want to get something "off their chest," or, perhaps more commonly, they feel they have knowledge of a situation that should be brought to the attention of the public.

When interviewing such people, remember two critical points:

- There is a temptation to believe that when someone says something negative about himself or herself, the information is true. It is likely, of course, that such negative information bears a greater ring of truth than positive information. But sometimes people do confess to things they have not done, for reasons usually known only to themselves. So it is wise not to take an "unburdening" entirely at face value.

- When someone discloses information to you voluntarily, you need to know why the admission is being made. Does the person have an ulterior motive, an "axe to grind"? If so, the information is suspect. For example, you may speak with someone from the law enforcement community who offers the information, on condition of anonymity, that a prominent official is under investigation but higher authorities are hushing up the investigation. This informant may be offering you this information because he or she is legitimately outraged that a high official is getting away with something. Providing such information could rightly be considered a public service. However, there is also the possibility that your interviewee has a personal grudge against the person allegedly under investigation and is using you and your station as a weapon.

Now that you're more aware of the ways in which an interviewee's perspective and motivations can alter the character of information you receive, you are ready to plan the basic structure of the interview.

Appropriate Structure for an Interview

Several factors are involved in determining how an interview will be structured and carried out. Among them are the intended use of the interview, the availability of the subject, and the cooperation of the subject.

Intended Use of the Interview

There are three primary types of news interview: interviews meant for use as background, as an actuality or sound bite, or on a talk show.

The *background interview* is conducted simply for the purpose of compiling information that may be useful in the story's production. This information, though, will probably not be used directly on-air. For example, a medical reporter might call physician friends and ask them about general trends and new information in the medical field. Everyone is aware that these sessions are simply conversations, meant for brainstorming and not for attribution. The physicians certainly would never speak freely or give strong and provocative opinions if they expected to be quoted. Likewise, reporters do not use material from such encounters as literal fact. They *always* verify the information with an on-the-record interviewee, because when people are not quoted, they are not held directly accountable for their statements—and this opens the door for them to exaggerate, slant, or even lie.

The actuality or sound bite interview is designed to produce a segment of audio that can be inserted into a radio voice actuality or inserted directly into a newscast read by the anchor. The goal of an actuality or sound bite interview is to evoke an answer that is short, to the point, and able to stand on its own. You can use several techniques (discussed in the following section) to elicit a usable actuality or sound bite response.

A talk show interview must usually run for a specified period of time and must have a flow—a sense of continuity. That is, it must move from one subject to the next with some sort of progression. The guest on a talk show can speak at much greater length than he or she can during an actuality interview.

Availability of the Subject

The same quality that makes people newsworthy also limits the amount of time they have available to the news media. This, in turn, affects how you will structure the interview. How will you arrange to meet the interviewee? Will you visit the interviewee in person at a remote location, have him or her come to your station, or do the interview over the phone?

An in-person interview at a remote location, often the subject's office or the site of an event in which the subject is participating, is usually the ideal choice for broadcast news gathering. For one thing, it captures the subject in his or her native environment and provides some of the physical or aural trappings that add color to the interview. Often, too, this is the only way you'll gain access to the person.

Having the interviewee visit the station is not a common option in most news-gathering operations. Although certainly convenient for the reporter, most newsmakers simply do not have time to make themselves available in this manner. The most frequent exceptions, of course, are guests who appear on talk shows. A talk show may or may not be a news-related production, but don't forget that you can usually arrange to use cuts from the talk show in a newscast should the program involve a newsworthy guest.

Often, a journalist must resort to a telephone interview. Radio stations, which usually have limited staff, frequently exploit this method of news gathering. A telephone interview is also much more convenient for an interviewee, and it may be the only method that will gain you access to him or her.

But telephone interviews have significant disadvantages. Because recorded phone conversations are instantly recognizable as such, some journalists feel they don't convey the immediacy or presence that makes radio such a powerful medium. Some radio stations go so far as to forbid the use of phone interviews and insist that a reporter gather every piece of actuality in person, using a high-quality microphone and recorder. However, most stations allow the use of phone interviews when that is the only logical alternative, such as for interviewing a local citizen trapped in an overseas war zone.

Cooperation of the Subject

For various reasons, interviewees might not want to speak with you or may be willing to cooperate only to a certain extent. The structure of the interview, then, may revolve around this factor. Two particular problems arise:

1. Getting a subject on mic. In rare cases, you'll have to "ambush" the person on the street. A street is legally considered a "public forum," meaning that a reporter has a greater right of access to the subject than if the person were on private property. The ambush interview should be considered only when repeated attempts to arrange a standard interview have been rebuffed. Remember that an ambush often arouses sympathy for the subject, whom the public may perceive as the "victim" of the ambush.

2. Circumventing a "no comment." Media-savvy public figures frequently have no reluctance to exercise their constitutionally guaranteed right to keep their mouths shut. Although some critics argue that airing a "no comment" can make an innocent person appear guilty, many news veterans observe that people who exercise their no-comment option can and do avoid accountability for their actions.

Setting aside that argument, which cannot be resolved here, remember that a "no comment" does not make for particularly informative or compelling news. When structuring an interview, there are three primary methods of getting past the no-comment stone wall:

- If the subject refuses to consent to an interview, inform him or her that you will *report* the refusal. This is a highly effective method of attitude adjustment. It may not necessarily circumvent the "no comment," but often it does prod the interviewee to talk.

- If, on-mic, the interviewee replies "no comment," ask *why* he or she is refusing to comment. Should the interviewee respond, the explanation of the "no comment" might be the answer you wanted in the first place.

- A variation on the "no comment" routine is the "no interview" dodge. If you cannot even get the interviewee on the phone—let's assume Mr. Big is always in a "meeting"—inform Mr. Big's secretary that you would like your phone call returned *at a specific time.* Be sure you are there to receive the call should it indeed be returned. Should Mr. Big not return the call, give this tactic one more try—but be certain to inform Mr. Big's secretary that if your phone call is not returned, you will air that fact. (An alternate option: Find out the name of Mr. Big's boss and

ask Mr. Big's secretary to transfer the call to that office. Mr. Big may suddenly materialize.)

After you have (a) determined the motives and perspectives of your interviewee and (b) determined the proper structure for the interview, it's time to actually execute the interview. The act of producing usable answers is a direct result of asking properly phrased questions. Certain techniques can help you gather reliable, direct, and compelling quotes from interviewees.

Questions to Evoke a Meaningful Response

A "meaningful" response means, simply, an answer that will serve your purposes and the purposes of the viewing or listening public. A meaningful response must be

1. useful within its technical context—for example, a meaningful part of a voice actuality;
2. a direct response to the question and to follow-up questions; and
3. illuminating to the listener or viewer.

Technical Context

A rambling answer will be of little use to you if you need a 20-second reply for insertion into a 90-second voice actuality. Also, the interview segment won't be very functional if it is too complex or too simplistic for the audience. If you are interviewing a guest for a longer segment, such as a talk show, you must elicit responses that will sustain the listener's or viewer's interest for an extended period, perhaps half an hour or even an hour.

Following are suggestions for making the message fit your medium:

- When asking a question for a brief sound bite, don't be reluctant to ask the same question several times. You may get some quizzical looks from your interviewee, but you will also obtain varied responses and, sometimes, better responses.

    If you're interviewing for radio, you can obtain several alternative audios for radio newscasts.

    When you use the technique of asking the same question several times, you can actually alter the questions slightly, so it appears that you're asking a different question when you actually are not. Alternately, you may elect to inform your interviewee in advance.

    "Sometimes, I ask the same question more than once," you might say, "so don't be surprised if you hear me repeat myself. I do this just in case there's a technical problem."

YOU'RE ON! • TECHNIQUES FOR EFFECTIVE ON-AIR PERFORMANCE (CONTINUED)

■ When you want a short answer, ask a short question! If you are looking for a 10-second sound bite, ask the mayor, "What's the most pressing item on tonight's city council agenda?" Don't ask, "Mayor, could you explain the priorities you've established for tonight's city council meeting—how do you plan to deal with all the items on the agenda, and how did the schedule get so packed in the first place?"

■ If you want a simple answer, ask a simple question. For example, you'll probably want to ask a physician, "How does cholesterol harm the body?" Unless you're producing a piece for a specially trained audience, don't start with, "Doctor, what is the mechanism by which cholesterol contributes to atherosclerosis?" The latter question raises some interesting points about the entire interviewing process. Regardless of the type of interview—sound bite, talk show, or background—the beginning question sets the tone for the entire interview. If you start the interview on a complicated theme, you probably will never get your expert back on a simple track.

■ Remember that no matter how much knowledge you have obtained during your research, your audience will essentially be starting from ground zero. Note, too, how the question about the "mechanism by which cholesterol contributes to atherosclerosis" forces the interviewee into deeper waters than you or your audience might care to venture. By asking about the "mechanism" by which cholesterol does damage, you are inquiring about a complex and still poorly understood process, but your physician interviewee will probably begin his or her answer from that point. It will be virtually meaningless to the audience, who simply wants a general idea of what cholesterol might do to their abused arteries.

■ If you are doing a talk show (that is, a show with an opening and closing and a predetermined length), remember that a talk show is essentially an imitation of a social situation. This means that the audience expects to be introduced to the guest. The topic should start on a general level and become more specific; the conversation should begin more formally and then become more personal; the questions should become more pointed as the conversation wears on. There are two reasons for observing this convention: First, if you lead with an abrupt, challenging question, you may appear rude and boorish. Worse, you may force your guest into a defensive shell and be faced with 29 uncommunicative minutes of remaining program time.

This isn't always the case, of course. On occasion, you will want to cut right to the heart of the matter. That depends on the interview and the interviewee. However, most experienced interviewers know that it's safer to warm up the interviewee with some slow pitches and to save the hardballs until the end.

Extracting a Direct Response
People evade questions for a variety of reasons. Sometimes, they are trying to hide something. More often, they are simply uneasy and afraid of being misinterpreted, and they may avoid your question or become inclined not to elaborate on the subject. It is a journalist's job to elicit a meaningful response despite these obstacles. Usually, this is a three-part task, involving obtaining a direct answer, focusing the issue, and stimulating further response.

Obtaining a direct answer means getting the respondent back on track. In these days of media advisors and public-relations counselors, shrewd public figures are often taught to evade a question by giving the answer they want—irrespective of the question that was asked. For example, you may be forced to ask a direct yes-or-no question because you are getting nowhere in your interview with a political candidate. You come right out and ask:

Q: Do you plan to fire the aide who leaked the information about your opponent?

A: We're going to run an honest, straightforward campaign. It's important that we keep our efforts on track, because economic conditions in this city ...

You're responsible for getting the interview back on track. "I'm sorry," you might say, "but I didn't quite understand your answer. Are you firing him or not?" This is one tactic. Here are some others.

■ *If the question is not being answered, say so.* Start by simply repeating the question. If that does not work, mention that the question was not answered and ask it again. Should you still not get an answer, directly ask the interviewee why he or she is ducking your question.

■ *Do not get drawn into a debate with your subject.* This strategy— making you a part of the issue—is a method of evading a question. For example, your interviewee may respond to your question by giving a basically irrelevant response, and then asking you, "Is that fair?"

- *Don't ever let the interviewee ask questions; that's your job.* Just turn the question around again, or say, "My feelings aren't important. What is important is your action on the bill before your committee … Now, once again, do you intend …"

Focusing the issue means getting the interview back on track when your interviewee has wandered off the subject, either accidentally or on purpose. Sometimes you need to focus the issue simply because your interviewee is speaking gibberish. Two techniques are particularly useful.

- *Use a paraphrase to force a clear response.* If you are not getting a clear answer, sum up what you *think* the interviewee said and repeat it to him or her. Then ask, point blank, "Is this what you are saying?" For example, if a public official has just told you something to the effect of "We need to re-evaluate the enhancement capabilities lost to us in the number of transactions which take place in certain economic categories, and reconsider the revenue structure of …", you should paraphrase what you think you heard: "Mr. Representative, did you just say you favor an increase in the sales tax?" This method will allow you to force an answer in plain English.

- *Use a transition to get back to the subject.* Guests, especially in long-form interviews such as talk shows, may accidentally or purposefully wander into the areas *they* want to talk about. You can get them back on the subject without appearing abrupt or obstinate by relating what *they* want to talk about to what *you* want to talk about. For example, the head of a city hospital who has been charged with running a sloppy operation may want to shift the subject to the fact that the city council has yet to draw up a firm budget for the year. Link the two subjects and force a transition back to your original topic:

Hospital Manager: "… since January, and still no action."

You: "Does the lack of a firm budget have anything to do with the charges that you are almost six months behind in your billings?"

Maybe there *is* a link between the two; maybe not. Either way, you've prevented your guest from wandering off on a self-serving polemic.

Stimulating further response is necessary to keep the interview rolling and to allow you the time and opportunity to dig for real answers. A number of techniques have proven successful.

- *Don't ask dead-end questions unless you are forced to do so.* Most books on interviewing advise you not to ask yes-or-no questions because such questions won't stimulate further response and will produce an awkwardly short answer. That, to an extent, is true, but there are times when you must call for a *yes* or a *no*. If your interviewee is evading an issue, don't be afraid to pose a yes-or-no question.

- *Master the art of out-waiting your interviewee.* If you receive a curt, nonresponsive answer to your question, don't switch to another subject just because you feel the need to keep the conversation moving. Let the recorder roll, keep the microphone in the subject's face, and wait. Usually, he or she will break down and start talking before you do.

- *Be careful about letting your subject catch on to your pattern of taking notes.* In other words, don't let the interviewee know when you have become excited by the information, because he or she will probably clam up. Former basketball star Larry Bird, for example, reads reporters very well; when they stop writing and look up at you, he maintains, that's a good time to shut up because the subject is getting "too deep." Interviewees are generally quite concerned about what you write—with good reason—and can make your job difficult when they ask, "Aren't you going to write that down?" The opposite situation can arise when an interviewee makes a stunning statement and you scramble to write it in your notebook. The interviewee will be struck with the magnitude of what he or she just said and will move to retract or mitigate it.

Therefore, when you are doing a notebook interview—that is, news gathering that does not involve the immediate presence of a microphone—don't tip your hand by letting your interviewee discern your writing habits. One way to hide your note-taking pattern is to write all the time, even if you are just doodling in the notebook. This gives the interviewee no clue as to what you think is important and what is not, and avoids the "aren't you writing that down?" and "wait, I didn't mean" syndromes.

SOURCE: Portions of this feature were adapted from Carl Hausman's book *Crafting the News for Electronic Media* (Belmont, CA: Wadsworth, 1992).

EXERCISES

1.   Have another student read a newspaper article. Then interview him or her about the article as if your partner were a spokesperson for one of the parties involved in the article. (Your partner should keep the clipping handy for reference.) Try to present a logical discussion of the subject. Because your partner is not really an expert on the topic, he or she will be unresponsive on occasion, but that is exactly the situation you'll run into from time to time in radio news. Your goal is to convert the discussion into a graceful 3- to 5-minute interview.

2.   Take the interview you've created, edit out a section, and write up a voice wrap. Make the voice wrap deal with a particular newsworthy segment of the interview, and make it about 60 seconds long.

3.   Come up with two new leads (new heads and orientations), and redo the story. Rewrite it and re-cut it as if you were freshening up the story for two upcoming newscasts. Incidentally, mechanical practice on equipment you're likely to use will be valuable, so if you have the opportunity to practice, use it. Record an audio feed, for example, and practice taking audio off the telephone. Becoming familiar with the operation of portable cassette machines will be beneficial, too.

14

Remote and Sports Production

Remote and sports production forms only a portion of the radio station's program day, but these areas put radio production people in the proverbial hot seat. Remote work, whether it involves covering a news conference or a football game, is a difficult undertaking that requires a great deal of preparation. In a time when radio programming is increasingly syndicated, the remote is the product that provides the station's local identity, so it's critical to get it right. Knowledge of equipment and production techniques also comes into play because the operational aspects are important in getting the signal back to the station.

Remote broadcasts often include sporting events, which is why we include a discussion of sports coverage in this chapter. Other common remotes include having a staff announcer play music from a car dealership, a new store, a restaurant, or some other business. The goal in such cases is to give the client (who has paid a fee to have the remote originate from his or her business) exposure and increased business. Less frequently, remotes involve news coverage, such as live broadcasts of press conferences. Music presentations are sometimes done remotely; usually, however, concerts are recorded on-site and are not fed live over the air.

Considerations of hardware and technical facilities will largely be determined by the equipment your station has on hand and by the technical qualifications of your engineering staff. Rely on your station's engineers for technical advice; they are the experts and will make many of the choices and installations.

Your role as a producer involves the planning, execution, and branding of these events. Although the engineering staff can give you help with the technical arrangements, you, the producer, must have an understanding of all the program elements and the kind of effects that make remote broadcasts successful.

Combined with a basic knowledge of radio production equipment, your knowledge and planning will be the key ingredients in a good remote broadcast. Your responsibility is to put the remote together in a way that produces the best quality and provides the sound you need to keep up the standards of your station.

REMOTE RADIO EQUIPMENT

Most remote equipment used to mimic a studio operation, such as playing music, is pretty much the same as that found in studio applications, though smaller models are favored. For remote work, you may still find a few old turntable consoles in operation, but more often than not a portable computer with fast hard drives will provide the audio sourcing capabilities needed for a remote.

Submixers are also used in remote productions, especially when a number of different microphones must be used and the inputs on the console are limited, as they usually are. Submixers are usually referred to as *portable mixers*. Portable mixers, such as those manufactured by JK Audio, Shure, and Sony, are especially useful in news remotes. They are essentially small audio consoles (some are the size of a brick) that can accommodate several mic or line inputs. Volume controls allow the operator to set a correct mix level (see Figure 14.1).

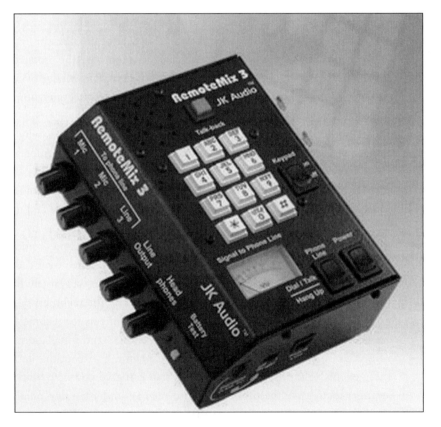

FIGURE 14.1

Some remote mixers combine audio functions with a telephone unit to simplify connections.

SOURCE: Courtesy of JK Audio

Incidentally, some portable mixers can be *ganged*, meaning several inputs can be combined in one mixer, and the output of that mixer can be fed into another mixer, along with other audio sources. This is a particularly useful tactic when you are confronted with the prospect of trying to run ten mics into one console.

Digital cart machines or MiniDiscs are generally not brought to the remote site because spots are played back at the studio. Newscasts are generally done at the studio, too. Back at the studio, the signal from the remote usually comes in on a remote pot, and the board operator handles coordination of other program elements originated from the studio. Sometimes program material from a remote location can be microwaved either to the station or directly to the transmitter. Microwave units are becoming increasingly common in radio broadcasting. Larger stations may have dozens of mini-transmitters in strategic locations throughout the city. Some stations have experimented with streaming back the remote on an Internet-based communication device. Although that is an exciting strategy and probably will be the method of choice in the future, it will take a while for the type of equipment needed to work its way into most medium- and small-market stations.

Telephone Lines

Telephone lines are still the medium of choice for a remote that covers a considerable distance. Specialized short-distance, two-way transmitters are typically used for shorter distances where signal loss or interference is not an issue. However, in major cities even short distances can be a problem if there are buildings in the way.

The landline is still an appealing option because it is easily accessible at almost all locations and because a device for putting the signal onto the telephone line and capturing it back at the studio, often referred to as a *codec*, enables better signal quality over standard telephone lines. (See Tuning In To Technology later in this chapter.) Additionally, telephone lines themselves have improved in recent years thanks to the widespread adoption of digital technology, so you can rent a high-quality "loop" from the phone company, or if the remote is to be conducted at a business, you may be lucky enough to find a high-speed line already installed.

And yes, you can do a remote using cell-phone service, although only certain types of services work well enough to offer the type of high audio quality you would need for an extended on-air program, as opposed to a quick news report. Best results are obtained by renting a high-bandwidth channel from the telephone company and using a microwave transmitter or a digital codec that connects to either telephone or Internet connections.

The vocabulary used by phone companies is confusing because sometimes the names of different lines and services vary from firm to firm, but the following terms are more or less standard and are useful to know if you are the one attempting to rent or locate a telephone line for a remote.

How do you get a signal back to the station, or to the antenna? In large markets, where the distance to be covered is not too great, the choice is usually a two-way transmitter such as the Marti unit (see Figure 14.2). (Marti is a trade name used by a firm that supplies a wide range of such devices.)

A two-way transmitter is a simple and reliable method, but there are situations when it doesn't work well. With so many people using the radio spectrum for short-distance transmissions, there is the possibility of interference. Some buildings—notoriously, shopping malls—play havoc with the transmission. The signal doesn't carry very far, and multiple transmission points must be arranged to retransmit the signal if you are attempting to cover many miles. You can make arrangements with broadcast engineers from different radio stations to avoid frequency duplication and interference. Learn more about this by visiting http://www.sbe.org/sections/freq_index.php, the website of the Society of Broadcast Engineers.

Transmitting over POTS lines, oddly, is at the forefront of something of a technical revolution. The reason is a device called a codec. Codec is an abbreviation for coder-decoder. (In the same type of verbal shorthand, modem is an abbreviation for modulator-demodulator.) What codecs do, essentially, is to put sound (and for other applications, video) into a digital format and then compress that information so it can be transmitted through the relatively narrow pipe of a telephone landline or cell-phone. The codec on the other end is able to unscramble the compressed data and turn it back into sound again. The better the compression, the better the speed, and the better the quality—just like with your garden-variety computer modem.

Companies that manufacture POTS codecs have made tremendous strides in compression methods in the past few years. POTS codecs, such as those made by the firm Comrex, produce quality more than adequate for transmission of something like a baseball game from a distant city (see Figure 14.3). And you can't beat the convenience; it's almost as simple as plugging in a phone.

Many codecs work with ISDN and switched 56 lines (a switched 56 line is a high-capacity line designed to handle large data flow). High-quality lines are often a permanent installation, with both the terminal for the line and the codec left in place. The applications for permanent remote installations vary from something as simple as a codec left in a church for broadcast of a weekly service to a switched 56 line running between a major radio station in New York and an

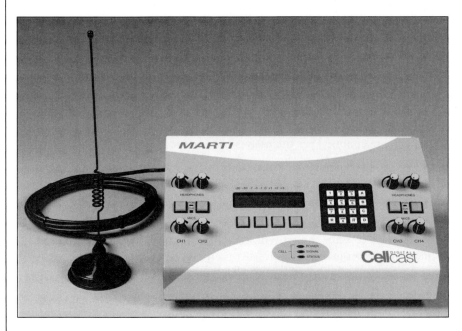

FIGURE 14.2

This complete remote unit uses cell-phone technology for transmission.

SOURCE: Marti Electronics

announcer's apartment in Dallas. That's how WCBS Radio in New York set up an arrangement with an announcer it hired to voice the station's promos and IDs. Today, ISDN and switched 56 services are giving way to more efficient Internet transmission systems.

Cell-phones are a very appealing option for the remote producer. There are codecs that plug into any standard cell-phone, and others that are specially designed for high-quality GSM service, which is available in many large metro areas but not universally offered across the United States or Canada. Many high-quality codecs allow you to choose among several transmission options.

Software-based codecs are the latest and perhaps the most intriguing of all options. Transmitting a remote over the Internet is technically feasible, and new equipment has been introduced over the past two years that makes this technology a reality.

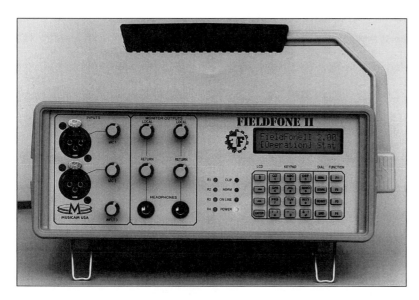

F I G U R E 14.3a

Digital remote equipment makes it possible to provide high-quality remote feeds using standard phone lines.

SOURCE: MUSICAM, USA Holmdel, NJ

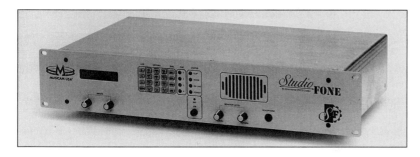

F I G U R E 14.3b

This codec allows stations to transmit high-quality audio over telephone and ISDN lines.

SOURCE: MUSICAM, USA Holmdel, NJ

POTS   An acronym for "plain old telephone service." This means a standard phone line, which will usually provide pretty limited levels of information transfer—usually in the range of 33 kbps (kilobytes per second).

ISDN   An acronym for "integrated services digital network." This is a high-quality line that can often feed voice, data, and video at rates up to 64 kbps. ISDN lines are common in many businesses, although you may not have the option of appropriating one for your remote because the firm probably depends on the line for transmission of information. Newer packet-based technology telephone systems are making ISDN systems less useful today.

GSM   The type of cell service most adaptable to remote transmission. GSM is often referred to as the "global system for mobile communication," but the acronym actually is derived from the French words **Groupe Spécial Mobile**, a research group founded to develop an international standard for cell communication. While GSM is the standard for Europe, it is less widely used in the United States and Canada. GSM works well for remotes because it does not send information in packets as most other cell systems do. The technicalities are beyond the scope of this chapter, but in basic terms, GSM provides a signal that is less likely to suffer data loss when transmitting material such as music. In recent years, service providers have made it difficult for broadcasters to use GSM with broadcast equipment.

DSL and **Cable Modems**   Digital subscriber line (DSL) service is a very high-speed connection that uses standard telephone line wiring to provide digital services. Cable modems are essentially interconnection boxes to high-speed Internet service provided by the local cable company. Many small businesses use these services to access high-speed Internet services. Modern broadcast remote equipment can use a business's Internet service to provide remote capability to radio stations. The remote producer simply connects a CAT 5 cable from the broadcast encoder to the local business's Internet. (Some newer equipment even works on wi-fi networks.)

Other Equipment for a Remote

Most stations use a telephone codec encoder and decoder or a microwave transmitter. A *codec encoder* is a device that converts the sound waves to a digital stream, which is then sent to the studio. The decoder, located at the studio, then converts the stream back into sound waves that the station can use.

It is important to have as many channels of communication back to the studio as possible. Remember, you'll need a method to talk off-air. A cellular telephone is handy, too, so that the remote on-air person will have a backup method of communicating with the studio. When broadcasting from a store, you may elect simply to use an available telephone—if the store owner will let you—and keep the line open to the board operator at the station. In less accessible locations, the telephone provider can install a separate telephone when the transmission line is installed.

Although a remote announcer can communicate back to the station by talking over the air line when the remote signal is in cue (back on the station console), that type of operation can be risky because the communication might wind up on the air. Sometimes, though, the remote announcer and the station board operator aren't able to take time out to chat. Some system of signals or protocol should be worked out in advance to avoid confusion.

Microphones are, of course, part of the equipment needed for a remote broadcast. You will do well to use rugged moving-coil mics because remote work can be rough on equipment. Determining whether or not to use a cardioid mic depends on the physical environment and on how much background noise you want included. Overuse of microphone directionality can detract from the broadcast; after all, if you are on remote from a store, you want it to sound like a store, not a studio.

Mic technique is also a consideration outdoors. **Wind filters** (also known as **pop filters**), such as the one shown in Figure 14.4, are useful in eliminating wind noise, which on a mic doesn't sound like wind at all but more like the rumble of a foundry. Be aware that ribbon mics are much more susceptible to wind noise than the moving-coil microphone types. When using a microphone for field production, choose a mic with a built-in shock mount to reduce hand-holding noise.

In some instances, you might want to add a mic to pick up wild sounds. In a basketball game, for example, mics are often placed near the backboards to capture the genuine sound of the game. Separate mics on the crowd also provide color and give additional flexibility to the balance of announcer and crowd noise because the volume of the mics can be controlled separately on a console or submixer. Sportscasters frequently wear a *headset mic*, a combination microphone-headphone that allows announcers to hear themselves or cues from the studio.

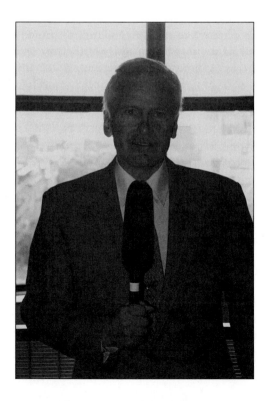

FIGURE 14.4

Carl Hausman illustrates the use of a mic with a wind filter.

SOURCE: Philip Benoit

Picking up a speaker is often a problem in remote news coverage, whether it is for a remote broadcast live or for recording on the scene. You will be at an advantage if the speaker at a press conference, for example, is standing or seated at a lectern. By placing your mic on the lectern, you can usually obtain reasonably good audio quality.

Placing your mic on a lectern often involves taping it to a group of other reporters' mics, so a roll of masking or duct tape is an essential element in your package of remote equipment. If there is no other mic on the lectern and you don't have a table or floor stand, you can improvise with the tape and attach the microphone in a jury-rigged manner. Be careful whenever you tape a mic to a lectern, though, because unless you want to dismantle it during the speaker's remarks, you will be pretty much committed to staying for the entire presentation.

Be sure to pack enough cable to reach your recorder, mixer, or other equipment. We offer more details on planning and packing for a remote later in this chapter.

Another way to pick up audio from a speaker is to tap into the public address (PA) system. (PA mics are generally not the best quality, however, and you may wind up with a poor-quality signal.) Many PA systems were set up with this function in mind. If you can't have advance access to the PA block, make sure to bring a variety of connectors; although most PA terminals have standard XLR outputs, some do not.

A variation on the PA terminal is the *multiple*, which is often set up by savvy public relations people to allow reporters to tap into audio. Public relations people often provide this as a way to keep the lectern free of a forest of microphones. Professionally supplied multiples often have both mic-level and line-level outputs for the convenience of broadcasters.

In sports applications, headset microphones are used. In addition to providing excellent noise cancellation (because of the physical qualities of the mic and because the element is close to the speaker's mouth), these are ideal when the announcer will be in a noisy situation, such as a ringside seat in a boxing arena. Headset mics also leave the announcer's hands free and don't crowd the table, a definite asset when you have many statistics and other items to keep track of (see Figure 14.5). Some headsets are wireless and transmit an FM signal. The director's private line can usually be fed into one earphone, simplifying contact between production and talent—an option primarily used in television. Some have a built-in cough switch to turn the mic off if the announcer needs to cough, clear his or her throat, or communicate with someone off-air.

PLANNING THE REMOTE

A remote must be well planned. Indeed, one of the major sources of trouble in remote broadcasts has been and continues to be lack of advance planning. A great deal of detail work is necessary for proper execution of remote broadcasts, and quite a bit of pressure is associated with these events. Much advertiser money is at stake, along with the prestige of the station. Sometimes a station remote is done with a nonprofit organization and the station uses the remote as part of its public service commitment to the community. In many cases,

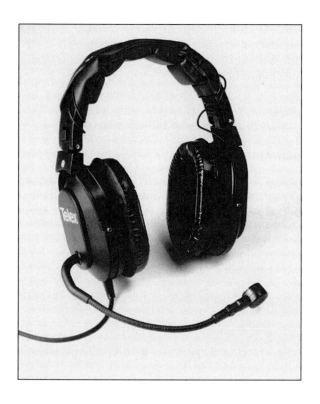

FIGURE 14.5

Many announcers prefer a sealed headphone-microphone combination when working in a noisy environment.
SOURCE: Telex

rights for a sports broadcast have been purchased in advance, so the producer must be prepared to protect the station's interests by providing a well-considered and airworthy product.

Signing Contracts

The first step in planning is to secure the contractual arrangement, which might involve a merchant signing a contract with the sales department or the administration of a college contracting with your station for rights to a sporting event. This is the time to make sure you understand the conditions that will exist at the site from which the program will originate. It is essential at this point to have a clear understanding of what will and what will not be provided for the broadcast: Will you have access to electricity, telephones, and a physically secure enclosure for your equipment? When will you have access to the event site?

Preparing the Site

The next step is to survey the site. This should, ideally, be done twice: before and after installation of the codec or remote transmitter. On the first visit, you can familiarize yourself with the area and make a rough plan showing the locations for various pieces of equipment. During this visit, you will also want to determine the availability of power and to assess external noise and wind conditions.

On the second inspection, made closer to the air date, you verify that the phone line (or other transmission facility) is in place, and you ascertain that conditions have not changed since your first visit. Check to make sure, for example, that new sources of noise have not been introduced or that the recently erected broadcast booth isn't facing directly into the wind. It's not always possible to make two checks, especially if you are planning a remote to another city, but the truism of better safe than sorry certainly applies to remote radio broadcasting.

Preparing the Equipment

For the lack of a connector, the broadcast could be lost. The same caveat applies to microphones, cables, and power cords. Take an inventory of equipment before you leave for the site and immediately after you arrive. Although particular needs will vary, your inventory list will probably resemble this one:

- Codec or microwave transmitter
- Console or mixers
- Microphones
- Wind filters
- Cable (at least twice as much as you think will be needed)
- A variety of connectors and adapters (male to male, female to female, and male to female)
- Power cords and adapters for two-prong and three-prong outlets
- Tape (electrical, masking, and duct)
- Cell-phone for back-channel communication with the studio
- Portable and accurate electric clock
- Portable radio for local pickup of the signal
- Recorders, if used
- Headphones
- Mic stands and clamps
- Screwdrivers, scissors, and other tools.

Don't forget to use the duct tape to secure wires and keep people from tripping on them (see Figure 14.6). Better yet, string wires from the ceiling if possible.

Preparing a Communication System

One of the most embarrassing and unprofessional situations in broadcasting can develop when the remote announcer and the board operator back at the station can't figure out who is supposed to do what. Much of this confusion can be avoided by planning out a protocol in advance.

Your role as producer may include acting as either remote announcer or board announcer; if so, work out in advance what will be aired at the studio and when. Is the weather to be read from the studio? If not, how will the weather forecast find its way to the remote announcer? The board operator and remote announcer should have a clear understanding about such matters.

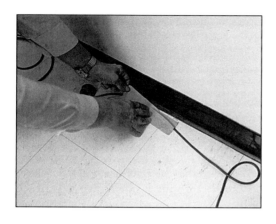

FIGURE 14.6
Using tape to secure cable to the floor is a good safety measure.
SOURCE: Philip Benoit

The remote announcer can also keep the production flowing smoothly by giving cues to the station board operator, such as, "In a moment, we'll go back to the station for the local news, but first let's talk to Joe Robinson, who is manager of the …" Preparing the communication system also can involve establishing the separate phone line we mentioned earlier. Although the individual details will vary, advance thought about the site, equipment, and method of communication is always a necessary part of the successful remote radio production.

Next, let's examine some of the particular requirements of sports broadcasting.

THE SPORTS REMOTE

Planning for the sports remote is critical. The producer of a sports event, who in smaller markets may double as the announcer, will be responsible for assembling, for the announcer's use, rosters of players, color information, and statistics; he or she will also be responsible for the physical set-up. Practice is very helpful. If you can possibly arrange it, try sample coverage (record it on-site for your reference) of a similar sporting event, preferably one held in the same location.

In preparation for the sports broadcast, check all connections and mics. Be especially careful of the location of the crowd mic, and be prepared to move it or have another one already strung up; one raucous or obscene fan can badly foul up all your plans.

Talk to the announcers about who will handle the starts and stops of the broadcast: who will announce the commercials, who will start talking when the remote starts, and who will be responsible for communicating with the studio in the event of equipment problems or other difficulties. Plan who will toss the program back to the studio for play of taped segments, such as commercials and station identifications.

Finally, there are two additional factors to consider when planning for the event: Large crowds can make parking difficult. Make sure you know where you are going to park on the day of the event. Also, be aware that outdoor sporting events are subject to rainout and rain delay. Work out in advance when and if the program will go back to the station in the event of rain delay. Will the board operator be ready to resume regular programming? Will the announcers fill in with talk and feature pieces?

All sporting events offer unique challenges to the producer. Following are some suggestions for the individual problems posed by various sports.

Baseball

Baseball is a wonderful game for radio. It essentially features one player at a time, and it benefits from a facile announcer who can tell interesting stories that captivate the fans. Many listeners grew up with radio baseball and find it has an appeal unequalled by other sports in other media. Bob Costas notes that the resurgence of baseball on radio—primarily due to satellite radio, which can bring a hometown experience to people all over the world, wherever they may have moved—is a "cutting edge technology that brings in the past." Listening to baseball on radio, he says, is "exactly what I did when I was 11 or 12, taking the keys to my dad's car, sitting in the driveway and trying to pick up games in different parts of the country through the crackle."[1] There's no question that the evocative skills of a good announcer, backed with a production staff that furnishes him or her with support and information, can make baseball first-rate radio fare. In fact, in the days before remote broadcasts of baseball games were technically feasible, announcers doing the "away" games for the home team were amazingly innovative, as described in the Radio Retro in this chapter.

But the same informal pace that makes baseball an ideal radio game also presents problems. Baseball games, unlike football, are stopped for bad weather, so use the preceding guidelines to make contingency plans. As a producer, remember that baseball games have many portions of little or no action, so selecting an eloquent and conversational announcer is essential.

From a technical standpoint, the sounds of a baseball game don't always travel back to the point of the announcer's mic. (This is a problem common to many sports.) A shotgun mic or a **parabolic mic** (a mic positioned in a reflective bowl) can be used to pick up the crack of the bat or the slapping of the ball into the catcher's mitt.

Hockey

The producer of radio coverage for a hockey game must select very good air people. The action is so fast that it's difficult for an inexperienced announcer to keep on top of it. An action mic adds interest because the sounds of the hockey game aren't very loud. But be careful, because hockey fans tend to be raucous and can shout things that are inappropriate for broadcast.

Football

Producers of radio football coverage should be aware that their listeners are among the most technically oriented fans in sports. In-depth analysis is usually called for, and you'll need someone who can handle this task. Further, football

---

1. L. Jenkins. "Baseball Rediscovers Its Radio Days," *New York Times*, June 12, 2005, D-1.

sportscasts benefit from a fairly large staff; if you can find someone to keep track of statistics, downs, and penalties, you'll help the announcers do a better job.

Be sure the announcers have *depth charts*, which are diagrams of the players as they will line up on the field, with first- and second-stringers listed. Having a depth chart is very helpful in determining who ran the ball or made a tackle.

Basketball

Basketball is subject to many audio problems. A gymnasium packed with cheering people is a difficult environment from which to broadcast. A half-empty gym can be even worse because of reverberation problems. In high-school coverage, you probably won't have access to a press box. Even in many college games, coverage is done from a table set up on the gym floor. The mic must be selected with an ear toward eliminating noise from people next to the announcer and presenting decent acoustics at the floor level.

One option is to use a directional mic or headset mic for the announcer and have a separate crowd mic. The two can then be mixed to provide a better-sounding balance. You may suspend the mic from the press box or even elect to string mics from the structure holding the backboard; this will add some interesting sounds to the coverage.

Basketball involves a great deal of statistical information, so the announcer(s) must have the ability to keep numbers straight. For example, listeners will want to know how many fouls or rebounds a certain player has as the game progresses, and it takes a well-organized announcer—or an announcer with some competent help—to have those stats at his or her fingertips.

Field Sports

Sports played on an unenclosed flat field, such as field hockey, soccer, and rugby, usually are difficult to cover for a number of reasons. First, bleachers or seats to lift the announcer above the action and offer a proper perspective may not exist. Second, wind noise is often a factor when there is no stadium to block air currents. Crowd noise is also a problem because there may be no place to hang a crowd mic. Spectators may be hundreds of feet away or, conversely, five feet from your mic. Power and line availability can also be problems.

In field sports, one of the best options available is to have a parabolic or shotgun mic on hand to pick up **ambient noise** from the crowd and from the athletes. (Wind filters are usually a great help.) You can create a small platform to elevate the announcer if no vantage point is available. The top of a building usually works in a pinch. If you can't rig up a platform and the playing area is far from any structure, the bed of a pickup truck is better than nothing.

A FINAL NOTE

The day of a remote is typically a tense one for the people responsible for its execution, and the degree of tension is usually in inverse proportion to the amount of advance planning.

RADIO RETRO • CALLING THE GAME YOU DON'T REALLY SEE

From the 1920s through the 1960s, many hometown baseball announcers would actually re-create games played in distant cities from their own studios. The crack of the bat was often reproduced by the announcer using a piece of wood to hit an empty cardboard roll that had held the teletype paper. Crowd noise was recorded at a previous home game and kept running throughout the studio re-creation. Attentive listeners would occasionally notice a loud voice in the crowd cheering for a player who had been traded three years previously. The information about what was really happening came from the teletype machine, basically a big, noisy, automated manual typewriter. The teletype was kept behind glass, but listeners could usually hear it churning away in the background.

According to a wonderful account by Pat Doyle, who was a broadcast assistant to Rochester Red Wings announcer Tom Decker in the 1950s and 1960s, the teletype would provide only the sketchiest of information, and the announcers would take it from there. As Doyle recalls,[2] this is what would come over the teletype:

"Burton up.

B1OS.

B2LO.

S1C. S2 Foul.

Out. Flied out to right.

The hitter, Ellis Burton, took two pitches for balls, one outside and one low. He took a called strike and then fouled off a pitch. No mention was made of the type of pitches or destination of the foul ball. Burton ended the at-bat by flying out to right field, again with no description of short, deep, lazy fly, line drive, or any other helpful information.

The rest of the inning would follow.

Frey up.

S1C.

Hit. Single to left.

Oliver up.

B1HI.

B2OS.

S1S.

S2 Foul.

B3OS. Wild pitch, Frey to second.

Out. S3C.

Easter up.

S1C. B1IS.

Hit and out. Single to right, Frey out at home 9-2.

Buffalo 4, Rochester 2.

With the briefest of descriptions, we learned that Jim Frey had singled to left, moved to second on a wild pitch, and was thrown out at home to end the inning. The nature of his hit, the description of the wild pitch, and the details of the play involving his being thrown out at home plate were left unstated. With Luke Easter batting, the hit could have been a dribbler between first and second or a line drive off the wall. For the aged Luke, any hit that wasn't a homer was a single.

At the microphone, Tom Decker and his fellow announcers would enhance the facts with details that may or may not have matched reality. Decker, a native of Buffalo, would have the advantage of being able to visualize the playing field on Offerman Stadium and its surroundings. All three were free to create scenes as they wished, limited only by the results that were printed on the yellow paper."

---

2. Pat Doyle, "Baseball Broadcasting from Another Day," Baseball Almanac, http://www.baseball-almanac.com/minor-league/minor2004a.shtml (accessed June 14, 2006).

The most important factor in doing a remote broadcast, especially a sporting event, is getting there on time. Arriving on time is a frequent problem in coverage of major sports. Why? Because what is normally a 10-minute drive to the stadium can take 2 hours on game day, when the thoroughfares are choked with traffic. If the event is in your hometown, you'll have a good idea of travel time to the site on game day. If it is an away game, try to book accommodations within walking distance, or plan to leave very far ahead of schedule to ensure that you're on-site in time for the broadcast. One broadcaster of our acquaintance recalls with horror the day he was scheduled to announce play-by-play for a major college game. Traffic was terrible, and he had the distinctly unpleasant experience of hearing the national anthem over his car radio as he waited in traffic, vainly trying to get to the stadium on time.

In conclusion, we'd like to bring up the planning issue again. Problems can and do occur, but advance preparation can make the difference between an inconvenience and a horror story. Having backup equipment can make the difference between executing a quick repair and not going on the air at all.

SUMMARY

Sports and remote production are usually small parts of the job of a typical radio producer, but they tend to be expensive and important affairs that require careful planning.

A variety of remote equipment is available, including codecs that make POTS lines sound—if not studio quality—at least acceptable for many applications.

Planning in advance is extremely important. Remember, a great deal of advertising money is at stake.

For producing a remote, the rule of thumb is to calculate every piece of equipment you might conceivably need, double that amount, and pack it. Be aware that you will need a communications system back to the studio. Work out all the details in advance.

Sports present a wide range of production problems. The most immediate problem in any sports event involves selecting a competent announcer.

After that, the producer must be concerned with arranging mic placements that eliminate extraneous noise.

Finally, plan to be in place well in advance of the scheduled start of the event. More than one remote has been ruined because key personnel were stuck in traffic.

APPLICATIONS

SITUATION 1/THE PROBLEM The producer for a remote inside a grocery store had a great deal of difficulty coping with noise from the air-conditioning system directly above her location. The set-up couldn't be moved, so a directional mic was substituted. Now, however, there was no ambient noise whatsoever. The goal of the remote was to present a program from the new grocery store, but the broadcast might as well have come from a closet.

ONE POSSIBLE SOLUTION A mic was suspended from the ceiling over the cash registers, and the ambient noise was fed into a mixer. A proper balance was struck between the announcer's mic and the ambient mic. Now, there was a sense of location to the remote.

SITUATION 2/THE PROBLEM Live reports from the local golf tournament sounded flat and lifeless.

ONE POSSIBLE SOLUTION The radio producer borrowed a technique from television and used a parabolic mic to pick up the swish of the clubs swinging and the plink of the ball dropping into the cup. Now, when the announcer said, "We're standing near the 18th green, where Lee Leonard is about to putt for an eagle," listeners could hear the ball being struck and dropping into the cup.

EXERCISES

1. Test out the sound qualities of various locations by taking a portable tape recorder and mic into various areas and business establishments. Try recording a test (with permission from the manager) in an auto dealer's showroom, a supermarket, a locker room, a restaurant, a shopping mall, an open field, and other locations you want to try. Briefly jot down the characteristics you feel each location has, and note the problems each might present for a remote broadcast.

2. Write down some of the special problems you think might be encountered in the following situations. Then propose possible solutions.

    For example, imagine broadcasting from a booth at the fairgrounds. You may encounter such problems as a rowdy crowd or a heavy wind from the west. To solve these problems, you should ask the fairgrounds manager to station one of the police officers on duty near the booth, and put the remote console against the west-facing wall to keep wind from hitting the mic.

    Now, think of problems and solutions for the following:

    - Coverage of a high-school swim meet
    - Remote from the construction site of a new building
    - Remote from the opening of the Lilac Festival, held in a city park

3. Plan and execute a remote from the hallway or a room adjacent to your production studio. You and your partners can invent any situation you want, but there is one ground rule: You cannot iron out problems by opening the door and conversing. Any communication must be done by wires that you and your instructor or lab assistant run yourselves, or by intercom or telephone. Set up mics and a laptop, if possible, and run their output back from the hallway or other room into the board in the production studio. Assign some duties, such as playing commercials or reading the news, to the board operator in the studio.

15

Advanced Radio Production

This chapter on advanced production will serve as a jumping-off point for your exploration of various specialized areas. Multichannel recording of music, for example, is a specialty within itself, and many schools offer entire curriculums devoted to this subject. We can offer only a basic introduction in this chapter. As part of that discussion, we deal with stereo recording and briefly explore the relationship of a stereo signal to radio broadcasting. Engineering and other technical operations are specialties, too. Without writing a primer on electronics, we will introduce a few basic terms, techniques, and concepts that might be useful to radio production people interested in expanding their knowledge in these areas.

The applications of audio in other media are wide ranging, and although those applications typically involve the principles dealt with in this book, many are outside its scope. There are a number of comprehensive guides to these applications, as well as to more advanced applications of the principles put forth in this book. Check the suggested readings at the end of the book.

MULTICHANNEL RECORDING

Multichannel recording can be accomplished in several ways. Today, many digital audio workstation (DAW) programs incorporate multitrack production capabilities within the software set-up. These software programs may allow you to mix as many as 128 tracks of audio, although you'll need a high-powered computer for that much capability. Digital workstations can take the place of multichannel recording consoles in some situations. However, the number of tracks that can be recorded simultaneously is usually limited by the hardware set-up of the computer. In other words, if the sound card has only a stereo input, you can only record two tracks at a time, despite the fact that your software can accommodate more tracks. Audio cards that accommodate eight inputs are fairly common in small multitrack setups. Because of this limitation, some radio stations have incorporated multichannel recording equipment in their studio operations, particularly if they feature live, local talent on their station. Multitrack systems allow high-quality recording and mixing of music and other complex audio projects, such as adding sound tracks to multimedia presentations.

Multichannel means pretty much what its name indicates: The console and recorder are capable of isolating a number of channels, depending on the channel configuration and the track configuration of the record-playback system. It's important to make a distinction between tracks (which are associated with recording equipment such as multitrack recording tape machines or workstations) and channels, which may be associated with consoles as inputs and outputs.

In multichannel recording, a separate audio source can be placed on each of these channels and then mixed into the final product at some later date. In music recording, for example, drums may be isolated on one, two, or more channels; the lead vocalist on another channel; and guitar on yet another. These individual channels could be directed to separate tracks that keep all the sources discrete. This allows the producer to balance the sound sources properly when the final mixdown of sources occurs afterward. Multichannel audio consoles typically offer a variety of sound shaping effects that can alter the coloration of the sound. Digital audio workstations with multitrack capabilities may provide a wide variety of sound shaping and effects controls for each channel (see Figure 15.1c).

Common formats for multichannel tape recording include arrangements of 4, 8, 16, 24, and 32 tracks. The number corresponds to how many tracks are placed on the tape. In high-quality recording facilities, 24- and 16-track studios are two of the more popular formats, whereas 4-track and 8-track studios are more common in broadcast stations. Modern tape recorders are digitally based systems. Figure 15.1a shows a console used for complex multitrack recording. Figure 15.1b shows a digital 8-track tape machine, which means it can record and playback any combination of 8 tracks simultaneously. Figure 15.1c shows virtual tracks on ProTools, a DAW with 16 playback tracks assigned. Today DAWs have replaced most tape systems.

Why is multichannel recording used? Because it gives the producer much greater flexibility and control. In music recording, for example, recording on a multichannel system offers a distinct advantage. If the recording of a music ensemble were done on only one track (or on two tracks in stereo, as we discuss later in the chapter), the result of the initial recording would be the final result. If the mic position caused the horns to sound too loud, little could be done. With multichannel recording, the horns can be miked and recorded separately, and then their volume level can be increased or decreased during the following session, called the mixdown, when the musical elements are remixed.

The advantages of multichannel recording don't stop there. Suppose that the horn part was hopelessly bungled during the recording. When each instrument is separately miked and recorded on a separate track, another musician can be brought in to re-record nothing but the horn part, which would then be mixed into the final product. Such flexibility also allows a singer to cut

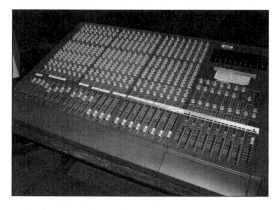

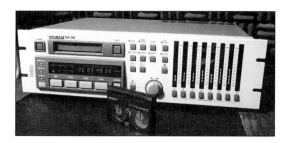

b. This digital multitrack recorder uses a cassette and can record up to eight tracks simultaneously.

SOURCE: Fritz Messere

a. Multitrack recording console.

SOURCE: Fritz Messere

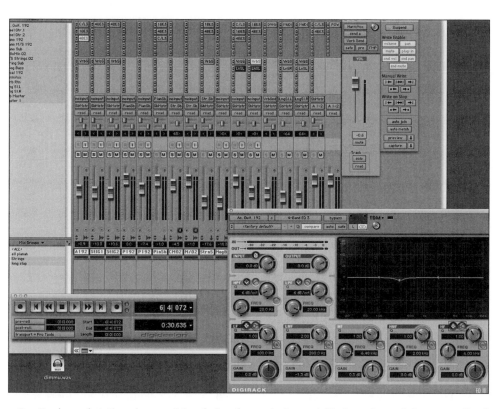

c. Pro Tools workstation shows mixing faders for each channel. Various channels have equalization or effects programmed. Here channel one has a 4-band equalizer assigned.

SOURCE: Digidesign, Inc.

FIGURE 15.1

Equipment for multitrack recording.

several versions of a song until the desired sound is achieved. A singer can also **overdub** her or his own voice, adding a harmony part, for instance, to a previously recorded song.

Multichannel consoles also allow sound shaping; that is, a variety of electronic devices can be used to alter the quality of the audio signal both during the recording and at the mixdown. Modern DAWs also offer the same sound shaping capability (and sometimes more). Sound shaping software such as the equalizer shown in Figure 15.1c can be assigned to each channel, allowing the producer to bring out the best sound for each channel.

Rendering is the time it takes to accomplish a specific task. Computers need to perform tens of thousands of computations within the software to put a reverb or echo on a sound, and as a result, sometimes you won't hear the effect immediately when you place it in the audio channel. Usually, the rendering time is tied to the speed of the computer and the number of effects you put on a sound. Increasingly, however, with modern multi-core processors, rendering time has becoming instantaneous for audio, allowing the producer to hear the results immediately. For video, however, rendering can still take time depending on the complexity of the video frame.

Before discussing multitrack features, let's look at a typical console set-up. The console pictured in Figure 15.2a is an 8-channel model with 24 inputs that can be assigned to any or all of the 8 channel outputs. It works using the same principles as do 16- and 24-channel consoles. Always remember that regardless of the intricacy of the hardware, the principle is the same; namely, in a multichannel mixing console, you usually have a double–duty board. One side of the board controls inputs. The other side controls outputs. This structure relates to and reflects the functions of a recording engineer and a recording producer; the engineer makes sure that the inputs are correct and the meters are reading properly, whereas the producer, sitting to the right, governs the mix and remix of the output of the console.

Input Modules

The input side (see Figure 15.2b) of the board takes in the signals from the mics (or other sources) and sends them through a series of circuits. A signal is routed through a series of circuits known as *modules*, the controls for which are located in vertical columns. There are modules for both input and output channels on the console. The circuits in the input modules (not listed in the order of signal flow) include the following.

The Vertical/Slide Fader   Multitrack consoles use vertical/slide faders rather than circular pots, ostensibly because the position of a bank of slide faders is easier to perceive at a glance than are the positions of several dials. Most producers also find it easier to control many faders than to control many dials.

Input Selection Controls   These include mic-level and line-level selectors. In addition to selection of sources, multitrack consoles offer a trim control

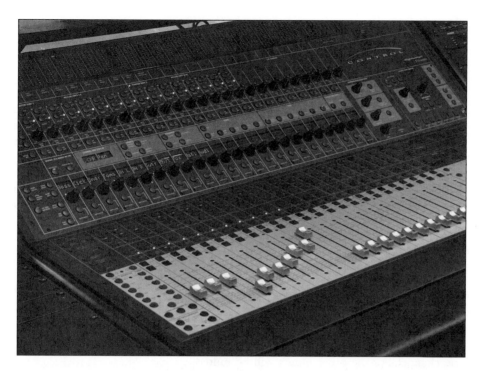

a. This multitrack console with 24 inputs can be controlled either manually or by computer software.
SOURCE: Fritz Messere

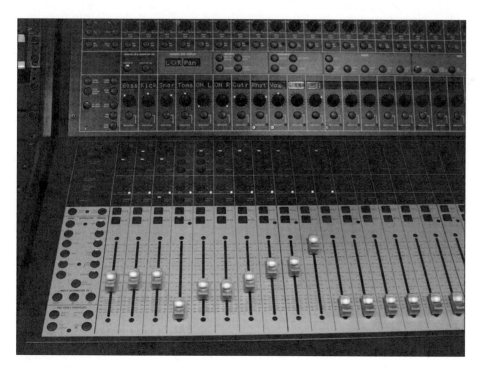

b. The faders on this board can be assigned by the operator. These assignments are shown on the LED readouts above each channel fader.
SOURCE: Fritz Messere

F I G U R E 15.2
Typical console setup.

(sometimes called a pre-fade level or PFL)—a fine-level adjustment of the input volume that allows you to keep sliders in the optimal control area.

In digital workstations, output of the fader usually feeds a series of I/Os (inputs and outputs), where the recording engineer can manipulate the sound.

Sound Shapers   Equalizers and filters are types of **sound shapers**; both are located on the input modules in physical consoles or are assigned to an I/O on a DAW. An **equalizer** alters the frequency pattern of an audio source; it can, for example, boost a certain range of frequencies. A **filter**, on the other hand, eliminates frequencies of a certain range. An effects or auxiliary pot may be found on an input module as well. Effects or auxiliary pots allow the engineer to apply special effects, such as reverberation, to a specific channel.

Pan Pot   The **pan pot** varies the amount of signal sent to each side of the stereo signals. Panning the pot to the left will send more of the signal to the left channel, and vice versa. A pan pot is used in the final mixdown.

Solo   The **solo** mutes other inputs so that the channel being soloed can be heard alone. This is useful for the engineer as she tweaks the sound on just that one channel. All the other inputs will be muted.

Bus Delegation   Bus delegation controls the sending of the signals from the input modules to the board's output modules, which are known as *buses*. A **bus** is a junction of circuits. Any number of input channels can be routed into a particular bus in the output section of the console. For example, six channels of drums (snare, tom-toms, bass drum, cymbals, two high-hats) can be directed to two bus channels during a mixdown, one for left and the other right in a stereo mix. Remember that in Chapter 2 we discussed program and audition on a radio board. Program and audition, too, are buses.

Digital workstations don't have bus switches because channels can be recorded separately. Each time a new track is recorded, a new track will appear in the DAW display (see Figure 15.4).

Output Buses

Output buses (see Figure 15.3) send the signal to the recording machine or DAW and to the monitors (though there are additional controls for the monitors, usually above the output buses). The bus feature allows the signals assigned to each bus to be altered in volume and panned, and some effects can also be added at the output level. Unlike input channel I/Os, when effects are added at the output bus, the effect will be applied to all signals on that bus. The important thing to remember is that the output buses correspond to track numbers on the recording device used.

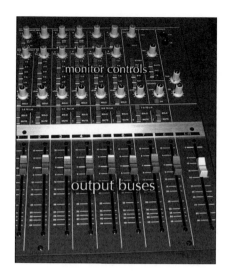

FIGURE 15.3

This console has eight channel outputs and a master fader. Monitor controls provide flexible monitoring options for the producer.
SOURCE: Fritz Messere

Monitor Controls

In the multitrack board output area, the signal flow to the loudspeakers is governed by the monitor controls.

A Further Note about Multichannel Consoles

The variety of hardware available for multichannel recording is mind-boggling, and a discussion of hardware usually winds up surveying the latest technical wonders on the market. However, the important thing about multichannel recording is not the technical features offered. What you should remember is that multichannel consoles provide great flexibility because they have discrete input and output sections. The input circuits shape the audio signal and assign it (and any other inputs you designate) to a particular recording track. Once the recording process has been completed, the input section of the console then plays back the recorded tracks and directs them to assigned bus outputs. The output bus is a circuit junction that feeds the final mixdown to a digital workstation or a master recorder of some kind (e.g., CD recorder, hard disc, etc.) and allows the producer to hear the final mix. Today, it is possible to master recordings in stereo or 5.1 surround sound.

A multichannel board can send signals to a recording device through the same pots that are used for mixdown. Some channels can be premixed; drums, for example, are often put on only one or two tracks even though four or more separate mics may have been used for recording the drums. Because of its ability to shape sound and assign particular signals to certain tracks, a multichannel recording system gives great flexibility to the person doing the recording and allows remixing of the program material.

Although hardware may vary, the principle won't. If you understand the principle, you'll be able to adapt with a minimum of instruction to the particular configuration of any multichannel console. Software-based multichannel recording packages mimic the way consoles work, with separate recording tracks and mixdown panels displayed on the monitor. This gives the recording engineer and the producer the same flexibility as hardware-based consoles.

Role of Multitrack Recording

Radio stations frequently use the multitrack recording capabilities of digital workstations for recording commercials, promotional spots, and voicers. Jingles and recording and mixing music presentations are frequently done on digital workstations or multitrack recorders (see Figure 15.4). Even though you may record only one or two sources at a time, multitracking allows the producer to layer one sound on top of another. Multitrack recording also has wide application in a number of related audio areas, such as multimedia production and television and movie soundtracks, but it is primarily the domain of the music recordist (the recording engineer who may also be the producer and/or the musician). Music recording is sometimes encountered by radio station personnel.

Although multitrack mixing does offer great flexibility in music recording, it is not the only way to record music. Some musical presentations are recorded simply by mounting a pair of microphones (or a stereo mic) above a musical ensemble. Most music recording is in stereo, so we deal with stereo recording and miking next. Then we wrap up the discussion of music by demonstrating mic techniques used in multitrack recording.

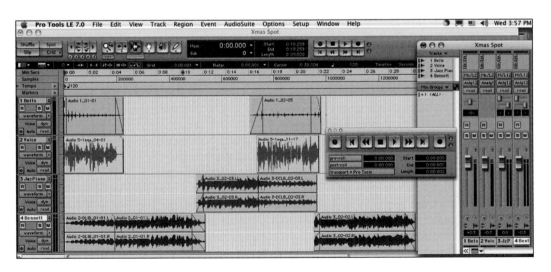

FIGURE 15.4

This is a 30-second spot created on a DAW multitrack. Cross-fades and ducking are executed in the software controls.

SOURCE: Digidesign, Inc.

STEREO

Any console routes signals into one or more master channels. For stereo, there are two master channels, usually designated as the left and right channels. Stereophonic sound gives a sense of depth and locale to the program material, in much the same way as two ears or two eyes give a sense of depth.

Stereo gives a feeling of location in space because of the differences in sound between the left and right channels. In a symphony orchestra, for example, violins are seated to the left, horns are centered, and cellos are on the right. In a stereo reproduction, the sound of the violins emanates primarily from the left speaker, giving the listener the same sense of spatial orientation as at a live performance. Horns are heard from both speakers and cellos from the right speaker. This sense of spatial orientation occurs because our ears are attuned to decoding the very slight difference when sound reaches the ears. Our ability to locate sound around us is very good. That's why we're able to tell the approximate position of someone speaking to us even if we're blindfolded.

A feature of multichannel recording that we've not yet mentioned is that it allows you to artificially assign a spatial relationship to a particular sound. Because each instrument or voice can be recorded on a discrete track, the producer can decide where to locate that sound (left, right, middle) in the final mixdown. Do you want the guitar to come from the left and the sax to come from the right? It's a simple matter of manipulating the pan pot controls. Stereo consoles used in broadcasting are able to process the stereo signal. They have a separate VU meter for each master channel. Operating a stereo broadcast console is essentially the same as operating a monaural console or a multitrack console, but you can control the left and right channels with one fader instead of two.

There is a significant difference between stereo and monaural recording processes, however. We've presented the information in this chapter in a specific order, leading up to a discussion of music-recording mic techniques, because the explanation of stereo mic techniques should clarify the roles of sound, stereo, and mixing. Understanding the basics of music recording helps illuminate our understanding of all areas of audio.

RECORDING MUSIC

There are two ways to record music in stereo: total-sound recording and **isolated-component recording.** Total-sound recording involves, for example, setting up two mics (one for the left channel and one for the right) and recording a symphony concert. As we mentioned, this method is a one-shot deal: Your product is essentially the final version. In isolated-component recording, you set up a number of mics on various sections of the orchestra and mix the inputs with a multichannel console.

Which do you choose? Total-sound recording is often used for symphony concerts because the mics pick up the symphony and the ambiance of the concert hall. It is also simpler to set up mics, and—some people contend—this

---

RADIO RETRO • THE BIRTH OF MULTITRACK RECORDING

Multitrack recording has become the norm today, and it's hard to believe that just two generations ago most recordings were done by putting an entire group of musicians and singers in front of a microphone. Elvis and Johnny Cash were originally recorded in the small one-room studio at Sun Records with a mono (one-channel) recorder. While that approach has some artistic advantages, it limits the recordist's opportunities to tweak the final project or make changes in the sound of the mix. In the 1950s, recording engineers frequently moved singers and musicians closer to or farther from a mic to achieve the final mix. If the producer wanted to double track a singer's voice, the original tape was played while the artist sang onto a second tape recorder!

The first person to use multitrack recording for a major project was the same man who invented the electric guitar, Les Paul, who died in 2009 at age 94. Using the evolving technology that allowed mixing multiple tracks on one tape, during the 1940s and 1950s, Paul would record a guitar track, re-record another, and eventually create a guitar chorus using one guitar. His development of the electric guitar occurred in parallel with his experimentation with feeding and mixing signals to a tape recorder.

During the 1960s, three tracks were frequently used to record musical instruments in stereo with mono vocals mixed in on one track, but two pop groups signaled a new interest in using technology to enhance pop music. Brian Wilson started layering many tracks together with songs like "Good Vibrations," and the Beatles elevated multitrack recording to the art form it is today with the release of *Sgt. Pepper's Lonely Hearts Club Band,* which was recorded on four tracks. Paul McCartney was impressed by the multitrack work done by the Beach Boys in *Pet Sounds* and used that technology to craft the still-astonishing *Abbey Road* album, which featured cuts such as "Come Together," "Maxwell's Silver Hammer," and "Octopus's Garden."

Every once in a while multitracking technology still does something to astound us. A notable example is the "duet" with Natalie Cole and her father singing "Unforgettable"—truly unforgettable because Nat King Cole had died many years before Natalie cut the duet using his old recordings.

Today's complex mixes may entail hundreds of sounds on 128 or more tracks. Thanks to the computer and highly evolved software, artists are limited only by their imagination.

---

approach does not impart an artificial sound to the music. Total-sound recording also eliminates a lot of problems associated with multiple mics, such as phasing. Isolated-component recording is more common in the recording studio and is most often used for popular music.

Both methods can produce excellent results. For many radio production applications, isolated-component recording is more useful because the music (or other program material) can be remixed—a highly practical feature for recording commercial jingles and voice-overs. For example, if you have a client who has paid for the creation of a music bed/jingle, you would want to have the bed and voice-over on separate tracks so the commercial message could be changed whenever it was appropriate while retaining the musical bed.

Total-Sound Recording Microphone Techniques

When confronted with an orchestra or a chorus, producers usually place the mics on the ceiling above the audience section, facing, of course, the orchestra or chorus. Cardioid mics are commonly used, but in middle–side recording, a bidirectional mic is added to the mix. The most popular methods of orienting the mics are called *coincident*, *spaced-pair*, and *middle-side*.

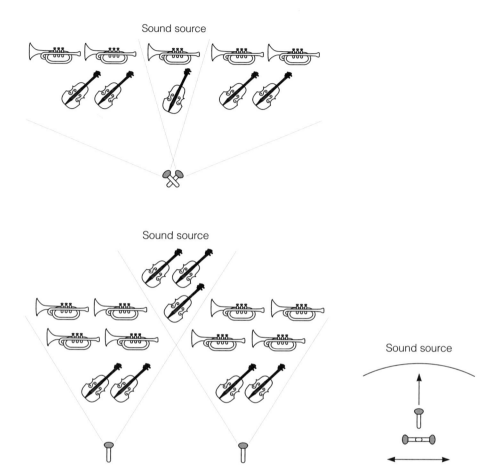

FIGURE 15.5

Microphone orientations.

Coincident Miking Setting up **coincident mics** (see Figure 15.5a) involves crossing two cardioid mics, usually at about a 90-degree angle. This imitates the way the ears hear and results in the kind of sound you would hear sitting in the middle of a concert hall. Why? Because the mic for the left channel picks up most of the sounds from the left side of the stage, the mic for the right channel picks up most of the sounds from the right side of the stage, and the sounds emanating from the middle are balanced between the two. If the mic angle is too narrow, the spatial illusion is lost; if the angle is too wide, there is a "hole" in the middle of the orchestra.

Spaced-Pair Miking When the mics are parallel, usually 1 or 2 feet apart (see Figure 15.5b), you get a very broad sound. Having **spaced-pair mics** heightens the stereo effect, though the mics are subject to some phase-cancellation problems because their pickup patterns have quite a bit of overlap.

Middle-Side Miking   The technique known as **middle-side miking** involves using a bidirectional mic to pick up sound from either side, with a cardioid mic facing the middle (see Figure 15.5c). Middle-side miking results in an extremely spacious sound, but it requires a special device known as a *phase inverter* to add the signals together properly.

These techniques can be used successfully in a variety of applications for total-sound recording. In addition, they can be used to mic one instrument in isolated-component recording, though most instruments are generally picked up with one mic because the pan pot on the console will be used to orient the instrument spatially.

Isolated-Component Recording

The most common question posed about isolated-component recording is, "How can the mic pick up only one instrument?" Isolating instruments from one another in the sound studio often involves using baffles or isolation booths or physically moving one instrument to another room. However, the use of a mic on one instrument results in considerable isolation from the sounds of other instruments, a factor that is often surprising to the first-time recordist.

The following mic techniques are useful in isolated-component recording.

For Singers   Most popular vocalists are comfortable with a relatively close mic distance, whereas classical singers prefer a larger distance. In any event, the distance is almost always less than a foot, with the mic placed roughly at mouth level. It is generally not considered good practice to let the vocalist handle the mic because of the possibility of noise from hand holding the mic. For popular singers, an acoustic filter is frequently put between the vocalist and the mic to minimize the possibility of mic popping or sibilance.

For Drums   Miking drums can be a very complex affair, involving as many as a half-dozen mics. Many recordists favor a separate mic for each unit (high hat, cymbal, snare, tom-tom, and so on), whereas others prefer to mike the whole drum set from above, often with a crossed pair. It's largely a matter of experimentation and individual judgment.

For Pianos   In the method shown in Figure 15.6, one mic is pointed toward the lower strings and another toward the higher strings. This results in a broad mix of the sound. Other methods include pointing a mic toward the open top of a grand piano or sticking a mic into one of the sound holes. Sensitive condenser mics, such as the AKG C451B shown, are often favored for piano recording.

For Strings   An electric guitar (and, for that matter, an electric synthesizer) can be miked by pointing a microphone at the loudspeaker that is fed by the guitar. Direct connection boxes can be used to route the signal from the guitar directly

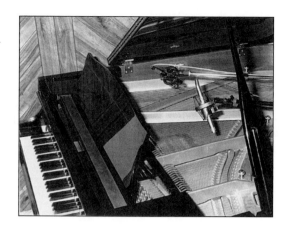

FIGURE 15.6
Miking a piano.
SOURCE: Philip Benoit

into the console. Acoustic guitars are generally miked by pointing a mic toward the sounding hole. The Rode RT1A and the Audio-Technical AT2020 are good choices because they are sensitive to the range and subtle sounds of vibrating strings.

For Brass   Brass is usually miked near the bell because all the sound exits from the bell. A Sennheiser E908 clips right to the bell of the instrument. However, a standard broadcast mic such as the EV RE20 is also a good choice because this durable moving-coil mic won't be overpowered by the full sound of a trumpet. In addition, its characteristic warm sound tones down some of the trumpet's blare.

For Woodwinds   Most of a woodwind's sound exits from the finger holes (not from the bell), so that is where the mic belongs. The famed Neumann U87 is very sensitive to the warm breathiness of a clarinet and gives an excellent response (see Figure 15.7). Many new large-diaphragm condenser microphones have been introduced in recent years that provide very good audio characteristics, and these may be considered in place of the expensive Neumann U87. New small condenser mics such as the AKG C519ML are becoming popular with recording engineers for both woodwind and brass.

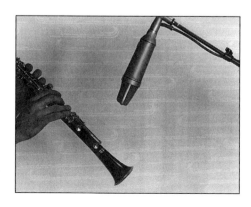

FIGURE 15.7
Woodwinds are best picked up by placing a mic near the finger holes.
SOURCE: Philip Benoit

For Ensemble Work   With small rock groups, you can easily place a mic on each instrument. However, unless you have a large collection of microphones, you'll probably want to designate a mic for different sections of an ensemble: one for the violins, another for the brass, and so on. It's largely a matter of experience and experimentation. As you get more practice in recording music, you'll develop techniques that work well for you.

Depending on the studio acoustics and the selection of microphones available to you, the actual distance between the mic and the instrument may be subject to some trial and error before the best results are discovered. Getting the mic into the right position, often called finding the "sweet spot," is really a matter of trial and error until you develop some experience in the recording process.

ELECTRONIC EQUIPMENT AND ITS USE IN RADIO PRODUCTION

Radio is an ever-changing field, and the equipment used can be highly complex. We now introduce some of the more advanced radio gadgetry and some of the more interesting applications of technology to producing radio and creating an effect. A radio production professional must stay current with advances in equipment. Read journals, attend conferences, and talk to colleagues in many areas. Radio is a state-of-the-art profession, and it pays to keep abreast of developments.

Equipment

First, let's look at ancillary devices or software modules. Digital audio workstation software may contain some essential effects components that used to be discrete devices. Other third-party devices, called *modules* or *plug-ins*, can be purchased separately. These software tools provide additional capability and flexibility for the sound engineer or the producer. Hardware versions of equalizers and compressors are more likely to be used in live sound reinforcement today while software versions will be found in radio control rooms.

Equalizers   One effects unit that you'll find extremely useful is the equalizer. Equalizers used to be "outboard" devices (see Figure 15.8a), meaning that they were not part of the console but were added to the audio chain after a pre-amp or after the console output. Essentially, an equalizer alters the frequency response of an audio signal. It can be used to boost or to cut down certain frequency ranges. The effect of an equalizer is to change the character of an audio signal. An R&B (rhythm and blues) or urban producer who wants to give a high-energy piece more "punch" (sound more bassy and powerful), for example, could use an equalizer to boost the bass frequencies.

On one common type, called a **graphic equalizer**, the controls allow you to set a graphic representation of the response curve you would like to create. By looking at the positions of the frequency curve, it is possible to boost or cut selected frequencies within the audible range. Often the range of frequencies affected are one or more octaves of music. For example, a graphic equalizer with a 6-dB curve would boost or cut the frequency of 1000 Hz by 6 dB relative to 500Hz and 2000 Hz.

Modern software gives the producer great flexibility over sound shaping. In Figure 15.8b this equalizer allows the user to choose several types of EQ (EQ is part of radio lexicon, meaning "to equalize" or "equalization"). In this illustration the Low-Mid Peak (LMF) controls are set to boost frequencies centered around 188Hz by nearly 9 dB (see the gain setting on the LMF controls). Notice that the frequencies affected are approximately one octave above and below the center frequency. At the same time, the producer can use the High Frequency (HF) controls to act like a "shelf." All frequencies above 5kHz are being reduced significantly. The settings here have been exaggerated to show their capabilities, but a producer might use the shelf to cut out unwanted background noise in the sound file.

Also commonly used in audio is the **parametric equalizer**. The difference between graphic or peak EQ and parametric EQ lies essentially in the amount of selected frequencies that can be manipulated. A parametric equalizer allows you to select one frequency and boost or cut just that frequency or that and surrounding frequencies (see Figure 15.8c). You accomplish this by choosing the range above and below the selected frequency you want to EQ using a bandwidth control. For example, you could remove an unwanted 60-Hz hum from a remote broadcast better with a parametric equalizer than with a graphic one because you would adjust it not to cut adjoining frequencies (it might be desirable to do so because adjoining frequencies add depth to your remote broadcast sound) (see Figure 15.8d). Trying to accomplish this with a graphic equalizer might make the remote sound tinny and weak because it would eliminate the entire octave around the 60-Hz hum.

Because most audio workstation set-ups provide equalizer capability within the software, the engineer can apply separate equalization to separate or multiple channels of audio. Figure 15.13 shows a number of effects available to users of BIAS's Peak Pro 7. This gives the producer much more control over the entire mix than if one equalizer was used after all channels were mixed together.

Filters   Sometimes a producer wants to delete a whole range of frequencies. A hiss, for example, can sometimes be eliminated by a **low-pass filter**, which allows lower frequencies to pass but chops off selected higher frequencies. A **high-pass filter**, which will cut low frequencies, might be used to eliminate some wind noise or a low rumble. Figure 15.8e shows a software-based variable high-pass filter. Care needs to be taken to assure that when using a filter, you do not remove too much content with the noise. A filter that is set for a single narrow frequency range is called a *notch filter* (see Figure 15.8d).

Some electronic components called *noise gates* can also act as filters when there is no audio signal in the circuit. For example, a noise gate is frequently used in studios with a background noise such as air conditioning, which, though

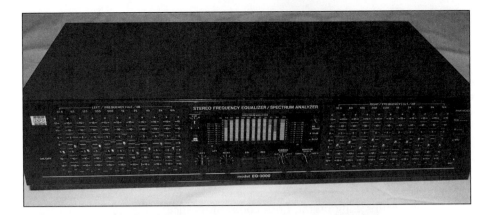

a. This graphic equalizer also displays the frequency spectrums of the different audio bands.

SOURCE: Fritz Messere

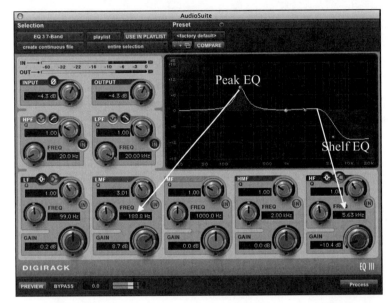

b. Software applications provide great flexibility to the producer. This module provides 5 bands of frequency adjustment in addition to low and high frequency filters.

SOURCE: Digidesign, Inc.

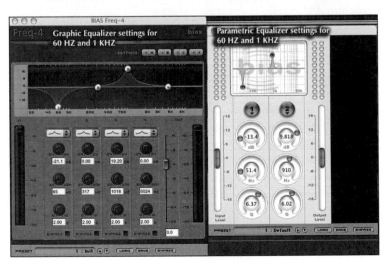

c. DAW equalizers combine the power of both graphic and parametric equalizers to shape sound. Pictured here are both kinds centered around 60 Hz and 1 kHz. Notice that the graphic equalizer affects a wide range of frequencies around 60 and 1 kHz. The parametric equalizer does not.

SOURCE: BIAS, Inc.

F I G U R E 15.8 (continued)

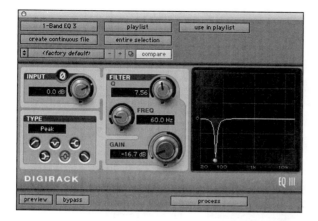

d. Software allows the user to create a useful 60-Hz notch filter.

SOURCE: Digidesign, Inc.

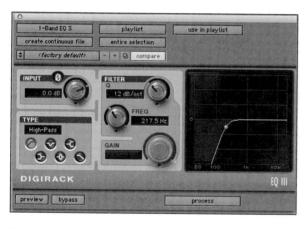

e. The high pass filter shown here will attenuate frequencies below 200 Hz but pass all frequencies higher.

SOURCE: Digidesign, Inc.

F I G U R E 15.8 (continued)

lower in intensity than an announcer's voice, would otherwise be heard whenever a mic was open and no one was speaking. A noise gate acts as an on-off circuit and is triggered by the volume change between the announcer's voice and the air-conditioning noise. Whenever the announcer stops speaking, the gate closes, preventing the noise from passing through the circuit. When the announcer begins speaking again, the gate opens and passes the audio (at which time the announcer's voice masks the background noise).

Compressors and Limiters These devices are often found in the equipment rack in radio control rooms and in audio software packages (see Figure 15.9). A compressor shrinks the **dynamic range** of the audio signal. Low-volume parts are boosted; high-volume parts are lowered. The result is to make the audio

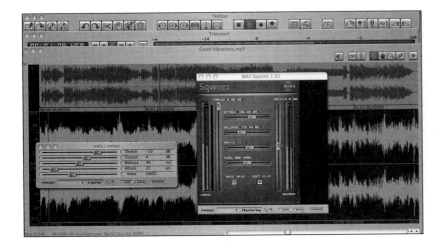

FIGURE 15.9

Peak Pro 5.0 allows users to choose between several different types of compression.
SOURCE: BIAS, Inc.

level more consistent throughout the piece, although some of the dynamic range of the music will be reduced.

Compression has a number of factors that can be set and varied, including the **attack time** (the length of time it takes for the compressor to kick in after a particular sound affects it) and the **release time** (the length of time the compressor takes to let the signal return to its previous level). A **limiter** is a compressor that severely restricts high-volume noises (or transient peaks in music) and has a high ratio of compression. Limiting is useful for keeping sudden loud sounds from overmodulating the signal. (In fact, the Federal Communications Commission [FCC] demands that radio stations keep their signals within certain tolerances to avoid overmodulation.) Compression is often used in radio stations to maintain a relatively constant signal that won't sink low enough to "fall off the dial."

Software That Enhances or Reduces Noise Reduction   A number of devices produced by **Dolby** Laboratories reduce noise usually associated with analog tape recording. In professional units, such as Dolby S, the frequency spectrum is divided into several bands. Each band is pre-emphasized (raised in volume) by a certain degree during recording, which lowers the noise floor relative to the signal. Dolby units in professional applications are usually rack-mounted and installed in the audio chain between the output of the board and the recording device. These devices are not likely to be seen in digital recording situations, but Dolby SR is frequently used in the motion picture industry. Today Dolby Digital Plus is being used to deliver surround sound in broadcasting.

There are many audio archives in transcript form or on audiotape that are not available on CD. Software programs such as SoundSoap can be used to remove audio hiss, clicks, and crackles from these legacy recordings. Such programs can dramatically improve the sound quality.

Effects Processors   With multichannel effects processors, you can alter the sound in a variety of ways. These units usually provide a number of standard effects such as *reverberation*, which means creating multiple, blended repetitions of sounds that add depth to the original sound. *Echo* (sometimes called slapback echo) is a distinct delayed repetition of the sound, whereas a *chorus effect* is a recirculated sound with a short delay between the original and the delayed signal. With *flangers*, you can create a mirror image of a sound and then shift it slightly; this throws the two sounds out of time and phasing and creates a bizarre effect that's been described as something like water rushing through a voice.

Most effects processors allow you to mix and match these effects in many different combinations, creating numerous possibilities for you to make a special effect. However, these special effects need to be used wisely (and not too often) or they will lose their impact on the listening audience.

Spatial Enhancers   By mixing and subtracting components of the stereo signal, **spatial enhancers** produce a signal that gives the impression of having greater presence or a larger spatial environment. The intent is to reproduce more detail in the music, giving it a more natural sound. Spatial enhancers usually work by shifting the phase relationships of the different frequencies in the sound. For example, adding a very small delayed signal and mixing it with the original produces a "wider" stereo image.

Units made by Behringer, Aphex, BBE, and others provide psychoacoustic (meaning refinement of the audio signal to maximize its effect in terms of how the human ears and brain process the sound) enhancements to audio signal processing (see Figure 15.10a). A radio station may use these spatial enhancers along with compressors or peak limiters to provide a unique sound.

Software effects can be chained together so one effects unit will feed another in a chain that can be arranged and controlled by the producer. Peak Pro 7 allows the user to simply arrange the different processors by dragging and dropping them into the desired order (see Figure 15.10b).

Techniques

Here are some advanced techniques for special effects that a producer might find useful. Some of them use complex equipment, and some of them don't.

Reverb   Reverberation, also called **reverb**, is both a technique and a reference to a particular piece of hardware called a *reverb unit*. Some production people claim that reverb is the single most important special effect available to the producer. Most DAWs provide reverb in the special effects section of the software. Reverb differs from echo in that it is accomplished by adding back an electronically delayed copy of the sound to the original signal. Reverb units have a control called *depth*, which allows the producer to vary the amount of original signal mixed back in. Reverberation parameters can be adjusted. This is useful for increasing or decreasing the impression of the room size, and it is frequently added to increase vocal clarity in a production.

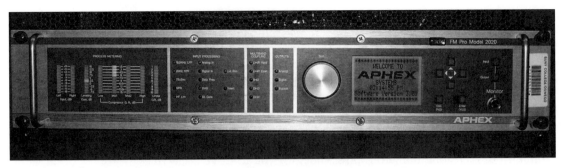

a. Sound enhancement units use a variety of techniques to improve sound quality.

SOURCE: Fritz Messere

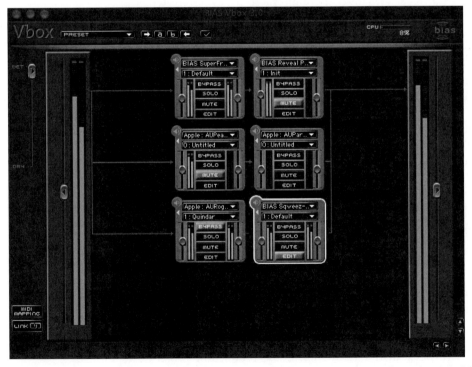

b. Vbox allows a producer to arrange the order of effects used. The arrows show the signal flow from input to output. Note that it is possible to mute and solo any of the effects so as to gauge the impact of one or more applications in the sound chain.

SOURCE: BIAS, Inc.

FIGURE 15.10

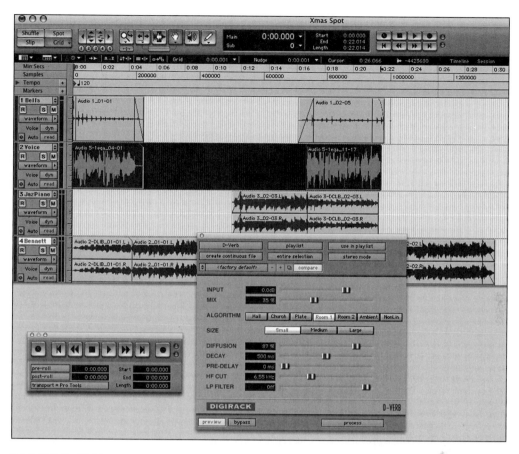

FIGURE 15.11

Echo has been added to the voice track on channel 2.

SOURCE: Digidesign, Inc.

Echo   The echo effect can be created within the special effects section of software or in a separate electronic effect unit. Echo is the feedback of the original signal from the playback head, passing back through the audio. In essence, it produces the same effect as yelling "Hello" into a stony cavern. Figure 15.11 shows the delay effect that has been set to create an echo of the original sound.

Reverse Boomerang Effect   This effect was originally created by playing audiotape backward and mixing it with audio. Many people credit the Beatles with inventing the effect on albums such as *Revolver* and *Sgt. Pepper's Lonely Hearts Club Band*. Today this effect can be accomplished using software effects in some DAWs. The effect, when used sparingly, can add surprise, eeriness, and disorientation for the listener.

Forward Echo   With **forward echo**, the echoes appear before the original sound and lend excitement. In a rock format ID, for example, echo can lend excitement because the echo builds up before the call letters are given. Accomplishing a forward echo is a little tricky, but once you see what's happening, it will make sense. This effect must be accomplished on a DAW capable of bouncing tracks. First, you record your voice track *dry* (without reverb or effects). Then you copy that track to a new track, which we'll call the effects track. Using the *reverse* effect, convert the track to a backward version of your original. Then apply an *echo* (also called delay) to the reversed track. Once you've added the delay, reverse the effects track again. Subsequently, playing back the original and effects tracks together will give you a forward echo. Some audio software also allows you to create dramatic effects by using *ping-pong delays*. You will need to do some experimenting with your system to ascertain its capabilities.

Pan Potting   Also known as **channel bouncing**, this technique takes full advantage of stereo's unique ability to capture the attention of a listener who is not expecting an announcer's voice to move from one location to another within a spot. Pan potting can be used to create a dramatic illusion of motion (such as a train whizzing by). It can also be used with reverberation to make the background sound change while keeping the main stereo image the same. These effects can be used by bringing the reverb unit into the board as a separate input and panning the reverb signal back and forth at a constant rate.

Changing Pitch   Most audio workstations have an effect that allows you to change the pitch of the audio file. The effect can be widely varied to make a voice or instrument very slow, or it can create a high-pitched "chipmunk" effect (see Figure 15.12). In a commercial for a medicine, for example, the copy might begin, "Are you feeling out of sorts?" with the announcer's voice getting slower. The effect would reinforce the message.

Doubletracking   An interesting special effect that is relatively simple to produce, **doubletracking** involves recording a voice and then altering a copy of that narration on a second track—perhaps by equalizing, by delaying slightly a copy of the original, or by changing the pitch slightly. Both voices, which are giving the identical narration, are played back together. The effect gives the voice an eerie, attention-grabbing aspect.

Gating   Compressors can be used to produce crisp sound by reducing the natural reverberation in a sound effect. Sound effects, drum rolls, cymbals, and even voices can be successfully modified using compressor techniques that "dry" the sound and provide punch.

Stuttering   Voices that have been gated can be pasted over and over into a DAW to create a stuttering effect that is commonly used on urban and modern rock stations.

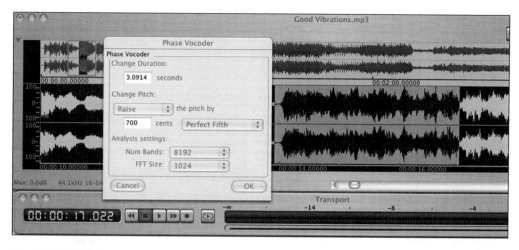

FIGURE 15.12

DAW software provides many capabilities for manipulating audio. Here the voice's pitch can be raised to make it sound like a chipmunk.

SOURCE: BIAS, Inc.

Normalizing   Digital audio workstation software frequently allows you to normalize all the tracks in an audio file. This can be a useful tool to bring several different audio sources, pasted into the sound file, up to the same audio level.

SUMMARY

We've presented only a limited amount of information on the technical end of radio, even though modern software has tremendous capability (see Figure 15.13).

There's a reason for our approach. Very often radio instruction becomes a discussion of hardware, and though that's interesting on some levels, it can be counterproductive. Super-sophisticated equipment and the equally sophisticated talk that surrounds it seem to cloud the issue of radio production.

Radio production is, in our opinion, an art form. Like any art form, it requires a thorough understanding of the techniques and tools of the trade. But it is more than stringing equipment together and using gadgetry to produce an audio novelty. To those of us who have spent much of our lives involved with radio, the medium is a very personal form of communication. It's a communication medium that enters the house, travels with us in the car, and even keeps us company while we jog. Radio production is the art of achieving the effects that make radio such an intimate, magical medium.

Multichannel recording is used when many sound sources must be recorded, mixed, and remixed separately. A typical multichannel board has input modules on

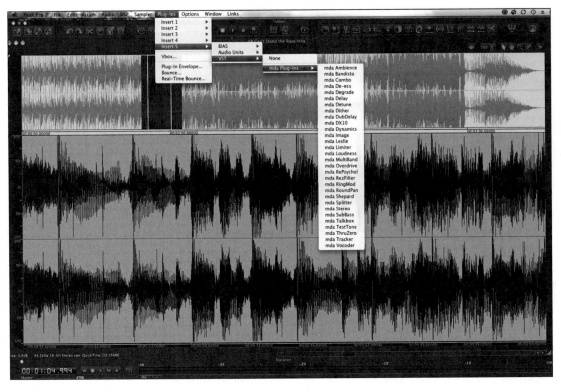

F I G U R E 15.13

In addition to the standard digital sound processing (DSP) functions associated with Peak Pro 7, there are many additional plugins available that can shape the sound file, providing great flexibility for the audio producer.

SOURCE: Bias, Inc.

one side and output buses on the other. The input side takes in the signals from the mics; the output buses send the mixed signal to some mastering record machine and the audio monitors. Each side has a variety of sound shaping controls.

The most popular techniques for recording stereo are coincident miking, spaced-pair miking, and middle-side miking. Total-sound recording is accomplished by placing one or more mics in a central place to record the sound as the listener would hear it. Isolated-component recording involves placing separate mics on each sound source and mixing the inputs together. This allows much greater flexibility and offers you a chance to repair bad takes when the music is being performed.

A wide variety of software effects and electronic components can be used to shape the signal, including equalizers, filters, compressors, limiters, noise-reduction equipment, special effects units, and spatial enhancers. Some DAWs provide many of the same capabilities to shape sound using built-in software but add flexibility because control is added to each input channel. Techniques used in advanced radio production include effects such as echo, reverb, forward echo, pan potting, and doubletracking.

APPLICATIONS

SITUATION 1/THE PROBLEM The producer of a program was recording a church choir for later playback. She miked each vocal section separately and planned to mix the program. The director of the choir listened to a test recording and was not pleased with what he heard. "The choir," he said, "sounds like a group of jingle singers."

ONE POSSIBLE SOLUTION Why did the sound vary so much from what the choir director was used to hearing? Because close-up miking of the sopranos, the altos, the tenors, and so on did not allow the music to reverberate through the architectural spaces of the church. Consequently, the effects of the acoustics—and the sound of the church choir—were altered. The producer opted for a crossed pair of cardioid mics above the tenth row of pews and was able to achieve a richer, more realistic sound.

SITUATION 2/THE PROBLEM A group of jingle singers and musicians were performing a commercial for an ice-cream parlor. Gay Nineties music was called for, with a banjo and piano. Unfortunately, the sound coming through the mics featured the booming, rich tones of the studio's grand piano, which had mics pointing toward its raised top.

ONE POSSIBLE SOLUTION The producer repositioned the mics to a spot directly above the hammers. Now, a lot of hammers were heard, and the piano sounded much more honky-tonk than grand.

EXERCISES

1. Mic a piano in several ways, noting the effects of different mic placements. Position the mic(s) at any or all of the following locations, noting how the mix of mics at various locations changes the character of the sound.

    - Behind the soundboard on an upright piano
    - In one of the sound holes inside a grand piano
    - Pointing at the raised cover
    - Above the keyboard

    If an acoustic guitar is available, try miking the guitar at the sound hole and then at the frets. Note the differences in sound as the mic is moved from one location to another.

2. If your digital workstation allows you to record multiple channels, record a musical group under the supervision of your instructor or lab assistant.

Remix the recording twice using whatever equipment is available. The goal is to make two recordings of the same program material that sound radically different because of the mix.

3. As a variation of Exercise 2, split the class into two groups, and have each group separately record the same performers doing the same musical number. See if the two versions are identical or how they differ.

16

Production, Programming, and the Modern Format

At no point in radio's history has the sound of the station been more important than it is now. With so many choices for entertainment and news, including new radio venues on the Web, podcasts, and satellite programming—not to mention the competition from other media—it is critical that the product clearly meet the needs of the audience.

Sometimes this can seem counterintuitive, as some of the hottest "new" formats may appear to be no format at all. Nevertheless, these free-form formats are designed to reach the clear needs of a precise audience—in this case, more music, less talk, and a wider playlist. But in most cases the format is sharply defined, and it's the role of the producer to keep that definition in focus.

What exactly is programming? There's a fine line between production and programming. We've defined all the parameters of production in the preceding chapters, and we have touched on the designs of current formats and how they relate to production.

Programming, for our purposes, simply refers to the selection and arrangement of music, speech, and other program elements in a way that appeals to the station's listeners.

This chapter specifically deals with the radio audience, the basics of the narrowcasting (meaning, reaching a small segment of an audience in the hopes that the small segment will have particular interests that will be attractive to an advertiser) format, and production techniques used in specific formats. We have placed this highly detailed, programming-oriented chapter later in this book because it serves as a starting point for the practice and study of other aspects of radio. Those aspects include music selection, delivery style, and blending of elements—those factors we often refer to as parts of the programming effort. In addition, the chapter deals, by necessity, with some management functions, including audience development and measurement.

We'll start with a close-up of the modern audience before discussing production specifics.

THE AUDIENCE AND THE FORMAT

Why bother elaborating on the nature of the audience and how that audience is measured? Primarily because identifying and capturing an audience is the heart and soul of on-air and off-air production.

We did touch on format in Chapter 1, but detailed examination of formatics would have been premature before we laid the groundwork for a thorough understanding of on-air and off-air production practices. Now that we've built the foundation, we can examine the superstructure of radio: the audience and methods of measuring audience.

The Audience

Pop quiz: The success of a radio station depends primarily on the number of people who listen—right? The answer: not exactly. In fact, program directors are as likely to complain about too much "wasted" audience as they are about too few listeners.

Although that may sound unlikely, it's a good illustration of the predicament of many of the modern media. Radio has become a medium designed to reach certain audiences to the exclusion of others. A radio station sells an audience to an advertiser (or, in many cases, to an agency representing advertisers). Prove it to yourself: In most major American cities, you have access to 20 or more radio stations, as well as literally thousands of venues on the Internet and satellite. How many different stations do you actually listen to? Two or three at most, for the majority of listeners.

A large, ill-defined audience is not a particularly attractive commodity for an advertiser who might be selling

- cosmetics to young women, or
- expensive foreign autos to successful businesspeople, or
- auto parts to young men.

This is not to say that size is unimportant. Once you have a clearly defined audience, the bigger the audience, the better. However, in these days of the super-segmented audience, the programmer or producer wants to be able to "capture" the right demographic (a statistical segment of an audience).[1] A profitable demographic can mean that a station can have a smaller audience than another station in the same market but make more money. For example, the all-news station WINS in New York City is rarely at the top of the pack in actual numbers of people listening. However, it is usually at or near the top stations in market advertising revenue, handily outdistancing rock and current hit radio (CHR) stations that command much larger audience shares.

The reason is the type of listener: An all-news station typically gathers a more affluent, business-oriented market than does a CHR station and can therefore charge more per spot. In this case, the more affluent listener translates into more money for the station.

Methods of Measuring Audience

Because numbers and the people those numbers represent are important tools in the radio salesperson's arsenal, it's not surprising that the methods of measuring audience are fairly complex. Our purpose here is not so much to offer a primer on ratings as it is to establish a common vocabulary for understanding some of the audience measurement factors that affect a station's sound and, therefore, its programming and production strategy. In other words, when we start throwing around terms such as *TSL*, *reach*, and *cume* when discussing format-specific production, it won't seem like an arcane conversation in a foreign language.

So we'll quickly define and identify audience rating services, those companies that collect data about radio station listenership; the total survey area and the metro survey area, the landscape on which ratings are taken; and the units of measurement, including ratings, share, average quarter-hour persons, cume, reach, time spent listening, turnover, and persons using radio. Though we don't refer to all these terms and concepts in this chapter, it is necessary to understand those that we do discuss before others can be defined.

Audience Rating Services   Several firms provide information about listenership, but Arbitron Inc. is the major player in audience measurement. Arbitron's primary tool is a diary in which listeners record their day's listening, although Arbitron is in the process of introducing electronic devices that can sense the station a person has tuned in (through frequencies embedded in the station's signal). The diary method is one reason stations go to such lengths to make their station's "signature" memorable. Have you ever noticed, as you drive through different areas, how many stations bill themselves as "Kiss (frequency)" or "Lite (frequency)" when their call letters may bear only a passing similarity to the spellings of Kiss or Lite? Part of the reason is to develop the station's identity in general. Another major factor is that Arbitron will generally accept Kiss or Lite in a diary entry as proof that the listener was tuned to that station.

---

1. As you remember from earlier discussions, *demographic* means a statistical representation of a population such as age, income, education, and so on. We use the term here in an informal sense to represent the composition of an audience.

Station WAAA

Hour By Hour

Metro Survey Area AQH (00)

	5:00 A.M.	6:00 A.M.	7:00 A.M.
	6:00 A.M.	7:00 A.M.	8:00 A.M.
WAAA			
P12+SHR	9.7	9.4	8.0
P12 +	136	136	125
W18–34	26	24	24
M18–34	60	62	58

WAAA Total Mon–Sat 6 A.M.–10 A.M. All Adults 25–49

AQH and CUME estimates

Adults 25–49

	AQH	AQH	AQH	CUME
	PRS	PRS	PRS	PRS
	(00)	RTG	SHR	(00)
WAAA	157	1.9	10.2	1980

F I G U R E   16.1

This is an example of a ratings report for hypothetical station WAAA.

SOURCE: © Cengage Learning 2013

A sample ratings report is shown in Figure 16.1. None of the ratings services reports actually looks precisely like this, but we've incorporated aspects of several so that any ratings report will look fairly familiar to you once you know what to look for.

A ratings report generally includes more than one station so that comparisons among stations can be made, but we've listed only WAAA to make the illustration simple. The hour-by-hour report lists shares and the estimated number of persons listening as totaled by the **average quarter-hour (AQH)** method. The (00) means that numbers listing "persons" should be multiplied by 100—or simply have two zeros added. Looking at the first column, 5:00 AM–6:00 AM, you can see that the P12 + SHR (people older than 12 share) is 9.7 percent. The figure is then broken down into estimated listeners, the total number of persons 12 and older (add two zeros), and the numbers of estimated listeners in various age and gender groups. (W18–34 is women aged 18–34.) Most ratings reports list several age and gender demographic groups.

Another type of report breaks down the total day's listenership for another hypothetical station. AQH PRS (00) means average quarter-hour persons, along with the ratings points, share, and total cumulative audience. The entries will become understandable as you read through this section, so please refer to the figure from time to time.

Other radio research services provided by Arbitron include RADAR, an acronym for Radio's All Dimension Audience Research, which uses telephone interviews to measure network radio penetration, a complex job now that "networks" can be formed simply by aiming at a satellite. An industry wide organization, the Radio Advertising Bureau, also provides a variety of research on audience, radio usage, and other metric information.

The electronic *portable people meter*, which will measure real-time radio use among differing venues, including television and online, was introduced in 2006. Arbitron plans to have people meters replace the diary in radio's top 50 markets by 2010. The meter is a passive measurement device, about the size of a cell-phone, which can track consumer exposure to a wide variety of media, including broadcasting, cable, and online radio. It is carried by randomly selected participants. At the end of each day, participants connect the unit to a dock that extracts codes that indicate what media the user has encountered.

Total Survey Area, Metro Survey Area   These are areas in which audience measurement is undertaken. The total survey area usually includes several counties that are served by two or more stations from within a metropolitan area. The metro survey area is a local area defined by the city and its immediate environs. Remember that most discussions about ratings center on the metro survey area, which is a far more useful measuring area now that most stations serve concentrated population centers rather than broad areas comprising several counties.

Rating   A *rating* is a percentage of the total available audience. Sometimes, the number of listeners is expressed as just that—a total number, estimated from statistical interpretation of results. Strictly speaking, a rating will be a percentage of an available audience. The available audience is, in ratings terms, known as a *universe*.

Share   The *share* is the percentage of people who are actually listening. This is the most commonly used measurement in radio. The share is frequently broken down among different genders and age groups, such as "women 18–34." When you see shares listed without any specific reference to age, the figures usually refer to all persons age 12 and older.

Average Quarter-Hour Persons   The quarter-hour is the basic unit of measurement in radio audience measurement. AQH persons is the number of listeners who tuned in during a specific quarter-hour for at least 5 minutes. A problem with AQH is that you cannot simply add up the AQH figures to obtain the total number of people who are listening during the day because the AQH figures will include some of the same people. AQH is important, however, in figuring gross rating points, as you'll soon see.

Cume   Cumulative audience measure, or *cume*, solves the problem of determining the total number of people listening by using statistical interpretation to determine the number of unduplicated audience listeners.

Turnover *Turnover* is a relatively self-explanatory term even though its derivation is somewhat complicated (which is why we did not include it in Figure 16.1, the hypothetical ratings report). The turnover ratio is a measure of how many people out of the entire audience leave the station during a given period.

Time Spent Listening Time spent listening (TSL) is a measure of the average time an individual listener tunes in to the station.

Calculating How Efficiently a Station Reaches Its Audience

Embedded in the total format structure is its efficiency in producing an audience that conforms to the needs of the advertiser. This will be clarified in a moment, but first let's nail down the basic vocabulary relating to how an advertiser buys spots and what the advertiser expects from the buy. There are several ways of calculating and expressing the effectiveness of a commercial. Remember, even though the total number of audience members is important, it is not the only calculation in the formula.

Gross Impressions The most basic unit of measurement for a commercial is gross impression, which is the total number of exposures to a commercial. Gross impression is calculated by multiplying AQH persons during the times the commercial was run by the total number of spots. Remember, this figure reflects duplicated audience. The same person may be hearing the commercial a number of times (which is not necessarily a negative factor, as we discuss shortly).

Gross Rating Point Gross rating point is simply a way of expressing gross impressions as a rating figure. Multiply AQH ratings by the total number of commercials played in those quarter-hours to determine the gross rating points. Many advertisers buy radio time based on a calculation of how many gross rating points they want to achieve over a given time.

Reach The *reach* is a measurement of how many different listeners hear the commercial. It is calculated by using the cume figure. The calculation itself is too complex to merit discussion here because adding cumes requires some statistical weighting. Just remember that reach represents the number of different people exposed to the spot.

Frequency Frequency is the average number of times a theoretical listener hears a commercial. It is determined by dividing the gross impressions by the cume.

Paying for Efficiency

The aforementioned formulas are used to calculate the effectiveness of an advertiser's purchase. They generate numbers that give advertisers a relative cost they can compare to costs of other stations. Those relative costs are typically expressed in one of three ways: cost per thousand, cost per point, or optimum effective scheduling.

Cost per Thousand   Cost per thousand (CPM) is simply the cost of reaching a thousand listeners. (*M* is the Roman numeral for one thousand.) This figure is derived from numbers that include new listeners in a certain period and listeners who may have heard the commercial before, so it includes, in radio vernacular, duplicated audience.

CPM is calculated by dividing the cost of all spots by the gross impressions after you have divided the gross impression by 1,000.

$$CPM = \frac{\text{Cost of All Spots}}{\text{Gross Impressions} \div 1,000}$$

If you spent $500 for 100,000 gross impressions, you would divide the gross impressions by 1,000 (to express the figure in terms of thousands) and divide the cost of all spots ($500) by that number to produce a CPM of 5. This means that it costs $5 to reach 1,000 listeners.[2] If an advertiser knows the CPM, he or she can compare the cost of running ads on all stations in a market or among various markets. The CPM will also be broken down by gender and age of listeners.

Cost per Point   Cost per point (CPP) has become the most commonly accepted way of measuring ad placement efficiency in radio. Cost per point is a measure of how much it costs to "buy" one rating point in a particular market. CPP is determined by dividing the cost of all spots by gross rating points.

$$CPP = \frac{\text{Cost of All Spots}}{\text{Gross Rating Points}}$$

As you remember, gross rating points are the product of the number of spots run multiplied by the AQH rating. For example, if you run five spots, one each on days Monday through Friday in a quarter-hour with a 1.5 rating, you will purchase $5 \times 1.5 = 7.5$ gross rating points. If each spot cost you $125, you have spent $625. Divide $625 (cost of all spots) by 7.5 (gross rating points), and you have a CPP of $83.33 per point.

Optimum Effective Scheduling   Some advertisers and radio executives argue that cost per point is not a particularly effective way of measuring the effectiveness of radio advertising because CPM and CPP do not quantify the segment of the audience that hears the commercial more than once.

As we mentioned, a duplicated audience is not always a negative because radio spots often require several listenings for the message to "sink in." A measure

---

2. These examples are adapted from another book by the authors, *Radio Station Operations: Management and Employee Perspectives* (Belmont, CA: Wadsworth, 1989).

to compare advertising efficiency is gaining some acceptance as a replacement for CPP and CPM. **Optimum effective scheduling** (OES) is a mathematicalformulation that determines the number of people who hear the spot three or more times and shows that figure as at least 50 percent of the total audience.

For the record, OES is determined by multiplying the turnover ratio by 3.29 and the cume by 0.46. Let's leave it there; the derivation of those figures takes too long to explain. However, the basic principle is simple. Most of a station's listeners listen between 5 and 8 hours a week, so OES calculates how many spots it takes to give those listeners three repetitions of a spot. Suffice it to say that though OES has its admirers, it also has critics who say that the formula works best for comparing buys in small markets and that it forces advertisers into excessively large purchases. (The average purchase for a run of spots calculated by OES was about $450 in the 1990s; today that figure would be higher.[3])

So what was the point of this dissertation? It's not necessary for someone involved in production to understand the intricacies of audience measurement, but, as we mentioned earlier, the vocabulary of audience measurement and composition is intrinsic to understanding the modern format and how production fits within that format.

Armed with the knowledge you've picked up in these few pages, you can now evaluate format design and production within those formats as a program director evaluates them: as strategies to capture and keep a large, loyal, and (in the case of commercial radio) affluent audience.

New media/radio combinations show great promise for ensuring the health of radio, but at present the technologies pose a formidable challenge: how to reliably measure audience.

In some ways, the Internet has revived old-style methods of audience measurement—in particular, the diary. Diaries were often viewed as unreliable because people would not carry the diary with them or were negligent in writing down notes of their habits. But today, ubiquitous Internet use is reviving the diary method, particularly in Europe. Proponents say Internet diaries are reliable methods for recording podcast and telephone use, devices not easily registered with electronic monitoring systems.

Having said that, personal people meters have proven very successful for the ratings company Arbitron, and their digital mechanization can also enable researchers to match products consumers buy after being exposed to commercials.[4]

The online world presents problems with audience measurement, the most difficult being the "eyeballs versus action" dilemma. Internet advertising can produce staggering raw exposures, but because every Internet environment

---

3. See "OES Gets Results through Effective Reach," *Broadcasting*, January 27, 1992, 32–33.

4. Matthew Flamm, "No static for Arbitron as people meters thrive; Radio industry falters, but stock is a buy as firm dominates field." *Crain's New York Business*, November 12, 2007, 4.

is a worldwide universe, it can be difficult to track action in the same way that a radio commercial can gauge results by a "tell them Charlie sent you" test.

However, as online measurement grows in sophistication, it is clearly poised to become far more enlightening than any other collection of metrics about advertising. *Click-through,* meaning a measurement of how many people actually click on the ad and visit the sponsor's website, is a good test of action versus eyeballs, but such systems are still awaiting more refinement.

A particular problem for radio is that with the number of impressions for new media growing, CPM declines. It is likely to become increasingly difficult to convince media buyers of the necessity to pay a relatively high CPM for radio advertising.

THE SPECIFICS OF THE RADIO FORMAT

Why is the format, this tool designed to capture and keep an audience, so complex? After all, can't a reasonably intelligent programmer simply pick some music, announcers, and newscasters and let the show run itself?

Perhaps. But formats live and die on conditions external to themselves (competition and changing demographics are among them), as well as the format itself. The programmer, and the production manager, must take all these factors into account when creating the sound of the station.

Defining Current Formats

If you really tried (and some have), you could probably come up with more than a hundred variations of program strategies that qualify as formats. Some who track formats have tried, but most have given up the attempt to classify each and every variation of program strategy. Today, we tend to use broad categories descriptive of formats and apply qualifying adjectives to further delineate those formats. (For example, a "light" adult contemporary [AC] features less rock than a "hot" AC.)

Billboard magazine and Arbitron have divided formats into more than a dozen categories for their format share reports. It's worthwhile to define some of these formats. Combining an understanding of typical formats with the audience measurement concepts we explained earlier will allow us, in the final section of this chapter, to take a relatively detailed look at the role of production in reinforcing the format. The following definitions mirror the descriptions introduced in earlier chapters but introduce more types of formats and explain how some terms relate to the construction of the format. We'll also briefly mention the primary characteristics and desirability of the demographics. The information on CPM is not essential for a producer, but it does provide some insight into the type of listeners and level of affluence.

RADIO RETRO • WHERE DID FORMATS COME FROM?

Radio didn't always have formatting formulas that helped programmers pick music for their listeners. In the early days of radio, most of the airtime was devoted to so-called *block programming*, where one portion of the day would be devoted, say, to classical music, then the next block to dance music, and so forth.

Not surprisingly, this didn't engender high audience loyalty or listenership.

Who invented the modern format? No one knows for sure, but the most popular version of history holds that an Omaha radio station owner named Todd Storz was in a bar in the early 1950s and noticed that people using the jukebox kept selecting the same records over and over. Legend has it that he decided to pattern the programming of his radio station after the jukebox, which held 40 records. (The jukeboxes of the time used 45s, small records that only held one song.)

The Top 40 format was refined by another radio station owner, Gordon McLendon of Dallas, who in the mid-1950s evolved the concept of rotating a small number of top hits and melded it with "personality" disc jockeys and contests.

The Major Formats

As of the fall of 2008,[5] Arbitron measured these formats, listed in alphabetical order:

80s Hits
Active Rock
Adult Contemporary (AC)
Adult Hits
Adult Standards/MOR
Album Adult Alternative (AAA)
Album Oriented Rock (AOR)
All News
All Sports
Alternative
Children's Radio
Classical
Classic Country
Classic Hits
Classic Rock
Contemporary Christian
Contemporary Inspirational
Country
Easy Listening
Educational
Family Hits

Gospel
Hot AC
Jazz
Latino Urban
Mexican Regional
Modern AC
New AC (NAC)/Smooth Jazz
New Country
News/Talk/Information
Nostalgia
Oldies
Other
Pop Contemporary Hit Radio
Religious
Rhythmic AC
Rhythmic Contemporary Hit Radio
Rhythmic Oldies
Smooth AC
Soft AC
Southern Gospel
Spanish Adult Hits

---

5. Arbitron, Inc., "Radio Station Formats," http://www.arbitron.com/home/formats. htm. Accessed November 29, 2008.

Spanish Contemporary   Talk/Personality
Spanish Contemporary Christian   Tejano
Spanish News/Talk   Urban AC
Spanish Oldies   Urban Contemporary
Spanish Religious   Urban Oldies
Spanish Sports   Variety
Spanish Tropical   World Ethnic
Spanish Variety

The Latest Trends in Formats

Formats come and go, often in concert with broader trends in society. Here are some interesting developments that emerged as this book was going to press:

1. Latin radio is one of the fastest-growing media segments. Spanish formats comprise more than 10 percent of all U.S. listeners age 12 and older.

2. On the downside, formats aimed at teens are tanking. Radio listenership among 12- to 17-year-olds has declined to about 8 percent of all listeners, capping a steady decline in the last decade. Teens' use of alternative listening devices, such as MP3 players, appears to be the root cause.

3. News/talk remains the dominant format, with a 17.6 percent share of listeners age 12 and over. Adult contemporary is second, with a 14.8 percent share, followed by Hispanic (11.2 percent), CHR (10.7), urban (10.1), and country (9.2), according to the Radio Advertising Bureau's most recent *Marketing Guide and Fact Book* (2007).

Here's a brief description of some of the major formats:

Adult Contemporary   Adult contemporary (AC) is a wide-ranging format that generally includes a few current popular hits, called *currents*; recent hits, known as *recurrents*; and older songs, known as *oldies*. AC ranges from rocking, hot AC to light, or easy, AC. Some AC declares itself a mix, using a mixture of types of songs and eras of songs. Adult contemporary formats are usually designed for general listeners rather than those listening strictly for only one genre of music. There are hot AC and light AC variations. AC has a relatively affluent demographic. CPM is high. This format scores particularly well among women around 30 years old.

Adult Standards   Adult standards is pretty much the same format as middle-of-the-road (MOR). (MOR is still an extant format, but *adult standards* is the term used by *Billboard* and Arbitron.) In any event, adult standards usually means music such as Tony Bennett and Brenda Lee. However, this format is no longer synonymous with World War II music. Selections from the Platters and even the Carpenters are often heard on adult standards stations. Remember, fans of the Carpenters who were in their late twenties when the Carpenters were in full flower are now in their fifties. Time marches on. CPM runs high, but raw numbers are declining, and adult standard stations are frequently found on the AM band.

Classical   The classical format usually includes orchestral, opera, and occasional show music. Some classical stations feature modern orchestral pieces, but most tend to stick with Bach, Brahms, and Beethoven. CPM is very high; the audience is typically highly affluent. Public radio stations often program this format.

Classic Rock   This used to be a splinter format of album rock but now has its own distinct identity. Classic rock might best be defined as the top hits from the best 100 rock albums of all time without new releases. Selections from Cream and the Moody Blues are examples of classic rock mainstays.

Contemporary Hits Radio (CHR)   CHR, also known as Top 40 or current hit radio, used to be what the secondary title says: the top 40 songs repeated over and over. But that strategy is hopelessly vague for a station that wants to distinguish itself in the marketplace. Today's CHR/Top 40 typically features heavy day parting—specially designed formats for the changing listenership during the day. Some CHR/Top 40 stations also mellow their playlist to capture a broader audience, whereas others play rhythmic Top 40 to skew toward the younger audience. These formats often use heavy promotion to build their audiences.

CHR/Top 40 has a fairly low CPM because its audience generally does not have much money, but again, young people have very active spending habits.

Country   As we defined earlier, country is a format with rural roots, but it is not limited to rural listeners. Country melodies typically have a *twangy* feel, and the lyrics often deal with the struggles of everyday life. Country music was rocket-hot in 2005 and is still among the most popular formats today. Oddly, that's a mixed blessing to country programmers and radio producers, who must tread the delicate line between ignoring the new material and alienating long-time listeners. (The word *producer* is a good substitute for *programmer* because planning airplay is really a matter of on-air production. We use *producer* with increasing frequency.)

Country is not regarded as having a particularly affluent demographic, although the format has made significant inroads among the affluent and the young, thanks in part to the huge success of several country crossover stars. Remember that the young are not particularly affluent on an individual basis, but they do spend a great deal as a group.

Modern Rock   Modern rock, also called new rock, features very progressive music, including many selections that would be characterized as alternative new rock. Music tends to be current with bands that have gained prominence within the last 5 years. CPM is highly variable.

New AC/Smooth Jazz   This music features jazz and compatible vocals. These stations play easy-going music designed to create a jazzy feel or mood. Music tends to be medium tempo, and it is sometimes referred to as new adult contemporary. CPM varies widely.

News/Talk   According to *The Radio Book*, the combination of call-in, live interview, and news programming called *news/talk* is the most successful format on the AM band. Although durable and popular, this format relies on good talent and is somewhat market driven. When times are not turbulent, talk ratings decline. Luckily for news/talk programmers, we seem to be realizing the ancient curse of "living in interesting times." In 2011, news/talk was neck and neck with country as the highest rated of all formats.

News/talk has a fairly affluent demographic. (All-news has a very affluent demographic.) It's particularly strong among businesspeople. Listeners tend to be older (35 and up) rather than, say, in the 18-to-34 demographic range.

Oldies   Just what constitutes an oldie is debatable, but to most producers, an oldie is a cut released at least two or three years ago, and of course, many oldies date back much farther than that. Some stations use rotations from all eras of recorded music, but the oldie market is segmented, too. You'll find that most rotations (the scheme of music played) in oldie formats center on an identifiable 15-year period. Many of these stations play music from the early 1960s through the 1970s for baby boomers.

Oldies CPM often runs a little higher than average, and some oldies formats are quite successful; highly specific oldies formats, such as classic rock oldies, have sizable and loyal audiences. Starting in 2004, some oldies stations began losing audience share.

Religious   The format is self-explanatory, but do note that the format can take on aspects of other formats. Some contemporary Christian music, for example, is virtually indistinguishable from that played on adult contemporary formats. Many of these stations are non-commercial, so CPM is either not applicable or, in the case of commercial religious stations, varies widely.

Rock   Rock, usually called album-oriented rock (AOR), features longer heavy-rock cuts and is primarily aimed toward a fairly young male audience. Album rock has many variations on its basic theme, but it essentially features older music, longer cuts, and longer sweeps (back-to-back music segments) than Top 40 does.

AOR has a low CPM because its audience is viewed as being less affluent and less likely than other audiences to buy a broad range of products.

Spanish   A variety of Spanish formats have become red-hot because of the growing number of Latinos in the United States. Radio station producers took note of this when they saw the results of the most recent census, and there has been good growth in Spanish stations. (In some Mexican border communities and southern Florida, of course, Spanish stations have been broadcasting for years.) Spanish formats have splintered into subformats as the genre becomes increasingly popular.

CPM can be good in many areas when there is a mating of easily identifiable products with this Latino audience.

Urban   Urban formats feature R&B, rap, hip-hop, hard rock, and other formats particularly designed to appeal to young, urban audiences, often blacks and Latinos. Not surprisingly, urban is a popular format in large cities. Like all formats, urban varies in the content and thrust of its programming. Many urban outlets also feature a healthy dose of Top 40 cuts and are nicknamed "churbans" or rhythmic Top 40. (If you hear, say, a Whitney Houston cut on an urban station, you're probably listening to a churban-leaning urban.) The rhythmic oldies format tends to be a mix of urban oldies interspersed with early rap and upbeat Motown hits. Urban CPM can be quite respectable because the format moves certain products very well.

Remaining Formats   There are dozens of other formats, including all-news, various ethnic formats, and even an occasional all-Elvis station (including one on satellite). Of particular interest is the all-sports format, which is proving successful for WFAN in New York and WEEI in Boston. The Internet allows incredibly narrow formatting, though business models for many of these formats are not fully developed. The most unusual format we know of is DogCatRadio.com, which programs music for pets to listen to when their owners are away. While it received much publicity, it was never regarded as a ratings blockbuster.

There is a great deal of overlap among formats. It's impossible to surgically separate, for example, a hot AC from a light Top 40/CHR. Note that new formats constantly merge and that many of today's large-scale formats were splinter or hybrid formats just a few years ago.

Filling the Niche: Today's Trends

After examining the range of formats available, we can see that finding and keeping an audience is not something that can be done in a vacuum. Changing tastes of the audience, rearrangement of competitors' formats, seasonal variations, and other external factors affect the viability of niche programming.

Here are some of the more noteworthy trends in radio programming in 2011:

1. Programmers were renewing their focus on content and (to some extent) personality. Terrestrial broadcasters were looking to capitalize on their strengths and provide what iPods and cell-phone radio stations don't—local focus and personal connections.

2. While there was some movement toward strong personality orientation, there was movement at the other end of the spectrum, too. The so-called Jack format, which has an extremely broad playlist—up to 1,200 songs spanning four decades—features no personalities and very little clutter. The jury was still out on the Jack format. While it proved successful in some

markets, programmers questioned how many radio formats survived in the past without dependence on personality.

3. Overall, adult hits, all sports, and classic hits saw improvements in market share, as did Mexican and Spanish formats. Also on the rise were specialty formats for children's, educational, Spanish adult hits, ethnic, and new country.

ON-AIR AND OFF-AIR PRODUCTION
IN THE MODERN FORMAT

Here's where audience measurement and format characteristics coalesce: The producer, on- or off-air, must blend the sponsor's desire for a clearly defined audience with the audience's desire for an attractive format.

We'll deal first with the fundamental issue of avoiding tune-out—a principle that applies to all formats—and then specifically examine production techniques in some major formats that you are most likely to encounter at some point in your radio career.

Production and Tune-Out

The producer's job is twofold: Get the listeners, and avoid doing anything to make them tune out. You want to build time spent listening and limit your turnover. Three major factors are involved here: avoiding dead spots, avoiding jarring transitions, and keeping the listener tuned in through quarter-hours.

Avoiding Dead Spots Suppose you have a tight CHR/Top 40 format, slick and well-timed work by the announcer, and you throw in a low-key commercial with no music in the background. Chances are you might lose a few listeners, which is why so many CHR spots are constructed with good production music.

In fact, almost all formats use high-quality production music. The days when you could grab a disc off the shelf and track any old instrumental underneath your commercial are gone. Today, lively production music that fits the format is an absolute necessity.

A variety of firms lease production music that projects a certain mood within the constraints of various formats. The cuts come on compact disc and are listed by selection. Some libraries of production music are now updated very frequently with new releases so that the music beds reflect current trends.

Avoiding Jarring Transitions An on-air producer must take care not to jolt the listener out of his or her seat. A soft cut back-to-back with a bold, loud song may keep your listeners awake, but it may also wake them up enough to change stations.

Some program directors make it a point to listen to ends and beginnings to see if they mesh. If not, some rearranging is in order. For example, a very loud, up-tempo intro is a bad choice to follow a soft song ending, but it is a good choice to back up to the end of a high-energy newscast.

Some program directors match keys of songs. A *key* is the musical scheme in which the notes of a song fall. In simple (and admittedly simplistic) terms, the key of a song is the first note of the scale used to write the song. That note and the note three notes above (the *third*) and the note five notes above (the *fifth*) sound natural and complete. The notes not on the base note (called the *tonic*) or on the third or fifth do not sound complete and hold us in suspense, waiting for the piece to be "resolved." Some keys simply do not segue well into one another. A key usually segues well with itself and with a song with a tonic key based on a note found in the first key. Audio specialist Stanley R. Alten has compiled a list of compatible keys—keys that can provide a good-sounding segue from one to another (see Figure 16.2).

For those of you without musical training, the preceding paragraphs are probably baffling. To be frank, one of the authors of this book, who has worked as a professional classical musician, usually cannot tell the key of a piece of music simply by listening. However, anyone with a decent ear can judge whether a segue between two songs is jarring because of a wide key change. Simply listen; if the beginning of the next selection sounds jarring, dissonant, or sour when lapping over the first selection, the keys don't mesh and it's best to rework the song selection.

Music in this key will segue with	First choice	Second choice	Third choice
A	A	D	E
A♯ (B♭)	A♯ (B♭)	D♯ (E♭)	F
B →	B	E	F♯
C	C	F	G
C♯ (D♭)	C♯ (D♭)	F♯ (G♭)	G♯ (A♭)
D	D	G	A
D♯ (E♭)	D♯ (E♭)	G♯ (A♭)	A♯ (B♭)
E	E	A	B
F	F	B♭	C
F♯ (G♭)	F♯ (G♭)	B	C♯ (D♭)
G	G	C	D
G♯ (A♭)	G♯ (A♭)	C♯ (D♭)	D♯ (E♭)

FIGURE 16.2

Compatible music keys.

SOURCE: From Alten. Audio in Media w/Info Trac, 6E. © 2002 Wadsworth, a part of Cengage Learning, Inc. Reproduced by permission. www.cengage.com/permissions.

Keeping the Listener Tuned in Through Quarter-Hours   Remember that Arbitron, counts listeners by numbers who are tuned in during a portion of the quarter-hour. As a result, part of a producer's or programmer's job is to keep the listener tuned in through those critical quarter-hour mileposts.

Production for Adult Contemporary

AC needs a particularly cohesive production strategy because there's so much competition. If you're running an easy AC that gets too hot, be assured that there is another easy AC in the market ready to usurp your listeners.

On-Air AC Production   AC stations usually have 6 to 14 currents in the main rotation—that is, 6 to 14 current songs that will be regularly inserted into the playlist. The hotter the AC format, the more currents. In general, AC relies on Top 40 to introduce records in a market, but the hotter ACs today are taking it on themselves to introduce new music.

Song selection is critical because a hard rock cut can drive listeners away. AC production directors listen carefully and may even disqualify a cut because of one portion of the song. "It seems like everybody has to throw something in a song to make you nervous," says consultant Bob Lowrey.[6] Very hard leads or dense rhythms, for example, often make the song unacceptable for the AC format, but don't forget that the situation cuts both ways. Too soft an AC selection ("Feelings" comes to mind) may drive listeners away from radio altogether.

Incidentally, try to have music sweeps briefly back-announced (identified after they are played; another word for this is *backsell*.) Research shows that lack of song identification is increasingly irritating to the AC audience.

Off-Air AC Production   Your selection of music beds for commercials must reflect the programming strategy of the station. In general, it is hardly ever a good idea to use a current as a music bed. Currents are only a small part of a rotation, so you'll be distracting the listener from the sound of the station and disrupting the format at the same time.

If you are producing a commercial, remember to use a good selection of female voices. Your audience is likely to be heavily female, a factor we sometimes forget. Light ACs are popular with women aged 18 to 34, and very soft ACs are popular with women aged 30 to 50. The commercial voice is often the representative of the listener, so be sure your audience has enough spokespersons.

Production for Album-Oriented Rock

Album-oriented rock (AOR) programmers want solid TSL in their numbers. AOR needs a loyal core audience.

---

6. Quoted by Sean Ross. "Soft AC Reconsiders Its Sources," *Billboard*, February 8, 1992.

On-Air AOR Production   Long sweeps are the rule. The basic strategy of AOR is to present long-form music, so frequent stops are audience killers. Although strong personalities are important, a growing body of research shows that AOR listeners are becoming bored by incessant chitchat among the on-air crew, so many stations are keeping intramural banter to a minimum.[7]

Off-Air AOR Production   This does not mean, though, that personalities don't count. Indeed, AOR still heavily depends on the intimate jock who projects a lifestyle. Remember that AOR spot production must have that intimate feel, usually produced by a high-quality mic and a close-in announcer. Appropriate music beds are OK, and some hard-hitting, compressed audio (for example, "Monster trucks at …" is often appropriate). But don't let your spots veer too close to Top 40.

Production for Country

Time spent listening is probably the most important consideration for country. Country's strength is strong TSL; in practical terms, that means that avoiding tune-out is especially important.

On-Air Country Production   Country stations have a peculiar problem: an embarrassment of riches. Country is making a comeback among young listeners, and dozens of hot young country singers are topping the charts. So what's the problem? Country fans are very loyal to the old standards, and you risk damaging your TSL and audience base if you alienate them with too much new music. Many stations are finding that one solution to this problem is to insert a new cut between a gold and a recurrent. This "eases in" the new music without turning off the audience that expects to hear the old standbys.[8]

Off-Air Country Production   Again, currents are not the best choice for music bed use. You're probably better off using the beds supplied by the music production houses. Those libraries come with music beds slanted toward the full range of country, from hot to highly traditional.

Don't always feel compelled to use a music bed. Country does not demand wall-to-wall music (as does Top 40). A good, intimate spot read by one of your station personalities can be highly effective.

"Intimate" nicely describes good country because probably nowhere in radio is personality–listener contact more important. Country production directors go to great lengths to make their on-air staff accessible to the public, so take advantage of that known quantity.

---

7. *Ibid.*

8. See "Programming: How to Get What Country's Got," *Radio Only*, December 1991, 24.

Production for News/Talk

News/talk depends heavily on frequent tune-in to build cume. Time spent listening is important, but news/talk programmers know that the listeners who tune in and out are the backbone of their numbers. Fresh ideas and fresh presentation are vital for building listenership.

On-Air News/Talk Production   We know the audience will be coming and going, so it's important that they be given the opportunity to do so without losing the flow of the program. In talk segments, for example, it is wise not to let your conversations lap over the stopsets. A listener tuning in during a stopset will not be able to follow the flow after the set concludes, and, as a result, the cume-building tune-in factor may be weakened.

If you have a regular feature, make it easy to find. WCBS-AM in New York (which is all-news, not news/talk, but the example we cite holds for both formats) plugs its "News and Weather Together on the Eights." Not only does this help reinforce listener recall of the frequency (88 on the dial), it induces anyone stuck in traffic in New York to tune in at 8 minutes after, 18 after, 28 after, 38 after, and so on. Seduce those listeners into hanging on for 5 minutes, and you've got some very high cume numbers.

Off-Air News/Talk Production   A music bed often detracts from the spots, so be judicious. Ideally, commercials and public service announcements (PSAs) should sound like the news/talk product itself: punchy and authoritative. The program hosts, and sometimes the news people, if station policy permits it, are usually better choices to voice the spots than anonymous announcers. If you do use music beds, remember that your audience is skewed toward older, more conservative listeners. Hard-rock beds are a no-no.

Production for CHR/Top 40

When you produce and program for CHR/Top 40, you're fighting turnover. In general, Top 40 advertisers want the best of both worlds: high gross impressions (reach) and a good many repeat listeners (frequency). Why? Because so many of the staple products advertised on Top 40 need to be distinguished from their competitors.

Soft drinks, for example, need an advertising strategy that has a relatively high frequency. Soft drinks are basically all the same product (you'd be hard-pressed to tell them apart blindfolded) and rely on audience perception for sales. Building an image requires that the message be repeated often enough for the image to sink in.

CHR/Top 40 does not have a particularly affluent demographic, so CPM is low.

On-Air CHR/Top-40 Production   How do you keep those numbers and keep them loyal? You have less flexibility in programming because CHR/Top 40 has a limited playlist. In general, your goal is to keep the production tight, keep on-air chatter to a minimum, and make sure your station has a distinct identity.

The "identity crisis" sometimes involves you in a direct maneuver to get listeners to remember your station. Liners—catch phrases read during the program, often over the intro to the music—are vital. Pounding home the liner helps reinforce your image and gives listeners something to remember when they fill out their diaries.

"Hot Hits 100—It Sizzles" is particularly useful if your call letters resemble the word *hot* and your frequency is near 100 MHz. Be careful, though, because if diary respondents make up their own call letters (if they think they're listening to WHOT when your station is really WHTS), you may start losing credit for diary entries.

Though CHR/Top 40 does not allow great flexibility in playlists, that does not mean that you can't vary your rotation of power cuts—the cuts at the very top of the chart—and oldies. Many Top 40/CHR stations incorporate a good selection of oldies, especially in dayparts where there may be a good share of older listeners, such as afternoons.

Off-Air Top 40/CHR Production   Hot music beds and heavy compression are a virtual must. In this format, a moment's departure from wall-to-wall music is often seen as a heavy tune-out factor.

The personalized approach does not work as well in CHR/Top 40 as in other formats. Jocks are basically second fiddles to the music, and the audience loyalty is generally to the music, not to the jock. So a no-music, personalized appeal from the jock will generally be less effective on this format than on a country or AC format.

Production for Urban/Churban/Rhythmic Top 40

Rhythm is the key to the urban format, and trendiness is essential.

On-Air Urban/Churban Production   Rap charts are volatile. What's in favor one week may drop off the charts like a stone the next, so the programmer or producer must keep a finger on the format's pulse. Although one-song sets used to be the staple of urban programming, many station programmers and producers are finding that sweeps are effective in building audience and keeping audience past quarter-hours.

Incidentally, there's a trick to appearing more current than the competitors. A number of urbans, churbans, and CHR/Top 40s have discovered that front-selling new music—that is, announcing cuts in advance—helps reinforce their reputation as innovators. This involves moving new cuts to places where they can conveniently be front-sold, such as immediately after a stopset.[9]

9. See "Programming: How to Bring It Back," *Radio Only*, November 1991, 22.

Off-Air Urban/Churban Production   Rhythmic music beds are important for commercial production, although strong personality spots, some without music, are not out of the question. Urban formats lend themselves to strong on-air jocks better than CHR/Top 40 does, so don't be afraid to inject a personal touch into commercial or PSA production. Don't go overboard, though, because losing the beat often means losing the audience.

PUTTING A FORMAT ON AIR

We will conclude this chapter with a discussion of how one becomes a programmer—putting all the pieces together, implementing a playlist, and putting the format over the air.

If you are instructed to "program" your station, one of the first tasks is to construct the program clock and the playlist. The program clock is not always a physical entity hung on the studio wall. It is often more of a theoretical structure into which program elements are inserted. Remember the important, overarching principle: The program clock is simply a structure that creates consistency through each *sound hour* and through each broadcast day.

The Format and the Sound Hour

Your goal is to make the station recognizable and to put the audience in a comfortable listening mode. Each part of the sound hour will have a purpose. For example, here is a typical sequence from an AC sound hour, detailing what happens and why:

- A short news segment and station ID at the top of the hour—give the audience news when they expect it and take care of the legal requirements for identifying the station.
- Lively vocal—give the audience a boost back into the programming.
- Oldie—provide an upbeat, feel-good memory.
- Two commercials—pay the bills.
- Bulleted (rising) hit—get the audience's attention again after the commercials; show them that the station is in step with the current music.
- Lighter vocal—you can't be intense every minute; the audience needs a break.
- Weather, commercial, and station promo—give the audience what they are interested in, pay the bills, and let them know they are happy listening to your station.
- A *B-list* song, one fading from the charts—keep consistency in the playlist by letting the audience gradually taper off on the fading hits.
- A Top 10 hit—keep things lively and current.

TUNING IN TO TECHNOLOGY • NEW MUSIC AND COLLEGE RADIO

It's a fact that college radio stations have traditionally thought of themselves as the places where new music is played and made. During the 1980s and 1990s, some of rock's biggest acts, such as U2, R.E.M., the Police, Talking Heads, and INXS, emerged from the college music scene.

Currently, there are about 800 stations licensed to colleges and universities and a number of unlicensed carrier stations that make up the music scene. Many of the jocks are students of broadcasting, but just as many are simply music aficionados who find taking a turn at the mic an exhilarating experience.

Indie Music Is *In* Now, but How Did It Start?

During the latter part of the 1970s, Robert Haber, the founder of the *College Music Journal* (*CMJ*), created a space where music directors from college stations could share their playlists. Prior to founding *CMJ*, he was the music director at WBRS, Brandeis University's radio station. Haber discovered that the music industry was practically ignoring the trends emerging out of the college music scene. Believing that the time was right to empower college programmers, Haber started *CMJ* out of the basement of his parents' house. His idea was pretty simple, but like many other successful things, the time was ripe.

The rationale for his idea was that new music discovered in Seattle, like Nirvana, might not be getting much airplay in Syracuse because students at that

station might not have been exposed to the grunge sound. As major record labels began to understand the importance of the college music scene, though, *CMJ* became a good barometer of the pulse of new music. Thus, over the past two decades *CMJ* has grown into a bible of sorts for college music programmers. Every year, its Music Marathon is a four-day sellout event featuring some of the hottest up-and-coming acts.

Today the *College Music Journal* is a significant force in determining new music; however, it is not the only source.

The New Music Scene

In the last few years, the new music scene has changed. Napster spurred a computer revolution in which people discovered that it was possible to share music over the Internet. Using file-sharing technology, it became easy to put an MP3 file on a server and let the world access it. While Napster made file sharing easy, it also made record companies angry since their product was essentially available for free. After the courts shut down Napster, Grokster, and other illegal file-sharing sites, legal systems began to develop.

Today's college students seem to have adopted laptops and iPods with a vengeance—students can search for new music anytime they have a connection to the Internet. There are thousands of music websites on the Internet, but Apple Computer's iTunes is perhaps the most successful example of a commercial site.

And so it goes. The mechanics of this clock probably would not be apparent to the listener, but the effect will be.

Different formats will have different goals. In a dance format, the goal will be never to let the rhythm stop. In a nostalgia format, the goal may be never to leap across decades and, oddly, never to use the word *nostalgia* (and thus to avoid reminding listeners how old they are).

Constructing the Playlist

How does a programmer decide what music to play? An important decision-making mechanism is to monitor industry publications to assess the popularity of certain cuts. *Billboard* and *Radio and Records* maintain very detailed charts of sales and airplay. A programmer also monitors local record store sales and, of course, what music is currently popular among Internet purchasers.

The trickiest part of constructing the playlist is introducing new music. Audiences tend to tune out when they hear unfamiliar music, so it's incumbent

In 2010 Apple announced that it had achieved more than 10 billion songs downloads from iTunes, and you can find a wide variety of musical genres to surf. (In fact, the iTunes top playlist for alternative music frequently mirrors the *College Music Journal* charts!)

Podcasting and Beyond: Finding New Music

Podcasting has made it possible for a variety of musical "experts" to provide information about new music. Some of the shows available highlight discussions about punk, electronic, Latino, and many more musical styles. Smaller record labels highlight upcoming releases, and the radio section of iTunes features more than 40 streams of school radio stations.

While iTunes may be the most successful music website, it's certainly not the only way to learn about new music. Napster.com (now legal) allows subscribers to listen to complete songs and to share their impressions on the Narchive. Live365 is another alternative source for hearing new music. Live365 lists more than 600 stations in the alternative category, and now claims to service several million listeners per month. Indie bands can upload at the website's music library, which enables the various Live365 radio stations to have access to these songs. MP3.com provides a music service similar to other music sites, except that you can hear the entire song. All of these services can

be useful to station music directors searching for the next big sound.

Indie music websites can be very useful resources for music programmers. Indie-Music.com and Allmusic.com are great websites for identifying new musical acts and for spotting trends. Click the Play Radio option for Indie-Music.com to access a selection of music based on the genre chosen. Whole selections are played through the computer's music player. Allmusic.com provides a wide assortment of useful features, including artist biographies, musical influences, and information on just released albums.

Pandora.com is a very interesting website that can help listeners broaden their knowledge of a particular genre. When you access the site, a pop-up asks you to identify a musical artist you like. From there, the website will take you on a musical journey that plays music related to that artist or genre. The musical selections presented are refined from the Music Genome Project, which claims to evaluate music based on a complex set of parameters. (If you're starting a job at a station that plays music that you may not be terribly familiar with, this would be a really useful site.)

As the Web continues to evolve, it is clear that music directors will have enhanced ways of discovering new artists and genres of music. Technology continues to provide us with broader music horizons. This will be a boon to the new generation of music programmers for college radio stations.

on the programmer to make sure the new cuts will appeal to the "old" audience.

The following Tuning In to Technology box contains several hints on rotating new music into the schedule.

We would like to close this discussion with a quote from Jim Robinson, the president of ABC Radio Networks. Robinson told *Billboard Radio Monitor* that one reason iPods and other listening devices have gained such a foothold is that "programming choices on the radio have become a bit more narrow and predictable than consumers would accept in a world where they have much more choice. So, today, we have an opportunity to assess our creativity and our presentation. This is our opportunity to show our resourcefulness as an industry."[10]

10. Tony Sanders, "Jazzing Up ABC: Jim Robinson." *Billboard Radio Monitor*, July 8, 2005. Accessed at http://www.allbusiness.com/services/motion-pictures/4487181-1.html. Accessed on November 29, 2008.

Remember: It is radio's ability to be there while we do something else that makes it such a vital part of this age. We can listen at work or in the car or while jogging.

And the producer will continue to mastermind this journey through time and space.

SUMMARY

Finding and serving a specific audience is probably more important to radio now than at any time in its history.

Radio ratings are generally taken in quarter-hour periods. Both duplicated and unduplicated audience data are important to radio stations because stations need to reach large numbers of listeners, but the very nature of the medium makes it important that they reach each listener a number of times with a given advertisement. Arbitron, a company that uses listener diaries to measure audience behavior, provides most radio rating.

The major methods of calculating advertising efficiency are cost per thousand, cost per point, and optimum effective scheduling.

There are many types of formats. One particularly useful categorization defines them as adult contemporary, news/talk, country, CHR/Top 40, album-oriented rock (AOR), urban, oldies, Spanish, classic rock, adult standards, easy listening, adult alternative, religious, classical, modern rock, and other formats.

A major factor in radio production is avoiding tune-out. This is done by avoiding dead spots, steering clear of jarring transitions, and giving listeners the music and talk they want. It is particularly important, because of the way radio ratings are taken, to keep listeners tuned in through the quarter-hours.

Even though radio has had some tough times recently, the medium is recovering, and the natural shaking-out process is, some believe, restoring the medium's basic mission: to give listeners what they want.

EXERCISES

1. We've purposely avoided showing an array of program clocks because they tend to provide a superficial and not entirely useful conceptualization of what an individual station actually does. But Figure 16.3 provides a sample program clock.

    Using it for reference, construct your own station clock by monitoring a particular station for one hour. Use the vocabulary we've defined in this chapter (current, recurrent, and so forth) along with the obvious descriptors (news, commercial stopset). This is an ideal class project since you can compare the various formats and, perhaps, individuals' different perceptions

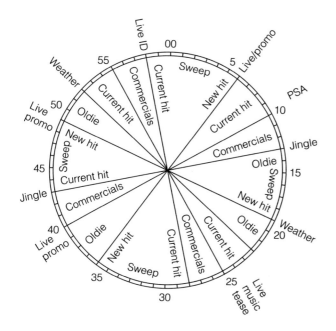

FIGURE 16.3

Program clock.

SOURCE: S. R. Alten, *Audio in Media*, 3rd ed. (Belmont, CA: Wadsworth, 1991).

of the same station during the same hour. It might also be useful to clock a *non-commercial* station, such as your local National Public Radio affiliate. Your instructor will assign stations to class members.

2. Write and produce a 30-second commercial for a product of your choice and produce it three ways: for a soft AC, a CHR/Top 40, and a country station. Don't assume that your choice of background music alone will suffice, and don't burlesque the announcing. (Sounding like a stereotypical character from *The Beverly Hillbillies* won't make for a good country commercial.) You are free, and encouraged, to change the copy itself for the three commercials.

17

Radio and the New Digital Infrastructure

Arbitron, the audience-measurement company that is the radio industry leader in measuring ratings, calls the new digital infrastructure "the infinite dial." Radio can now be paired with the Internet to be "streamed" (definitions follow), podcast, sent through mobile devices, and distributed in tandem with mobile smartphone technology and social media.

It comes as no surprise that many listeners, particularly young ones, listen to radio on the Internet via computer. But that is not the only option on the horizon. Arbitron, in a report on the future of digital radio,[1] noted that one in four Americans have listened to an iPod or other MP3 player connected to a car stereo, and a significant percentage of young consumers anticipate listening to Internet radio in their cars. Additionally, iPod/MP3 penetration has reached about 44 percent of Americans. About 40 percent of listeners age 12–24 say they would listen to more FM radio if their smartphones had a compatible tuner.

ITEMS ON THE INFINITE DIAL

There is a fundamental difference between the two major types (the major types as of this writing) of systems for distributing Internet audio.

Streaming is the creation of a program that is broadcast live or played back in real time. It is not stored by the device receiving it, and it is in most respects

---

1. www.arbitron.com/study/digital_radio_study.asp

similar to the transmission of a traditional terrestrial radio station. System software is typically provided by firms that specialize in streaming Internet radio, such as ShoutCast. But other sources of streaming software include computer and major software manufacturers. Both Apple and Microsoft offer proprietary streaming systems.

Podcasting involves shrinking an audio file into a highly compressed format. The most common and familiar is called MP3. MP3 is a proprietary format that stands for MPEG–1 Audio Layer 3. MPEG, in turn, stands for "Motion Picture Experts Group," an enterprise that developed and standardized compression formats for electronic media. "Podcast" is somewhat of a confusing name in that it was developed as a play on the name iPod, which is the proprietary name of an Apple product. However, any MP3 player available (and there are dozens) can play back this form of compressed audio file.

The nice thing about podcasts is that they can be saved, redirected, and stored in a databank. Apple, for example, allows customers to mount podcasts at its iTunes store. They can be retrieved, listened to, or transferred to portable MP3 playing devices.

Another digital innovation in radio is known as HD Radio. HD actually stands for "hybrid digital," although many people assume it stands for "high

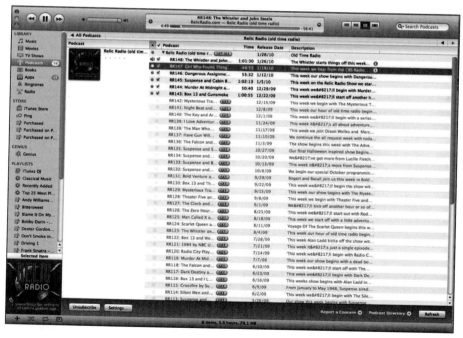

FIGURE 17.1

A podcast menu from Apple's iTunes.

SOURCE: Screen shot from ITunes

definition." However, the term *HD Radio* is actually a trade name and, according to the trademark holder, it doesn't stand for anything anymore.

HD Radio allows broadcasters to split the existing signal, which in analog form covers a fairly broad bandwidth, into several discrete stations. Such an option allows, for example, a news radio station that carries a baseball game to continue the all-news broadcast on a different channel.

Digital delivery systems also allow extraordinarily segmented radio. Pandora (See Figure 17.2), for example, streams more than 800,000 songs that are based on the preference of the listener, who, through various feedback mechanisms, continually refines the specificity of stream. In fact, a listener's mood can be accommodated by creating multiple channels, which are user-selected with the click of a mouse.

Pandora has an impressive 80 million registered users. Millions listen to various incarnations of Internet radio—about 73 percent of persons 12 and older. However, remember that terrestrial radio reaches more than 90 percent of people 12 and over on a regular basis, giving it, in broadcasting terms, a huge "reach."

What, then, makes relatively small audiences attractive to advertisers? While advertisers are still warming to the concept, the attractiveness of small audiences involves an idea dubbed "the long tail."

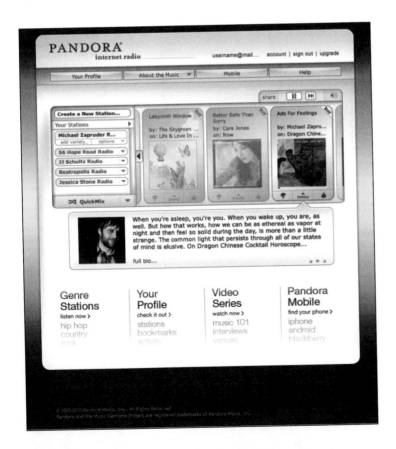

FIGURE 17.2

Pandora's "Profile" page lists personal listening preferences from a selection of more than 800,000 choices.

SOURCE: Pandora.com

RADIO AND THE LONG TAIL

The long tail is a consumer demographic concept coined by *Wired* editor Chris Anderson, who uses it to describe the concept that while a graph of the buying public would show a big bump where most buy a small number of major products, the graph would have a long, sloping tail that includes many more customers with more specific preferences.

Amazon.com is an example of a long-tail retailer. While it sells its share of blockbusters, it also sells millions of relatively obscure books, many sold by independent contractors who use Amazon to sell their products and in return turn over a share of their proceeds to Amazon.

Long-tail consumerism is possible because there is no shortage of supply of virtually anything in the digital world—books, advertising space, or music content. With computer-generated content, it is essentially just as easy to sell a million different items and a million copies of an identical item. If, for example, ads are stored in a computer memory, they can be delivered after a computer program compares them with the presumed characteristics of the listener—not such a hypothetical calculation if you have gathered information on song, listener age and gender, preferences based on actions predicated by other ads, and so forth.

The long-tail concept can apply not only to songs chosen by computer algorithms but to preferences for certain types of information served up by text messages or ads sent to applications, or "apps."

HOW THE INFINITE DIAL AND THE LONG TAIL CAN CREATE A MARKET

While the possibilities are still being sorted, placement of advertising by networks, such as Google, can provide new-media venues with a prefabricated advertising structure.

The way that much of Google's advertising works is that advertisers bid on keywords for searches or for what is known as "context-sensitive" advertising. To oversimplify—but not by much—if an Internet radio station plays music of the 1950s, it can be an attractive venue for reaching customers in their sixties and seventies. Any advertiser with a product geared toward that age group could find an easy access point to serve up tailored ads via digital media.

A TURN OF THE INFINITE DIAL

If you have not done so already, a quick Web search on "Internet radio" will turn up thousands of examples. Some are streams that duplicate terrestrial radio broadcasts. Others are part of an existing terrestrial radio station or group of stations that offer unique content. Others are freestanding.

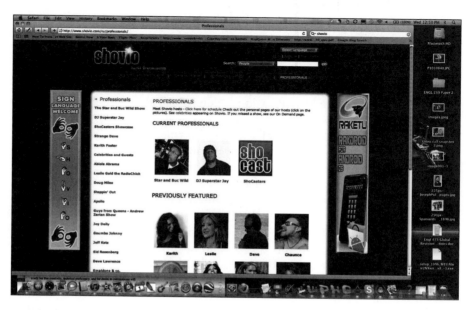

FIGURE 17.3

Internet radio service Shovio radio personalities are showcased on its website.

SOURCE: Shovio

But some are so inventive that they defy easy description, meaning that they may be true pioneers of a new digital age in radio. One particularly inventive site is Shovio.com, which was formed by a group of high-profile broadcasters but doesn't simply duplicate broadcast content. The system reaches listeners and viewers over the Internet and also can be fed on mobile phones.

Shovio.com is a new type of product in that it mates radio with social media and video. Hosts can interact with guests and vice versa, exchanging text comments and audio and video messages.

Shovio (See Figure 17.3) has various packages within the reach of anyone who wants a digital platform. It also features highly produced programs on "Shovio Studio" hosted by well-known broadcasters such as Star and Buck Wild, who also syndicate their program on a number of websites dedicated to hip-hop.

The configurations possible in such new media offer advertisers highly targeted and trackable advertising, including clickable targeted video ads, "live reads" by program hosts, banner ads, product integration into the shows, and promotion through social networking.

SUMMARY

The only thing certain in the evolving digital infrastructure is uncertainty, but it's a safe bet that creativity, technical proficiency, and the desire to communicate will always be coin of the realm in any type of radio, whether it be "radio" as we know it or some new system that may evolve even before the next edition of this text.

This chapter has primarily addressed the role of the digital infrastructure in broad strokes and as it applies to established commercial enterprises. But the real excitement of digital radio centers around the fact that entry costs have hit the basement—meaning you could be part of the first major wave of radio entrepreneurs, a topic discussed in Chapter 18.

There is no question that the new digital infrastructure has rewritten the playback for all media, including radio. Some aspects are clearly detrimental, including the drain from local advertising revenue caused by targeted and search-based Internet ads.

On the other hand, radio stands poised to benefit from some of the same technologies. A particular strength of radio is that it is one of the few media that can be consumed during the working day in many employment environments. In that regard, the ability of Internet radio to reach the inside of office buildings couples with the ability to overcome a traditional weakness of radio—the inability of the terrestrial radiated signal to penetrate into office buildings.

That's only one example, of course, but it's a good illustration of how media technologies are often dual-edged, and the industries that profit from the leading edge are the ones who exploit new opportunities.

APPLICATIONS

SITUATION 1/THE PROBLEM An advertising salesman for a station that covered a large metropolitan area was having trouble with one of his biggest sponsors, a foreign car dealership that specialized in high-end, high-performance models. The dealership's owner complained that he needed not just a series of ads but a way to keep potential customers loyal and engaged.

ONE POSSIBLE SOLUTION The station created a weekly podcast about the racing scene, narrated by an announcer familiar with the sport. The podcast contained spots for the dealership, and was offered on a regular Really Simple Syndication (RSS) feed. While it would be difficult to measure precisely how many sales were generated from the podcast, it did create the desired result—a stronger connection between the dealership and customers.

SITUATION 2/THE PROBLEM A news/talk station in a medium market had a difficult division of loyalties among its listeners. Some were avid fans of the local minor-league baseball team, while others wanted a steady diet of the talk shows that brought them to the station in the first place. The baseball games, though, were profitable because they were an appealing venue for many local advertisers. How could the station continue to carry the games but not cause tune-out among its most loyal base?

ONE POSSIBLE SOLUTION The station broadcast the games over the terrestrial channel and sent out the regular talk show on the HD channel. It was not a perfect compromise, as not everyone could tune in the HD, but it did present a viable option and allowed continuity among the station's offerings.

EXERCISES

1. Spend some time researching the way that traditional local advertising can come in conflict with Web-based advertising. For example, use your favorite search engine to look for locksmiths, and then compare the results with your local Yellow Pages. You may find that the locksmiths that appear near the top of your search engine results are not local at all, or at least carry no local address in their listings. The reason? National firms that hire local freelancers have become masters at optimizing search results to get exposure at the top of the list, a situation causing consternation among established local locksmiths. This is but one example of how search advertising has changed the landscape for advertisers and merchants. Check out what the *New York Times* had to say about this: http://www.nytimes.com/2011/07/10/your-money/lead-gen-sites-pose-challenge-to-google-the-haggler.html?_r=1

2. Make a log of context-sensitive Internet ads that appear on radio stations' websites or Internet-only radio stations. While there is no certain way to determine if it is a context-sensitive ad, you'll generally be able to tell because the ad will be one of many that have the same general layout and change when you repeatedly log into the site. List ten sites and ten ads that you encountered, and do your best to come up with a correlation between the content and the ads. Don't be surprised—or think you're doing something wrong—if the connection seems tenuous at best. Computer programs that generate the ads often make wild and sometimes wildly off-target guesses.

3. Prepare, either individually or as a class project, a podcast. Make it a weekly update on a particular issue. One suggestion would be search engine optimization, one of the hottest topics facing modern media. Your instructor will determine the level of complexity of the podcast, but you might want to include some interviews or commentary from multiple voices.

18

Entrepreneurial Radio

The nature of entrepreneurship has always been difficult to define. While most of us think of an entrepreneur as someone who is self-employed and starts a new venture from the ground up, there is no question that people work in an entrepreneurial fashion in existing businesses.

In any event, there probably has been no better time in recent history to take on a new venture revolving around media. For the person with start-up aspirations, the future is promising because investors are generally aware that new media will profoundly change media economics, but they—like virtually everyone else—have no road map to follow. Existing media operations often look for their staff to come up with new ideas to exploit emerging technology. And if you are a traditional-age college student, you will find not only your technological skills but your cultural connections valued. Media operations covet the 18–25 age demographic, and they frequently look to their entry-level staff to penetrate this dynamic market.

Most of this chapter will address radio as a potential start-up venture for entrepreneurs, although the basic principles can be applied in virtually any configuration.

THE NEW WORLD OF THE MEDIA ENTREPRENEUR

A new media visionary named Jeff Jarvis contends that the "old" model of media was one based on value provided by scarcity. In the case of traditional radio, the elements were valuable because

a. Radio spectrum space is scarce. Only a few stations could exist in a particular market due to licensing restrictions. This is due to the fact that too many stations would interfere with each other and would make it impossible for any station to operate and be heard through the interference.

b. Radio inventory is scarce—meaning the number of commercial spots available. Radio ownership in the traditional sense is clearly a product of scarcity, too, and a very expensive business to enter as an owner. Radio owners must pay for expensive antennas, production facilities, real estate, and so forth.

But in the new media model, scarcity is hardly an issue. Virtually anyone can start some sort of a Web-based venture. The cost of entry can be modest or, if you're creative, near zero. But the problem, at least from a profit standpoint, is that virtually anyone can start a Web-based venture. The owner of a traditional media operation typically had a built-in market. For example, if you owned a radio station in a medium-size city and were the only country music format in town, you pretty much "owned" the demographic associated with that format.

(This is not meant to imply that owning a radio station guaranteed a profit, or that all commercial time can be sold. It simply means that in the world of terrestrial radio, supply and demand are relatively standard concepts and are inextricably linked with legacy media economics.)

So how does one make money in new media? One model involves exploiting the "long tail" and offering a highly specific product that, while it appeals to a limited percentage of people, can

a. Appeal to a reasonable number of people looking for a specific type of media.

b. Find a way to sell that audience.

Essentially, points (a) and (b) are involved in what's called monetizing content.

MONETIZING INTERNET MEDIA CONTENT

Connecting an audience with advertisers who desire that audience is hardly new, but the apparatus to make that connection has evolved astonishingly in the past decade or so. The old way is expensive: You needed to hire salespeople to call on clients and convince them to buy, let's say, a commercial on your radio station. If your radio station was popular and offered good value, a fair percentage of your customers would call you. Still, it could be a tedious and labor-intensive process.

The direct sale of advertising is used for many Internet-based businesses, but the connectivity of the Internet has enabled media entrepreneurs to sell advertising on their sites with very little effort. At the same time, such arrangements often result in very little, if any, profit.

GOOGLE'S ROLE IN MEDIA ENTREPRENEURSHIP

Preeminent in Internet advertising for start-up sites is Google, which makes the lion's share of its income from search results. Google offers two programs, similarly (and some would say confusingly) named Adsense and Adwords. They are really opposite ends of the same transaction, though. Adwords is the service that allows those who want to sell ads to "buy" a keyword or phrase. An example might be "microphones." Search on the word in Google and a series of ads will appear on the right-hand column and a few at the top of the left-hand column. Manufacturers have paid for placement in the ad columns (the search results themselves are not ranked by payment), indicating how much they will pay for each click-through on the ad. Essentially, the keywords and phrases have been auctioned off to the highest bidder. While there are other factors that relate to how the results are ordered, the bid on the word or phrase is the primary factor.

Adsense is the flip side of the coin. Google pays proprietors of Internet sites to let Google ads appear on those sites, and Google funnels what Google's computers consider relevant ads to those sites. Sites then receive a cut of revenues from the clicks on the ads Google placed on their sites.

Sites that have large numbers of visitors and specific, attractive content are typically the venues that make the most income from the Adsense program.

Revenue generated by sale of the keywords on Adwords is used to buy advertising on Adsense.

Google is certainly not the only source of revenue for a website (more on that in a moment) but it is probably the most easily accessible source of revenue for the new media start-up. While there are no guarantees, media sites that draw many visitors and provide highly targeted content can and do generate significant revenue.

OTHER MONETIZATION MODELS

Generating an income on the Internet isn't easy, and in fact has proved an elusive process even to some (maybe most) major media companies. However, inventive entrepreneurs have used a variety of models to monetize content. Among them are the following:

Direct sales of advertising space, usually banners. Banner advertising is often viewed as intrusive and marginally effective, but nevertheless it is a proven technique for selling Internet page real estate. Many sites post "rate cards"—details of advertising costs—directly on their sites and usually spell out the cost for a banner of a certain size or frequency. The plus of this approach is that if the banner sale is direct, with no middleman involved, the site proprietor can keep all the profits. Usually, design of a banner is not particularly demanding or labor intensive, and some advertisers will design and provide their own.

Sales of merchandise related to the site. Many Internet radio stations, and similar media sites, sell hats, T-shirts, and other paraphernalia (sometimes dubbed "swag") to fans. Other sites sell products directly related to the theme of the site; for example, guitar amps on a site promoting independent music. There can be considerable profit related to this model, although carrying an inventory can be expensive and bothersome. Some Internet-based businesses avoid this problem by dealing with "drop shippers," firms that will, for a cut of the sale, ship the product from their factory or warehouse, saving you the trouble of putting it in your inventory.

Affiliate programs. Some large marketers will offer commissions from sales to place advertising on your site. Amazon.com has a well-known affiliate program. A radio entrepreneur might, for example, carry an ad for a particular artist's work with a link to Amazon.com, which will make the actual sale while providing a small commission to the site owner.

Personal appearances and other services. A site can produce significant income simply by being the conduit between the owner and what the owner has to sell. Many Internet radio station proprietors, for example, promote and sell remote DJ appearances through their sites. Authors promote books, consultants promote consulting, and motivational speakers promote and arrange speeches.

Fees for access. Known as putting content behind a "paywall (colloquial word based on the term 'firewall' meaning a barrier behind which content is available only to those who have paid for it)" this is a strategy that has met with limited success. For a variety of reasons, people are reluctant to pay for Internet content. Perhaps this has to do primarily with the fact that as the Internet developed, many media companies placed content on sites for free, thinking that advertising would eventually pay the bills. That particular model of advertising has not lived up to expectations (though Google's context-sensitive advertising has been a spectacular success). Having noted that, delivery of Internet-based media on the computer as we know it may one day, and possibly one day soon, be a thing of the past. Tablets and mobile devices could subsume a substantial share of media consumption, and perhaps consumers will be more willing to pay directly for such fare. Major media companies are banking on the attractiveness of tablet-based subscriptions, and firms specializing in delivery of mobile content are optimistic that customers will pay for media-related "apps."

Grant money and donations. Some sites, including many Internet radio venues, simply ask for donations. Other sites solicit grant money, a process that sometimes requires a special federal designation as a nonprofit entity.

Other network arrangements. Some media sites have created their own networks. While the arrangements are varied, one common structure is the "curated" network, in which one parent site links to other sites that have related content, and the sites share their audience. The sites, of course, link back to the parent and to other sites in the network. Such an arrangement can exponentially multiply interested and relevant audiences.

For free. Not everyone or every institution wants to make cash from a site. The "income" and "monetization" might come in the form of personal satisfaction or promotion of one's business or institution. As an example of the latter function, note that many high schools have created radio stations to keep students in contact with one another and to link the institution with students and parents.

SERVICES FOR INTERNET RADIO

A variety of firms offer hardware and software for starting an Internet radio station. The only concrete constant is that if you want to play music, you must either play music that does not need clearance to play or you must obtain the clearance, usually through payment of a royalty.

Note that many Internet radio stations are created solely for the purpose of playing independent music, and the music creators assign the stations the right to use that music. Many of these stations, in fact, are created by the creators of the music.

While it is possible to do what commercial radio stations do and make arrangements with music licensing firms, it may be more practical to deal with a firm that includes royalty/licensing coverage as part of its service. Such services generally also provide the software needed to program a station so it operates in the owner's absence—meaning that your Internet station will not have to be staffed 24 hours a day.

There are many such services. One is called Live365.com. (Again, there are many; this is only being used as an example.) Live365 offers services for professional and what the firm calls "personal" broadcasting. Rates are based primarily on how many listeners you want to accommodate at one time.

Also, check out Shoutcast.com, which sells software for streaming media and space on its servers.

SUMMARY

Internet radio may not be a guaranteed profit center, but it does generate listenership and does not typically involve a consuming investment of time and/or money. For example, a station called Radio Swing Worldwide (operated through the Shoutcast network) in year 2010 received more than a million tune-ins in one month. It is supported by modestly priced spots—$60 for eight spots a day for one month. A well-known Internet radio station called SOMAFM is entirely listener supported and broadcasts no fewer than 18 different channels of music. And in various cities across the nation, veteran terrestrial broadcasters are choosing to start their own Internet-based operations.

While Internet radio and new media in general are typically not a road to quick riches, they are part of an evolving media system that likely will include so-called legacy media for some time to come.

Earlier in the chapter, we mentioned Jeff Jarvis, often considered the preeminent authority on new media models. As Jarvis points out in his book *What Would Google Do?*, much of his income is derived from assuredly old-fashioned sources. His book made more than his blog, and his consulting, teaching, and speaking engagements generate more money than his book.

The new media marketplace seems to be turning into a venue where small pieces of a pie are digitally connected to make a symbiotic whole—meaning that in the best of all digital worlds, we reach and affect an audience through multiple, additive platforms.

The role of advertising is obviously critical to a radio entrepreneur, and understanding that role requires some grounding in the "infinite dial" and "long-tail" concepts discussed in the previous chapter.

If the new media economy seems opaque and confusing to you, don't despair. It's that way to everybody.

But don't the titans of new media have a firm grasp on audiences, their tastes, and their economies? Not exactly. Look at the free-fall that's sinking MySpace.com, which only a couple years ago was viewed as a masterpiece of a site that could read and please an audience. But audiences are fickle, technologies change rapidly, and advertiser dollars flee when there's trouble.

The point: Everyone has a chance to succeed—or fail—in the new digital economy, and that includes radio professionals.

APPLICATIONS

SITUATION 1/THE PROBLEM A local band was having trouble generating publicity. While it mounted a Facebook and MySpace page and posted some videos on YouTube, it faced the same problem as several other local groups—piercing the media clutter.

ONE POSSIBLE SOLUTION Bands that have similar approaches and styles of music are, without a doubt, competitors. However, they also are collaborators in the sense that if their style of music becomes popular, the pie becomes bigger and everyone can take a bigger slice. So in this case, four local groups of roughly the same genre started their own Internet station. The investment was small, the maintenance was minimal, and the product was always on display and lent some prestige to their marketing efforts.

SITUATION 2/THE PROBLEM A voice-over announcer was finding her freelance market drying up. Because many voice-overs are produced by exchanging audio files over the Internet, she no longer had a lock on local clients.

ONE POSSIBLE SOLUTION The announcer searched for blogs, online newsletters, and other public-relations material produced by local businesses, and she approached those businesses with a proposal for producing a podcast. Several clients, after hearing a demo, signed up. In some of the podcasts, she included a brief interview segment with a representative of the firm. The podcast became a viable and creative auxiliary product that could be offered by the firms and created a reasonable profit for the producer. After all, a high-quality podcast can be created using a standard computer, a reasonably priced microphone suitable for voice, and a quiet room. In this case—a real one—the producer did not have a quiet enough area and recorded her voice narration in her car! (Think about it: Cars have very sophisticated engineering to keep noise out, and the interior of a car has excellent sound-absorption qualities. Moreover, if you're parked in a noisy location, you can always drive somewhere else.)

EXERCISES

1. One of the emerging realities of modern media—especially journalism and, in some cases, music—is that the person is more central to the enterprise than the organization. Today, it's not unusual to find an expert in a topic (e.g., personal finance, technology, politics) freelancing to a variety of media organizations as well as maintaining a personal Web presence. Your assignment is to pick a specialty, or perhaps two specialties, and prepare a five-year plan on how you will make a living. Identify and describe at least five articles you would write, sketch out an idea for a radio program, describe a blog, make up a plan for speaking engagements you'd seek, and list websites to which you would link.

2. In about 1,500 words, profile a media entrepreneur. It doesn't have to be an internationally known celebrity, and it can be someone who operates in very nontraditional media as long as his or her work is involved with radio.

    Focus on two aspects:

    ■   The work—what makes it tick, why it is appealing, why you like it. Give examples and weave them into the text of your paper. Provide links to audio, video, or other content.

    ■   The person—how the media entrepreneur got started, background, strategies, future plans, and why he or she chose a particular specialty.

    Include an interview if you can get it. Most of the time, you can. Email interviews are fine as long as you identify them as such.

3. Prepare a business plan for a venture you would like to start. Formats for business plans vary widely, and your instructor will give you some guidance on the eventual form. But every business plan contains these items:

    ■   Background of the founder and qualifications

    ■   A description of the business

    ■   Clarification of potential customers

    ■   Expectation of income and sources of income

    ■   Plans for growth

    ■   Possible strategic alliances (partnerships or collaborative deals with other businesses that will produce a win for both)

Appendix A

A Play by Richard Wilson

Production of this play can serve as a good exercise in understanding the construction and flow of an outstanding drama. It probably will—as intended—pose a great technical challenge. In fact, we considered less difficult and less sophisticated plays for inclusion in this appendix, but we decided that the challenge presented here would provide an excellent learning experience. It also graphically demonstrates what we mentioned in Chapter 11 about the need to maintain a "fabric of believability."

The late Richard Wilson was a prize-winning author of fiction and nonfiction. He won the Nebula award of the Science Fiction Writers of America for his novelette *Mother to the World*. Wilson wrote more than one hundred published science fiction stories and three novels. He also wrote a history book and was a reporter and editor in Chicago, Washington, New York, and London. And now, a one-act play titled, Another Time …★

Sound: Keys in door, door opens, two men walk into room.

NEIGHBOR	(Don) Come up to my place and have a nightcap, Harry. It's still early.
HARRY	No thanks. I've had too much already.
NEIGHBOR	You only have a birthday once a year.
HARRY	Is that all? Lately they seem to come along more often.
NEIGHBOR	None of that, now. Fifty-three is young. Besides, you don't look a day over 52. This is a nice apartment. You've lived here a long time, haven't you?
HARRY	About 30 years. Me and my memories.
NEIGHBOR	Of Helen? Sorry, but people in the building do talk.
HARRY	It's all right. Helen died here. We were going to be married.

Meanwhile, we were living here. The Ninth Avenue El was still up then. The trains rattled right outside these windows. What a racket they made! But we didn't mind. We kept the shades down and felt all the more secluded.

NEIGHBOR   I didn't mean to stir up painful memories.

HARRY   It's never painful to think of Helen. I miss the El, though. They started tearing it down the day of her funeral.

Sound: Neighbor shuffles nervously.

NEIGHBOR   Look, I better go.

HARRY   It's all right. I live in the past a lot, except when somebody snaps me out of it, like you. Thanks for the pub crawl, Don. It's been years since somebody dragged me out.

NEIGHBOR   Don't mention it. I've got to go.

HARRY   Want some coffee or anything? Want to sit with me and watch TV?

NEIGHBOR   No thanks. Good night, Harry. Happy birthday.

HARRY   Good night.

Sound: Door opens, neighbor exits.

Sound: Harry pulls up chair, snaps on television, twists TV channel dial. Through sound of television speaker, commercials come on. They are chanted and build to an offensive crescendo.

VOICES   Better! More! Bigger! Newer! Best! Most! Biggest! Newest! Pain! Pain! Pain! Relief! Get relief! Get instant relief! Cramps? Irregularity? Aching back? Hurt? Hurt? Eat! Smoke! Drink! Diet! Lose weight! Exercise! Go! Come! RUN! ASK YOUR DOCTOR! ASK YOUR GROCER!! ASK YOUR—

Sound: TV clicked off. Footsteps as Harry walks across room. Click of radio being turned on. Characteristic sound of stations sliding past as dial is twisted.

VOICE   (calm and friendly as Harry moves the dial): We have brought you the Atwater Kent concert …

NEW VOICE   (as dial is turned): This is station WEAF signing off …

NEW VOICE   (as dial is turned): And so it's good night again from those sweethearts of the air, May Singhi Breen and Peter de Rose …

NEW VOICE   (as dial is turned): This has been Raymond Knight, the Voice of the Diaphragm, enunciating.

NEW VOICE   (as dial is turned): Tune in again tomorrow to WJZ for Billy Jones and Ernie Hare, the Happiness Boys.

Sound: Harry clicks off radio.

HARRY   (not believing it): WEAF. WJZ. I'm back in the past … when I was happy … young. When life was uncomplicated. (Laughs).

I am *happy*. I am *young*. (*He begins to believe it.*) It's true. Why not? As long as I want it to be it's true, here in this room, right now. As long as I don't look in the mirror—as long as I don't switch on the TV. And I'm 25! Helen's alive! But where is she? She's gone down to the corner, I guess. She'll be back in a minute with our midnight milk and oatmeal cookies ... Maybe a couple of charlotte russes.

Sound: In distance, the rumble of the El. It grows louder, louder, and closer.

HARRY   The El ... but if I look, it won't be there.

RADIO VOICE   *Yes it will.*

HARRY   Who said that? The radio? You ... but ... I want it to be, but it isn't.

RADIO VOICE   *Yes it is.*

HARRY   I have to meet it halfway. Have faith. I have to go out. Then it will be there. *I know. I know.*

Sound: The vague rumbling of an El platform.

HARRY   This is the El platform ... And the gum machine ... and the mirror—I'm *young*. (*His voice is reflecting change in age.*)

APRIL   Of course you are. Handsome, too.

HARRY   Who are you? Are you Helen?

APRIL   Helen? No. Have you got a buffalo nickel? To get me through the turnstile?

HARRY   Buffalo nickel?

APRIL   Jefferson won't do. He hasn't been minted yet. *You* know that.

HARRY   I'm not sure I know what you mean.

APRIL   Yes you do. Have you got two buffalo nickels for a Roosevelt dime?

Sound: Clink of coins as they exchange.

HARRY   How could you know about Roosevelt dimes? He wasn't—isn't even president yet. FDR, I mean. Wouldn't he still be governor of New York?

APRIL   I'm not good at current events, but I think it's later than that. Just a minute, let me get through the turnstile.

Sound: Coin drops at turnstile and turnstile turns. April's footsteps.

HARRY   You're not from here either—are you? Your clothes look right, though. How did you get here? (*Laughs.*) I don't even know what year it is. It was too dark to see the license plates and I couldn't find a newsstand—to buy a paper.

APRIL   You don't need a paper.

HARRY   I seem to be about your age. How old are you?

APRIL	Twenty-four.
HARRY	And I'm 25. Let's see—I was born (*he figures to himself*)—and if I'm 25 this is 1936. Is that right?
APRIL	It doesn't matter. Everything is relative in the duoverse.
HARRY	In the what?
APRIL	Never mind. You don't have to understand.
HARRY	I really don't want to—to push it too far. It's too fragile.
APRIL	It's not, really. But I can understand your feeling.
HARRY	Can you? I was listening to the radio—it's an old Atwater Kent—because I was mad at the television … You know what television is?
APRIL	Yes, of course.
HARRY	That's right. You know about Roosevelt dimes and Jefferson nickels. Maybe you know about Helen. She died, but if this is …
APRIL	I'm sorry. You won't find Helen. You can reverse time but you can't cancel death.
HARRY	I didn't *really* think you could.
APRIL	You said you were listening to the radio—steeping yourself in the past.
HARRY	I didn't say that.
APRIL	That's the way it happens.
HARRY	It happened to you, too?
APRIL	Not exactly *happened*. I planned it.
HARRY	Well, I certainly didn't—what's your name?
APRIL	April.
HARRY	(*formally*): Hello, April. I'm Harry. Where are you going, April?
APRIL	I'll be going with you … while you do your sightseeing in 1936. Then I'll go home with you.
HARRY	(*surprised and embarrassed*): Oh? Home with me?
APRIL	It'll be all right.
HARRY	(*not so sure*): Of course. But—home where the TV set is? You'd be—wouldn't you be—old—?
APRIL	Don't worry about anything, Harry. Enjoy yourself. That's what you came back to do, isn't it? Aren't you happier?
HARRY	(*after a pause*): Yes, I am.
APRIL	Where do you want to go?
HARRY	First? First to the Staten Island Ferry. Because—because it was there—
APRIL	You don't have to explain. Not in the duoverse.

Sound: Train rattles into station … Sound dissolves to wind, lapping waves, harbor sounds such as foghorns in distance.

APRIL	I'm glad you had two buffalo nickels for the ferry.
HARRY	I'm really here? Literally?
APRIL	What do you think?
HARRY	I don't know. Here—now. It's too—could I meet myself? If I looked, could I find another Harry? The one who's living through 1936 the first time?
APRIL	No. You're the only Harry in this 1936.
HARRY	This 1936? I—is that what you mean by—what do you call it—the duoverse? There are more than one?
APRIL	Yes, but you mustn't think I understand everything I have a name for. I do know you couldn't be here—and neither could I—unless there was something controlling the paradoxes. That's the duoverse, they tell me—a twin universe to keep time travelers from running into themselves.
HARRY	(*troubled*): Who tells you that? No … don't tell me. I don't need to know. I'm just so glad I found you.
APRIL	I'm glad I found you. I'd been looking for so long.

Sound: Foghorn.

HARRY	(*almost as a prayer*): Let's not lose what we've found. Let's keep it forever.
APRIL	And thou beside me—under the branches of the time-tree … ? Something like that? Oh, Harry!

Sound: They embrace and kiss.

APRIL	(*with infinite regret*): It's impossible, Harry … I'm going the other way.

Sound: Harry and April walking to door of Harry's apartment. Sound of El in background.

Door opens. Sound of Harry and April walking in.

APRIL	We haven't done much sightseeing in your beloved past. We haven't seen the Hippodrome—the streetcars on Broadway—
HARRY	No, don't turn on the lights yet. You're all the past I want. (*Concerned.*) Is it all right for you to be here?
APRIL	It's the way it has to be. There's no other.
HARRY	But here I'm old—and you—?
APRIL	Not till we turn on the TV, Harry. Not till then. I'll turn on the lights now.

Sound: Light switch.

HARRY	I'm still young. I'm—sit down, please. What can I get you?

APRIL   Coffee?

HARRY   I just have to heat it up. It's already been percolated once.

Sound: Walks across room.

APRIL   (*calls to him*): I might have known you'd have real coffee. No millions of tiny flavor buds for you, eh, Old Timer?

HARRY   (*calls to her*): I don't have the room.

Sound: Harry walks back into room, sound of cups clinking and Harry and April drinking.

Harry starts to say something, but El train drowns him out. Finally:

APRIL   (*puts down cup; sound of her chair scraping back as she stands*): Thank you for the coffee—and everything.

HARRY   (*sound of him jumping up*): Don't go! Please!

APRIL   I must. It's a long way. Turn on the TV, please.

HARRY   No—I won't! I won't make you old!

APRIL   You don't understand.

HARRY   Please! It's too early. There's nothing on. Wait …

APRIL   I *have* waited, Harry. You don't know how long.

Sound of El. Sound of April moving past and turning on TV. Sound of TV voice. As TV voice comes on, sound of El dies out.

TV VOICE   —And now, kiddies, it's time for your Uncle Jack to tell you about a wonderful surprise waiting for you and your mommies in the supermarket …

Sound: TV clicks off.

HARRY   (*the age once again in his voice*): You're the same! I'm old—but you're 24! Even though we're back in the present!

APRIL   (*sadly*): I told you we were going different ways. Your way was back. Mine was—is—forward. Oh, my dear, I'm sorry. I had to use you. I had no choice.

HARRY   You came from the past—but in 1936—you weren't even born!

APRIL   I wish—I'm so afraid this will hurt you—but I'm not from your past, or even your present … I'm from the future.

HARRY   The future—then I'm just—a stop on your journey … where you're going … I'm dead!

APRIL   No, Harry. It's all—relative. It's what you are *now* that matters. Not what will be, or what was.

HARRY   I know I hoped for too much. I wanted my youth and I wanted you—and I can't have both. I can't have either.

APRIL   (*distressed at his unhappiness*): It was to have been so simple, so scientific. I was to go back—they have machines—and make notes. Saturate myself in the atmosphere of the past. Oh, it doesn't matter! You're what counts. I've hurt you, and all I wanted was to give you what happiness I could, in passing—

HARRY   It doesn't matter. I'm just a phantom in your life—in your real present. Where you belong, I'm only a corpse in the graveyard.

Sound: April starts to cry.

HARRY   Let me finish. Be realistic. I'm just a complicating factor who got in your way. You mustn't compare yourself with—with someone who doesn't exist in your own time, but think of me occasionally ... up there in twenty-hundred and—whatever it is.

APRIL   Harry, stop it! Don't kill yourself in your own lifetime ... I'll stay with you, my dear. I will! I can't do this to you.

HARRY   No, I won't let you. Look, I'm a sentimental man who's been privileged to know his youth again. Knowing that youth, I know yours. I won't let you sacrifice yourself—for a phantom who died before you were born.

Sound: April sobs.

HARRY   Come on, child. Wash your face. Off with that lipstick. Cupid's bows are passé. (*Indulgently, fatherly*) Scoot! You've got to fix yourself up and find somebody who can make change for a coin that hasn't been minted yet ... Forgive my vanity, but I hope this time it's a woman.

Sound: April walks to bathroom, distant sound of water running. Sound of walking back into room.

HARRY   When you go, don't say goodbye.

APRIL   All right.

HARRY   I hate long goodbyes. Leave as if—as if you were going down to the corner—to get some—some milk and oatmeal cookies.

APRIL   (*tries to pretend*): All right. I guess I'm ready. Is there—anything else you want while I'm out?

HARRY   Maybe a charlotte russe?

APRIL   (*the pretense fails*): Oh Harry, I don't even know what that is!

HARRY   Never mind.

Sound: Door opening, April walks out. There is silence. Suddenly, the door bursts open. April's footsteps as she runs in.

HARRY   You didn't go!

APRIL	(*panting, barely able to speak*): Y-yes.
HARRY	You couldn't have, and been back so soon.
APRIL	(*panting*): I could have come back to yesterday, if I'd wanted, traveling in time. At least there is a yesterday.
HARRY	Of course there's a yesterday. That's where we—you mean where you went back to—ahead to—whatever you say—it's not—it's been—?
APRIL	There's no tomorrow.
HARRY	What do you mean?
APRIL	Where I was going I'd have been a corpse—without even a graveyard. I mean when I got close to where I wanted to go I realized it wasn't even there any more. Something wiped it out —or it finally blew itself up—I don't know what. I just know it's gone.
HARRY	… and so you came back to me.
APRIL	That's not very flattering, is it? I'm sorry.
HARRY	You're here. The details don't matter.
APRIL	You're the one I turned to.
HARRY	That matters. Very much. You're welcome. But the one you've turned to is an old man.
APRIL	Hush. You're not old. You've lived in a suspended life. I'm the one who's aged, dashing back and forth between the centuries.
HARRY	You lie—adorably. But stay with me. At least until you find your bearings in this crazy time.
APRIL	I *want* to stay with you. You're the same person I met on the El platform. Do you think you've changed—inside?
HARRY	(*lightly*): Inside, I always think of myself as 19—much too young for a mature woman like you.
APRIL	Oh, Harry, I *can* love you. I will. Just give me a little time.
HARRY	You have all the time I have left.
APRIL	… I want to stay with you forever, Harry. And if we only listen to the radio all our remaining years, that'll be all right, as long as we're together. And one night, Harry, who knows— we'll turn on the old Atwater Kent—and hear the Street Singer or the Happiness Boys—and then the program will be drowned out by the Ninth Avenue El—I can almost hear it—rattling its way through that magic time when you're 25 and I'm 24.

Sound: The El is heard. Its sound swells and then fades to silence.

Appendix B

A Capsule History of Radio: Past Meets Future for the Modern Producer and Programmer

Throughout this text, we have tried, where appropriate, to demonstrate how much of radio's modern practice is tied to the past. But because this is a radio production text, the amount of space in the main chapters that can be devoted to history was limited. In this appendix, we can take a more expanded view of radio's development. Our goal is to show how radio as it exists today developed because of cultural changes, advances in technology, and changing demographics. Further, although we cannot really predict the future, certain elements of history do repeat themselves, and perhaps we can discover some keys to the future of radio production and programming by examining its past.

To radio's early listeners, invisible signals flashing through thin air seemed to be nothing short of magic—a type of wizardry that not only moved messages with lightning speed but also eliminated geographic barriers. Distance no longer imposed geographic limits on one's awareness of human events. Information could pass through space, penetrating walls and mountains. Any form of human expression that could be communicated through voice, or music could reach the most distant farmhouse as well as a Manhattan penthouse. A simple box could turn one's home into a theater, a concert hall, or a classroom. The romance of the idea is powerful and undeniable.

This is a short story, beginning little more than a hundred years ago.

THE BEGINNINGS OF THE MAGIC MEDIUM

Radio traces its origins to the theoretical physics of James Clerk Maxwell. Maxwell's *A Treatise on Electricity and Magnetism*, published in 1873, postulated the existence of electromagnetic waves. Using mathematical formulae, Maxwell determined that an invisible energy existed in the universe, an energy that behaves like visible light.

About a decade later, a German physicist named Heinrich Hertz conducted a laboratory demonstration that confirmed Maxwell's theory. Hertz's demonstration of the existence of electromagnetic phenomena, however, provided no clue to any practical application of this form of energy. In fact, it was doubted at the time that these waves would be of any practical benefit.

About a hundred years ago, a young Italian tinkerer named Guglielmo Marconi was the catalyst for translating these academic discoveries into a means of transmitting information. "Hertzian" waves fascinated the young Marconi, who outraced other scientists attempting to manipulate these waves to send telegraphic messages. Marconi used an on-and-off method to transmit the code developed by Samuel Morse, and within a couple of years Marconi developed a method to transmit signals powerful enough to cross great distances, including vast expanses of water. The development of ship-to-shore "wireless," as it was called, promised to be a considerable advantage in an age of growing interoceanic travel and commerce.

Marconi brought his discoveries to the Italian government, which expressed no interest. Marconi's mother, who earned a reputation as a wily and persistent businesswoman, brought Marconi to England instead. The British government was entranced by radio technology because it offered a rapid communication system to its far-flung empire. Marconi's product showed every promise of becoming a practical success, and a company was formed with Marconi as one of six directors and a major stockholder. After patents and licenses were obtained, radio became a financial success as well.

Marconi repeated this success in the United States, where the Navy had a strong interest in acquiring a technology that promised to give it a tremendous strategic advantage. Marconi formed an American company, and radiotelegraphy, as the industry was called, became an American commercial venture that would soon form the basis of an entire industry.

RADIO FINDS A VOICE

Other inventors and experimenters were intrigued by radio but disenchanted with dots and dashes. The challenge was to discover a way to manipulate radio waves so that sound could travel through space the same way it travels through wires. An inventor named Reginald Fessenden believed that the physical nature of the on-and-off interrupted wave—which worked fine for Morse code— would prevent the interrupted wave from ever transmitting sound. Fessenden teamed up at General Electric with F. W. Alexanderson, and together they developed a device called an alternator, which could transmit a continuous wave. Fessenden put the alternator through a test-drive on Christmas Eve at Brant Rock, Massachusetts. He played his violin, read from the Bible, wished the audience a Merry Christmas, and told them that he would broadcast again on New Year's Eve. No doubt this came as quite a shock to the small audience of shipboard wireless operators, who previously had heard only the staccato of dots and dashes.

In the early years of the twentieth century, many experimenters moved radio forward. One of them, Charles D. Herrold, who operated a college of engineering in San Jose, California, transmitted regular programs and provided listeners with a written schedule. Herrold's operation ended when World War I began, but after the war others took it over. Today, KCBS Radio in San Francisco traces its lineage to Herrold's small, low-power transmitting facility.

That low power, incidentally, remained a serious problem for early radio stations wanting to transmit voice and music. An interrupted wave carrying Morse code could travel many miles, but waves carrying sound produced a weak signal. An experimenter named Lee de Forest worked to improve the capability of the new medium by amplifying the signals. His invention was called an "audion tube," and in theory it was really quite simple: The signal was transmitted across an electronic grid, and a more powerful signal was sent through that grid, picking up the imprint of the first signal but greatly amplifying it. The device operated most efficiently in a vacuum; hence it was later called the vacuum tube.

De Forest also provided early radio programming to a scattered group of experimenters and amateurs. Early listeners heard a wide variety of live musical performances, lectures, recordings, and reports of events. The hum and babble over the airwaves was fascinating, in part, because it was so novel—much the same as early Internet transmissions. It was an exciting time, with wireless companies sending out dots and dashes and legions of amateurs "playing radio," broadcasting from their bedrooms or barns or chicken coops. The government began to issue licenses for radio stations in a vain attempt to sort out some of the confusion, because those who "played radio" often arbitrarily chose a frequency and did not give much thought to the problem of interference.

The days of playing radio soon came to an abrupt end. With the advent of World War I, the Navy and Army shut down the amateur stations and took over the commercial wireless operations. Because of the expertise they had developed, amateurs were in demand by the armed services.

RADIO AFTER WORLD WAR I

During World War I, technology advanced rapidly, and after the war's end, several American firms resumed exploring the commercial possibilities of radio. Several major companies were involved in one aspect or another of wireless technology. Among them were General Electric, AT&T, Westinghouse, and, of course, American Marconi.

During the war, numerous contentious patent disputes were put aside as the firms concentrated on filling military orders. Following the armistice, American Marconi found itself to be an unwanted player in the communications sweepstakes. America was turning isolationist, and the British owned American Marconi. Communications technology was considered too important to be in foreign hands. So a deal was made, and a new American corporation was created. Shareholders of Marconi were given a piece of the action. Its articles of incorporation stipulated that no more than 20 percent of the stock could be held by foreigners and that only U.S. citizens could be officers or directors.

General Electric, AT&T, Western Electric, and Westinghouse picked up large blocks of the stock. The name of this new corporate behemoth, established in October of 1919, was the Radio Corporation of America (RCA). Many of the former American Marconi employees moved over to RCA. One of them was David Sarnoff. At RCA, Sarnoff resumed the campaign he had begun at Marconi, trying to generate interest in his "radio music box" idea. As before, there were no takers. But it wouldn't be long before RCA realized it was missing the boat.

RADIO CARRIES A TUNE

Why did it take so long for the radio industry to catch on to the seemingly obvious potential of radio? At the heart of the problem was a classic chicken-and-egg scenario: Listeners had no easy way to pick up the signal short of building their own sets. This meant very few radio receivers were in existence. Companies were reluctant to invest in manufacturing receivers, however, because there wasn't much actual radio for listeners to pick up. Schedules were still catch-as-catch-can, and programming was decidedly uneven. From the standpoint of the companies that could provide radio programming, there really was no point in developing a regular, high-quality schedule until there was a critical mass of listeners and a way to make money off them.

The Westinghouse Company cracked this particular egg. Westinghouse, located in Pittsburgh, Pennsylvania, had carved out a strong role in communications and electric power. During World War I, the firm had acquired many government contracts for radio and related communications. But when the war ended, Westinghouse was at a competitive disadvantage because RCA and the American Telegraph and Telephone Company (AT&T) dominated the market. RCA and AT&T controlled the lion's share of the radio-related patents.

The man who helped Westinghouse crack that barrier was Frank Conrad. Conrad had only a seventh-grade education, but he learned on the job and became one of Westinghouse's most valued employees. His bosses told him, however, that amateur radio work was on his own time. Using his call letters, 8XK, he talked from his garage to other hobbyists, who often commended him on the technical quality of his transmissions. As interest grew, Conrad began to present programming for a short time every Saturday night, using records from a local music store, to which he gave free mentions. He also carried some live saxophone and piano recitals. Keep in mind that radio was still a novelty, mainly for experimenters and hobbyists. But with a big boost from Frank Conrad, radio was about to take the country by storm.

A local Pittsburgh department store ran a newspaper ad mentioning Conrad's programs, noting that the transmissions were picked up by a "wireless set" operating at the store. The ad pointed out that similar sets were for sale at the store for $10. Conrad's boss, Westinghouse vice-president Harry Davis, saw the ad and had an idea: If enough interesting programs could be provided, radio could move beyond the stage of being a hobby for technically oriented people and become a medium for everyone to enjoy. In short, radio could become a mass consumer product, and Westinghouse could make the radios—and the profits.

Davis called Conrad into his office and outlined a plan. Conrad would build a new transmitter to be located at the Westinghouse plant. A regular (though limited) schedule of programming would be instituted and publicized in advance. Davis figured that, with some regularity of programming, people would want to buy radios. (Hindsight tells us he was absolutely right.) He had an additional idea for maximizing publicity: He wanted Conrad and his coworkers to have the new transmitter up and running in time for the approaching presidential election.

Time was short, but Conrad said it could be done. In the last week of October, the U.S. Commerce Department assigned the call letters KDKA to the Westinghouse station. The *Pittsburgh Post* agreed to telephone wire service results to the station, and on November 2, 1920, KDKA broadcast the election returns that put Warren Harding in office as the 29th president of the United States.

RADIO AFTER KDKA: THE COMING CHAOS

Across the country, people were talking about this phenomenon called radio. Companies and entrepreneurs were opening up radio stations. Manufacturers were turning out radios as fast as they could. Secretary of Commerce Herbert Hoover described it as "wireless fever" and called it "one of the most astounding things that [has] come under my observation of American life." In those exciting and chaotic early years, radio programming was a hodgepodge proposition. Station operators relied in large measure on free talent. Musical groups, soloists, and lecturers were happy to go on the air for the exposure radio provided. Other commercial stations sprang up quickly, but the term *commercial station* meant only that they were licensed by the U.S. Department of Commerce. Advertising played no role in radio as yet.

Many newspapers, colleges and universities, and religious organizations soon opened radio stations, even though those stations did not produce revenue. (Again, it is impossible to keep from making a comparison to the companies that started sponsoring websites for publicity and goodwill, with no immediate financial benefit.)

The situation became something of a stalemate. Station owners were not about to pay for programming when they didn't have to. Besides, there was no firm notion on how, exactly, stations should support themselves. The idea that advertisers could pay for commercial announcements was not widely accepted. Many thought such advertising would not only be crass but would also discourage listeners from tuning in to stations. Political leaders as well as many radio broadcasters were adamantly opposed to "selling out" to sponsors. Hucksterism was to be avoided.

But the idea that stations existed to sell radios was on the wane. As listenership increased, so did the demand for improved technical quality. Station owners felt the need to purchase better-quality professional equipment instead of relying on jerry-built studios and transmitters. This was going to cost money. What's more, the better performers were becoming less enthusiastic about appearing on the radio for nothing. And the listening public was becoming more sophisticated and demanding about the kind of programming it expected.

Something had to happen. There was talk of following the British system of financing broadcasting by charging radio owners annual user fees. That concept didn't fly in the United States. Another failed idea involved radio stations making direct pitches—asking listeners to send in money to support the station. That tactic didn't generate much interest, though public radio and TV stations use it even today.

Commercialization of the airwaves was about to begin. It would start fairly unobtrusively, then gain momentum and boldness. It would turn radio into a cash cow for many owners. It would also allow radio programmers to hire the best talent available, from symphony orchestras to first-rate Hollywood and Broadway stars.

AT&T DEVELOPS TOLL BROADCASTING

The first inkling of radio's new commercial potential came in 1922, and the company behind it was AT&T. The concept was radical: AT&T—the telephone company—would provide no programs, only facilities. In the same way that the company provided customers with telephones—and a telephone network to plug it into—it would provide broadcast facilities to paying customers for whatever they wished to put over the air. AT&T's profits would come from the charges made for this service, called toll broadcasting. Under AT&T's concept, programming would be supplied by paying customers. If you wanted to perform or lecture on the air, you could do so for about $50 for 15 minutes of airtime. The company originated this concept at a station in New York City with the call letters WEAF.

But AT&T discovered a flaw in the concept—the same flaw marring the entire radio industry. If there was no attractive programming, there was no audience. AT&T decided that it needed to supply a certain amount of programming to prime the pump, so to speak. And soon, WEAF began to attract paying customers.

An area real estate company decided to give toll broadcasting a try. Its message stressed the appeal of country living, and the firm, with apartments for rent in the "country" (actually the suburbs), was happy with the response it received. As the months progressed, other companies paid for the privilege of getting their messages out to the public by radio. Commercial broadcasting was on its way to becoming the means of support for the great majority of radio stations in the United States.

Exit AT&T

Ironically, just as radio's commercial and very profitable future was taking shape, AT&T got out of the radio business, selling pioneer station WEAF to RCA for one million dollars.

The phone company's decision came after a good deal of wrangling among the principal players in the fledgling industry, specifically those companies that had bought stock in RCA and reached agreements on cross-licensing of patents. AT&T had been contending that it held the exclusive right to sell commercial airtime. In addition, it controlled the higher quality phone hookups that allowed two or more stations to carry the same program simultaneously, a concept known at the time as "chain broadcasting." Other broadcasters had to use inferior telegraph lines.

Clearly, a resolution of the tensions was overdue. The feuding parties agreed to submit to binding arbitration. AT&T did not fare well. The decisions favored RCA, GE, and Westinghouse. After further discussions, the phone company agreed to a plan under which it would essentially leave the radio business but would have the sole right to set up wired interconnections (networks) among stations.

DEVELOPMENT OF THE NETWORKS

Broadcasting pioneer David Sarnoff, who would later become the president of RCA, demonstrated the potential of network broadcasting as early as 1921 when radio was still in its "hobby" stage. The occasion was a championship prizefight with international appeal: heavyweight champion Jack Dempsey versus French champ Georges Carpentier. The event would take place in Jersey City, New Jersey. Using a borrowed transmitter and an improvised antenna, Sarnoff arranged to broadcast the fight through radio sets and loud speakers in theaters, halls, and barns connected together in a "network" throughout the eastern part of the country. It is estimated that some 300,000 people listened to the big fight. It was an important day for radio, but not nearly as good for Carpentier, who lost by a knockout in the fourth round.

The next year AT&T hooked up its flagship station in New York, WEAF, with Boston station WNAC for a musical program. By 1923 there was a mini-network of six stations and, by 1924, a chain of radio stations reaching from coast to coast. RCA, Westinghouse, and General Electric likewise ventured into "chain broadcasting." Because they had access only to lesser quality telegraph lines, they were not as successful as AT&T—although their time would come.

NBC and CBS

By the mid-1920s, the significance and potential of radio broadcasting was apparent to all but the most diehard skeptics. RCA, which had ignored Sarnoff's prescient "music box" memo just a few years earlier, now was ready to take the big plunge. With Sarnoff's continual prodding, RCA established a permanent network called the National Broadcasting Company (NBC).

Just a few months later, NBC set up a second network. The original one was dubbed the Red Network and the newcomer was called the Blue Network. The federal government eventually forced NBC to give up the Blue Network because the government feared too much concentration in the hands of one company. The Blue Network would eventually become the American Broadcasting Company (ABC).

The idea of radio networking made sense on several fronts. If many stations, instead of just one, were carrying the same programming simultaneously, the cost of the program could be shared. The quality of programming could be upgraded, thus attracting more listeners, and the larger the audience, the more appealing the program would be to sponsors. It seemed to be a win-win situation for all concerned, except, perhaps, for those who felt community-oriented programming was being squeezed into smaller and less desirable time periods. (Many believe those people had a valid point.)

NEW COMPETITORS SET THEIR SIGHTS ON NBC

NBC could look over its corporate shoulder and see competition moving in.

A struggling company called United Independent Broadcasters (UIB) was offering some programs. But it wasn't much to worry about. NBC was clearly the king of the hill, and UIB most likely wouldn't last—and it didn't. UIB acquired some stations, but eventually folded. The Columbia Phonograph Record Company bought what was left of UIB and renamed it the Columbia Phonograph Broadcasting System (CPBS).

The new name didn't help. Sponsors were hard to come by, as most radio advertisers preferred to be associated with NBC, the "quality network." New investors, including WCAU owners Isaac and Leon Levy, jumped into the breach as the CPBS, piling up debt, was about to call it quits. At about this time, the name of the network was changed to the Columbia Broadcasting System (CBS).

PALEY TAKES OVER CBS

William S. Paley was 26 years old and an executive in his family's Congress Cigar Company, a firm that had advertised on WCAU and on the CBS network. He was impressed by the power of radio advertising. With the encouragement of the Levys and the blessing (and investment) of his family, Paley decided to see if his instincts about radio were right. He moved to New York as president of the Columbia Broadcasting System. David Sarnoff didn't know it yet, but he now had good reason to look over his shoulder. Part of that story is revealed in the sidebar, which profiles two of the most fascinating—and contrasting—personalities who shaped broadcasting.

ADVERTISING COMES OF AGE

In the late 1920s, radio was still uncomfortable with its growing commercialization. That radio came into the living room dictated, according to the thinking of the day, a certain decorum. Hard-sell messages were looked down upon. Network executives fretted over the content of commercials: Was toothpaste a distasteful product to advertise on the air? Should one mention the actual price of the product? One interesting practice in the effort to advertise without really advertising involved a rather circular approach: To gain the advantage of frequent on-air mention without the unseemliness of actually presenting a commercial message, entertainment groups were frequently named after their sponsors. The Cliquot Club Eskimos, for example, were named after a beverage company.

The raw power of the medium meant that subtlety would not last. Slowly, the commercial sales pitch became a common feature of radio. Many stations that had been started as goodwill and publicity vehicles by newspapers, department stores, or other business ventures made the move into commercial sponsorship.

As a result, advertising agencies (companies that design a firm's advertising, advise where to place that advertising, and negotiate the sale of advertising time or space on various media) began to play a major role in radio. In fact, ad agencies began to create and produce programs as well as sponsor them. Radio departments were created at leading ad agencies, and agency personnel coordinated scripts and hired talent. The networks, which received revenue for the airtime, were enthusiastic about this arrangement.

By the mid-1930s, radio was being taken seriously as a major economic power. In fact, some newspapers saw radio as a threat to the very existence of printed media and engaged in such futile protests as refusing to print radio station broadcast schedules. Despite this tactic, radio only became stronger, cresting in popularity during what was known as its "Golden Age."

THE GOLDEN AGE AND MASS ENTERTAINMENT

What intrigued advertisers about radio was the massive audience—both national and local—that the medium could attract week after week. But what troubled radio executives was how to reach and hold this broad and diverse audience. The regular schedule of radio programs could chew up enormous amounts of material, and all this newfound popularity was straining an industry that actually wasn't quite sure what it was supposed to be providing. What was the ideal radio program? There was no existing "tradition" of radio programming, so radio programmers had to look to other models. For example,

- Newspapers knew that columnists appearing in the same part of the paper each day attracted a regular readership, as did comic strips, which provided readers with running stories that needed only small development week after week.

- The motion picture industry had exploited the serial with great success. Multipart adventures and dramas drew regular crowds who faithfully followed the adventures of Tarzan or "The Perils of Pauline."

- A type of stage show known as vaudeville attracted audiences who craved the variety of different acts rapidly performed, one after the other.

These types of programs, adapted for the airwaves, became mainstays of radio in the 1930s and into the 1940s. And radio developed these forms into program styles that were uniquely radio—combining the appeal of the serial with radio's relentless (if still sometimes indirect) advertising message. For example, *Jack Armstrong, All American Boy* was sponsored by Wheaties, a cereal that touted itself as the "Breakfast of Champions." Serials gave listeners the opportunity to become familiar with a cast of characters who would develop over time. The characters actually carried most of the shows; the plots were generally devices to provide the characters with situations and predicaments to negotiate. Imaginative dialogue and sound effects were used, but the real magic took place inside the listeners' heads, who added their own imaginations to the mix and created unseen characters in the theater of the mind.

Vaudeville's radio version evolved into the variety format. Instead of the lighted stage in the darkened theater, the magic sound of laughter emanated from a stage the listener could only imagine. A cross between variety and serial—the situation comedy—soon became a mainstay of radio's Golden Age.

Audiences became devoted fans of stars they had never seen, and some series, such as *Amos 'n Andy*, were so popular that many motion picture theaters would interrupt their schedules when the program came on so as not to suffer a drop in movie attendance.

Programs like situation comedies and escapist adventure, as well as game shows, provided good times in an era when good times were scarce. Radio's Golden Years were terrible times for the nation as a whole. The 1930s and 1940s were a time of deep economic depression followed by a huge overseas war. That war would soon provide a new stage for radio.

RADIO COMES OF AGE

Though some early broadcasts featured news items, such as election returns in 1920 on KDKA, regular reporting of news did not develop quickly. Radio, which had few reporters, was in no position to compete with newspapers, an industry that had two centuries of collective experience and tradition to draw upon, a solid economic base, and a vast network of news providers. In fact, news on radio was often used as filler if announcers were obliged to fill airtime when a performer failed to arrive at the studio. (As often as not, the announcer would read the news right out of the local paper.)

Certain events pointed to radio's potential. One of the most dramatic demonstrations of the power of radio news to cover breaking events—and score a huge "scoop" over newspapers—took place in 1933 when a reporter was describing the expected routine docking of the dirigible *Hindenburg* as it arrived in Lakehurst, New Jersey. The airship exploded while the announcer was on air live—and the announcer's wrenching description of the scene, as burning passengers fell to earth, became a vivid and memorable example of what radio could do.

Before World War II, there was major development of the role of commentators. One of the best known was H. V. Kaltenborne, who had a background as a newspaper editor. Kaltenborne began to give "talks" on the air—which sometimes contained withering criticism of the government. There was some movement to stifle him; after all, the government, in the public interest, licensed radio. Was it proper for Kaltenborne to use public airwaves to roast public officials? Kaltenborne won out and established himself as the dean of radio news commentators; but the fundamental issue of how a private individual can use public airwaves remains more or less an open question today.

As the war in Europe heated up, Americans began to experience the full force of radio. When a CBS radio administrator named Edward R. Murrow began his famous broadcasts from London in the 1930s, radio had been broadcasting from Europe for almost a decade. CBS, led by the young William Paley, had emerged as a competitive force against the powerhouse NBC. A CBS news reporter named Caesar Searchinger pioneered its European broadcasts, which allowed Americans to hear the live voice of the British monarch and later that of playwright George Bernard Shaw, who used the opportunity to castigate the American social system.

But it was Hitler who made Europe seem relevant for Americans. The voices of Hitler and other European leaders such as Churchill, Mussolini, and Chamberlain were literally brought to the American dinner table and living room. Thanks largely to radio, European events began to seem more like American events, and just as important. The isolationism that had characterized American foreign policy since the end of World War I melted away as the world became, figuratively, a much smaller place. Americans increasingly realized that what affected Europe affected America.

When Germany began its Blitzkrieg (German for "Lightning War"), Edward R. Murrow was on hand to describe—in a live broadcast, as it happened—the nightly bombing raids. He conveyed to Americans, sitting in the comfort and security of their homes, the stark, ravaging fear that accompanied the sound of the air-raid sirens. Radio listeners heard the sirens, the explosions, and the screams, while Murrow's rich, clipped baritone described the scene in economical phrases that captured the sights, the sounds, and even the smells of his surroundings:

> This ... is London. (*Bombs explode in background.*) There are no words to describe the thing that is happening. The courage of the people, the flash and roar of the guns rolling down the streets, the stench of the air raid shelters.

Gradually, Americans became aware that Hitler must be stopped. Europe had been at war for years, while America sat on the sideline. Americans, sickened by the devastation of World War I, justifiably wanted no part of another European conflict. President Franklin Delano Roosevelt believed that America must enter the war, and he used radio as a medium to present this view. Roosevelt recognized the value of radio as a mass medium with an intimate quality. He broadcast what became known as "fireside chats," friendly, encouraging conversations, which originally dealt with his plans to work the country out of its Depression troubles. Later, his topic turned to war. Americans in cities, in towns, and on farms all over the country tuned in to hear their president, often speaking like a father, offering bits of hope.

Then, in early December of 1941, President Roosevelt spoke before a joint session of Congress, his speech carried live by radio.

> Yesterday, December 7th, 1941, a date that will live in infamy, the United States of America was suddenly and deliberately attacked by naval and air forces of the Empire of Japan ... I ask Congress to declare that since the unprovoked and dastardly attack by Japan ... a state of war has existed between the United States and the Japanese Empire.

Congress acted on the President's request, and the United States went to war. Sons, brothers, husbands, and fathers volunteered or were drafted. The families who stayed behind relied more and more on radio to keep them in touch with developments. Reports from overseas were sent by shortwave radio to network control rooms in this country, which then fed them out to their affiliated stations.

By the end of the war, radio journalists had become proficient at gathering news that was startling in its immediacy. Murrow and a seasoned team of correspondents formed the nucleus of a news organization that would come to represent a major force of excellence in American journalism. CBS became the model for other networks as they developed worldwide news organizations of their own.

Radio news, and radio, entered the 1950s at a crest of power, prestige, and popularity. Then the roof fell in.

TELEVISION LOWERS THE BOOM

Television had been demonstrated at the 1936 World Fair (covered by the *New York Times*, which offered the observation that television's commercial possibilities were doubtful). It was perfected in the 1940s and became a household fixture in the 1950s. At first, many in radio were openly skeptical of the possibility of television's becoming a respected and respectable medium. Many of the star newspeople at CBS avoided the medium because they viewed it as a short-lived gimmick.

That gimmick crushed radio like a steamroller. Stars who could be seen had much more appeal than those who could only be heard. Personalities like Jack Benny made the crossover to television and saw their audiences increase dramatically. Television began to exploit its own technical advantages, becoming more than just radio with pictures. Milton Berle, for example, used elaborate sight gags to produce his own variety of slapstick. Ernie Kovaks used special effects, often tying up breathtakingly expensive studios for hours to produce a visual that would last only a couple of seconds.

Radio's magic appeared to be gone; it simply could not compete with a medium like television. But it could leave the mass audience to television and reinvent itself as a medium that appealed to a more targeted listenership.

Radio targeted its audience through airplay of recorded music, song after song. This was not exactly a new practice, having been "invented," according to radio legend, in the 1930s when an announcer named Martin Block popularized the format in a program called *Make-Believe Ballroom*. Block reportedly came up with the idea when a studio orchestra failed to show up and he needed to fill time. He is credited with developing the modern "disc jockey" format, which was later adapted into programs like *Your Hit Parade*. These programs played the most popular tunes of the week and were in part responsible for the evolution of the Top 40 format.

Music on radio was generally an eclectic mix well into the 1950s. Disc jockeys might play some classical, followed by jazz, followed by big band, and then followed by whatever the disc jockey wanted to play. Disc jockeys had developed considerable skill in weaving all this together. They became consummate professionals, able to entertain, persuade, and motivate. What's more, they had fun doing it. And when television threatened to dismantle the radio industry, the talent of the emerging corps of disc jockeys was melded with a powerful new force: rock 'n' roll music and the lifestyle that went with it.

ROCK SAVES RADIO

As rock evolved from rhythm and blues, the youth of the nation became captivated with this new form of musical expression. Rock in the 1950s was rebellious, a refreshing change from the heavy cloak of conformity that settled over the postwar United States. Young people wanted more of a role in society. Coincidentally, they also were developing quite a bit of disposable income during these prosperous years.

Radio stations sensed this new awakening, and as millions tuned into the sounds of early rockers like Bill Haley and the Comets, Carl Perkins, and Ferlin Husky, radio programmers discovered something of enormous importance: This was more than music. Rock was a lifestyle.

The old hit-parade format—playing the most popular songs of the week according to record sales—was now used to program stations' broadcast schedules. It was a relatively easy format to implement, even in the tiniest radio station: All you had to do was read one of a number of record industry publications and play the top 40 most popular cuts.

As it turned out, making money off Top 40 was fairly easy, too. Soft drink manufacturers, traditionally heavy advertisers, found that they had a direct pipeline into the youthful lifestyle—in one case, they called it joining the "Pepsi Generation." Grooming products and the rapidly growing fast-food market all fueled radio's comeback.

Radio had found a new and eloquent voice. Disc jockeys such as Allen Freed, who developed the concept of "personality" as an essential component of Top 40 radio, became stars. Radio itself became a powerful force in the music world, so much so that some radio programmers engaged in an unethical and illegal practice called payola, where—in return for a bribe from the record company—they would give a certain cut heavy airplay.

The youth culture was the biggest, but not the only, segment of the population to be intrigued by the newly rediscovered music box. Adults found radio to be a fine companion; development of new, small components called transistors (replacements for the bulky vacuum tubes invented by de Forest) meant that radio could travel to the beach, to the backyard, and, most notably, in the car.

RADIO TUNES INTO ITS AUDIENCE

Programmers became aware that enormous numbers of commuters were driving to and from work in the morning and evening, and once radios became commonplace in cars, the programmers exploited this lucrative "drive time." Soon a station could be identified by its format, a term that came to mean the type of

SIDEBAR • DAVID SARNOFF AND WILLIAM S. PALEY

Among other things, David Sarnoff liked to be remembered for his role in an international tragedy when he was in his early twenties, long before he became known for his contributions to radio and television broadcasting. Sarnoff had come to this country from Russia with his family at the turn of the century. He took a job with the Marconi Wireless Telegraph Company of America and became a highly competent operator, sending and receiving the dots and dashes of Morse code. According to an official biographer's story, Sarnoff can take the credit for notifying the world on April 14, 1912, that the luxury ship *Titanic* had struck an iceberg in the North Atlantic and had sunk, with the loss of more than 1,500 lives. Sarnoff allegedly stayed at his post for 72 hours with almost no food or rest, acting as the information link between the scene of the disaster and the mainland.

We say "allegedly" because there are serious questions about whether the account of Sarnoff's heroism is accurate. Later information shows that Sarnoff may have been carried away when he spoke with his biographer and portrayed himself as the only link to the *Titanic* when, in fact, other operators may have played significant roles as well. Like many great men, Sarnoff had an impressive ego, and his knack for self-promotion likely led him to play with the facts.

Nonetheless, his place in history is assured. From very humble beginnings, he moved successfully through the Marconi Company to the Radio Corporation of America, where he served as chief executive officer from 1947 until his death in 1971. He was an early proponent of radio broadcasting when others failed to see its potential, and he was a major force in the development of television.

William S. Paley grew up in comfort, unlike David Sarnoff, the man who would become his great business competitor. But Paley wasn't really satisfied as an executive in his family's cigar company. He found the challenge of his life in the young and not-at-all prosperous radio network, the Columbia Broadcasting System. Paley was urbane and could be a charmer, but he was also a shrewd businessman who nursed CBS to health and then built it into a colossus. In the late 1940s, during the Golden Age of radio, Paley made a swift and dramatic move on NBC. He staged a "talent raid" on the other network, luring many of its top stars to CBS. In both radio and television, Paley was noted for his programming genius and his appreciation of talent.

As World War II approached, Paley supported establishment of a serious radio news operation for CBS. CBS News, initially in radio, then in television, became known as the premier broadcast news division. With the help of correspondent Edward R. Murrow and colleagues Eric Sevareid, Charles Collingwood, William Shirer, and others, CBS set journalistic standards for the broadcast industry. Paley was proud of his news division, which was not expected to be a profit center. It was "the crown jewel" in the CBS empire.

Under Paley, the respected CBS Labs developed the long-playing record. But there were also some missteps along the way. In the 1940s, the CBS-developed color television system lost out to the RCA version. In the 1960s, during a period when many corporations went on a diversification spree, CBS bought up several companies, including the New York Yankees (which then dropped from first to last place in a scant two years), a guitar company, and a toy company. In later years, CBS divested itself of most of these not-very-successful acquisitions, deciding to concentrate on its core businesses. Despite these setbacks, Paley, like Sarnoff, is a truly historic figure in the saga of broadcasting.

"Sarnoff and Paley" was written by Michael C. Ludlum exclusively for *Modern Radio Production*. Used with permission.

music played on the station. A station was usually known as Top 40, or Country and Western. Those that chose a middle path were called middle-of-the-road (MOR).

Through the 1960s, methods of sampling the audience became more sophisticated, and the distinctions among audiences were fine tuned. By the late 1960s, whereas previously perhaps four or five stations had dominated a major metropolitan area, now there was room for many more because of the niche markets that had been discovered and cultivated.

Almost all this growth came on the AM band. (AM stands for amplitude modulation.) There were several reasons for AM growth. The FM (frequency modulation) band had been available for years, but confusion over assigning frequencies had caused that technology to languish. Getting an FM radio for your car was an expensive proposition, and home sets equipped to receive FM often did not work very well.

In the late 1960s, significant advances were made in the quality of receivers as well as the capability of stations to transmit a high-quality FM signal. Once FM was perfected, it outshone AM in sound fidelity, because the signal is less prone to interference and because FM stations are assigned a broader range of frequencies, meaning that their signals can carry more sound information. Once-unused FM frequencies became dominant powerhouses, and AM suffered. However, after incurring severe losses in the 1980s, AM radio stations have returned to relative health, many of them by programming talk and news, two formats that have continued to increase in popularity.

Glossary

AC See *adult contemporary*.

acoustics The study of sound. Also, the properties of a studio, room, or concert hall that contribute to the quality of the sound heard in it.

actuality The sound of an event, recorded or broadcast at the time the event took place. Also called a sound bite.

ad-lib To speak over the air without a prepared script.

adult alternative A radio format featuring jazz and compatible vocals.

adult contemporary (AC) A wide-ranging radio format that generally includes a few current popular hits, recent hits, and older songs.

adult standards A middle-of-the-road radio format, generally featuring older music, including show tunes and durable vocalists.

air monitor A source on the console that monitors the output of the station as it is received over the air. It monitors the actual output of the transmitter rather than an output from the console or any other piece of equipment along the audio chain.

airshift Period during which any particular radio operator puts programming on the air at a radio station.

album rock A radio format that features long, heavy-rock cuts and is primarily aimed toward a fairly young male audience. Also called album-oriented rock.

album-oriented rock (AOR) See *album rock*.

AMBER alert America's Missing: BroadcastEmergency Response. A system developed by broadcasters to alert citizens to, and provide information about, missing children.

ambient noise Noise randomly occurring in an environment.

amplification The raising of the volume or strength of a signal.

amplifier A device used to raise the volume or strength of a signal.

amplitude The property of a sound wave or electrical signal that determines its magnitude.

analog In radio, a type of recorded sound source that produces a sound wave similar to the original wave. Traditional methods of reproducing sounds, such as phonograph records and standard audiotape, use analog methods rather than digital recording.

analog-to-digital converter (A-to-D converter) An electronic device that converts analog audio into digital electronic pulses.

AOR See *album rock*.

ASCAP American Society of Composers and Publishers, a music-licensing agency.

ATRAC (Adaptive Transform Acoustic Coding) A method of compressing digital audio sound files using psychoacoustic principles.

attack time The length of time an audio processing unit takes to activate the compressor after a particular sound affects it.

audio Electronically transmitted or received sound.

audiotape Thin tape used to record sound that has been transduced into a magnetic signal.

audition A mode of console operation in which sound can be channeled into a speaker without being fed to the on-air transmitter. Also, assessing material or talent in advance of production.

automation Using machinery to put program elements on the air; typically reduces the need for human workers.

average quarter-hour (AQH) persons The number of listeners who tuned in to a specific quarter-hour for at least five minutes.

back-announce Identify musical selections after they are played.

backsell See *back-announce*.

backtracking Counterclockwise rotation of a disc on a broadcast turntable; part of the sequence of functions used to cue a record.

bed See *music bed*.

bidirectional A microphone pickup pattern in which sound sources are accepted from two opposite directions—in front of and in back of the mic—but not from the sides.

billboard A rundown of information to be fed by an audio service; usually printed but sometimes spoken.

binary The digital computer's method of using two pulses—on and off—to encode computer language.

bit A binary digit. The smallest portion of computer language.

BMI Broadcast Music International, a music licensing agency.

board An audio control console.

broadcast wave format (BWF) .WAV audio files that carry metadata that can be used by broadcast automation systems.

bus A junction of circuits where the outputs of a number of sound sources are mixed together.

BWF Broadcast WAV format sound file. See *WAV format*.

bytes Digital words made up of 8 bits that can represent values between 0 and 255. CDs use bytes per sample to detail frequency and loudness values.

capacitor A device for storage of electrical signals, used (among other functions) as an element in a condenser microphone. *Condenser* is an old-fashioned term for *capacitor*.

capstan A revolving metal post on a tape deck that determines the speed of the tape's movement. It turns the pinch roller.

cardioid A microphone pickup pattern that is unidirectional and heart-shaped.

carousel A circular, rotating device for automatically playing cartridges.

cartridge The element of a turntable assembly that converts vibrations of the stylus into electrical energy. See also *cartridge tape*.

cartridge machine A unit that plays and records cartridge tapes. Today the term *cart machine* often refers to a hard disk recorder that functions like an analog cartridge machine.

cartridge tape A continuous loop of recording tape housed in a plastic case. Usually called a cart.

cassette Two small reels of tape enclosed in a plastic case.

CD See *compact disc*.

CD–DA file (compact disc–digital audio) The sound file format standard for compact discs.

central processing unit (CPU) The brain of a computer; the circuitry that performs calculations.

channel The route followed by a signal as it travels through the components of a system. Also, an input or output designation on an audio control console.

channel bouncing A production technique that moves sound from one speaker to another. Sometimes called pan potting.

classic rock A radio format featuring album rock without new releases.

classical Music format that plays standard-form orchestral and choral pieces; also referred to as concert music.

codec An abbreviation for coder/decoder, a device that encodes audio signals into digital pulses for use with the public telephone system. At the station the decoder translates the encoded signal back into audio.

coincident mics Two cardioid mics set up to cross at approximately a 90-degree angle; a standard method of recording.

coloration The nuances of sound that give it a particular character.

combo Simultaneously operating the audio console and announcing over the air. Doing this is usually called working combo.

compact disc (CD) A disc that is recorded digitally and played back by laser-beam readout.

compact disc (CD) player A device to play back a digitally encoded disc using a laser that reads the code on the disc.

complex waveform A visual representation, usually on a computer or an oscilloscope, of the various sound waves that make up a particular sound.

compression Process used to minimize distortion by reducing the differences in level between low- and high-volume segments of a recorded or broadcast sound.

condenser mic A microphone that contains a capacitor as an element and typically requires an external power supply. Changes in the position of the vibrating diaphragm of the mic alter the strength of the charge held by the electrical element.

console A device for amplifying, routing, and mixing audio signals.

contemporary Christian A religious format featuring Christian rock and up-tempo songs.

contemporary (current) hit radio (CHR) See *Top 40.*

cost per point (CPP) A measure of how much it costs to "buy" one rating point in a particular market.

cost per thousand (CPM) The cost of reaching a thousand listeners.

country A radio format with rural roots but not limited to rural listeners.

CPM See *cost per thousand.*

CPP See *cost per point.*

CPU See *central processing unit.*

cross-fade Gradual replacement of one sound source with another. One sound is faded out and the other is simultaneously faded up. At one point, their sound levels are the same.

crossover A song that bridges two categories of music, such as country and pop.

cue To ready a record or tape playback device so that it will play at the first point of sound or at some other desired starting point. Also, to indicate by hand signal or other means the desired time to begin a performing activity. Also, a channel on a console that allows you to hear a sound source without putting it on the air.

cue tone A sound meant to convey a signal to an operator or to an automated device.

cume Cumulative audience measure. A measure that uses statistical interpretation to determine the number of unduplicated radio audience listeners.

current hit radio See *Top 40.*

cut A segment of recorded sound on a disc or tape. Also, to record a segment of audio production, such as a commercial or public service announcement.

cycle One complete movement of a sound or electrical wave through its naturally occurring pattern to its starting point.

databurst Series of digital pulses that activates the station's Emergency Alert System monitor.

daypart Segment of the broadcast day. Dayparts include morning drive (6–10 A.M.), midday (10 A.M.–3 P.M.), afternoon drive (3–6 P.M.), and evening (6 P.M.–12 A.M.).

dead air Silence over the air.

dead-potting Starting an audio source with the pot closed; usually done at a carefully calculated moment, with the goal of finishing the audio source (such as a song) at an exact time.

decibel As applied to sound, a relative measure of volume.

delegation switch A device that allows the operator of a console to choose which of two or more sources is to be controlled by a particular pot.

demographics Statistical representation of a population; usually used in radio to refer to the characteristics of the listening audience.

diaphragm The portion of a microphone that vibrates in response to sound.

digital Based on the translation of an original sound source into binary computer language.

digital audio workstation (DAW) A computer with audio recording software or a standalone digital interface connected to a computer designed to record, edit, and play back digital sound files.

digital audiotape Audiotape combined with an audiotape recording system that allows sound to be recorded in binary computer language.

digital-to-analog (D-to-A) converter An electronic interface that converts digital sound files into analog audio playback.

directional mic A microphone that picks up sound from only one direction. Also called a unidirectional mic.

DIRS Disaster Information Reporting System. Used in conjunction with the Emergency Alert System to report information about local infrastructure during times of national or regional disasters.

disc A phonograph record or compact disc.

disc jockey (DJ) A staff announcer who acts as host of a music program.

distortion A change or alteration in the quality of sound that impairs the listener's ability to identify it with its source.

Dolby Trade name of a noise-reduction system.

donut In radio production, a recorded audio segment that provides an introduction, an ending, and a music bed. An announcer uses the segment as a production aid by reading copy over the music bed, thereby filling the "hole" in the donut.

doubletracking Recording a voice and then recording another version of the voice that has been slightly altered electronically. When both voices are mixed and played back, an eerie effect results.

downlink The method by which a receiver on earth can pick up a transmission from a satellite.

dubbing Recording sound from one recorded source to another. Also, the process of copying a digital sound file.

ducking Fading music or sound effects tracks under voice.

DVD Digital Versatile Discs (also Digital Video Discs). Digital medium that provides for high-resolution sound playback, including surround-sound formats.

dynamic mic A mic in which a coil moves through a magnetic field in response to sound vibration sensed by the diaphragm of the mic.

dynamic range The difference in volume between the loudest and quietest sounds of a source.

echo Repetition of a sound, usually caused by the reflection of the source bouncing off a hard surface. Also, an electronic special effect created by using a delay unit or by feeding back the output of a tape machine's playback head while recording.

edit point A location on a DAW timeline or other playback source where the producer wants the edit to begin or end.

editing In audio production, the alteration of a structure of a recorded sound—most commonly through the electronic manipulation of audio segments or files.

Shortening, reordering, and replacing audio segments are common editing functions.

editing and production structures Patterns of editing commonly used in radio production to establish music, voice under, voice up, cross-fade, voice out, music up, music wrap, voice wrap, and various combinations of these patterns.

electromagnetic field An area containing patterned magnetic waves produced by electricity.

electronic splicing (editing) The removal of portions of a recording and the subsequent reassembly of the remaining material by means of electronic equipment rather than by physically cutting or splicing the tape.

element The part of a microphone that transduces sound into electrical energy.

Emergency Alert System (EAS) A federal network for broadcasting information to the public, activated in times of war, natural disaster, or other dire circumstance.

equalization Alteration of a sound source as a result of varying its frequency balance.

equalizer A device for boosting, limiting, or eliminating certain frequencies of audio.

erase head The part of the head system of a tape unit that removes the recorded signals from tape.

establish To play a recognizable and noticeable portion of a sound source. For example, a producer may establish a music theme before potting it down.

extracting Importing a sound file into a DAW from a different recorded medium such as a CD. Also called ripping.

fact sheet A listing of facts given to an announcer as a guide for delivering an ad-lib commercial.

fade To bring a sound source up or down on an audio console at a given rate of speed (usually slowly).

fader See vertical/slide fader.

false ending In some recorded material, an apparent end of the recorded segment that is in fact not the end.

feedback Reamplification of a sound, resulting in a loud squeal from a loudspeaker; often caused by mic pickup of the output of a speaker that is carrying the sound being picked up by the mic; also occurs when the record head of a tape machine receives the output signal of the same recorder.

filter An electronic system that reduces or eliminates sound of designated frequencies.

flanger Device for throwing a sound and its mirror image out of phase to produce unusual sound effects.

flanging Slightly delaying reproduction of a source and then mixing the reproduced sound with the original source of the sound to produce a special effect.

flash memory Storage devices that use electronically erasable programmable memory (EEPROM) to store digital files. Flash memory may be used over and over again.

flat response A faithful response by a microphone.

format A radio station's programming strategy, evolved to attract a particular audience; the mix of all elements of a station's sound, including the type of music played and style of announcing.

formatics The study of developing and applying generic programming concepts for radio.

forward echo An echo in reverse, used as a special effect; the echo comes first, and the sound follows.

frequency The number of times a sound wave repeats itself in 1 second—expressed in cycles per second (cps) or hertz (Hz). Also, the average number of times a theoretical listener hears a commercial.

frequency response The range of frequencies that can be produced by an audio system.

front-selling Announcing upcoming musical selections before they are played.

full track A method of recording in which the signal is placed over the entire width of a tape.

gate An electronic device that can open or close based on a threshold of sound. Used in recording to dry up tracks and prevent unwanted extraneous noise.

generation In analog recording, the term used to refer to how many times a copy of a sound file has been made from a master tape. The first generation tape would be a direct copy of a master tape. The second generation would be a copy of the first copy.

geostationary Staying in an orbit over the same part of the earth, as a result of moving in tandem with the earth's rotation.

graphic equalizer A device for tailoring sound; the controls produce a visual representation of the frequency response, hence the term *graphic*.

grooves The continuous narrow channel in a phonograph record that is tracked by the stylus.

gross impression The total number of exposures to a commercial.

gross rating point A way of expressing gross impressions as a rating figure. AQH ratings multiplied by the total number of commercials played in those quarter-hours determines gross rating points.

GSM (Groupe Spécial Mobile) Cellular Type of cellular phone service that can support remote transmission.

half-track A method of recording in which signals are simultaneously placed on two tracks (one-half of the tape width each) of a tape, thus making stereo recording possible. Also called two-track.

hardware The physical equipment of a computer system, or the machinery connected to a computer system.

hardwired When referring to equipment, this means physically wired together.

harmonics Frequencies related to a fundamental frequency that are multiples of the original. The mixture of harmonics with the fundamental gives a sound its particular timbre or tonal color.

heads The devices on a tape machine that impart a signal to the tape; they generally consist of an erase head, a record head, and a playback head. The erase head scrambles the iron oxide particles on the tape, the record head arranges the particles in order, and the playback head reads the pattern formed by the record head.

headset mic A mic that fits directly on the head, using earpieces; useful for sports announcers.

headstack A post on which multiple recording heads are placed one on top of the other.

hertz (Hz) A unit of frequency (identical to cycles per second) named after Heinrich Hertz, whose discoveries made radio transmission possible.

high fidelity Giving high-quality, faithful reproduction.

high-pass filter A filter that allows only high frequencies to pass, chopping off lower frequencies; used, for example, to eliminate a low-pitch rumble.

hot-potting Starting a sound source with the pot open.

hypercardioid A microphone pickup pattern that is very narrow, heart-shaped, and unidirectional.

inverse pyramid A method of news writing whereby the most important details of a story are given at the beginning or top. The story can then be cut from the bottom.

iron oxide Rust; the substance on a magnetic tape that holds the signal.

ISDN Integrated services digital network. A type of data line used by broadcasters to link remote locations of network affiliates.

isolated-component recording Recording various components of an orchestra, or other multiple-component sound source, using a separate mic to record each component. The output of each mic is recorded on a separate channel. These are mixed after the recording session.

jazz Music format characterized by syncopation and melodic variations, frequently improvised by the performer.

key On an audio console, the device for turning a pot (and through it, a sound source) on and off. Also, the musical scheme in which the notes of a song fall.

lavalier mic A small mic that hangs from a string around the announcer's neck or clips to the announcer's clothing; not widely used in radio production.

lead The beginning sentence or sentences of a news story—ostensibly the most important part of the story.

levels The volumes of signals, usually as read by a VU meter.

limiter A device used to suppress dynamic levels of a reproduced sound above a preset limit in order to provide a more constant output level.

line level signals Audio signals sent to a console from playback devices such as computers, CD players, and other external devices with their own electronics.

live assist A method whereby automation is used to help an operator perform tasks more simply and efficiently.

log The station's official record of what was aired during a broadcast day.

loops Small audio segments that can be repeated or strung together to create longer musical beds. Also, small midi files that accomplish the same purpose using a sequencer.

lossy A data compression scheme where some of the original data is lost.

loudspeaker A device for reproducing sound by transducing it from audio into sound.

low-pass filter A filter that allows only low frequencies to pass, chopping off the highs; used, for example, to eliminate a hiss.

magnetic tape In radio production, audiotape composed of a backing strip coated with iron oxide particles.

When the particles are aligned in response to a signal in an analog or digital recording device, the signal can be stored and later played back as sound.

master pot The potentiometer (volume control) that governs the entire output of a console.

metadata Information contained within a computer file. In the BWF format, information about the song title, time, and artist can be used for automating radio stations.

microchip A small circuit produced by a photographic process, used in computer technology.

microphone A transducer that converts sound energy into an electrical signal, which may then be amplified, recorded, or broadcast.

middle-side miking Technique for total-sound recording, involving a bidirectional mic picking up sound from the sides of the performing area and a cardioid mic in the middle; used to produce a very spacious sound.

MIDI A device for interfacing a number of sound-producing instruments with a computer and each other.

MiniDisc A magneto-optical recording system developed by Sony. Each disc can hold about 80 minutes of stereo recording on a maximum of 255 tracks.

MiniDisc Machines that can be used for recording, playback of spot announcements, and editing.

mix To combine a number of sound sources.

mix-minus Console circuitry that allows the producer to use the telephone to interview guests without creating feedback from the interviewer's mic in the control room.

modern rock A radio format featuring very progressive music.

modulation The electrical imprint of a sound signal on an audio or radio wave.

monitor Loudspeaker in a sound studio or control room.

motional energy Energy produced by movement, such as sound. Sound qualifies as motional energy because it is produced by a physical vibration in molecules in the air or in some other medium.

mouse A device for controlling the movement of information on a computer screen.

moving-coil mic A microphone whose characteristic element is a coil that moves through a magnetic field (thereby producing an electric signal) in response to the movement of a diaphragm, which vibrates in response to sound waves.

MP3 format (MPEG-1, Audio Layer III) Audio sound file format developed for use of Motion Picture Experts Group (MPEG) video. The format is a compressed audio format that lends itself well to Internet transmission. Many portable audio players use the MP3 format.

multichannel A type of console used in sound recording that is capable of isolating a number of channels from one another.

multiple A set-up that allows many mics to be plugged into a sound source; useful for public events where many journalists will be using tape recorders.

multitrack A device that records several audio sources, usually laid down on one tape.

music bed A segment of recorded music used as background sound in a broadcast production (usually a commercial). See also *donut*.

muting system A device that automatically cuts the control room speaker to prevent feedback when a mic is opened.

Mylar A substance used as a backing for audiotape; it stretches more easily than acetate.

needle drop The means of measuring usage of material from a licensed set of sound effects or music beds. Fees are charged "per needle drop."

network A linkage of broadcast stations in which a central programming source supplies material to the individual stations making up the system.

new rock See *modern rock*.

news/talk A radio format that is a combination of call in, live interview, and news.

newswire News feed from a service such as the Associated Press. Today, the term is a misnomer because the source is usually a satellite downlink, not a teletype wire.

normal connection The way in which an engineering staff routes a signal under normal circumstances. If you want to change the pattern, you can use a patchcord to "break the normal."

omnidirectional A microphone pickup pattern that is capable of picking up sound sources equally well from all directions.

optimum effective scheduling (OES) A mathematical formula that determines the number of people

who hear a radio spot three or more times and, at the same time, comprise at least 50 percent of the total audience.

output Anything that is fed out of an audio system.

overdub To add another audio element to an existing one. For example, a singer can listen to his or her previously recorded work while recording (overdubbing) a harmony part.

pan pot A control that allows a producer to move a sound source from the left stereo channel to the right one, or vice versa.

parabolic mic A microphone positioned in a reflecting dish that has a three-dimensional parabolic shape; used to pick up distant sounds.

parametric equalizer A type of equalizer that allows an operator to select one particular frequency and boost or lower that frequency.

patchbay A device in which patchcords are plugged for the purpose of routing signals.

patchcord A wire with an easily inserted connection, used to reroute signals for the convenience of the operator.

patching A method of changing the routing of a signal through an audio system. Also, a connection that is temporarily placed between audio inputs and outputs.

PFL Pre Fade Level Allows for the adjustment of audio signal before the audio console fader.

phase synchronicity When two or more sounds reach a mic at the same time, the sounds are said to be in phase, and their amplitudes combine. When the sounds reach the mic at different times, they are called out of phase, and they cancel each other. A similar principle applies to electrical waves.

pickup pattern A representation of the area within which a mic effectively picks up sound, based on a 360-degree polar pattern.

pinch roller A rubber wheel, driven by the capstan on a tape deck, that keeps the tape moving at the correct speed.

pitch The ear's and mind's imprecise interpretation of the frequency of a sound.

plate (platter) The part of a turntable that holds the disc and revolves.

playback head The part of the head system in a tape recorder or deck that reads the patterns created on tape by the record head and produces an electrical signal conveying this information to the rest of the playback system.

playback only Designation for a cartridge machine or other audio unit that does not have a recording capability.

podcast A radio program that is made to be streamed via the Internet to a small, portable device such as an iPod.

polar pattern A graph consisting of concentric circles that are assigned decreasing values toward the center of the graph; a pattern superimposed on the graph represents the area within which the microphone effectively picks up sound.

pop filter A wind-blocking screen in or on a microphone, designed to prevent the blasting or popping noise caused by announcers who pop their *p*'s and *b*'s.

popping An undesirable explosive sound caused by too-vigorous pronunciation of sounds such as *p* and *b*.

pot Short for potentiometer. A device on an audio console that controls volume.

potentiometer See *pot*.

preamp Short for preamplifier. A small amplifier that boosts a signal, usually up to line level. It generally accomplishes the first step in the amplification process.

preamplifier See *preamp*.

pressure-gradient mic Another name for a ribbon mic, which operates by measuring the difference in pressure between one side of the ribbon and the other.

producer A person who manipulates radio equipment to construct a program and achieve an effect.

production The process of manipulating sound elements with radio equipment to transmit a message and achieve an effect.

production library A collection of music or sound effects used in production. Production libraries are generally leased but sometimes bought outright; increasingly, they are appearing on compact discs.

program A mode of operation in which sound can be channeled through the console to the on-air transmitter.

programming The selection and arrangement of music, speech, and other program elements in a way that appeals to the station's listeners.

proximity effect A property certain mics have of accentuating lower frequencies as sound sources move closer.

public affairs programming Program elements in the general public interest.

public service announcements (PSAs) Program elements designed to provide the public with needed information.

quantization The process of converting a sound waveform into a binary computer word that expresses both frequency and amplitude.

quarter track A method of recording in which individual channels are laid down on each of four tracks of a tape.

RAM See *random-access memory*.

random-access memory (RAM) In a computer, the area in which software can be loaded and information can be loaded and retrieved.

range The portion of the frequency spectrum that a microphone or other audio element can reproduce.

rarefaction An area in which air molecules become less dense; the opposite of compression. Sound waves are carried through the air by a series of rarefactions and compressions.

rating A percentage of the total available audience.

rating services The companies that collect data about radio station listenership.

reach A measure of how many different listeners hear a commercial.

read-only memory (ROM) The area of a computer where information (especially that which has been factory installed) can be read but not accessed.

record head The part of the head system in a tape recorder that imprints the sound pattern on the magnetic tape.

release time The length of time it takes for an audio processing unit to let a signal return to its previous level.

remote Production done on location, as opposed to in a studio.

render The time it takes for a DAW to perform an effect or execute a software instruction.

reverb Short for reverberation. An effect produced with an electronic device that adds a time delay to a sound source and then adds it back to the signal.

reverberation See *reverb*.

ribbon mic A microphone with a paper-thin element that vibrates in response to the velocity of sound waves.

The element is suspended in a magnetic field that converts the sound into an electrical signal.

riding levels Keeping close watch on the strength of signals to ensure that the program is not overmodulated. Also known as riding gain.

rock Music format featuring electric guitars and drums. Subgenres include modern rock, classic rock, and alternative rock.

ROM See *read-only memory.*

routing Channeling an audio signal.

routing switcher An electronic switch that can route the input and output signals. Routing switchers take the place of manual patch panels.

sample and hold circuit Electronic circuit used to convert analog audio into digitized audio.

sampling The process of converting analog audio into digital bits for use in a computer or synthesizer.

sampling frequency The number of times per second (expressed in Hz) a digital recording unit takes a sample of a sound source.

satellite An orbiting device that, among other things, retransmits signals to a broad portion of the earth's surface.

segue The transition between two recordings played consecutively without interruption.

SFX Sound effects.

shape As a component of frequency response, the level of response at various frequencies within a mic's range; basically, the form of the graph that indicates the mic's sensitivity at various frequencies.

share The percentage of people who are actually listening to a station.

shotgun mic A long, narrow mic that has a very narrow, highly directional pickup pattern.

sibilance The noticeable prominence of hissy *s* sounds.

signal-to-noise ratio The ratio (expressed in decibels) between the intended sounds of a recording or broadcast and the undesirable noise of a system.

sine wave A visual representation of a sound wave as it moves through its various values of compression and rarefaction.

slipcueing Finding the starting point of a disc by slipping it back and forth on the turntable plate without allowing the plate to move. Often used interchangeably (though somewhat inaccurately) with slipstarting.

slug A heading used by a wire service for quick identification of a story. (Example: WEATHER FOR SEVEN WESTERN COUNTIES.)

software The programs run by a computer.

solid-state Describes electronic equipment that operates without vacuum tubes.

solo A control on a multitrack console that mutes other inputs so that the remaining channel can be heard alone.

sound The perception by the ear or by some other instrument of waves resulting from the vibration of air molecules.

sound bite A piece of sound recorded at the scene of a story and integrated into a newscast. Often used synonymously with actuality, but the term *sound bite* is more commonly used in radio if the piece of sound is a sound effect, such as a siren screaming.

sound effect Any sound other than music or speech that is used to help create an image, evoke an emotion, compress time, clarify a situation, or reinforce a message. Abbreviated as SFX in scripts.

sound envelope The waveform that represents a sound. In modern usage, the term usually refers to the waveform representation on a computer screen produced by means of a MIDI or other digital editing device.

sound shapers Devices on a recording console that can be used to change the physical characteristics of the audio signal.

spaced-pair mics Two microphones set up parallel to each other, one or two feet apart; used in stereo recording to produce a very broad sound.

Spanish A popular program format that features musical styles with a distinctive Latin flavor.

spatial enhancers Devices used to alter the stereo signal to give the impression of a larger physical environment—that is, to create the impression of a very large hall.

splicing The process of joining together two pieces of recording tape, usually with the aid of an editing block and adhesive tape made specifically for this purpose, in order to edit recorded material or to repair broken tape.

spot A prerecorded announcement (usually a commercial).

stereo Using two channels for sound reproduction in order to create the illusion of depth and spaciousness.

stinger A brief musical opening designed to attract attention. Increasingly, stingers are produced by digital technology.

stopset The time when an announcer talks or commercials are played after a music set has played.

streaming Technology that allows an end user to listen to an audio file as the signal is being transferred from a remote server. Quicktime and Real Audio are examples of streaming technology.

stylus The portion of a phonograph that makes contact with the grooves in a record and vibrates in response to the shape of the grooves. The vibrations create an electrical signal in the cartridge, and this signal is subsequently fed into an amplifier and distributed within an audio system.

submixer A miniature console through which several sources can be output to one of several submasters on a full-size multichannel console.

supercardioid A microphone pickup pattern that is narrow, heart-shaped, and unidirectional and falls somewhere between a cardioid pattern and a hypercardioid pattern.

supply reel The reel on a tape recorder from which tape spools during play.

supply spool The part of the DAT cassette that contains the audiotape. Tape unwinds from the supply spool across the head and onto the takeup spool.

surround sound Audio format that uses five or more channels to reproduce audio with a 360-degree sound perspective. Different systems include Pro Logic or Neural Audio surround sound.

syndicators Firms that distribute programs or program material to individual radio stations for a fee.

synthesizer An electronic musical instrument that resembles an organ but can produce a wide range of sounds.

switched 56 Data service that supports transmission of digital information at the rate of 56 kilobits per second.

T-1 High-speed data line that supports program services such as Web streaming and podcasting.

takeup reel The reel on a tape recorder that pulls and collects tape during play.

takeup spool The part of the DAT cassette where tape is collected once it has been pulled across the recording head.

tape guide Equipment on a tape deck that keeps the moving tape in a precise position.

task-oriented sequence The arrangement of radio production tasks in the most convenient and efficient order for accomplishing them within the confines of the production studio. Thus, doing the ending of a commercial first may actually be preferable under some circumstances.

telco drop The point at which a telephone company terminates a transmission line for carrying a remote signal back to the studio from the site of a remote broadcast. The station's remote equipment is connected to the drop.

telephone hybrid Device that allows board operators to bring telephone calls into the audio console with good sound quality.

time spent listening (TSL) A measure of the average time an individual listener tunes in to the station.

tonearm The movable arm on a turntable unit that holds the stylus and cartridge.

tonic The fundamental note that determines the rest of the musical notes that will form a proper chord.

Top 40 A radio format that may include many of the most popular songs or heavy dayparting (specially designed formats for the changing listenership during the day). Also called contemporary or current hit radio (CHR).

total-sound recording Recording the entire sound output of, for example, a musical group, as a single sound source rather than recording separate sections or instruments with separate mics. Also see *isolated-component recording.*

track The portion of a strip of magnetic tape that is used for recording sound information. Also, of a phonograph cartridge, to trace with accuracy the grooves of a record.

transducer Any device that performs the function of converting energy from one form into another.

transmitter The device responsible for producing the radio waves that carry a station's signal.

trim control An adjustment control that makes very fine changes in the volume level on a console.

turnover A measure of how many people out of the entire audience leave the station during a given period.

turntable A system consisting of a plate, a drive mechanism, a tonearm, a speed control, and an on-off switch; used to play conventional disc recordings.

two-track A two-channel stereo recording where each track uses one half of the recording tape.

uncompressed audio Digital audio files that are sampled and saved without using technology that reduces the size of the file.

unidirectional A microphone pickup pattern capable of picking up sound sources clearly from one direction only. Also called *one-directional*.

uplink The piece of equipment that sends a signal to a satellite.

urban A radio format featuring rap, hard rock, or other format particulars designed to appeal to young, urban audiences.

vertical/slide fader A pot that slides up and down a linear slot rather than turning on a projecting axis (as does the traditional circular pot).

virtual instruments Musical instrumental sounds produced by audio synthesizers in conjunction with sequencer software. See *MIDI*.

voice actuality A report from a journalist with an actuality segment inserted in its midst.

voice report (voicer) An oral report of a news item, spoken by a journalist who signs off with his or her name, sometimes the location from which the report emanates, and sometimes the name of the news organization. (Example: "This is Bob Roberts reporting from Capitol Hill for WAAA News.")

voice slate An announcement at the beginning of an audio file that designates the take number for that file (e.g. "File Name, take 2").

voice-tracking Using a computer program to insert voice-over segments into radio programs, thereby eliminating the need for a disc jockey.

voice wrap An editing and production structure that begins with one voice, which gives way to a second voice, which gives way finally to the first voice until the conclusion of the spot.

volume The level of sound, perceived as varying degrees of loudness.

volume–unit meter (VU meter) A device that provides a visual readout of loudness. The most important use of a VU meter is for taking zero on the scale as a reference level for the proper audio output level.

wave A complete cycle of electrical or sound energy.

waveforms Visual representations of physical waves.

WAV format Digital sound files stored in a Windows pulse code modulation format. Typical settings for a WAV format is a 16-bit, 44.1-kHz stereo file.

wild sound Ambient sound used to enhance the atmosphere of an actuality or a sound bite.

wind filter A filter that fits inside or outside a mic and blocks the blasting noise caused by wind.

wire service A news-gathering organization that supplies news copy and audio reports to subscribers, who use the wire-service material to supplement their own news-gathering resources. The name is something of an anachronism since most of the material is delivered by satellite today rather than by wire.

wow The sound a record or tape makes when the audio portion is heard before the playback device has reached full speed.

XLR A type of three-pin connector commonly used in radio.

Suggested Readings

Listed in this section are books that will be of particular help in understanding radio in general and production in particular. Some may be out of print, but many of the older books are readily available in libraries or from Amazon.com.

PRODUCTION AND TECHNICAL WORKS

Stanley R. Alten. *Audio in Media*, 9th ed. Boston: Wadsworth, 2010. In the authors' opinion, the most comprehensive guide available on audio; much of the content is applicable to radio production.

Antony Brown. *The Focal Easy Guide to Adobe Audition 2.0.* New York: Elsevier, 2006. Good overview of many audition features and operations.

Frank D. Cook/Avid Technology. Pro Tools 101, version 9.0. Boston: Course Technology. Cengage Learning. 2009. Latest version of Pro Tools explained in depth.

Todd M. Howard. *GarageBand '11 Power!: The Comprehensive Recording and Podcasting Guide.* Course Technology PTR. 2011. Good overview of the software written in a conversational, easy-to-understand style.

Peter Kirn. *Digital Audio: Industrial-Strength Production Techniques.* Berkeley, CA: Peachpit Press. 2006. Very good reference focusing on recording and recording techniques.

Drew O. McDaniel, Rick Shriver, and Kenneth Collins. *Fundamentals of Audio Production.* Allyn and Bacon. 2007. Straightforward explanations of basic recording for broadcasting, film, and live sound.

Alec Nisbett. *Use of Microphones*, 4th ed. Stoneham, MA: Focal Press, 1994. A very thorough study of the sound studio. Useful for radio, though probably more useful to recording-studio engineers.

Bobby Owsinski. *The Recording Engineer's Handbook.* Course Technology PTR. 2nd ed. 2009. An excellent handbook of all aspects of recording technology.

David E. Reese, Lynne S. and Brian Gross. *Radio Production Worktext*, 6th ed. Stoneham, MA: Focal Press, 2009. A workbook approach to radio production.

GENERAL RADIO, RADIO OPERATIONS, AND SURVEY TEXTS DEALING SUBSTANTIALLY WITH RADIO

Erik Barnouw. *A History of Broadcasting in the United States.* New York: Oxford University Press,1966, 1968, 1970. Three-volume history; comprehensive and readable.

Joseph Dominick, Fritz Messere, and Barry Sherman. *Broadcasting, Cable, the Internet and Beyond*, 7th ed. New York: McGraw-Hill, 2010. A well-known, all-in-one guide to understanding the broadcasting, cable, and electronic media world. In-depth discussion of formats.

George H. Douglas. *The Early Days of Radio Broadcasting.* Jefferson, NC: McFarland Publishing, 1987. Narrative of radio's troubled birth and childhood.

Geller, Valerie. *Beyond Powerful Radio*, 2nd ed. Stoneham, MA: Focal Press, 2011. An all-in-one look at radio programming.

Michael C. Keith. *The Radio Station*, 8th ed. Stoneham, MA: Focal Press, 2009. A heavily illustrated guide to radio.

Lewis B. O'Donnell, Carl Hausman, and Philip Benoit. *Radio Station Operations: Management and Employee Perspectives.* Belmont, CA: Wadsworth, 1989. A comprehensive guide to many aspects of radio, including physical facilities, station programming, operations, production, sales and advertising, and management.

Christopher H. Sterling and John M. Kittross. *Stay Tuned: A History of American Broadcasting*, 3rd ed. Hillsdale, NJ: Lawrence Earlbaum, 2002. More than just a history—an easy-to-use, quick-reference guide to many aspects of broadcasting.

Gilbert A. Williams. *Legendary Pioneers of Black Radio.* New York: Praeger, 2008. An interesting and readable work about black disc jockeys, often unheralded shapers of the industry.

RADIO PROGRAMMING

Susan Tyler Eastman and Douglas Ferguson. *MediaProgramming: Strategies and Practices*, 8th ed. Belmont, CA: Wadsworth, 2008. A broad but concisely analytical study of programming, with specific references to radio.

Murray B. Levin. *Talk Radio and the American Dream.* Lexington, MA: Lexington Books, 1987. An exhaustive study of radio talk shows. Includes transcripts of broadcasts.

Quincy McCoy. *No Static: A Guide to Creative Radio Programming.* Backbeat Books, 2002. An interesting book about practicing the craft of creative programming.

RADIO NEWS

Carl Hausman. *The Decision-Making Process in Journalism.* Chicago: Nelson-Hall, 1990. A guide to principles of news judgment.

Brad Kalbfeld. *The Associated Press Stylebook and Briefing on Media Law*, 44th ed. New York: Associated Press, 2011. Thorough style guide to writing and staying out of trouble.

C. A. Tuggle. *Broadcast News Handbook: Writing, Reporting and Producing in a Converging Media World*, 4th ed. New York: McGraw-Hill, 2010. Covers all aspects of news gathering today.

Ted White, Adrian J. Meppen, and Steven Young. *Broadcast News Writing, Reporting and Production*, 2nd ed. New York: Macmillan, 1996. An incisive guide that goes beyond writing and shows the entire range of radio (and, of course, television) news operations. Excellent examples of how news is gathered and scripted for broadcast.

ANNOUNCING AND PERFORMING

Carl Hausman, Philip Benoit, Fritz Messere, and Lewis B. O'Donnell. *Announcing: Broadcast Communicating Today*, 5th ed. Belmont, CA: Wadsworth, 2004. Many of the techniques discussed are applicable to radio; some chapters deal specifically with radio announcing.

Stuart W. Hyde. *Television and Radio Announcing*, 11th ed. Boston: Houghton Mifflin, 2008. A durable book, now updated.

COMMERCIALS AND ADVERTISING

Terri Apple and Gary Owens. *Making Money in Voice-Overs: Winning Strategies to a Successful Career in TV, Radio and Animation.* Los Angeles: Lone Eagle, 1999. Practical and interesting career advice.

David Ogilvy. *Confessions of an Advertising Man.* New York: Atheneum, 1989. A revealing insight into the world of professional advertising by the founder of one of the world's most successful advertising agencies. Useful for anyone who wants to design advertising of any type.

Charles H. Warner and Joseph Buchman. *Broadcast and Cable Selling,* 2nd ed. Belmont, CA: Wadsworth, 1991. A very useful guide primarily aimed at selling time, but much insight is provided into producing effective advertising.

Sherilyn K. Zeigler and Herbert H. Howard. *Broadcast Advertising: A Comprehensive Working Textbook,* 3rd ed. Ames: Iowa State University Press, 1991. Step-by-step guide, a good reference for a producer.

Web Links

Listed in this supplemental section are websites that will provide more information about radio in general and production in particular.

Chapter 1

How Radio Works: http://www.howstuffworks.com/radio.htm

Web Radio locator: http://www.web-radio.fm

Windows Media.Com: http://www.windowsmedia.com/MediaGuide/Home

Apple iTunes and Podcasting: http://www.apple.com/itunes

Apple QuickTime Player: http://www.apple.com/quicktime/mac.html

SiriusXM Satellite Radio: http://www.xmradio.com

AOL radio: http://music.aol.com/radioguide/bb

Pandora: http://www.pandora.com

Chapter 2

Audio Articles from Broadcast Engineering Magazine: http://broadcastengineering.com/audio/

Wheatstone Production Consoles: http://www.wheatstone.com

Logitek Production Consoles: http://www.logitekaudio.com

Harris Audio Consoles and Networks: http://www.broadcast.harris.com/default.asp

Chapter 3

Turntable history: http://www.djsociety.org/Turn%20History.htm

How CDs work: http://www.howstuffworks.com/cd.htm

Differences between DVD audio and CD: http://electronics.howstuffworks.com/question344.htm

Vintage Audio History: http://www.videointerchange.com/audio_history.htm

Chapter 4

Sound recording history: http://www.recording%2Dhistory.org

How hard disk drives work: http://www.howstuffworks.com/hard-disk.htm

Recording History Page: http://www.recording-history.org/

How MiniDiscs work: http://www.minidisc.org/first_minidisc.html

How Flash Memory Works: http://electronics.howstuffworks.com/flash-memory.htm

Chapter 5

How microphones work: http://www.howstuffworks.com/question309.htm

Multimedia Bluffer's Guide to microphones: http://home.pacific.net.sg/~firehzrd/audio/mics.html

How hearing works: http://health.howstuffworks.com/human-body/systems/ear/hearing.htm

Chapter 6

The tapeless studio: http://www.webdevelopersjournal.com/studio

Audacity—Free Open Source Recording Software: http://audacity.sourceforge.net/

Digidesign Audio: http://www.avid.com/us/products/family/pro-tools

BIAS Peak Software: http://www.bias-inc.com

Adobe Audition Software: http://www.adobe.com/products/audition/main.html

Chapter 7

American Society of Composers, Authors and Publishers (ASCAP): http://www.ascap.com/index.html

Broadcast Music Incorporated (BMI): http://www.bmi.com/

How podcasting works: http://computer.howstuffworks.com/internet/basics/podcasting.htm

Chapter 8

DJ Mix Tips: http://computer.howstuffworks.com/internet/basics/podcasting.htm

The FCC's Emergency Alert System: http://www.fcc.gov/pshs/services/eas/

Pams history and radio jingles: http://www.pams.com/history.html

Jinglefreaks.com: http://www.jinglefreaks.com

Chapter 9

How computers work: http://computer.howstuffworks.com/pc.htm

Apple's GarageBand: http://www.apple.com/ilife/garageband

Information about HD radio: http://www.ibiquity.com/hdradio

Shareware for radio production: http://www.hitsquad.com/smm/cat/RADIO_PRODUCTION

SmartSound-Royalty Free Music Creation: http://www.smartsound.com/sonicfire/

Chapter 10

Old-time sound effects in radio broadcasting: http://www.old-time.com/sfx.html

Free sound effects: http://www.stonewashed.net/sfx.html

Absolute sound effects archive: http://www.grsites.com/sounds

Chapter 11

Mercury Radio Theater: http://www.mercurytheatre.info

Collection of old time radio dramas and shows: http://radiolovers.com/

Old Time Radio Network: http://www.otr.net/

BBC Radio 3 Speech and Drama Programmes: http://www.bbc.co.uk/radio3/speechanddrama/

Chapter 12

Old Time Radio Commercials: http://www.old-time.com/commercials

Library of American Broadcasting: http://www.lib.umd.edu/LAB/

Bob and Ray Comedy Classics: http://www.bobandray.com/listen.html

Chapter 13

C-SPAN Radio: http://www.c-span.org

National Public Radio: http://www.npr.org

UPI news: http://www.upi.com

American Public Media: http://americanpublicmedia.publicradio.org

Associated Press Radio website: http://www.apbroadcast.com/AP+Broadcast/Radio/default.htm

Chapter 14

WBUR's It's Only a Game: http://www.onlyagame.org

ESPN Radio: http://espn.go.com/espnradio/

Chapter 15

Audio mixing info: http://www.answers.com/topic/audio-mixing

TweakHeadz Lab_The Perfect Mix: http://www.tweakheadz.com/perfect_mix.html

Soundprint: http://www.soundprint.org

Radio and Production Magazine: http://www.rapmag.com

Audio Mixing Tutorial: http://www.garritan.com/tutorial/AudioMixing.htm

Chapter 16

Radio Station World North American Radio Links: http://radiostationworld.com
Radio locator: http://www.radio-locator.com
Shoutcast: http://www.shoutcast.com
Live365.com: http://www.live365.com/index.live

Chapter 17

New media economics: http://www.buzzmachine.com/
Workings of new media: http://www.wired.com/magazine/

Chapter 18

Radio entrepreneur resource: http://www.live365.com/index.live
Center for new media entrepreneurship: http://cronkite.asu.edu/experience/knight.php

Index

NOTE: Page numbers in boldface indicate locations of definitions of terms.